over under and around

over under and around

ESSAYS IN PERFORMANCE AND CULTURE

RICHARD SCHECHNER

Seagull Books

calcutta new delhi 2004

ISBN 81 7046 262 2

Cover designed by Naveen Kishore
using a photograph by Richard Schechner

Published by Naveen Kishore, Seagull Books Private Limited
26 Circus Avenue, Calcutta 700 017, India

Printed in India by Leelabati Printers
P54 Ananda Palit Road, Calcutta 700 014

Welcome to India, Carol

CONTENTS

Foreword / CAROL MARTIN	1
Theatre into the Twenty-First Century	5
Performance Spaces: Ramlila and Yaqui Easter	54
The Performance Group in India: February–April 1976	73
Restoration of Behaviour	101
Performers and Spectators: Transported and Transformed	187
From Ritual to Theatre and Back: The Structure/Process of the Efficacy-Entertainment Dyad	225
Dixi, Namahage, and the Question of Folk Performance	273
Believed-in Theatre	285
Rasaesthetics	312
Appendix A: Rasabox Actor Training / MICHELE MINNICK	341
Appendix B: Experience Rasaboxes / PAULA MURRAY COLE	346

Acknowledgements

'Theatre into the Twenty-First Century' first published as 'Theatre for Tomorrow' in *UNESCO COURIER*, November 1997. 'Performance Spaces: Ramlila and Yaqui Easter', Wenner-Gren Foundation for Anthropological Research, unpublished; 'The Performance Group in India' was first published in *Quarterly Journal* of the National Centre for the Performing Arts, Bombay, 1976; 'Restoration of Behaviour' and 'Performers and Spectators Transported and Transformed' were first published in *Between Theatre and Anthropology* (University of Pennsylvania Press, 1985); 'From Ritual to Theatre and Back: The Structure/Process of the Efficacy-Entertainment Dyad' is reprinted from *Essays on Performance Theory* (Drama Books Specialists Publishers, 1976); 'Dixi, Namahage and the Question of Folk Performance' was first published in *Papers from the International Symposium on East Asian Folklore and Performing Arts,* Tokyo, 1995; 'Believed-in Theatre' first appeared in *Performance Research* 1997, vol. 2, no. 2 and 'Rasaesthetics' in *TDR* 2001, vol. 45, no. 3, pp. 27-50.

Appendix A:'Rasabox Actor Training' by Michele Minnick and Appendix B: 'Experience Rasaboxes' by Paula Murray Cole (first published as part of 'Rasaesthetics') are reproduced here with the permission of the respective authors.

Foreword

Even to Richard Schechner the constellation of his essays sometimes seems too vast to form a discernible pattern. Perhaps it is demonic energy that possesses him to write so much across cultures. Or perhaps it's the practising Jew converted to Hinduism and renamed Jayaganesh, after the affable protector of new endeavours, that propels him to never stop trying to know, to travel and to experimentally become that which he is and is not. It is almost as if he is living the image of a digitized face always morphing into other faces while continually returning to himself.

The essays collected in this book represent Schechner's lifetime in performance studies. In many ways his thought has held fast to a stable trajectory, in other ways it has radically changed. Political theatre, the avant garde, the secular and sacred rituals of performance, the nature of belief and its suspensions in theatre, aesthetics, performance theory, and performance studies have all been his recurring subjects. At the same time, his knowledge has changed and deepened as he has spent much of his life seeing all kinds of performances all over the world. So he is in a position to compare the incomparable—Yaqui and Ramlila, dixi and namahage—in a manner that furthers the study of ritual and indicates the ways performance is similarly and differently imbricated in different communities. Schechner has also learned that the avant garde is more than a historical occurrence localized in or originating in a single culture. Schechner asserts that we can also understand the avant garde as a particular kind of articulation of the traditional and the oral, performances that at first glance seem wholly different.

India figures deeply in many of these essays: Schechner first studied in India for four months in 1971-1972. During that time he witnessed many different kinds of performances, from jatra in Bengal to yakshagana in Karnataka, from pand pather in Kashmir to kathakali in Kerala. It was also during that sojourn that Schechner first came upon the *Natyashastra*—a text he later studied (in translation) in detail, forming the basis for his theory of 'rasaesthetics' published in this book. Schechner returned to India in 1976 when he experienced Ramlila in Ramnagar for the first time. That 1976 trip kicked off with The Performance Group touring northern India for three months performing Brecht's *Mother Courage and Her Children*. It was then that the links between the experimental, the political, the traditional, and the theoretical were already forged.

The 1980s brought Schechner to Japan, the U.S. Southwest, and China for three different kinds of traditional performances. In 1980, he studied namahage on the Oga Peninsula jutting into the Sea of Japan on its Western coast. For several years in the mid-80s, Schechner observed the Yaqui waehma (Easter) celebrations outside Tucson, Arizona. And in 1988, he traveled to Guizhou province in the interior of south central China where he saw a village performance of dixi, a masked form enacting old stories of women warriors, gods, and heroes. This book contains essays drawn from each of these field trips.

During all this time, Schechner continued to adapt and direct plays—first with The Performance Group and later independently and with East Coast Artists. These plays ranged from Schechner's cautionary version of Greek tragedy—*Dionysus in 69* (based on Euripides' *The Bacchae* and opening in 1968) and Seneca's *Oedipus* (in Ted Hughes' searing translation, opening in 1977) to Genet's *The Balcony* (opening in 1979) and his own version of the Faust legend, *Faust/gastronome* (opening in 1993). No doubt Schechner's thinking about performance is inflected with his work as a 'man of the theatre.'

The range and depth of Schechner's scholarly endeavour informed by his artistic practice has led him to think about the deep structure of performance and theorize its construction across cultures. He has tried to bring seemingly very different kinds of performances into the same conversation. Upon reflection, this endeavour is largely the outcome of one of his early theatrical experiences, working with The Free Southern Theatre in 1963-65.

Especially important was 'Freedom Summer,' 1964, when the Free Southern Theatre toured rural Mississippi, Alabama, and Louisiana with works as far-ranging as Samuel Beckett's *Waiting for Godot*, Martin Duberman's *In White America*, Bertolt Brecht's *The Rifles of Senora Carrar*, and Ossie Davis's *Purlie Victorious* (which Schechner directed). That summer, Schechner experienced theatre as a weapon, as entertainment, as education, and as a declaration of independence. He also worked closely with farmers and labourers, teachers and students, doctors and clerks who all joined together in the struggle to end racial segregation in America. Schechner learned from the Free Southern Theatre that division and discontinuity were the strategies of bigotry and oppression. In theatre scholarship, he encountered analogous divisions and discontinuities in assertions of the West's professional theatre's superiority. In both cases, he has worked hard to radically change the conversation, the ways of knowing, and to oppose the partitioning of knowledge into discrete realms of worth and worthlessness. This confluence of practice and scholarship where each realm wholly informs the other, is second only to Schechner's far ranging contact with diverse types of performance in generating his exceptional thinking on the meaning and importance of performance as the paradigm for the twentieth and twenty-first centuries.

As I suggested before, the essays in this book should not be read as an indication of any kind of developmental progression. The essays, despite their sometimes-radical proclivities, are more in the mode of traditional scholarship in which a writer revisits his subject again and again, each time newly enriched with passion, knowledge, and life experience. They are each rehearsals for further performances of the differences within the same, the similarities within the differences. They are Schechner's scholarly dharma, phases in the life cycle of a scholar/artist devoted to an existence of mind amidst theatre. And if one believes that life and work are cyclical, then life and work are never finished.

The operative metaphor is Radha constantly seeking Krishna to consummate her desire for a divine love whose ultimate essence cannot be known to her. In Schechnerian performance theory terms this is 'restoration of behaviour.' Players play and spectators experience the performance over and over to catch a glimpse, to live a moment of insight, to thrill with the love of something that is always repeating itself but not exactly the same, replayed but not ever fully grasped. To quote Schechner from one of his most well known essays, 'Restored behaviour is living behaviour treated as a film director treats a strip of film.' I can quibble a bit and say Schechner should have selected the film editor, not the director. The point, however, is, as Schechner points out, that in this process of editing, the original truth or motivation may be lost but the behaviour remains intact, albeit broken into bits that can be rearranged, reconfigured, and recontexted. This, I would like to propose, is Schechner's model not only for performance but also for his scholarship, if not his actual lived life. Collected here are ten discrete essays with thought that has been rearranged, reconfigured, recontexted, and expanded.

In his previous and, up to this point, his only book published in India (1983, Seagull Books, Calcutta), *Performative Circumstances From The Avant Garde to Ramlila*, Schechner dedicated the book to me. 'Welcome to India, Carol,' he wrote. And now in my foreword to his second book published in India by Seagull Books I reply, 'It's a breathtaking journey.'

CAROL MARTIN

Theatre into the Twenty-First Century

The future of theatre?—but which kind of theatre? There is the theatre of artists modelled on the Western style of staging the dramas of playwrights, plays made mostly of words and acted for the most part in a naturalistic style. There is the theatre of highly codified gestures, costumes, and makeup combining the spoken word with sung dialogues and songs—such as Japanese kabuki. There is the theatre that could also be called dance or opera because of its total integration of movement, gesture, song, and narrative—such as Chinese kunju or jingju or Indian kathakali. There is the theatre of ritual performances addressing, honouring, or entertaining the gods—as practised in many cultures around the world. There is the theatre of popular festivity and ritual where people build and wear masks and full-body costumes, such as Yoruban gelede, Hopi kachina, or Trinidad mas–Carnival. There is the theatre of religious narrative taking many days to enact such as Indian Ramlila, Yaqui waehma, or the Oberammergau cycle.

The theatres I have been most concerned with are avant garde or experimental theatres centred in Europe and North America but with counterparts extended throughout the world; and traditional theatres, especially in Asia, Native America, and Trinidad. The so-called 'mainstream' theatre—Broadway, the West End, Boulevard Theatre (the genre has several names)—has not been the focus of my scholarly study or artistic work. So when I talk about the future of the theatre, I am really talking about the future of the avant garde and the future of traditional theatres. Let me take each of these up by turn, and then see if there is any connection linking them to each other.

The avant garde or experimental theatre once was 'in advance of' what was following; work was attempted whose outcome was unknown and therefore had the character of experimentation. But it has been at least 25 years since that was so. The avant garde is no longer in advance of anything; nor do most of the persons working in the so-called avant garde risk failure in order to explore new boundaries of performance knowledge or practice. In fact, a strong argument can be made that all today's theatre is 'official,' paid for by the government, foundations, or other mainstream funds—or desiring to be paid for by these funds. Nowadays, work called 'avant garde' or 'experimental' is simply another style of theatre—one identified with a certain group of artists and a certain way of making theatre. At one point—up until the mid-1970s in the USA, perhaps until another date elsewhere—many of these artists were avant garde; their work broke new grounds, they took big chances and risked failure both aesthetically and in terms of commercial success. This is no longer true.

Of course, many works are still labeled 'avant garde.' In fact, this term does not refer to a single style or tendency, but to several. These I need to identify and say something about, briefly:

1. The current avant garde—whatever/whoever critics, audiences, and artists identify as belonging to the avant garde. The term 'avant garde' has a certain positive value; many people want to belong to the avant garde. Calling a theatre artist 'avant garde' is sometimes more a way of praising the artist than describing the work.

2. The historical avant garde—the line of development which began with naturalism in Europe in the 1880s and extended through many successive waves of experimentation, new ways of doing theatre (and indeed all the arts): symbolism, futurism, dada, surrealism,

Happenings, environmental theatre, performance art, and so on. Each of these claimed hegemony over all that preceded, each was destined to be absorbed into the mainstream one way or another. Works that were hissed off the stage by one generation, were honoured by the next; styles that were incomprehensible became meat and potatoes for the next generation of secondary school students. But at a certain point, the 1970s, the historical avant garde ended. There were no more waves of newness crashing onto shore. With the emergence of postmodernism, recycling dominated. Probably the end of the historical avant garde coincided with a certain finality to underlying scientific knowledge. New developments in science take on the characteristic of technical innovations, 'improvements,' rather than a shift in fundamental paradigms. A definite mode of stability reminiscent of the European middle ages is felt. Perhaps if newness is to become important again it will originate outside of the Euro-American cultural sphere. This is where the question of 'globalization' becomes determinant. Is there anywhere—since the end of the Cold War—that is really outside the Euro-American cultural sphere?

3. The forward-looking avant garde—enacts a future that is both amazing and sometimes apocalyptic. This branch of the avant garde celebrates the newest technology. As I write this, interactive telecommunications and CD-ROMs, the Internet, virtual realities, and multimedia dominate the forward-looking avant garde. The work of Robert Lepage and Laurie Anderson are examples of the forward-looking avant garde. Important theorists of this avant garde are Brenda Laurel (*Computers as Theatre*, 1993) and Jon McKenzie ('Virtual Reality: Performance, Immersion, and the Thaw,' *TDR* 1994, vol. 38, no. 4; and 'Laurie Anderson for Dummies,' *TDR* 1997, vol. 41, no. 2).

4. The tradition-seeking avant garde is the opposite of the forward-looking. Tradition-seekers eschew high tech. Instead they look toward 'ancient knowledge,' 'rituals,' and 'traditional performances' especially in non-Western cultures. Here the ideas and researches of Jerzy Grotowski are dominant. As Grotowski says his goal is: 'To re-evoke a very ancient form of art where ritual and artistic creation were seamless. Where poetry was song, song was incantation, movement

was dance. [. . .] One might say—but it is only a metaphor—that we are trying to go back before the Tower of Babel, and discover what was before. First to discover differences, and then to discover what was before the differences. [. . .] We can hope to discover a very old form of art, art as a *way of knowledge*' (in Zbigniew Osinski, 'Grotowski Blazes the Trails,' *TDR* 1991, vol. 35, no. 1, p. 91).

5. The intercultural avant garde—here there are two aspects, one that is positive, seeking out and synthesizing 'universals' and connections among cultures; and one that is ironic and probing, seeking out disjunctures and miscommunications 'at the borders.' In the first instance, the ongoing work of Eugenio Barba and his International School of Theatre Anthropology (ISTA) is exemplary. In the second, it is the practice and theories of performance artist Guillermo Gomez-Pena. At ISTA and in his writings, Barba attempts to show how at the root of all effective artistic performing are 'pre-expressive' positions, movements, and gestures. For Barba, these pre-expressives are most clearly seen in Asian dance-theatres such as kathakali, odissi (India), buyo (Japan), jingju, and kunchu (China). Gomez-Pena emphasizes the contradictions of living and working in more than one culture simultaneously. 'I physically live between two cultures and two epochs. [. . .] When I am on the US side, I have access to high-technology and specialized information. When I cross back to Mexico, I get immersed in a rich political culture. [. . .] I walk the fibres of this transition in my everyday life, and I make art about it' ('A Bi-National Performance Pilgrimage,' *TDR* 1991, vol. 35, no. 3, pp. 22-23). While Barba wants to find connections, Gomez-Pena and others like him explore both the links and the disjunctures, the ways cultures collide, fail to communicate—engaging fractures, difficulties, ideological contradictions, and crumbling national myths. Barba tends to work with traditional performers only; Gomez-Pena with both traditional and postmodern artists.

Of what use is dividing the avant garde into five? The categories overlap—the current avant garde includes work that is forward-looking, tradition-seeking, and intercultural. But analysing the avant garde in this way reminds us of two important facts: the complexity and multiplicity of today's avant garde; and how far today's avant garde is from the historical avant garde. Today's avant garde is neither 'in advance of' nor in 'opposition to.' Some work, of course, is oppositional or resistant to official culture; but much work that is called avant garde is supported by official or quasi-official money and structures. The principal goal of much of the historical avant garde was to expose, ridicule, and destabilize official art and official culture. The principal goals of the other four kinds of avant garde are too various to summarize—but revolution and rebellion are not today very important themes. Nor is there an attempt to present 'the shock of the new' that characterized the historical avant garde. The newest work in today's avant garde is highly technological—and these technologies are immensely popular and widespread, global even. They are innovative but not shocking; they tend to integrate rather than divide (as rebellious actions do); and they cost a lot of money, especially during the development stage—so there has to be a deep alliance with the social forces that have money.

With these things in mind, I can now return to the theme of this writing: Where is the theatre going? The question may better be put, 'Where are the various theatres going?'—for if nothing else is clear, it is that there are many different kinds of theatres, in many different cultures and contexts, and that these are not moving in lock-step. Once it was felt that perhaps theatre would disappear in the face of various other forms of dramatic entertainments and arts, movies and video especially. But the emergence of computer technology is more likely to see a collapse of difference among the various media arts. The use of the information chip instead of the strip of celluloid of magnetic tape, will mean an increasingly easy-to-use flow back and forth of images and actions from the computer to the film to the video—and also between the so-called live and the so-called mediated. I use the term 'so-called' because interactivity will allow for the immediate intervention of 'viewers' or 'audiences' who now become 'users' or co-creators. Hypertextuality will become very common. And although fixed-text media—movies and television—will be ubiquitous, interactives on the personal as well as highly artistic level will increase exponentially. Even today, when one goes to a university computer room, many students are not doing 'research' but connecting to the internet or conversing via email. Others are stitching together performances directed at private or small audiences; and some are making stuff for larger audiences.

As far as 'live theatre' goes, the emergence of chip technology and performance does not sound their death knell. It means only that the various avant garde will bifurcate still more. If today there are five avant gardes, in 25 years there may be 10 or more avant gardes. The theatre itself will take many forms. Collectively, there will be a lot of live performance, but each genre or subset will be very specific, 'local' not in the sense of being isolated in a certain place, but in the sense of having a relatively few clients scattered here and there and brought together first by means of the Internet and how it develops and secondly by local and regional 'festivals' or other occasions that gather into one spot for a limited time all those interested in a certain kind of performance. Culture will no longer be defined as localized in place, but as localized in taste and practice. One will be able to belong to a 'drama culture' or a 'performance art culture' wherever one lives; just as one can practise a specific religion wherever one lives (hopefully!).

This new definition of 'local,' defining it generically rather than geographically, will have an effect on traditional performance genres. At present, such forms as kathakali or noh, gelede or samba, wayang kulit or Yaqui waehma were tied to a particular place, particular social practices, and particular practitioners. But increasingly, at least some of these forms are opening to practitioners who might not be 'born to them,' and are frequently not only displayed but actually domiciled outside of their place of origin or primary practice. Global tourism exerts an extremely strong pressure. Governments and corporations—often indistinguishable from each other—are replacing traditional patrons. Already many traditional arts have been commercialized, globalized (uprooted and simplified), and 'smoothed out' to satisfy the tastes of tourists and 'art lovers' rather than the specific demands of their own histories and practices. Only those societies rich enough to establish categories comparable to the Japanese 'living national treasures' will be able to preserve their traditional arts as such. And even when thus preserved, the traditional arts exist more or less in venues that are like a museum or game park: strictly fenced off from the impact of ongoing life. Many traditional arts will cease to exist. No effective remedy has been put in place to stop this cultural extinction. Nor is it all bad—times and circumstances change; not everything that was can be preserved indefinitely. Sometimes the urge to preserve is a mask hiding the fear of change.

Nor ought we to underestimate people's inventiveness and creativity, especially the power of popular culture. Even as advanced economies preserve some traditional arts in their traditional forms, and other arts not so protected vanish, a new category of continuous creation of tradition through fusion and hybridity emerges. Throughout Latin America, for example, performances fusing African, European, and Native American religions are thriving as Santeria, Umbanda, Voudon, Samba, and so on. Other parts of the world show a similar creativity as new syntheses are formed. Over the past several centuries immigration and displacement has created the greatest movement among the world's peoples ever experienced. From assailed or displaced fragments of cultural practices, new vigorous performances have arisen. And soon enough, formerly 'artificial' or 'synthetic' practices are transformed into new wholes. We live in a period where older traditional arts exist side by side with new traditional arts, the fruit of both consciously 'invented traditions' and less thought-out but very robust hybrids. Furthermore, and very importantly, many theatre experiments have been in collaboration with, and/or deeply affected by, traditional performing arts and rituals. The 'roots' movement in India, the theories and practices of Suzuki Tadashi, the dramas of Wole Soyinka, the researches of Jerzy Grotowski and Eugenio Barba—and much other work along this line (what I dubbed the 'tradition-seeking avant garde')—is robust and thriving.

And what about 'ordinary theatre' (in Euro-American terms), the enactment of dramas written by playwrights and performed by actors? Of course, this kind of theatre is not 'universal' and 'omnipresent'. It is a specific cultural occurrence and as such it could go extinct. But I don't think it will. I once wrote that this kind of theatre would become the string quartet of the twenty-first century. By that I meant that ordinary theatre would have a small devoted audience. It would be for select tastes. Other rituals, entertainments, spectacles, and enactments would take up most of the room conceptually, financially, and spectatorially. A few people, in relatively small venues, would continue to make and enjoy 'ordinary theatre'. We would take from this art a certain pleasure—but it would not be important in the way it was, say, at the end of the nineteenth century when a new drama by Ibsen could shake up an entire continent. The important debates about public culture would be conducted outside of theatres—on TV, over the Internet, in new rituals convened and enacted electronically; or via mass movements assembled in the streets. But not in theatres. But this is not the whole story. The utopian electronic global village may suffer the same fate of non-existence as all previous utopias. The media and the internet are increasingly omnipresent without satisfying certain basic needs answered by live performance. In fact, live theatre will flourish to some degree *because* of the rapid development of media and instant information transmission. Note that I say 'information'—and perhaps ought to say 'data'—and not the more complex term, the more intriguingly knotted human, 'communication'. The media provides more information than communication, while live performance often offers more communication than information. Live performance is a very big category that can be sub-divided into non-theatre and theatre performances. Non-theatre performances include performance in everyday life, religious services, sports, and popular entertainments such as rock-music concerts and Disney-like theme parks. These are not the subject of this writing. Live theatre itself is a big category that can be divided in three: 1. Broadway, boulevard, and other large-scale commercial enterprises; 2. not-for-profit, subsidized mainstream theatres such as the stadtheaters in Germany or the regional theatres in the USA; 3. experimental theatre and performance art. Commercial theatre is self-supporting because it effectively exploits crossovers between media and live performance. Shows and stars exist both live and on tape, CDs, and film. In this sense, the pop entertainment industry is the most advanced performance genre economically and technically. The stadtheater system is the way the middle class tells itself that it is 'cultured' and 'responsible'. This system is equivalent to state operas, ballet companies, and symphony orchestras. Its repertory relies on 'classics' but includes some new works and the safer experimental artists who 'graduate' to official status, such as Robert Wilson or Peter Sellars.

Experimental theatre and performance art—as I noted earlier—is harder to pin down. Some performance artists such as Laurie Anderson or Spalding Gray become fairly large stars; occasionally a movie star such as Willem Dafoe continues to work also in experimental theatre. But basically, the experimental theatre and performance art—the 'contemporary avant garde' as defined earlier—takes place in small venues for tiny audiences. Yet this work serves a very important function. Live performance of this type continues to be 'dangerous'. By dangerous I do not mean performers who wound themselves onstage but that live performance includes working in front of audiences while making and recovering from mistakes and unforeseen circumstances. Live performance also is able to explore risky or taboo subjects. Large-scale performances, film, and video involve such amounts of money that often the money-givers do not want to take chances. Finally, live performances before/with small audiences allow for the experience of close contact physically, emotionally, and conceptually between actors and spectators. This experience of shared presence is irreplaceable.

Will there be money for this kind of theatre? Surely not enough. At one time, experimental performance got no public or official support at all. Maybe under those circumstances, the avant garde was most alive, dangerous, and important. Owing its existence to no one except the artists and the immediate audiences gave freedom to those involved. Of course, censorship and worse has always been a threat—and will continue to be. In more than one place, under more than one kind of government and police presence, experimental theatre—like the press and public speech—lives under threat. But the underground seems to find a way, thank god. And the need for an unofficial or anti-official theatre is real. Official theatre—no matter how beautiful—is always just that, 'official'. And in houses of worship—live theatre's closest sibling—laughter is scarce, especially of the sarcastic, ironic, parodic, and blasphemous kinds. Nor does church, synagogue, mosque, or temple abet bleak tragedy or atheistic scepticism. Official or corporate theatres, newspapers, and media, as well as state-sponsored religions, all require continuous challenge and critique. Corrective tones of unbelief, mockery, parody, horror, and delight are found in experimental theatre and performance art, what I have called the current avant garde. Also found there is dirty language, offensive acts, and risky imagery: stuff that lives, grows, and adds to the granaries of literature and thought. This is the kind of theatre I hope the next century will see plenty of.

Environmental Theatre: Space

> This earth is my body. The sky is my body. The seasons are my body. The water is my body too. The world is just as big as my body. Do not think I am just in the east, west, south, or north. I am all over.
>
> Killer-of-Enemies, Apache Hero

> Not every place was good to sit or be on. Within the confines of the porch there was one spot that was unique, a post where I could be at my very best. It was my task to distinguish it from all the other places. The general pattern was that I had to 'feel' all the possible spots that were accessible until I could determine without doubt which was the right one.
>
> Carlos Castaneda

In June 1970, I spent nearly three hours in the anechoic chamber at the Massachusetts Institute of Technology. After a period of very deep sleep, I awoke with no sense of how big the room was. I could see the walls, the floor, and the ceiling, but that wasn't enough to fix distance, and therefore size. How big was I? How big were the things in the room? When I spoke or shouted, there was no echo. I discovered how much I depended on echo to fix distance and how much I depended on distance to fix size. I crawled across the floor. It was like a big inner-spring mattress with no cloth covering. I measured the space with my body, but I had no assurance that, like Alice in Wonderland, I hadn't changed size. Then I lay still, and I heard gurglings in my stomach, my heartbeat, and an incredibly loud whirring and ringing in my ears. I felt my body try to expand to fill the space of the chamber, and I experienced my skin as a thin bag containing bones and a lot of sloshing fluid.

The fullness of space, the endless ways space can be transformed, articulated, animated—that is the basis of environmental theatre design. It is also the source of environmental theatre performer training. If the audience is one medium in which the performance takes place, the living space is another. The living space includes all the space in the theatre, not just what is called the stage. I believe there are actual relationships between the body and the spaces the body moves through. Much of workshop and rehearsal is devoted to discovering these relationships, which are subtle and ever-shifting.

The first scenic principle of environmental theatre is to create and use whole spaces. Literally spheres of spaces, spaces within spaces, spaces which contain, or envelop, or relate, or touch all the areas where the audience is and/or the performers perform. All the spaces are actively involved in all the aspects of the performance. If some spaces are used just for performing, this is not due to a predetermination of convention or architecture but because the particular production being worked on needs space organized that way. And the theatre itself is part of larger environments outside the theatre. These larger out-of-the-theatre spaces are the life of the city; and also temporal-historical spaces—modalities of time/space. At the start of the Open Theater's *Terminal*:

> 'We come upon the dying to call upon the dead.' We tried many routes to call up the dead: we invented some, and we studied procedures used by people who believe in invocation. What we chose finally was to knock on the door of the dead by tapping; with the feet on the floor, the door of the dead.

> There is no ground where underfoot—below the wood, below the stone—are not the bones of someone who once lived. The guides invited the dead below the stage floor to come through and speak through the dying. [1]

There is no dead space, nor any end to space.

The Performing Garage is roughly 50 ft by 35 ft, with a height of 20 ft. Photograph 1 shows the environment for *Dionysus in 69* during the pre-performance warm-ups. One of the two dominant towers is partially visible. The space is organized around a central area marked by black rubber mats. The audience sits on the platforms or on the carpeted floor. The only concentration of audience is a five-tier vertical structure on the north wall, which seats about one hundred persons. The lower levels of this tier can be seen in the upper right corner of the photo. Photograph 2 shows one of the dominant towers of the *Dionysus* environment. Pentheus, with his foot on the rail, is at the top of the tower addressing the audience and the performers. Spectators sit all around Pentheus. Diagonally across from this tower is its twin, separated by the black mats; about 15 ft separate the towers.

The action of *Dionysus* occurs in several areas and in several ways. Dominant actions such as the birth of Dionysus, the seduction of Pentheus, and the death of Pentheus take place on the black mats. Choric actions such as the taunting of Pentheus by the chorus, the planning of Pentheus' murder by the chorus, and the soliciting of help from the audience take place in various areas around the periphery, mostly among the spectators. Some actions such as the sexual relations between Dionysus and Pentheus and the initial meeting between Cadmus and Tiresias take place entirely out of sight of the audience, privately. Underneath the visible environment is a pit 35 ft by 8 ft by 8 ft; two trapdoors allow access to the pit. There are good hiding places underneath some of the platforms back close to the walls. These 'secret' places were used as well as the public places.

Most of the action is single-focus, but significant actions take place simultaneously [Photograph 3]. While Pentheus is trying to make love with a person from the audience, the chorus is whispering to other spectators: 'Will you help us kill him in ten minutes?' After Pentheus is killed, all the women in the company rush into the audience and simultaneously tell about their part in the murder. At the end of the play, weather permitting, the large overhead garage door is opened, and all the performers march out into Wooster Street, often followed by spectators [Photograph 4].[2]

Photograph 5 shows the same space reconstructed for *Makbeth* (1969). Here a series of tightly connected rectangles rises from a central table. On this table much of the major action of the play takes place. But scenes are also acted high in the ramparts, back in corners out of sight of most spectators, and in the pit, which is wholly open, making a trench down the north side of the Garage. The rugs of *Dionysus* are gone, and the bare wood rises from a cement floor. Unlike the open feeling of the *Dionysus* environment, *Makbeth* suggested closed-in spaces, 'cabin'd, cribb'd, and confin'd'. Photograph 6 shows Lady Makbeth at the opening of the play sitting in her place reciting quietly to herself the text of Makbeth's fateful letter.

In *Dionysus* the audience is free to sit anywhere and invited to move around the environment. One scene is a dance with the audience. Spectators frequently join in the action at various times during a night's performance. In *Makbeth* the audience is restricted to a thirty-inch rim at the edges of the platforms. Action takes place in front and behind the audience, but not with them. On only one occasion during the run were spectators invited to participate. I told the audience of about 50 who were gathered upstairs before the performance that they should feel free to move around the space, following the action, exploring the complexities of the environment. I warned them that most of the actions were clustered in bunches performed simultaneously, so that following one action meant missing others. I asked them to remove their shoes so that their movements would not unduly disturb the performers. Nevertheless most of the performers felt that the movement of the audience was a distraction, and the experiment was not repeated. Audience movement is used extensively in *The Tooth of Crime*.

Photograph 7 is of *Commune*. Here 'pueblos' are built in two corners of the Garage; these are connected by a four-foot-wide 'road' elevated to eleven feet. The centre area is dominated by a gentle Wave that rises, falls, rises, and falls again. Next to the Wave is a tub three feet deep and six feet in diameter. The Wave and tub are used during the performance as many things: boat, sea, land, house, blood, village, beach, yard. The audience sat mostly high in the environment, though on crowded nights a number of persons sat on the floor. There was some audience movement through the space. For one scene all the audience was asked to sit on the Wave, and most did so.

But more than in *Commune* or *Dionysus* spectators have the choice of sitting at the edge of a platform, deep in a pueblo, with other persons, or alone. The spectator can choose his own mode of involving himself within the performance, or remaining detached from it. The audience was offered real choices and the chance to exercise these choices several times throughout the performance. The spectator can change his perspective (high, low, near, far); his relationship to the performance (on top of it, in it, a middle distance from it, far away from it); his relationship to other spectators (alone, with a few others, with a bunch of others); whether to be in an open space or in an enclosed space. Surprisingly few spectators took advantage of the opportunities to change places. Even when the performers encouraged moves—such as saying to the audience when everyone was assembled on the Wave, 'When you return to your places, perhaps you want to go to a new place to get a different view of the events'—only a small proportion of the spectators went back to places different from where they'd come.

Photograph 8 is of *The Tooth of Crime*, from a gallery above the playing areas which are in and around a large houselike structure built entirely from plywood modules. For the first time TPG used a structure that blocks vision and has no single arena-like central playing space. Spectators move around the viewing gallery or on the floor in order to follow the action of the play. Also there are windows cut in the environment so that scenes can be seen framed in the environment—giving a filmlike shifting focus to the action. The patterns of movement in *Tooth* are irregular circles on the floor, with a lot of climbing into the modules. Each of the characters has a station in the environment; the characters move but often return to their stations. Some of the feel of *Tooth's* action is of a medieval play.

The *Tooth* environment is modular. Each of the plywood sides is perforated so that it can be joined to other sides in a variety of ways. Squares, rectangles, polygons, and near-circles can be built. Low, medium, and high platforms or towers rising to 16 ft as in *Tooth* are possible. The modules can be reconstructed in numberless variations. The entire system is non-mechanical: it can be entirely reconstructed by hand. Jerry N. Rojo designed this modular system because TPG needed flexibility in order to stage a number of works in repertory.

Rojo, in collaboration with the Group, designed all the environments for TPG discussed in this essay. He is, in my opinion, the world's leading environmentalist. A large portion of his genius is in solving all the formidable artistic-technical problems we put to him in requiring a flexible, transformational space without the encumbrance of heavy or expensive machinery.

I MET ROJO at Tulane University where he came in September 1966, on a leave of absence from the University of Connecticut. He had his Master's from Tulane and came back to work for his doctorate. The New Orleans Group was working on *Victims of Duty*. I was teaching a seminar in performance theory. Paul Epstein, Arthur Wagner, and Rojo were among those who attended the seminar. We had before us some of the work of Jerzy Grotowski, Happenings, examples of ritual theatre, and game theory—of both the mathematical kind and Eric Berne's. Wagner was teaching acting, Epstein was a musician, Rojo a designer. I recall nothing specific about the seminar, but I know it acted on my ideas strongly. I remember that Rojo said little. Over the year we got to be friends. He was the one 'technical person' at Tulane who was interested in my ideas. Then when we were finishing rehearsals for *Victims*, we ran into some technical problems. We wanted a pile of chairs spiralling from the floor to the ceiling strong enough for Choubert to climb on. I asked Rojo to come down to the studio theatre of Le Petit Théâtre de Vieux Carré where *Victims* was being staged.

He liked the environment very much. He solved the problem of the chairs by building an armature of very strong plastic-coated wires from which the chairs blossomed like tree leaves. The next year in New York TPG was in the middle stages of *Dionysus* rehearsals. Mike Kirby had drawn some towers that I thought would be a good central image for the environment. But Mike wanted towers of a certain shape placed in a certain way; and I wanted something else. I phoned Rojo at Connecticut, and he said he'd help. He made new designs for the towers. I liked them immensely. He went ahead and built the towers.

So that is Rojo with hammer and saw. I think my deepest respect for him comes because he knows that environmental design = construction. The ideas are okay, the renderings beautiful, the models exciting—but it all comes down to hammers, nails, materials, and making the space into the shapes you need.

I think it's the same with performing. The daily physical commitment is what counts. The spirit is the body at work.

After *Dionysus* I invited Rojo to design *Makbeth*. I also asked Brooks McNamara who, like Rojo, had been a student at Tulane. During the winter of 1968–69 they both worked on designs that ranged from Ziggurats to mazes to cattle runs. Finally, both Rojo's and McNamara's ideas were used. Then I asked Rojo to design *Commune*. Then he designed *The Tooth of Crime*.

THESE EIGHT PHOTOGRAPHS give some indication of the flexibility possible in a small space such as the Garage. Each environment has a different feel, though all are made from simple wood structures. The audience is arranged in different ways and the action flows through the spaces differently for each production. In *Dionysus* there are many circular movements centred around the black mats; the flow is basically uninterrupted and with few turbulent eddies. In *Makbeth* the moves are angular, there are many private actions, much simultaneity, sharp, disjointed gestures, and harsh sounds coming from several directions at once. Heights were used much more than in *Dionysus*. Commune returns to some of the circularity of *Dionysus*, but the circles are incomplete, broken off. Most of the action takes place in the centre area, on or near the Wave. *Tooth* flows in tight eddies, circles, and figure eights, and the characters often spy on each other from heights or hidden vantage points.

Each environment grew from detailed work with the performers. Work with Rojo begins after the work with the performers is well under way. I try to make the environment a function of the actions discovered by the performers. Of course a reciprocity develops between space and idea, movement and characterization. In the case of *Makbeth* the fact that so much of the rehearsing was done in Yugoslavia far from the Garage led to a production style that hampered the performance.

Environmental design comes from daily work on the play. The environment develops from workshops, discussions, drawings, and models. Models are important because no two-dimensional rendering can give an accurate feel of space. Rehearsals are held in partially finished environments because the performers' work will revise the plans even during the construction phase. After opening, the environment changes as new aspects of the work are uncovered. The Performance Group's work with both the *Dionysus* and *Commune* environments was superior to work with the *Makbeth* environment because many rehearsals, open and closed, were held in the partially completed environments. The space and the performance developed together. On the other hand, the Group returned from Yugoslavia to a totally finished, extraordinarily strong *Makbeth* environment—a marriage between the environment and the performance was never consummated.

Work on an environment may begin long before a play has been selected or a script assembled. The basic work of TPG is with space: finding it, relating to it, negotiating with it, articulating it.[3] Whenever the Group arrives somewhere to perform, the first exercises put people in touch with space.

> Move through the space, explore it in different ways. Feel it, look at it, speak to it, rub it, listen to it, make sounds with it, play music with it, embrace it, smell it, lick it, etc.

Let the space do things to you: embrace you, hold you, move you, push you around, lift you up, crush you, etc.

Let sounds come out of you in relation to the space to its volumes, rhythms, textures, materials.

Walk through the space, run, roll, somersault, swim, fly.[4]

Call to another person with words, with names, with unworded sounds, with unsounded breathing. Listen to the calls, try them from different places.

Then find a place where you feel most safe. Examine this place carefully, make it your home. Call from this place, this home, this nest. Then find a place where you feel most threatened. Call from there. Move from the bad place to the good place while singing softly.

I believe there is an actual, living relationship between the spaces of the body and the spaces the body moves through; that human living tissue does not abruptly stop at the skin. Exercises with space are built on the assumption that human beings and space are both alive. The exercises offer means by which people communicate with space and with each other through space; ways of locating centres of energy and boundaries, areas of inter-penetration, exchange, and isolation, 'auras' and 'lines of energy'.[5]

An exercise based on these assumptions was developed by the Group at the start of a summer residency at the University of Rhode Island in 1971.

1. Performers move slowly towards each other until they are compressed into a living ball. They pack themselves together more and more tightly. They collapse towards no space, towards infinite inward pressure [Fig. 1].

2. Then, an explosion of the primal mass into the space; an explosion with sound. Ideally, the primal mass is at the centre of the space, equidistant from walls, ceiling, and floor—so that the explosion goes in all directions [Fig. 2].

3. Each person comes to rest in a place where he feels safe, centred, defined in relation to space and others. From this centre each person

marks out his boundaries, finds the points where he confronts others, where there are contested spaces, where he harmoniously shares space. The space is structured by fields of personal energies [Fig. 3].
4. Each performer determines for himself a route through the space.

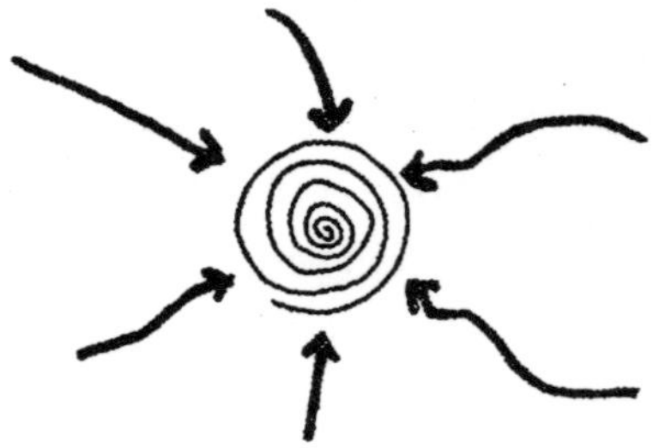

Fig. 1

He keeps this map to himself, and once it is set, it cannot be changed. The reason for this rigidity is so that the experience of one performer does not cause another performer to alter his route, his own experience. Of course the exercise can be done with people choosing maps

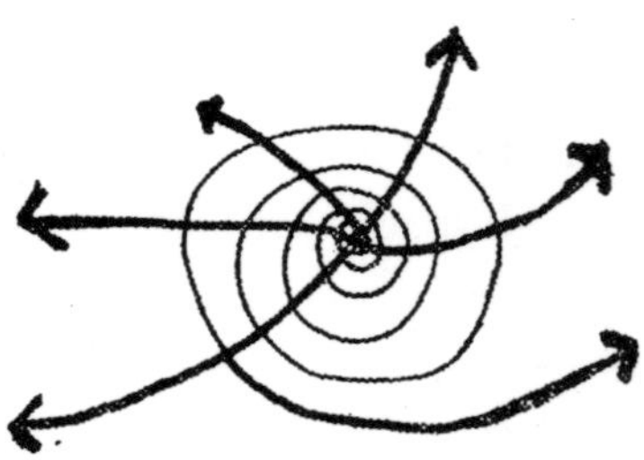

Fig. 2

on the moment. The map of performer *A* is shown in Fig.4.
5. Performer *A* passes through many different energy fields. Sometimes he is drawn in, sometimes pushed away, sometimes torn between two or more currents. As *A* makes his way, the others react with sounds, movements (without displacing the feet), and breathing

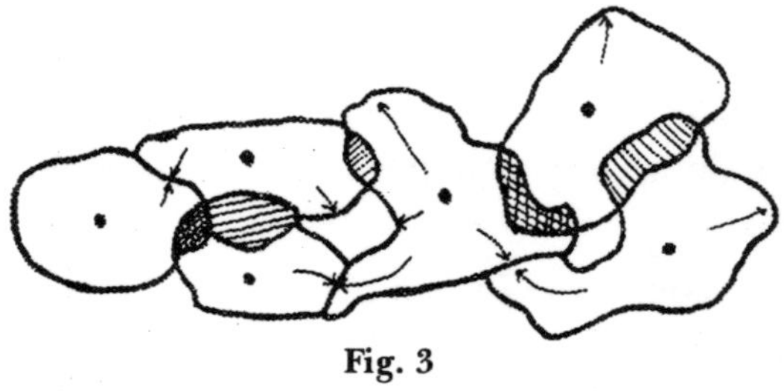

Fig. 3

rhythms. *A* moves either fast or slow, depending on the energies he feels; he makes sounds or remains silent [Fig. 5].

This exercise with its allusions to the 'big bang' theory of universal creation and to the voyage home of Ulysses through seas of temptations, dangers, and pleasures gives performers a sense of *how full space is.* The problem is identifying the constantly changing patterns of energy that radiate through spaces—energy that comes from people, from things, from the shapes of space.

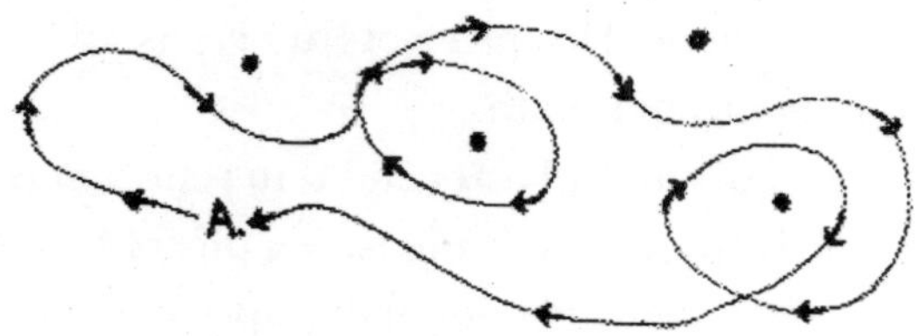

Fig. 4

Exercises like the two described help performers make space-maps—read space in many different ways. Western thought accustoms us to treat space visually. But acoustic, thermal, tactile, olfactory, and brain-wave maps can also be drawn. An olfactory map, for example, will not have the sharp edges of a visual map—it will be fluid, always changing, literally drifting on the wind, with eddies and intense centres shading off towards ill-defined edges.

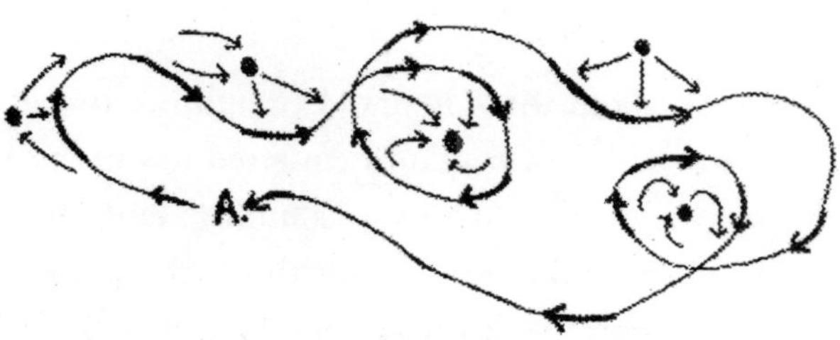

Fig. 5

In the spring of 1969 TPG explored the relationship between the snout—the nose and mouth, the cavities of the sinuses and throat, the gut, and the larger spaces in the theatre to the large gut spaces in the body. The work culminated with an exercise in June:

> Everyone concentrates on the fruit. Imagine biting into it, tasting it, smelling it. Then, one at a time, performers go to the basket and using only the snout take one grape or berry. Roll it around your mouth, under your tongue; play with it as long as you can. Then bite into it, feel its juices and flavour, chew it as slowly as you can. Swallow.
>
> One performer goes back to the basket, takes a berry or grape with his snout. This piece of fruit is passed around the circle from mouth to mouth.
>
> Everyone goes to the basket and with your snouts, making as many trips as necessary, bring back a pile of fruit for yourself. Then put as many berries and grapes in your mouth as you can keep count of. When you lose count of how many you have, bite. Let the juices run down your chin. Sit quietly.
>
> Look at the basket. Everyone at once, animal-like, making sounds, using only snouts, rush to the basket and take the fruit. Carry it to a safe place and eat.
>
> Find each other. Clean each other with your tongues, catstyle. Relax, make sounds, take each other in. Take in the whole scene: empty basket, white cloth, stained clothing, scatterings of fruit-leavings.

This exercise took about three hours. The lighting in the Garage was a spotlight on the basket of fruit and scattered low-intensity lights elsewhere. The *Dionysus* environment was standing, and the soft rugs helped the exercise. I recall the fierceness with which people took the fruit and devoured it. Then they rushed from the centre of the theatre to dens, perches, nests, lairs. Only after a long while did they return to the open.

Through a process I don't understand but accept, *the insides of the body perceive space directly*. This visceral space-sense is activated by exercises like the fruit-eating. Exercises in smelling also activate the visceral space-sense. Visceral perception is related to the actual wash of the guts inside the body. To get at this you have to let go of sight, hearing, and touching with the skin. Things must be tasted and smelled, touched with the nostrils, mouth, lips, tongue, anus, and genitals: those places where the viscera is on or close to the surface. Visceral space-sense is not about edges, boundaries, outlines; it is about volumes, mass, and rhythm. The exercise in which a performer moves through spaces energized by others is about boundaries. 'Fruit-eating' is about rhythm.

I can't draw all this material into a neat bundle because I don't have a theory that can handle it. But let me throw a few more things at you. Richard Gould says that Australian aborigines perceive landmarks as 'nothing less than the bodies of the totemic beings, or items connected with them, transformed . . . into individual waterholes, trees, sandhills, ridges, and other physiographic features, as wells into rock alignments and sacred rock-piles.'[6] This is very much like what S. Giedion finds in the prehistoric art of the caves:

> One could give an almost endless list of instances showing how forms of animals, imbued with mystic significance, were born out of the rock: the bison in La Mouth (Dordogne), where the whole outline of the back, and to a certain extent even of the head, had been formed by the natural rock; the bison of the cavern of El Castillo (Santander), where major parts of the body had been seen in a stalactite and only a few lines were necessary to bring out the image; the group of polychrome bison on the ceiling of the cavern of Altamira, whose unusual recumbent positions stem from the form of the rock protuberances . . . Rock, animal, and outline form an inseparable unit.[7]

Or the things Antonin Artaud saw in Mexico:

> Nature has wished to express itself over a race's entire geographic compass . . . I was able to grasp that I was not dealing with sculpted forms but with a specific play of light, which *combined* itself with the outline of the rocks . . . And I saw that all the rocks had the shape of women's busts on which two breasts were perfectly outlined.[8]

Artaud also saw heads, torsos in agony, crucifixions, men on horses, huge phalluses, and other images impressed on the rocks or rising from them. 'I saw all these forms became reality, little by little, in accordance with their rule.'

In all these cases not only is the separation between man and his environment transcended, but each is the image of the other. A recurrent claim of shamans is that they can take their guts out, wash them, and replace them; or that they have had their corruptible human guts replaced by eternally durable ones of stone.

The visceral space-sense is elusive, even for those who have experienced it. It is a communication from within the spaces of the body to within the spaces of the place one is in. You become aware of your body as a system of volumes, areas, and rhythms; as a coordinated collection of chambers, channels, solids, fluids, and gases; as a combination of resilient, hard, inner skeleton covered and held together by supple, tensile muscles and membranes—all this supporting and surrounding central, pulsating, life-source bays, gulfs, and bundles of mobile guts.

Donald M. Kaplan has carried these ideas to the point where he believes all theatre architecture is an expression of infant body-states. He thinks that the proscenium is a perfected form wherein the digestive guts seated in the darkened auditorium hungrily await the 'food' chewed and fed from the brilliantly illuminated stage (mouth). 'The interface of stage and auditorium is not a celebration of a maturational achievement, as certain other architectural forms are. A theatre reminds us of a dynamic condition.'[9] This condition is the digestive tract from mouth to stomach.

> Thus, as the theatre fills up and the performers prepare to go on, a voracity in the auditorium is about to be shaped and regulated from the stage by an active exercise of some kind of prescribed skill. At this point, we can begin to answer the question of what a theatre does kinesthetically, by observing that its geometrics and functions favour a juxtaposition of a *visceral* and *executive* experience.[10]

The visceral audience awaits satisfaction from the actors who feed the performance to them.

By putting everyone on stage, so to speak, the environmental theatre does away with the dichotomy Kaplan identified. The audience in environmental theatre must look to itself, as well as to the performers, for satisfaction of visceral needs. This less sharply delineated division of roles, actions, and spaces leads *not* to deeper involvement, not to a feeling of being swept away by the action—the bottomless empathy enhanced by darkness, distance, solitude-in-a crowd, and regressive, cushioned comfort of a proscenium theatre—but to a kind of in-and-out experience; a sometimes dizzyingly rapid alternation of empathy and distance.

The orthodox theatre-goer is snuggled. He can keep his reactions to himself, and he is more likely to get utterly wrapped up in the experience on stage. This is even truer in the movies, where there is absolutely no responsibility to respond, because the actors in a film are not present at the theatre. In the environmental theatre the lighting and arrangement of space make it impossible to look at an action without seeing other spectators who visually, at least, are part of the performance. Nor is it possible to avoid a knowledge that for the others you are part of the performance. And in so far as performing means taking on the executive function, every spectator is forced into that to some degree by the architecture of environmental theatre.

Spectators experience great extremes—of deep, perhaps active involvement and participation; then critical distancing, looking at the performance, the theatre, the other spectators as if from very far away. Sometimes a spectator will freak out, go so far into the experience that he is lost inside it. More than a few times I have talked someone back from very far places. But the other extreme also occurs. I have spent many hours watching performances from a detached, disinterested point of view; and I have seen others do likewise. This is not a question of boredom, but of focusing on aspects of the performance other than the narrative, or the feelings of the performers. These aspects technical, environmental, spectator behaviour—are masked in the orthodox theatre. You couldn't focus on them if you wanted to. In environmental theatre there are endless degrees of attention, subtle gradations of involvement. The experience of being a spectator, if you let yourself get into it, is not smooth but roller-coaster.

Many people, trained in the rigid reaction programme of orthodox theatre, are embarrassed by what they feel at environmental theatre. They think that the in-and-out reaction is 'wrong' or an indication that the play 'doesn't work'. People come up to me and say, 'I couldn't keep my attention focused on the play'. Or, 'I was moved by some of it, but I kept thinking my own thoughts. Sometimes I lost track of what was going on.' Or, 'Sometimes I felt good, but at other times I felt threatened'. Or, 'You know, I watched the audience so much I lost part of the play.' Or even, 'I fell asleep.' I think all of these responses are splendid.

IF THE BODY is one source of environmental theatre design, there are also historical and cultural sources. The body gives data for space-senses while historical or cultural studies give data for *space-fields*. Modern European-American culture is prejudiced in favour of rectangular, hard-edged spaces with clear boundaries and definite senses of right and left, up and down. There is only a blurry idea of what happens inside these boundaries. We fight wars to preserve boundaries, while letting the life inside our nations deteriorate.

Space may be organized without a single axis, as among the Eskimo where figures in the same field are 'upside down' relative to each other. Give an Eskimo child a paper to draw on, and he will fill up one side and continue to draw on the other side with no more thought of discontinuity than you have when you follow a sentence in this book from one page to the next. Space may be organized with a distorted or permutated axis as in surrealist art or topographic mathematics. Or it may be organized according to the X-ray technique of the Northwest Coast Indians who see the inside and outside of an object with equal clarity—a cow with her unborn calf in her belly, a fish with a hook lodged in its throat, a man with his heart beating in his chest.

Space can be organized according to time, so that sequence in space = progression in time, as in Egyptian panels, medieval tryp-

Space may be organized without a single axis, as among the Eskimo where figures in the same field are 'upside down' relative to each other. Give an Eskimo child a paper to draw on, and he will fill up one side and continue to draw on the other side with no more thought of discontinuity than you have when you follow a sentence in this book from one page to the next. Space may be organized with a distorted or permutated axis as in surrealist art or topographic mathematics. Or it may be organized according to the X-ray technique of the Northwest Coast Indians who see the inside and outside of an object with equal clarity—a cow with her unborn calf in her belly, a fish with a hook lodged in its throat, a man with his heart beating in his chest.

Space can be organized according to time, so that sequence in space = progression in time, as in Egyptian panels, medieval tryptichs, and the settings for morality plays in which the progress of history from the Creation to the Fall to the Crucifixion to Salvation or Hell was plain to all who had eyes to see. Space can be organized so that size, not distance, indicates importance. In Egyptian art the gods are biggest, the pharaohs next, and so on through many classes until we reach tiny slaves. Examples are without limit. Space can be shaped to suit any need.

The concept of *space-field* may be easier to grasp if I briefly present five kinds of performance space-fields: Egyptian, Greek, Balinese, Mexican, and New Guinean. The first two are historical, and the last three exist today.

The Egyptians staged periodic ceremonial spectacles. For these they built entire cities and floated great, ornate barges down the Nile. The river was not only the liquid, flowing stage for much of the Heb-Sed; it was itself the source of all Egyptian life, a living participant in the great drama of renewal. Time itself was stopped for the Heb-Sed festival. (We retain this idea of a holiday being time out.) The days of the Heb-Sed were not part of the calendar. The function of the mighty festival was to renew all of Egypt starting with the pharaoh. He himself played the major role in the drama. 'It was not a mere commemoration of the king's accession. It was a true renewal of kingly potency.'[11]

The theatre event was performed in a special place that existed in a special time. But through this specialness flowed the eternal Nile which was both sacred and profane. And like the Nile, everyday Egyptian life was transformed by the Heb-Sed and renewed [Fig. 6].

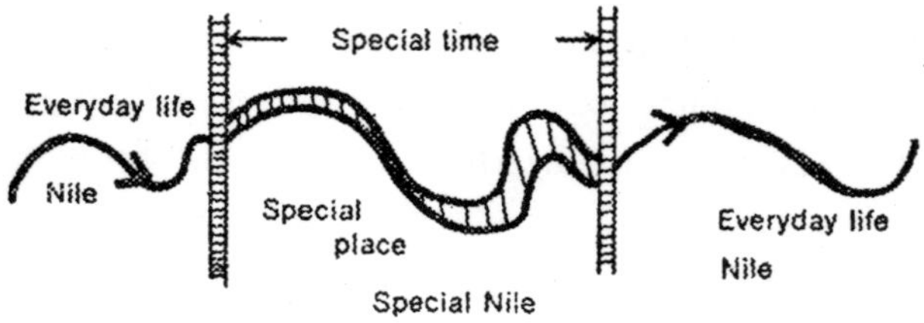

Fig. 6

Via Crete and other Mediterranean stepping-stones the Greeks took much from the Egyptians including the idea that the theatre is a festival: something that exists at a special time in a special place. But the Greeks were also influenced by prehistoric shamanistic ceremonies coming down from Central Asia and Europe. Animism, nature worship, and landscape were very important to the Greeks who, in this regard, were not so far from today's aborigines. The Greek theatre raised its audience in a semicircle around a full-circle dancing area. The audience area was made from a natural hill, and every Greek theatre gives a beautiful view over the skene to the landscape beyond. Thus the Greek arrangement included elements of holiday (= time out) and continuity with the landscape and the gods who dwelt therein [Fig. 7].

Furthermore, the Greeks liked watching the dances not as discrete moves but as completed sequences, finished figures—a kind of stepped-out destiny in movement. In some surviving Greek theatres there are pavements of different coloured stones tracing the dance routes: architectural scripts. These pavements help the memories of dancers and spectators alike. At any given moment the whole dance is known, and the dancers are seen as figures somewhere on the course. We tried for something like this in the *Commune* environment where different maps, figures, routes, and writing were marked on the floor and other parts of the environment. We used masking tape beçause that suggests the police reconstructing a crime and a stage manager marking the floor of a theatre.

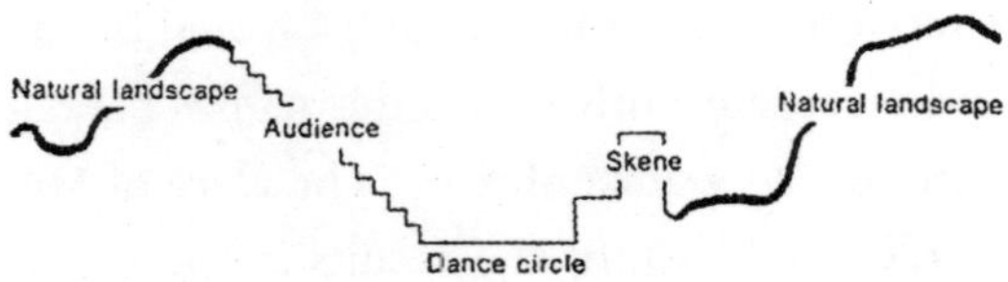

Fig. 7

Nothing could be farther from the Egyptian and Greek uses of space than the Balinese. The Balinese build nothing special for theatre. They do no seasonal plays. They perform in the village square, on temple steps, in courtyards, or on temporary stages thrown up for the occasion. And the occasion may be a marriage, a birth, a stroke of good fortune, a Hindu holiday, a need to placate the gods, or the means by which a rich man shows how rich he is. The performers are magnificently costumed and trained; they are professional in every sense except the commercial. But there is little formality surrounding a performance. Dogs eat some of the ceremonial food signalling the gods' acceptance of the offering, children play in the street in the midst of the trance-dancers, old men doze on their porches, women market, and those who want to watch the play do. Theatre in Bali accompanies everyday life. There is no time out for theatre. To the Balinese theatre happens anytime, anywhere, and its gestures are continuous with the rest of living [Fig. 8].

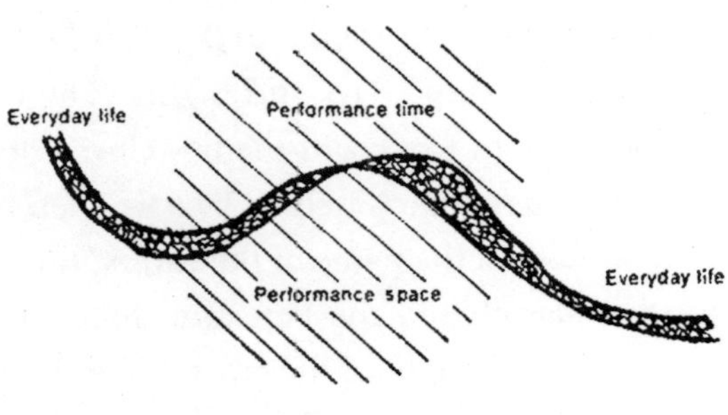

Fig. 8

This integration of ceremonial and everyday is present in many Oriental cultures. M. C. Richards describes the Japanese Raku Ware where a person makes a teacup, fires it, and drinks out of it 'all in a single rhythm'.[12] The high formality of Japanese theatre is a refinement of daily, courtly, and military gestures. There is no break existing village remains intact, but it is transformed by the drama into another time and place. Recently such a drama has been uncovered in the coastal mountains of western Mexico. The Cora of Mesa del Nayar were converted to Catholicism by the Jesuits in the sixteenth century. Then in 1767 the Jesuits were expelled from Mexico. No priest appeared on the Mesa until 1969. During the two hundred years without contact these Cora maintained many Roman Catholic rites, among them a Holy Week passion play.

> But they made them uniquely their own. For example, they had come to identify Our Lord Jesus Christ with their ancient deity Tatayu, the sun god . . . They took elements from the story of Christ's Passion, death, and Resurrection and made them into a ceremony designed to ensure the renewal and continuity of their communal life.[13]

In the Cora play a boy of about seven plays Christ. There is no Pilate, no Judas. The villains are called *borrados*, which means 'erased ones' in Spanish. The borrados are the Judeans responsible for the crucifixion. For the three days of the festival 'all authority, civil and religious, passes to a man called the Captain of the Judeans. He and his *borrados*—young men of the region—darken themselves with soot and mud and thus 'erase' their own personalities and their personal responsibility for whatever they are about to do.' Fortified with peyote, the *borrados* hold forth for three days and nights. The crucifixion is preceded by a chase through town with the boy-Christ doing his best to get away from the *borrados*. He is helped by a wooden cross that he brandishes. 'Three times—in the name of the Father, the Son, and the Holy Ghost—the *borrados* chased the boy, and three times they fell writhing to the ground at the sight of the cross.' Then they catch him, tie him, and bring him to the church. There women groom him, and he sleeps overnight. The next morning he is brought out by the *borrados* and made to stand in front of a cross in the churchyard. This is the crucifixion. The next day at noon the village governor arrives on horseback. He plays the role of the centurion. He rides among the *borrados* and breaks their bamboo spears. They fall dead to the ground and then get up, go to the stream, and take a purifying bath. 'Near the tie him, and bring him to the church. There women groom him, and he sleeps overnight. The next morning he is brought out by the *borrados* and made to stand in front of a cross in the churchyard. This is the crucifixion. The next day at noon the village governor arrives on horseback. He plays the role of the centurion. He rides among the *borrados* and breaks their bamboo spears. They fall dead to the ground and then get up, go to the stream, and take a purifying bath. 'Near the church all was mirth and happiness.' Many things are interesting about the Cora play: how it is integrated into the life of the village, the changes made in the traditional Christ story, the double quality of drama and initiation ritual.

The Central Highlands of New Guinea provides the fifth model of using space. Catherine Berndt observed an all-night ceremony and noted the changes that occurred in a large open field.[14] 'At first there were distinct clusters of dancers, although the edges of the clusters blur as people greet kin, attend to ovens, or rest on the sidelines.' The blurring continues leading to wholesale intermingling 'until it becomes impossible to distinguish groups. Nevertheless, a certain nucleus is likely to resist this tendency to disperse.' Finally, as the time to set off for home approaches, 'the various units reform (though less compactly then before) and set off' [Fig. 9].

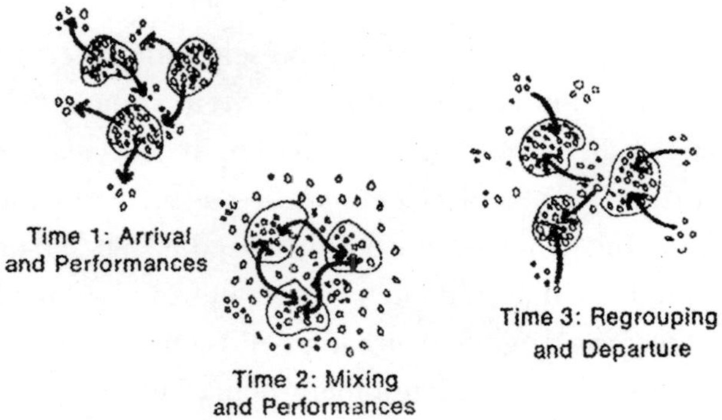

Fig. 9

This is not unlike what happens at a party—except that in New Guinea the gathering is the occasion for performances of farces, dances, and songs. These are ornately costumed and often carefully staged.

use suits the great formality and impressive scale of the Heb-Sed. What the environmentalist learns in studying these examples—and many others—is that space-time-action is a single, flexible unit. The first obstacle to environmental design is preconception. The great enemy of preconception is a knowledge of cultures and periods other than one's own.

THUS FAR I'VE SPOKEN of environmental design abstractly. I've said that it is related to body spaces, space-senses, and space-fields, but I have not been concrete in showing how. For one thing environmental design practice is ahead of theory. This is true partly because there are so many extraordinary examples of environmental design if we simply open our eyes to see. Whether the environmentalist looks at American Indian, Asian, Oceanic, African, Siberian, or Eskimo societies, he finds many models that may stimulate his creativity. Also he can look back in history as far as he can—to Altamira and the other caves; and then forward to Egypt, the Near and Middle East, Asia, and medieval Europe. In our own day he can study productions like Ludovico Ronconi's *Orlando Furioso*, Gilbert Moses' and Archie Shepp's *Slave Ship* (designed by Eugene Lee), Peter Brook's *Tempest* and *Orghast*, the work of Jerzy Grotowski, and the extraordinary work of Peter Schumann and the Bread and Puppet Theater.

What all of these works past and present, dramatic and ritual, in industrial and non-industrial societies have in common is that they each create or use whole space. Whether it is *Orghast* or Robert Wilson's *Ka Mountain* and *Guardenia Terrace* set amid the ruins of Persepolis and the mountains near Shiraz, or the Heb-Sed on the Nile, or an initiation rite that starts in a village, moves to a road leading to the river, climaxes along the riverbanks, and concludes back in the village, or *Akropolis* with its environment being built out of stovepipes during the performance, or a pig-kill and dance at Kurumugl in New Guinea—each example is of an event whose expression in space is a complete statement of what the event is.

Sometimes the space is broken into many spaces. Sometimes the audience is given a special place to watch from. Sometimes the space is treated fluidly, changing during the performance. Sometimes nothing is done to the space. The thing about environmental theatre space is not just a matter of how you end up using space. It is an attitude. *Start with all the space there is and then decide what to use, what not to use, and how to use what you use.*

Work on *Makbeth* began in October 1968, with workshops exploring Shakespeare's *Macbeth*. We did a lot of exercises about prophecy, laying on hands, witchcraft. We took the text apart and reassembled it in funny ways. We tried to find the main threads of action from both an individual and a group point of view. In December we had Rojo and McNamara down to the Garage. Both of them sat in on workshops and talk. Many models of the environment were proposed. We selected, finally, Rojo's—but did not discard McNamara's. After modification it became the Makbeth Maze: the way into the theatre from the second floor of the Garage. The Maze was a bit of Madame Tussaud, a bit of fun house, scraps of theatre history, mirrors, and information about the performance. It ended at an open hole in the floor, a narrow descent into Makbeth's hell.[15]

The mise-en-scène for *Makbeth* was worked out in six phases, the environment in five.

Mise-en-scène

1. October 1968–February 1969. Improvisations without keeping to Shakespeare's text. Search for basic actions, basic movement patterns. First determination of space-field as 'cabin'd, cribb'd, and confin'd.'

2. March-June 1969. Making of scenes not in Shakespeare. These expressed some actual situations in the Group. Using Shakespeare's text as raw material. Demystifying Shakespeare. First character groupings: Dark Powers, Founders, Doers, Avengers.

3. July–August 1969. Cast assignments. Decisions about the shape of the space, the nature of the music. Much work with Rojo and Epstein. End of group workshops. I worked alone assembling what we had into a coherent script.

4. September 1969. Rehearsals in Baocic, Yugoslavia, while Rojo built the environment in the Garage. Composition of music by Epstein in Philadelphia.

5. October–November 1969. Rehearsals in the Garage. Revision of script. Integration of music into the production. Opening.

6. December 1969–January 1970. Run. Few changes except tightening. Closing.

The second phase of work didn't yield an acceptable performance text, but it gave performers a handle on the language. The work overcame the scared feelings people have when first approaching sacred Shakespeare. Also the second phase made it clear how to organize the story and divide the roles.

Environment

1. October 1968–February 1969. Rojo, McNamara, and I discussed the themes of the play and possibilities for the environment. They came to a few workshops.

2. March–May 1969. Rojo and McNamara attended Wednesday night workshops devoted to text construction and environment. Drawings and models, many rejected ideas including ziggurats, corrals, and wire fences. Finally, Rojo's design is accepted, and McNamara's is transformed into the Maze.

3. June–August, 1969. Construction of working models. Decision to move Maze upstairs and use it as the way into the environment downstairs. Approval of final building plans before my departure for Yugoslavia in August. Also approval of costumes.

4. September I969. Construction of about 90 per cent of the environment while the Group rehearsed in Yugoslavia.

5. October 1969. Completion of environment, lighting, costumes.

The big mistake with *Makbeth* was that we rehearsed it in Baocic, and the space-field of that outdoor meadow stayed with us. It was

1 TOP. Performance warmups for Dionysus in 69. Performers stretch out on their backs for breathing excercises. Warmups take about one hour.

2 BOTTOM LEFT. One of the towers of Thebes. The spectators are citizens of Thebes as well as theatregoers. They share this identification with the performers.

3 BOTTOM RIGHT. Dionysus in 69.

All photos by Fred Eberstadt.

4 TOP LEFT. Taking *Dionysus* out into Wooster Street—exploding the space of the theatre. Photo by Fred Eberstadt.

5 TOP RIGHT. *Makbeth* environment, looking across the table to the stairway down which the audience comes entering the theatre from the second floor.

6 BOTTOM LEFT. Lady Makbeth as she appears while the audience is entering. Quietly she recites the text of Makbeth's letter to her.

7. BOTTOM RIGHT. Spectators and performers in the final scene of *Commune*, as a reporter interviews Spalding/Polanski conerning the death of Sharon Tate.

8 TOP LEFT. *The Tooth of Crime* environment, looking from the gallery to the centre structure.

9 TOP RIGHT. Kattrin in *Mother Courage*, scene 8, on a cold winter's night spent on the street in front of the Performing Garage. 1975. Leeny Sack as Kattrin. Photo by Richard Schechner.

10 BOTTOM. James Clayburgh's environment in the Performing Garage for Seneca's *Oedipus* in Ted Hughes' translation. Twenty-seven tons of earth were shoveled into the space making for a three-feet deep soil in which masks and other evidence of the past crime were buried. 1976. Photo by Richard Schechner.

11 LEFT. Swiss Cheese being hoisted aloft in *Mother Courage*, scene 3. 1975. The Performing Garage, New York, with Joan Macintosh as Mother Courage, Spalding Gray as Swiss Cheese.

12. RIGHT. Bertolt Brecht's *Mother Courage*, 1976, at Singjole, a village near Calcutta. Joan Macintosh as Courage.

All photos by Richard Schechner.

impossible to work effectively in the Garage environment. The Yugoslavian rehearsals broke in two our work on the play; and yet the rehearsals in Yugoslavia gave us the fundamental scenic actions. The production could not survive the contradiction. Ultimately the magnificent Garage environment was alien to a mise-en-scène worked out in Yugoslavia.

The Baocic meadow was large; performers looked across at adversaries who could be seen but not heard. There was a limitless ceiling of sky, the play of natural light, the sweet smell of clean air. In the meadow the Dark Powers transformed into birds hiding in the trees or woodchucks in the underbrush. The Makbeths lived atop a knoll near a large tree. Malcolm and Macduff, after the murder of their father, Duncan, took a long semicircular route through forests and shrubs to get at the Makbeths. I directed by running from one side of the meadow to another, ducking behind trees or rocks, flattened on my belly in the grass, watching, yelling directions, just keeping up with the action. I saw Banquo, trapped by the Dark Powers in a blind alley of shrubbery, vainly struggle before they bashed her head in with a rock. I hid nearby as the Dark Powers lured Makbeth into a dusky gully cut by a brook and whispered to him that he would never be slain by a man of woman born. I watched as Malcolm and Macduff, assisted by the Dark Powers, camouflaged themselves with grass and branches and advanced on Dunsinane. Only a few of these scenes were translatable into the Garage environment. The long, deep pit against the north wall served well as the gully-home of the Dark Powers; Banquo was trapped amid the wood columns supporting the environment; the advancing Malcolm and Macduff darted from column to column as in a forest as they approached Dunsinane. But the amplitude of the Baocic meadow could not be stuffed into Rojo's magnificent Garage environment. Furthermore, this amplitude did not suit the play we started the previous winter in New York.

What happened during the month's rehearsals in Baocic was that the performers developed the action according to the space-field there while Rojo built from what he perceived from workshops. The spacefield of Baocic contradicted the space-field of Rojo's environment. Disunity within the Group made it impossible to overcome or live with this contradiction. We could not use it creatively. I remember William Finley saying, when he first saw the Garage, 'It's great, really marvellous, but how do we work in it?' I panicked and resorted to blocking. Instead of taking the time to let the performers feel their way around, through, and into the space, I imposed actions and rhythms. Throughout its run *Makbeth* never felt at home in the Garage. I hope I've learned the lesson: *Text, action and environment must develop together*.

Rojo's environment had one supreme quality: it incorporated the tensions he sensed in the Group, conflicts that led to the dissolution of TPG early in 1970. The rehearsals of *Makbeth* coincided with the undoing of the Group. Daily, heavy personal things came down, and although no one said so out loud, I think we each knew that *Makbeth* was our last play together. Because of the way TPG works, our conflicts fed into the structure of *Makbeth*. It became an angry play of blood, power struggles, betrayals, fleeting contacts, brief flashes of quiet punctuated by screams. All of this is in Shakespeare's script. It also characterized the environment. Gone were the soft carpets and suffused lighting of *Dionysus* replaced by a concrete floor, bare wood platforms framed by iron piping, lighting that came in fitful bursts. The bare feet of *Dionysus* gave way to boxing shoes, nakedness to unisex costumes of crushed corduroy.

It was better with *Commune*. Rojo and I met during the spring of 1970 to talk over the play while it was in its very early stages. He visited New Paltz several times during the summer to watch workshops and present and revise his drawings and models. Sculptor Robert Adzema made several models that were helpful in getting the environment together. Everyone in the Group went over the models and made suggestions. At the end of July the Wave was built in New Paltz, and we rehearsed with it for the rest of the summer. We appropriated scaffolding and built an approximation of the environment Rojo was designing. He saw enough rehearsals to change his plans according to what was happening to the play. There were weekly open rehearsals to see how the audience reacted to the environment. By the end of August a plan was agreed on, and during September while TPG and

Wave were in residence at Goddard, Rojo built about one-third of the environment in the Garage. In October we did a few open rehearsals in the Garage working in the partially finished environment. Rojo learned from watching us work. He completed the environment in October while the Group was on tour—still with the Wave, our cumbersome environmental security blanket. When the Group returned to New York in November, everyone pitched in to paint the Garage. We painted the ceiling sky blue and the walls desert red-brown. The environment was finished. Later, during performances, spectators—given chalk—added much interesting graffiti.

Some of the graffiti is still on the ceiling, even for *The Tooth of Crime*. And lumber, fittings, scraps of every environment ever built in the Garage comprise part of whatever is most current. This is not only a matter of economy. Like new cities built on the rubble and from the rubble of older ones, the present recapitulates and transforms the past: there is a tangible tradition in the Garage.

There is no such thing as a standard environmental design. A standard design mocks the basic principle: *The event, the performers, the environmentalist, the director, and the audience interacting with each other in a space (or spaces) determine the environment.* Having said that, I offer a 'standard environmental design'. A theatre ought to *offer to each spectator the chance to find his own* place. There ought to be *jumping–off places* where spectators can physically enter the performance; there ought to be *regular places* where spectators can arrange themselves more or less as they would in an orthodox theatre—this helps relieve the anxieties some people feel when entering an environmental theatre; there ought to be *vantage points* where people can get out of the way of the main action and look at it with detachment; there ought to be *pinnacles, dens, and hutches*: extreme places far up, far back, and deep down where spectators can dangle or burrow or vanish. At most levels there ought to be places where people can be alone, be together with one or two others, or be with a fairly large group. Spaces ought to be open enough so that in most of them people can stand, sit, lean, or lie down as the mood directs. Spaces ought to open to each other so that spectators can see each other and move from one place to another. The overall feel of the theatre ought to be of a place where choices can be made. The feel I get from a successful environment is that of a *global space*, a microcosm, with flow, contact, and interaction.

This long list of 'ought to be's' is obliterated by the specific needs of a production. None of the TPG environments meets all of these 'requirements'.

As the environmentalist works, particularly if he is new at the game, he should ask himself questions. These questions are implicit in the work, different from questions an orthodox designer might ask.

1. Does the mass, volume, and rhythm of the whole environment express the play? Not the play as I abstractly conceive it, but as I have watched it develop in rehearsals?

2. Does the material out of which the environment is built—texture, weight, colour, density, feel—express the play?

3. Can spectators see each other? Can they hide from each other? Can they stand, sit, lean, lie down? Can they be alone, in small groups, in larger groups?

4. Are there places to look down on most of the action, to look across at it, to look up to it ?

5. Where are the places for performing? How are they connected to each other? How many places are used both by the audience and by the performers?

6. Are there efficient ways of moving up and down as well as in all horizontal directions ?

7. What does the environment sound like? How does it smell?

8. Can every surface and supporting member safely hold as many people as can crowd onto it? Are there at least two ways in and out of every space?

The thing about safety is that nothing should be disguised. If a ladder is hard to climb, make it look like it's hard to climb. In five years' working in the Garage there have been no major accidents and only a few scrapes and sprains. The worst that's happened has been a broken foot that occurred to William Shephard when he made a spectacular leap changing his course in midair to avoid demolishing a spectator.

The environmentalist is not trying to create the illusion of a place; he wants to create a functioning space. This space will be used by many different kinds of people, not only the performers. The stage designer is often concerned with effect: how does it *look* from the house? The environmentalist is concerned with structure and use: how does it *work*? Often the stage designer's set is used from a distance—don't touch this, don't stand on that—but everything the environmentalist builds must work. Stage designing is two-dimensional, a kind of propped-up painting. Environmental design is strictly three dimensional. If it's there, it's got to work. This leads to sparseness.

HAVE YOU EVER THOUGHT how *stupid* the proscenium theatre is architecturally? Start with the auditorium, the 'house'. A silly name for row after row of regularly arranged seats—little properties that spectators rent for a few hours. Nothing here of the freedom of arrangement in a house where people live—and can push the furniture around. And most of the places in the 'house' are disadvantageous for seeing or hearing. The first few rows are so close that the actors in their effort—to project to the back and up to the balconies—spit all over you; the seats to the side give a fun-house mirror view of the stage, all pulled out of proportion; the seats at the back of the orchestra under the balcony are claustrophobic and acoustically murder; the view from the second balcony makes the stage look like a flea circus. Only a few seats in the orchestra, mezzanine, and first balcony offer anything like a pleasing view of the stage. But this is no surprise. The proscenium theatre was originally designed to emphasize differences in class and wealth. It was meant to have very good seats, medium seats, poor seats, and very bad seats.

When people come late or leave early, they all but step on you, push their asses in your face, and disrupt whole rows of spectators. There is no chance to readjust your body, take a seventh-inning stretch, or extend your arms. During intermission everyone runs to the lobby to gobble food, drink, smoke, talk. Intermission is just about the only human thing going on. Also, of course, to see who's here—which undeniably is one of theatre's chiefest and oldest joys. Not just to look at or for famous people—but to look over the crowd, see who's out with you this evening. This looking is impossible in the darkened house that cruelly makes you focus straight ahead, as in church or at school, at a performance that, finally, may not interest you at all.

The worst thing about the 'house' is that it imprisons you away from the stage where there are many interesting things to see if you were only allowed. What's visible of the stage from the house is only a fraction of its total area and volume. For me the wonderful direction is up. To gaze up into the flies through rods and curtains and lights and ropes and catwalks and galleries into the immense space! Whenever TPG is asked to perform in a proscenium, I accept with enthusiasm. 'Bring everyone on stage,' I say, 'and turn a few lights upward so that people can see how high the flies are.' Also in newer theatres there are vast chambers to the left and right of the playing stage, and often behind the playing area, too. These are for 'wagons', a term as old as medieval theatre, meaning rolling platforms on which whole sets are built and then brought into place. And sometimes there is a turntable—a device Brecht loved. Usually there are trapdoors leading to a cellar under the stage, and doors going to the backstage, the shop, the dressing rooms, the greenroom. So the proscenium stage is a focused space surrounded on every side by other spaces attending on the stage like an old queen. How mean that audiences should be exiled from this royal realm of magic. Such exclusion is pitiable, cheap, unfair, and unnecessary.

My own preference is to do away with most of the machinery. It makes the theatre worker like a soldier trapped inside his burning tank. But I would keep the spaces—the overs, unders, and arounds.

Some new theatres designed by people who want to keep up to date try to keep 'the best' from previous ages. These theatres are like old trees weighted down by so many branches that they break. Such a theatre is the brand-new job at the University of Rhode Island, where TPG was in residence in the summer of 1971. The theatre wasn't even open to the public when I saw it. In the semicircular arrangement of seats in the house is the Greek amphitheatre, in the vomitoria leading from the house to the foot of the orchestra pit is the Roman stadium, in the space for wagons are the medieval moralities and pageants, in the fly system are the Italian scenic conventions of the Renaissance, in the slightly thrust stage is the Elizabethan theatre, in the proscenium posts is the eighteenth-century theatre, in the orchestra pit is the nineteenth-century opera, in the turntable is the early twentieth century, in the bank after bank of computerized lighting controls are contemporary electronics. Pity the poor student actor!

When the Group took one look at this monster, we decided to work in the scene shop—an honest, large, irregular space that could be made into anything. Not by building scenery or pushing buttons, but by putting down a plywood floor we could dance and run and jump on, some scaffolds to climb over, a few velours to soak up extra noise, and fewer than twenty lights to make it bright enough to see. The rest is performing.

THE SIMPLE FACT that in most theatres actors enter through their own door at one time and audience enters through another door at a later time architecturally expresses a strong aesthetic and class consciousness. The separate doors are entrances literally to different worlds. The stage door leads to all the equipment and facilities backstage. This stuff is not at all dressed up. Layers of paint, raw pipes, old scenery, costume racks, lights, wires, tools, are all laid out in ways that facilitate use and accessibility. Except on the stage things are arranged according to systems that make for easy indexing and use. On the stage, of course, things are arranged for the audience's eyes. The audience enters the theatre door into a plush, often ornate, and stylish lobby. This is so even off off-Broadway where, in their own way, the lobbies are modish. The house itself is as plush as the producers can afford to make it. From the house the audience views the stage where an illusion has been created. From the front the stage presents its false but pretty face. From backstage the scenery is ugly (if you like illusions) but working—supports, nails, ropes, and wires are visible—and the view of the stage from behind or the sides reminds me of nothing so much as a ship: a lot of equipment focused in a small space.

What if the audience and the actors were to enter through the same door at the same time? What if all the equipment of the theatre, however arranged, were available to public view at all times? What if we eliminated the distinctions between backstage and onstage, house and stage, stage door and theatre door? No theatre that I know of has done this, not absolutely. Once in Vancouver in August 1972, TPG experimented with a 'real-time' performance of *Commune*. I announced to our workshop and to some university classes that anyone would be welcome to come to the theatre at 6 pm—at the time of the performers' call. About ten students showed up, and they entered the theatre together with the performers. The visitors were free to go wherever they pleased. They watched warm-ups, listened to notes, helped the tech director check the lights, set the props, fill the tub, clean up the theatre. They watched the performers put on their costumes and saw the regular audience arrive at 7:45. Then the performance. After, the routine of closing up the theatre for the night: removing costumes and putting them in the laundry bag for washing, re-collecting props, emptying the tub, and all the other routines of ending. Out of the ten students only two or three stuck for the whole process that was over around 10:30. (*Commune* itself takes only about ninety minutes.) The performers were a little uneasy at their presence for warm-ups and notes. After the performance no one minded who was there. I felt funny, too, and performed a little for the 'real-time' audience. I wanted them to have a good time. Removing the 'magic' from theatre won't be easy.

A further experiment in this line is part of *The Tooth of Crime* production. Performers man the box office, greet spectators as they enter the theatre, explain aspects of the production: particularly the fact that spectators can get as close to a scene as they wish by moving throughout the theatre during the entire performance. At intermission performers prepare and sell coffee, talk to spectators, socialize, and let everyone know when the second act is beginning. The difference between show time and intermission is clear, but there is no attempt made at hiding the non-performing life performers lead even in the midst of a night at theatre. Strikingly enough, I find that the performers' concentration on their work and the audience's interest in the story is not at all diminished by the socializing. If anything, the playing of the play is enhanced. Roles are seen as emerging from a full constellation of activities that include economics, logistics, hostings, and one-to-one relationships. The performers are seen not as the magic people *of* the story but as the people who *play* the story.

WHEN I DESIGN an environment, I try to take into account the space-senses of the performers, of the text-action, and of the space we're working in. These make an irregular circle, an interconnected system that is always changing [Fig. 10].

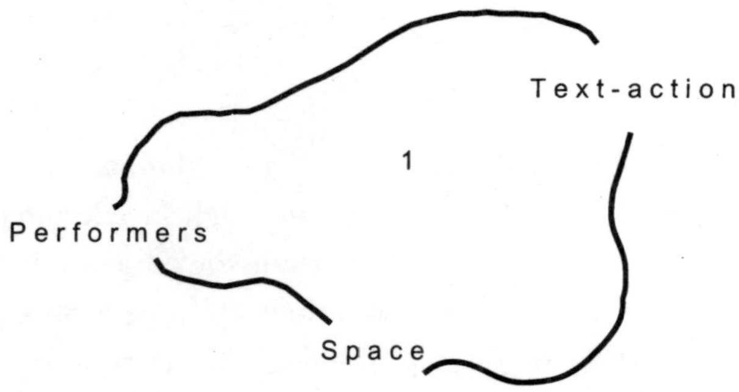

Fig. 10

In time the space gets set as the environment is built. Or doesn't get set. The finest thing about *Orlando Furioso* was the way the environment itself kept changing because the environment was the audience. As the big set pieces crawled or hurtled across the floor, the audience scattered or followed. I climbed a lighting tower and looked down from about twenty feet. Not knowing Italian helped me concentrate on the changing figures of movement. I thought I detected a pattern.

For gentle, quiet scenes the audience pressed in, heads and shoulders forward. Running away from a careening platform, they seemed to run in front of it instead of to the sides as one might expect. In other words, they challenged the platform to run them down—they played a game with the platform. They stood back from declamations, with hips thrust forward, head and shoulders back.

Once the audience is let into the environment, the basic relationship is changed. There are four points on the circle [Fig. 11].

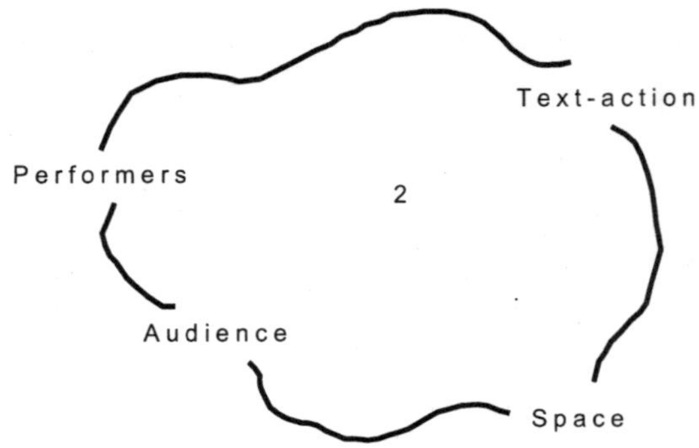

Fig. 11

This is as simple as ABC except that in orthodox theatre the audience is outside the circle. Fixed seating, lighting design, architecture: everything is clearly meant to exclude the audience from any kind of participation in the action. Even their watching is meant to be ignored. The spectators are put into the semi-foetal prison of a chair, and no matter what they feel, it will be hard to physicalize and express those feelings [Fig. 12].

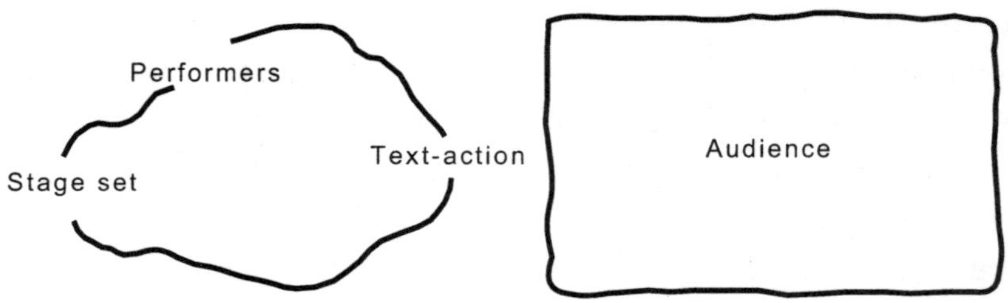

Fig. 12

I don't see any middle ground. Either the audience is in it or they are out of it. Either there is potential for *contact* or there is not. I don't deny that the spectator in the orthodox theatre feels something. Sure he does. *But he cannot easily, naturally, unconsciously, and without embarrassment express those feelings except within idiotically limited limits.*

When we say of a great performer that he or she has *presence,* that

When we say of a great performer that he or she has *presence*, that we are *moved* by the performance, that we have been *touched*, we are not speaking nonsense or entirely metaphorically. Many times I've seen an audience collectively catch its breath, shift position, become very still, change their points of contact and orientation to each other, or to the performers, quite unconsciously, without thought or intention. These changes in body positions, in expressive poses—the way a person fronts himself (or sidles, or turns his shoulder, or his back) on another—on an action is a delightful part of every performance in an environmental theatre. The theatre ought architecturally to offer a rich field for this kind of communication—not only to occur but to be observed by whoever has eyes for it. The orthodox theatre lets the audience see the actors making this kind of movement. But what about letting spectators see spectators and performers see spectators? Such open architecture encourages a contact that is continuous, subtle, fluid, pervasive, and unconscious. Lovely.

Three major tendencies of contemporary Western theatre are exemplified by the ways audiences are arranged and treated. In the orthodox theatre, including so-called open stages, such as arenas, thrust stages, and calipter stages, the stage is brightly lit and active; from it information flows into the darkened auditorium where the audience is arranged in regular seats. Feedback from the house to the stage is limited [Fig. 13].

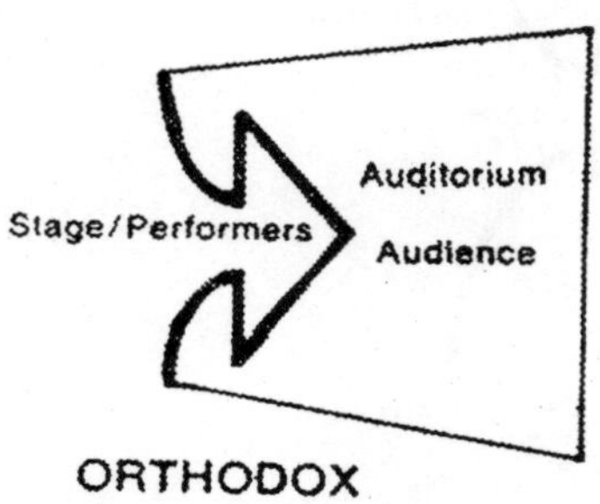

Fig. 13

Stage	*Auditorium*
bright	dark
active	passive
giving	taking
noisy	noisy
irregular arrangement	regular arrangement
costumed	everyday dress
magic space	plain space

Confrontation theatre, as in the Living Theatre's *Paradise Now*, uses orthodox theatre space for unorthodox ends. Many local scenes or confrontations take place both on stage and in the auditorium. The traditional uses of stage and house are frequently inverted. The aim of confrontation theatre is to provoke the audience into participating or at least to make people very uncomfortable about not participating. Confrontational theatre is a transitional form depending heavily on *épater le bourgeois* attitude and the need among the bourgeois to experience suffering as a relief of guilt [Fig. 14].

Stage	*Auditorium*
bright	alternately bright and dark
active	forced into activity
giving–taking	taking–giving
noisy	noisy
irregular arrangement	regular arrangement changed by attempts to use the whole space
usually in street clothes, sometimes naked	usually in street clothes, but sometimes provoked to nakedness or exchange of clothes
magic space made plain	plain space made magic

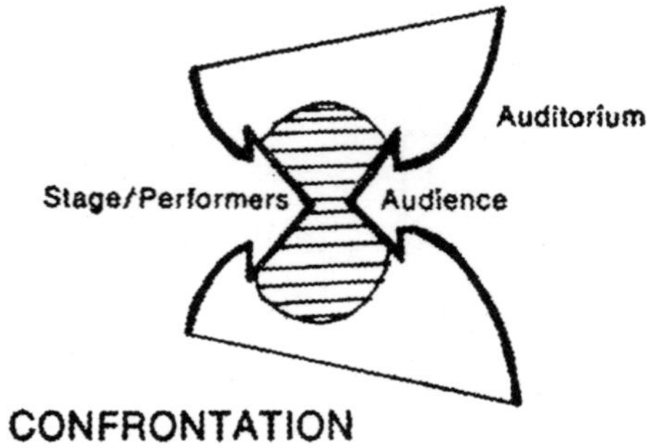

Fig. 14

Environmental theatre encourages give-and-take throughout a globally organized space in which the areas occupied by the audience are a kind of sea through which the performers swim in and the performance areas are kinds of islands or continents in the midst of the audience. The audience does not sit in regularly arranged rows; there is one whole space rather than two opposing spaces. The environmental use of space is fundamentally *collaborative*; the action flows in many directions sustained only by the cooperation of performers and spectators. Environmental theatre design is a reflection of the communal nature of this kind of theatre. The design encourages participation; it is also a reflection of the wish for participation. There are no settled sides automatically dividing the audience off against the performers [Fig. 15].

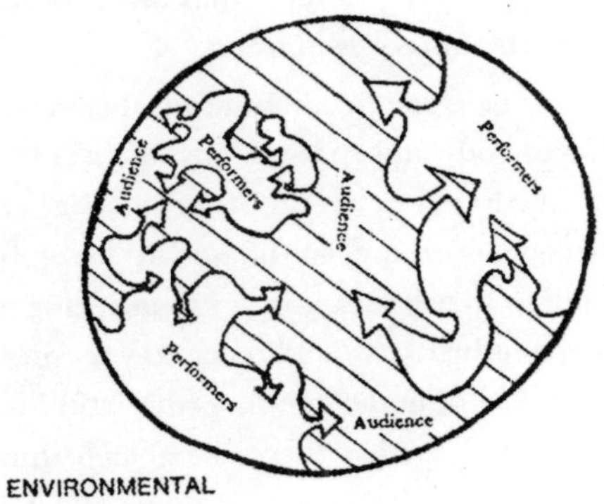

Fig. 15

I end this essay by proposing a few principles of environmental design. These have all been discussed. I gather them as a way of easy reference and summary.

1. For each production the whole space is designed.
2. The design takes into account space-senses and space-fields.
3. Every part of the environment is functional.
4. The environment evolves along with the play it embodies.
5. The performer is included in all phases of planning and building.

The Performance Group, Dionysus 69 (New York: Farrar Straus and Giroux, 1970). A film of the play taken in the Garage is also available.

3. Articulating a space means letting the space have *its* say. Looking at a space and exploring it not as a means of doing what you want to do in it, but of uncovering what the space is, how it is constructed, what its various rhythms are. Maybe staying still in it, as in the spaces of some cathedrals.
4. When an action is literally impossible—such as swimming or flying—the performer does it sonically, or in action with the help of others. If a person cannot fly by himself, he can be carried in such a way that he gets a sense of flying. If he cannot swim through air, he can make his breath find the rhythms of swimming.
5. Much work needs to be done in pinpointing the exact relationships between the human body and space. Many apparently mystical concepts will, I think, be found to have roots in fact. Just as the blind bat sees with high-frequency sound, so the human being has many ways of locating himself in space; means other than seeing and sounding. I believe that energy is broadcast and received very precisely and that we are at the threshold of understanding what and how. Also we are on the verge of conceding that there is no such thing as dead or empty space.
6. Richard A. Gould, *Yiwara: Foragers of the Australian Desert* (New York: Charles Scribner's Sons, 1969), p. 128.
7. S. Giedion, *The Eternal Present: The Beginnings of Art* (New York: The Bollingen Foundation, 1962), vol. 1, p. 22.
8. Antonin Artaud, 'Symbolic Mountains' (1945),in a translation by Victor Corti, *TDR* (1965), vol. 9, no. 3, pp. 94–6
9. Donald M. Kaplan, 'Theatre Architecture: A derivation of the Primal Cavity', *TDR* (1968), vol. 12, no. 3, p. 113.
10. Ibid., pp. 107–8.
11. Henri Frankfort, *Kingship and the Gods* (Chicago: University of Chicago Press, 1948), p. 79.
12. M. C. Richards, *Centering* (Middleton, Connecticut: Wesleyan University Press, 1970), p. 29.
13. Guillermo E. Aldana's extraordinary article 'Mesa del Nayar's Strange Holy Week' in the *National Geographic* (June 1971), has many unforgettable photographs. All quotations are from Aldana's article.

14. Quotations and drawings from Catherine H. Berndt, 'Ascription of Meaning in a Ceremonial Context in the Eastern Central Highlands of New Guinea' in *Anthropology in the South Seas* (1959), pp. 161–83.
15. The New Orleans Group had something similar in the lobby for *Victims of Duty* in 1967. The exhibit was mounted on billboards and contained hundreds of photos, newspaper articles, letters, birth certificates and other personal crap dealing with the private lives of the performers and directors—a takeoff on the trivia in theatre programmes. Also there was a short film, slides, and taped music counterpointing the Tulane NROTC band with Hitler marches. During the performance the exhibit was changed so that when the audience left, people were forced to duck under a sheet on which was written the famous Eichmann quotation: 'I am a victim of the actions of others and obedience to duty.' From the ceiling hung pictures of Eichmann all neat in his uniform.

Performance Spaces: Ramlila and Yaqui Easter

To speak of performance spaces is also to speak of time and function. Not only what spaces are used, but for how long and in what ways. And it is not always true that space follows function—that a particular arrangement of a performance space is the way it is because of the use to which it will be put. Certain shrines arise around special places: place comes first, and around it gather definite kinds of performances. No drama itself may be considered, among other things, a theatre of marking special places. Also to speak of performance spaces is to speak of rhythmicity: the alternation between activity and inactivity, sound and silence, fullness and emptiness. In a chart [Fig. 1] comparing a number of performances with regard to genre, space, and time in several cultures I find almost no limits to what a performance may be, where it may take place, how long it takes to complete, what its functions are. There are private performances for no audiences, or audiences of one; there are performances with a live audience of more than 100,000 and a media audience of many millions. There are performances that take place secretly, in hard-to-get-to places closed off from public view; and there are performances that aggressively try to reach as many persons as possible employing every available means of publicity and broadcasting. There are performances closely identified with specific places—so closely linked that a performance elsewhere is impossible; and there are performances that cannot be said to belong to any place.

The varieties, magnitudes, and functions of performances are so vast that it may not be helpful to generalize, except by providing Fig. 1. Instead I will look a little more carefully at a few examples. I will concentrate my remarks on Ramlila of Ramnagar, a 31-day cycle play of north India that tells the story of Ram's great war against the demon king, Ravana. Then I will examine aspects of Yaqui Easter, as celebrated in New Pascua, Arizona. The Yaqui Passion Play begins at Lent and ends Easter Sunday. Holy Week, and especially Wednesday through Saturday, are climactic. Finally I shall survey some experiments with performance space made by American theatre artists in the 1960s and 70s. I intend that this intercultural comparison will form the basis for a discussion.

Ramlila is a cycle play lasting 10 to 31 days performed outdoors in the Hindi-speaking region of north India. Its season is around the Dusserah holiday in September-October. Dusserah is Durga Puja in Bengali-speaking India. A very important day. Ramlila is based on Tulsidas' late sixteenth century epic poem, *Ramcharitmanas*, a Hindi version of Valmiki's Sanskrit Ramayana. Although thousands of Ramlilas are performed, of varying complexity and duration, I have studied only one carefully: that of Ramnagar, acknowledged throughout India as the fullest, most theatrically sophisticated, and holiest of them all.

Ramnagar is across the Ganga River from Varanasi, also called Benares, one of the most sacred cities in India. Due to the patronage of the Maharaja of Benares, who lives in Ramnagar, this Ramlila draws the largest audiences of any. The whole subject of Ramlila is vast, touching themes of *bhakti* (devotional worship), pilgrimage, reincarnation, nationalism, theatre, relationship between performer and role being performed, kingship, poetry, the secular government, and patronage. Here I will deal only with the space of the performance.

But in Ramlila even space is complicated. To discuss it involves consideration of pilgrimage, processions, the Maharaja as King and as performer, theatrical mise-en-scène, ancient and modern Indian history, the relationship between myth, theatrical space, and local geography.

Ramnagar literally means 'town of Ram'. Fittingly named because the town of Ramnagar is the actual setting for the enactment of Ram's deeds. During the first third of the nineteenth century, under the direct supervision of the maharajas of the time, numerous stage settings were built throughout the town in order to provide places for the various Ramlila performance events. Thus there is Ayodhya, the capital of Ram's kingdom; Janakpur, the home of Sita, his queen; Chitrakut, Ram's first residence in exile; Panchavati, the spot where Sita is kidnapped by Ravana, ten-headed demon king of Lanka; and Lanka itself, Ravana's kingdom and site of the great battles between Ravana's and Ram's armies. More than this, there are the pathways and main streets of Ramnagar used for processions; and the main town square used to depict the reunion of Ram, Sita, and Lakshman with their brothers when Ram's exile ends. And there is the outside and inside of the maharaja's fort, or palace, which becomes part of the drama in its final days.

Importantly, the actual orientation of these spaces, as well as their relative position in Ramnagar, is a more or less accurate model not only of India and Sri Lanka, but also of Ram's movement through the countryside. The Ganga River makes a loop at Benares (also called Varanasi and Kasi) so that the sun rises over the river, with Benares on the west bank, Ramnagar on the east. This helps in orienting the Ramlila environments so that actually Lanka is far to the southeast, Ayodhya to the northwest, Janakpur to far north and Chitrakut (also Rambagh: Ram's pleasure garden in the last night's performance) to the northeast, a direction of good luck.

The action of Ramlila is both physical and narrative. That is, the actual movement of the characters is itself a decisive part of the story: movement has significance. The first night of the performance, where the gods implore Vishnu to incarnate himself as Ram, is performed around the *kshir sagar*, in front of an ancient Durga temple near Chitrakut and Rambagh, in the auspicious northeast. When Ram goes into exile he crosses make-believe Ganga River—the holy river—as he heads from his capital at Ayodhya in the northwest back towards the northeast. When Sita is kidnapped, Ram's army moves steadily to the southeast. This move parallels the actual historical movement through India of the Sanskritic, Vedic culture the Aryan invaders of India brought with them. Among the poems they brought, merging into Dravidian and other native Indian traditions, was the Ramayana. After the climactic battles and cremation of Ravana at Lanka, battles that have looked just about the same for 150 years, Ram victorious and his party are loaded into a great cart hauled by spectators through the streets of Ramnagar first to the reunion with their brothers and later, in a conflation of time and place, to an actual meeting with the existing Maharaja of Benares who, assisted by his family, feeds visiting King Ram a sumptuous meal as thousands of townspeople look on.

At this point something very powerful theatrically and religiously is creating a unique social, even political, situation. Since 1949 when India became an independent, secular state, there has been, officially speaking, no Maharaja of Benares. All principalities were abolished, and a few years later, the privy purses were discontinued. Still every one calls Vibhuti Narain Singh 'Maharaja'. Why? The answer in no small way is to be found in Ramlila. For the Ramlila season, especially during the performance of the arati temple service that concludes each evening's show, the murtis—literally, 'images' of the gods—who are the boys playing Ram, Sita, Lakshman, Bharat, and Shatrughna—are thought by many in the audience to actually be the gods they otherwise represent. It is a miracle parallel to Catholic transubstantiation. Thus the presence of the murtis bestows on their patron and host a royalty that might by now be much diminished (as with some other Indian former Maharajas). But it's not quite that simple. There is more like a symbiotic relationship tied up as well to the whole physical setting of Ramnagar: to the fact that for a month, in a whole town, Ram lives. The Maharaja of Benares is the only person with enough religious-traditional force to sponsor a great Ramlila. And the Ramlila in turn validates the Maharaja's Maharajadom. The climactic visit of mythic-theatrical Ram to the Fort of the actual-theatrical Maharaja is an intersection of ancient and modern, mythic and theatrical, extraordinary and ordinary time and space.

In Ramlila there are three kinds of movements in three spatial spheres—a situation parallel to that of Yaqui Easter. The three movements are those of pilgrimage, those of the nightly performance, and those existing within a mythic narrative; and the three spatial spheres are of India, of Varanasi to Ramnagar and back, and of the Ramlila story. The three spheres are not concentric, nor does one replace or abolish any of the others. They all exist simultaneously in a palimpsest.

The most far-flung sphere is that of those in the audience who consider Ramnagar Ramlila a pilgrimage centre. Many people take a month out from their lives to attend Ramlila, and some travel from distances of more than 1,000 miles to get to Ramnagar. More immediately, on a daily basis, many thousands of spectators cross the Ganga from Varanasi to attend Ramlila in Ramnagar. At the end of the night's performance they cross back, often singing bhajans, devotional songs, in honour of Ram, as they row back across the sacred river. To immerse oneself in Ganga is itself an act of purification. To cross the river daily to and from Ramlila is a sacred act. More than one boat capsizes each year, and some people drown. At one level of experience this is a bad thing, at another level it is a good thing.

The third sphere of movement, also immediate and actual, are the processions and shifts of theatrical environment that comprise so much of Ramlila itself. At Ramnagar there are ten major shifts. And these movements are precisely analogous to the Ramlila narrative. To attend Ramlila, therefore, is to participate with Ram in his adventures. Many thousands of spectators go with Ram into exile, attend him and his army on their march through India and across the great bridge of stones into Lanka, and throng around triumphant Ram and his party as they return to Ayodhya. These movements are not incidental or cosmetic. They are the core of the performance.

The environments of Ramlila are surprisingly detailed: a correct model of the mythic narrative—even to being laid out in the correct directional orientation. Thus the performance, like the narrative, moves from the northwest to the southeast and back again to the northwest. Throughout the month of Ramlila each spectator is reminded that Ram's story takes place in an actual and a mythic India simultaneously—for the places in the narrative, Ayodhya, Lanka, Janakpur, Chitrakut, Panchavati—actually exist. And many spectators believe that by attending Ramlila they can visit these sacred places: to perform them in Ramlila is to bring them into existence for one month, just as the gods themselves, as murtis, exist for this same month. Thus to move through Ramnagar is to move through India—not the India of today, but the India of Ramraj—the time when Ram ruled. This is an epoch not like today's debased Kali Yuga, but of an earlier more perfect time. So the movement in space is also a movement in time—and many who attend Ramlila feel they have been literally transported both spatially and temporally.

So do those who perform in Yaqui Easter. The performance I saw at New Pascua near Tucson, Arizona, though more modest theatrically, is very much like Ramnagar Ramlila in terms of the use of space. At New Pascua the organization of space contributes greatly to the bringing into theatrical existence of beings and forces that otherwise would remain unmanifest. (And this process of making manifest the unmanifest is, I think, one of the links connecting aesthetic and ritual theatre. It is also the area—of training and mise-en-scène—where theatre specialists can exchange techniques with ritual specialists.) As with Ramlila, though not as extensively or with as many people, Easter is celebrated by Yaqui speaking peoples in the USA and Mexico. My study of Yaqui Easter has just begun, and I will rely both on my own observations and the writings of Muriel Thayer Painter (*A Yaqui Easter*, Tucson: University of Arizona Press, 1971) and Edward H. Spicer.

The Yaqui situation is complicated by the fact that the ceremonies in New Pascua are versions of earlier observances performed in other places. This is doubly significant because the Yaqui put strong emphasis on place. The 'original' eight Yaqui towns of Rio Yaqui in Mexico date from the early period of contact with the Jesuits in the seventeenth century. These towns, hundreds of miles from the Yaqui settlement in New Pascua, are both actual and mythical. They constitute an arena of Yaqui history as the Yaquis relate their history; they are also the place where Christ walked during the three days between his crucifixion and resurrection. But before the eight towns, and surrounding them, as if they were islands, is the *huya aniya*, the wildlands, home of the deer. As Spicer says:

> The *huya aniya* of the Yaquis is neither wholly separate from the Christian realm nor does it interpenetrate in a way comparable with that in the Christian-Maya synthesis. [. . .] Every ceremony devoted to a Christian supernatural required participation by ceremonialists whose power was associated with the *huya aniya*.[1]

Thus the Easter Passion Play incorporates Deer and Pascola dancing, and a very dense interplay of these with two other kinds of performance figures: masked Chapayekas who pursue and crucify Christ and unmasked beribboned Matachin dancers who celebrate Christ's triumphant resurrection. This resurrection is marked by the throwing of flowers—flowers that actually drive back, disarm, and unmask the Chapayekas who, defeated and transformed, burn their masks on a pyre piled up against one of the main crosses in the village square and then, unmasked, enter the church to gain the blessing of Christ. The symbolism is so dense because it is a dynamic system of conscious and non-conscious oppositions and interpenetrations: countryside vs town, flowers vs masks, masked vs unmasked, Deer vs Pascolas (ritual clowns), Chapayekas vs Matachins, ancient musical instruments vs instruments introduced by the Spaniards, men vs women, adults vs children, pre-Columbian ceremony vs Jesuit-introduced Catholicism. And so on. To list these as oppositions does injustice to the complexity of their inter-relatedness. I do not have time here to even begin to decipher this system. But I need to point out a few more 'movements' of the Yaqui that figure in their Easter performances—for these movements are recapitulated in the mise-en-scène itself.

The Jesuits entered Yaqui country in 1617. They were withdrawn

General Note

The Chart lists examples anecdotally. That is, many more examples could be given for almost every category. At this level what the Chart shows is the great diversity of performative events in terms of genre and use of time and space; and it shows the interrelatedness of events-time-space.

The chart can be read as a grid. For example, a PhD Oral Examination is an example of Private But Open Secular Ritual; a Town meeting held in a church is an example of a Secular Ritual taking place in a Sacred Space; the Macy's Thanksgiving Day Parade is a Calendrical/Cyclical event taking place in Found Space. And so on. All items can be located according to three axes: Event, Time, Space.

Not all items are so explained, but they can be. And some items, obviously, occur in more than one category. So, Ramlila is Multi-Time: Segmented plus Calendrical/Cycle plus symbolic Time plus Days in duration. But Ramlila is not so easy to locate in terms of whether or not it is Aesthetic Theatre of Sacred Ritual or social Drama: it is all of these, and at some moments more one than the others. Thus the Chart's weakness: it categorizes whereas many performances transform from one category to another, or slip across categorical boundaries. Still I have found making the Chart helpful in organizing my thinking about performance; and I hope that it will be of use to others.

Specific Notes

1. The Theatre on Chekhov Street is one of several in Moscow operating privately outside the control of censorship. A description of it, and other private performances, is found in TDR, 23:4 (December 1979). Private restricted performances are common in places qwhere public free expression is limited; it is also the mark of certain kinds of rituals that can be attended by certain people only.

spaces that attempt to bring the outdoors insde. Even more outfront in this intention are domed stadiums whose Astroturf looks like grass.

3. The Tiwi settle certain disputes by using a ritual duel stagtes in the main village square. The duel is described by C. W. M. Hart and Arnold R. Pilling in *The Tiwi of North Australia* (New York; Holt, Rinehart and Winston, 1966). Using their account I discuss the Tiwi duel in 'Actuals: A Look Into Performance Theory' in *Essays on Performance Theory* (New York: Drama Book Specialists, 1977). The Tiwi duel is a near-perfect example of Victor Turner's 'social drama'.

4. Stuart Sherman stages 'spectacles' on street corners, in theatre lobbies, in various other places not usually thought of as performance spaces. His spectacles are theatrically modest: a small table, an assembly of props all of which can fit in an attaché case, no dialogue; a total elapsed time of under 30 minutes. As he became more successful, Sherman began inside theatres, on stage, in more orthodox ways.

5. Sam Hsieh is a performance artist who specializes in 'one year performances'. According to Barry Kahn (Live 6/7, 1982, pp. 40-2): 'On 30 September 1978, Sam Hsieh began a year of solitary confinement inside an 11'-6" x 9' x 8' cell which he built within his studio. "I shall not converse, read, write, listen to the radio or watch television until I unseal myself." A friend, Cheng Wei Kwang, took charge of his food, clothing, and waste. At 5.00 p.m. on 11 April 1980, Sam Hsieh punched in on a standard industrial time clock he had installeld in his studio, an act which he repeated every hour on the hour until 6.00 p.m. on 11 April 1981. And on Saturday 26 September 1981, Sam Hsieh began his third one year performance: "I shall not go in to (sic) a building, subway, train, car, airplane, ship, cave, tent. I shall have a sleeping bag," his statement said.' During his one year performances Hsieh allows the public to view him at certain times. For the outdoor performance anyone who knows who he is can watch him.

6. The Orokolo of Papua-New Guinea used to perform a cycle play that took years to complete. It is described by F. E. Williams in *The Drama of the Orokolo* (London: Oxford University Press, 1940); and also discussed extensively by me in 'Actuals', Extended performances—or connected cycles of performances—are not uncommon. A sports season can be thought of as a cycle of performances. Major league baseball is certainly this way—with several high points: opening games, All Star Games, 'important series' near the end of the season, 'traditional rivalries', playoffs, and World Series.

7. Robert Wilson staged a seven day performance as part of the Shiraz Festival in 1972. It involved 50 persons and took 168 hours. It was staged on a mountain, and took the form of a kind of ascent of pilgrimage, *Ka*

	MINUTES OR LESS	HOURS	DAYS	MONTHS OR MORE	SINGLE TIME: ONCE ONLY	REPEATED	MULTI-TIME: SEGMENTED	CALENDRICAL CYCLE	EVENT-GENERATED TIME	SYMBOLIC TIME
	Execution	Theatre on Chekhov Street	Election of Pope	Some initiations	Execution	Theatre on Chekhov Street	Election of Pope	Some Aborigine performances	Election of Pope	Theatre on Chekhov Street
l	Puja at Hindu temple	Happenings; ballgames, etc.	Some happenings	Sam Hsieh 'Yearlong' performance[5]	Bar Mitzvah		Some happenings	Puja at Hindu temple	Some happenings; sandlot baseball	Some happenings
a	Stuart Sherman[4] street spectacle	Ordinary theatre and dance	Ramlila; Yaqui Easter	Orokolo cycle[6]	Some happenings	Ordinary theatre and dance	Ramlila; Yaqui Easter	Ramlila; Macy's Parade	Big league ball	Ordinary theatre and dance
sis;	TV commercials	Feature films	Olympics	TV soaps	Boxing title match	Feature films	Olympics	Olympics; World Series	World Series	Feature films
ere	Puja; eucharist	Ordinary church service	Election of Pope; Aborigine ceremonies	Pilgrimage	Bar Mitzvah		Yaqui Easter; Ramlila	Yaqui Easter; Ramlila		Ramlila; Yaqui Easter
e; all	Stuart Sherman Jewish circumcision	Ordinary theatre and dance	Wilson's *Ka Mountain*[7]	Hostage crisis	Wilson's *Ka Mountain*; hostage crisis	Ordinary theatre and dance	World Series; Olympics	World Series; Olympics	Baseball	Ordinary theatre and dance
ring s	Some happenings	Parades; some happenings	Wilson's *Ka Mountain*	Brook's theatre in Africa[8]	Many happenings and Performance Art		Aborigine ceremonies	Macy's parade; Aborigine ceremonies	Sandlot baseball	Schechner's *Philoctetes* on the beach[9]
; n	Execution	Ordinary theatre and dance	Murder trial	Orokolo cycle; pilgrimage	Some happenings	Ordinary theatre and dance	Ramlila; Yaqui Easter	Ramlila; Yaqui Easter	World Series	Ordinary theatre and dance
all	Some happenings; execution	Ordinary theatre and dance	Murder trial		Some happenings	Ordinary theatre and dance	Murder trial	Church services; folk Bugakū[10]	Indoor sports	Ordinary theatre and dance
	Stuart Sherman	Greek or Elizabethan theatre	Wilson's *Ka Mountain*	Orokolo cycle; pilgrimage	Some happenings	Elizabethan theatre	Ramlila; Yaqui Easter	Ramlila; Yaqui Easter	Baseball	Elizabethan theatre
ll	Execution	Ordinary theatre dance	Murder trial		Boxing title match	Ordinary theatre and dance	Murder trial	Folk Bugaku	Indoor sports	Ordinary theatre and dance
sis	Some happenings; some guerrilla th.	Some happenings	Olympics; Ramlila; Yaqui Easter	Orokolo cycle; hostage crisis	Hostage crisis	Ramlila; Yaqui Easter	Ramlila; Yaqui Easter	Ramlila; Yaqui Easter	World Series	Ramlila; Yaqui Easter

	AESTHETIC THEATRE	SACRED RITUAL	SECULAR RITUAL	SPORTS	SOCIAL DRAMA
PRIVATE AND RESTRICTED	Theatre on Chekhov Street[1]	Initiation rites	Executions in USA	Sports played at home	Election of Pope
PRIVATE BUT OPEN	Happenings and Performance Art	Bar Mitzvah	Ph.D. Orals	Sandlot baseball	Murder tri
LOCAL	Ordinary theatre and dance	Teyyam	Macy's Thanksgiving's Parade	Big league baseball	Turnerian social dran
GENERAL	National Network TV drama	Pilgrimage	Inauguration of US President	Olympics	Hostage cr wars
SACRED SPACE	B and P in St John the Divine	Religious events; Aborigine landscape	Town meeting in church	Aztec ballgame	Church wh Pope is elected
SECULAR SPACE	Ordinary theatre and dance	Jewish circumcision; home wedding	Macy's Parade; Olympics	Playing fields	Town squa legislative h
FOUND SPACE	Rooftops, beaches, streets, galleries	Sacred trees, rocks, rivers	Parade routes	Sandlot ball	Wars; US Embassy du hostage cris
TRANSFORMED SPACE	Stage set; environmental theatre	Churches; R L environments	Courtroom; execution chamber	Stadiums	Courtroom throne-roo
INDOOR SPACE	Theatres	Churches, temples	Courtroom; execution chamber	Fieldhouses[2]	Courtroom legislative h
OUTDOOR SPACE	Greek or Elizabethan theatre	Aborigine initiation grounds	Parade routes; US inauguration	Stadiums	Tiwi 'duel'
SINGLE SPACE	Ordinary theatre and dance	Church service	Courtroom	Stadiums, fieldhouses	Courtroom legislative h
MULTISPACE	Many happenings; environmental	Pilgrimage	Parades	Marathon running; Olympics	Hostage cr

Mountain is described in an article by Ossia Trilling in *TDR*, 17:2 (June 1973), pp.33-47.

8. From December 1972 through February 1973, Peter Brook and thirty actors, techinicians, and support persons travelled by landrover through Africa from Algiers, across the Sahara, into Niger, Nigeria, Dahomey, Mali, and back to Algiers. During their trip they staged improvisations, exchanged theatrical (songs, dances, skits, techniques, etc.) items with Africans, and showed their own work. They played in many different situations. A uniting, and signaling, item was their 'performance carpet'. 'We got out [of our vehicles],' said Brooki, 'unrolled our carpet, sat down, and an audience assembled in no time. And there was something incredibly moving—because it was the total unknown, we didn't know what could be communicated, what couldn't. All we discovered after was that nothing had ever happened resembling this before on the market [at In-Salah, in Algeria]. Never had there been a strolling player or some little improvisation. There was no precedent for it. There was a feeling of simple and total attentiveness, total response and lightning appreciation, something that, perhaps in a second, changed every actor's sense of what a relation with an audience could be.' See Brook's Africa, An Interview by Michael Gibson', in *TDR*, 17:3 (September 1973), pp.37-51.

In 1960 I staged Sophocles' *Philoctetes* on the beach of Truro, Massachusetts (near Provincetown, where I was running a summer theatre). The audience had to walk over a mile of sand duen to reach the place where the performance took place. Philoctetes himself roamed the dunes; Neoptolemus and Odysseus arrived by boat (we had launched them about a half-mile further down on the beach). The Truro dunes really conveyed the sense of desert island that the Sophoclels play asks for.

In December 1979 I observed folk Bugaku in Northern Japan (Kazano City), at a Shinto Shrine. Peasants, wearing traditional masks, including a famous golden one said to possess great power, danced for about 3 hours on a makeshift square elevated stage—like a boxing ring without ropes—set up in the center of the interior of the shrine. It was said that this same performance is done each year, and dates back many hundreds of years.

in 1767. Much of what is celebrated today by the Yaqui took shape from after the Jesuit withdrawal when contact with Euro–Mexican power was occasional and bloody. In the early twentieth century a climax was reached in the relationship between Yaquis and Mexicans. The Mexican revolutionaries wanted to bring the Yaqui (and other Indian groups) into the Mexican nation—but on strictly Mexican terms. The struggles that followed, and continue to this day, resulted in at least two major dispersions of Yaqui. Many Yaqui were sent as forced labourers to the Yucatan. Others fled across the Rio Grande to Arizona—and some of these settled near Tucson. Thus if the Jesuits introduced concentration—the establishment of the eight towns—the Mexicans forced diaspora. Most recently, in the 1960s and 70s, as Tucson grew and encircled the Yaqui settlements there, a group of Yaquis led by Anselmo Valencia, who is both their political and religious leader, established New Pascua and won for it status as a Federal Indian Reservation. New Pascua is today the largest single settlement of Yaquis in the USA.

Thus there is a recurrent pattern in post-contact Yaqui history. This pattern is of concentration and dispersion, settlement and diaspora, centre and beyond (*huya aniya*). This pattern comprehends space as something significant in itself, and dynamic. This sense of significant movement is at the heart of Yaqui Easter.

During the performance there are three main spatial spheres. These are concentric; and there is much power in each of them making for a complicated inter-relation between the centre, the midspace, and the beyond. The Easter ceremonies—though they can be studied from any number of perspectives—are extremely interesting as an unfolding relationship among these three spheres—for this relationship, theatrically speaking, can be discussed as a concrete mise-en-scène. The over-all movement of the Easter performance is from the outside in, finally climaxing in the combat and absorption into the centre of formerly disruptive but plainly ancient and native, and therefore necessary, forces.

Fig. 2 shows the arrangement of space for Easter in New Pascua. The food stalls are temporary structures. Local people sell various foods and drinks (non-alcoholic). The stalls mark out the difference between the beyond—where the stations of the cross (numbered 1 through 14) are, and beyond them, the outside world of Arizona and *huya aniya*—from the interior outdoor space of the village square. The unnumbered cross immediately in front of the open church door marks an area that includes the inside of the church. This is the most central area, the place where the final reconciliation takes place; and where the Matachins dance their celebratory steps.

There is another 'open door', that of the Ramada in the northeast of the square. In the Ramada dance the Deer and Pascolas—a kind of sideshow literally. The significance of the Deer to Yaqui Easter is explained by Spicer thus:

> The Deer and the Pascola are essentially secular, but I am sure that the Deer Dancer has not always been so. Because they are not sacred, they may be danced throughout the Lenten period at household fiestas. Their meaning, despite being joyous like the Matachin dances, does not conflict with the Fariseo ritual meanings. It is just outside the realm of the sacred, and therefore not incompatible with the austerity and discipline of the Fariseo ceremonial season.[2]

When the Deer dances publicly, on Holy Saturday night as part of the Fiesta that celebrates Christ's victory—actually, with the Yaqui, the victory of the 'little angels', young boys and girls whose thrown flower petals literally disarm and unmask the Chapayekas, both defeating and reconciling them—when the Deer dances he does so in the Ramada: its open door being parallel to, not in conflict with, but, as Spicer points out, different than, the open door of the Church. And the Deer brings with him the space of *huya aniya*, and the flower world: the wild, the beyond.

Of all the spatial manipulations visible in the Yaqui 40-day Passion Play, let me concentrate on two only: the appearance and actions of the Chapayekas from Lent through Holy Saturday and the representation of the Crucifixion itself on Good Friday. The first manifestation of the Chapayekas is the appearance of a single one who emerges from

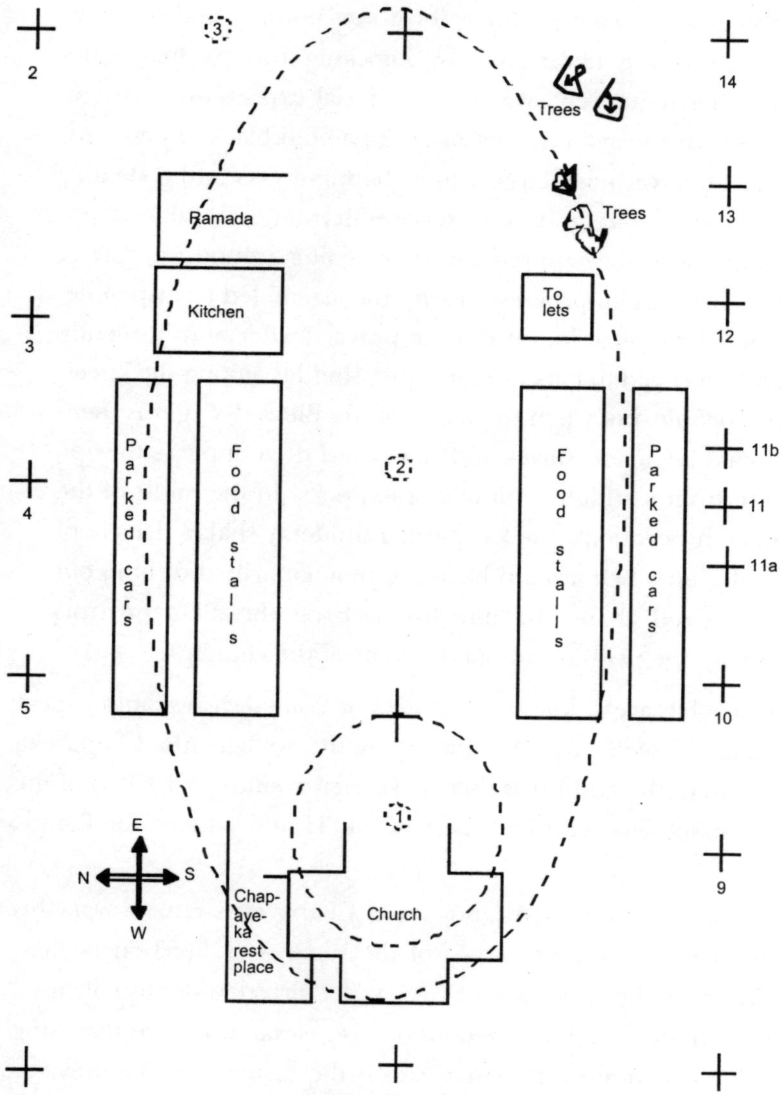

2
3
3
4
5
6
7
8
9
10
11a
11
11b
12
13
14
Trees
Trees
Ramada
Kitchen
To
lets
P a r k e d c a r s
F o o d s t a l l s
2
F o o d s t a l l s
P a r k e d c a r s
1
E
N
S
W
Chap-
aye-
ka
rest
place
Church

Fig. 2

under the Church altar on the first Friday of Lent.

> Slowly a figure emerges who is obviously out of place in the church. It looks around as though in puzzlement, but it is not easy to know what it thinks, for it says nothing and seems to be expressing uncertainty by knocking two painted sticks together tentatively. Moreover no facial expression is visible. The being wears a helmet of hide painted black, green, red, and white with two large loosely flapping ears and a slender pointed nose. It ignores the services in front of the altar where hymns and prayers preparatory for going around the Way of the Cross are in progress among the assembled townspeople. The Chapayeka goes up to the prayer leader and insolently cocks its head to look at him better, shuffles among the kneeling people, but when the name of the Blessed Virgin is mentioned begins to shiver and shake and then appears to wipe filth from its thighs with one of its sticks. In the midst of the solemn devotions, the Chapayeka suddenly shakes deer hoof rattles on a belt around his waist, momentarily drowning out the sacred chant. Turning his back on the altar, he trots among the people and out the door of the church.[3]

Then the Chapayeka joins the Soldiers of Rome, whose camp is next to the church [see Fig. 2]. Accompanying the Soldiers, the Chapayeka goes ahead of the faithful as they make their rounds of the Way of the Cross; the Soldiers surround the faithful. Thus a pattern for Lent is set.

On the following Friday two more Chapayekas enter town, this time from the northwest corner of the square—a direction farthest from Cross 11, the Crucifixion Cross; and a direction not usually used to approach the church whose door opens eastward, towards the rising sun. One of the entering Chapayekas is the being from the previous Friday, and both Chapayekas seem a bit disoriented. At the same time that they appear almost comical they also are sinister and scary. They carry their beating sticks. The sound they make is a leitmotif of Yaqui Easter. It will be heard throughout Lent and mark the marching of the Soldiers of Rome and the Chapayekas. The Crucifixion itself—the hammering of imaginary nails with a wooden hammer into a cross at Station 11—will echo this same sound of wood-on-wood. When the two Chapayekas see the church they become agitated and uncertain. Then from somewhere else in town two more Chapayekas appear. 'Now elaborate gesturing takes place. It becomes evident that these beings communicate by using their sticks, employing various gestures and rhythmic beats.'[4] The Chapayekas 'demonstrate that they have come from somewhere to the north [a direction from which wild things come] and are very reluctant to stay in town and especially to go near the church'.[5] The Soldiers of Rome invite the Chapayekas to join them in their enterprise—the pursuit and crucifixion of Jesus. The Chapayekas express interest mostly in food and fiesta, but agree to join the Soldiers who promise the same. Thus an alliance against Jesus is made. An alliance that is parallel to the alliance Ram makes with Hanuman, the monkey general, and Jambuvan, the bear. The Chapayekas are in some way acculturated by the Soldiers—and even as they join against Jesus they lay the groundwork for their eventual salvation.

But who are these Chapayekas who do not know what's going on? And why was the first one discovered inside the church they so evidently fear and avoid? I am not going to give an anthropological answer—that is, use Spicer's great authority to assert that the Chapayekas are linked to Hopi and Zuni kachinas (which would surely place them to the north). I would rather stick to the theatrical evidence close at hand because I can handle that kind of material more confidently. By not knowing what's happening the Chapayekas demonstrate their origins in a distant place both geographically and conceptually—they are literally out of touch with Jesus. By being discovered first in church—as a stray dog or even wild coyote might wander unknowingly into an improper place—the first Chapayeka demonstrates his innocence—the sophisticated Soldiers of Rome must educate the Chapayekas to their evil purpose. But his discovery in church also foreshadows the resolution of the drama: it is a prediction acted out rather than spoken (as befits the mute Chapayekas): for on two more occasions the Chapayekas will enter the church. First after they capture Jesus from Gethsemane they will guard him in church—taking over that holy space and converting it entirely to their needs. Then on Holy Saturday, the Chapayekas will enter the church again, but this time as supplicants and devotees of Jesus. And, strictly speaking, not as Chapayekas at all because their masks will have been discarded and burnt. So the Chapayekas in church show a definite progression: first as alien, unknowing, confused figures; then as sinister agents of the Soldiers who crucify Jesus; finally as transformed beings—townsmen who have shed their Chapayeka personae to become rededicated to Jesus. The flower power of the Little Angels literally unmasks and converts the Chapayekas into family men: for even as it is as lone males that they enter the town it is as men-with-their-families, their children and women, that they accept Jesus.

Each Friday during Lent more Chapayekas appear, until they number 35 or 40.

> They are all outfitted according to a similar pattern, although some may wear old overcoats instead of blankets and some are barefooted, while others wear the traditional flat Yaqui sandals. But there is great variety in the masks. Each Chapayeka makes his own mask, and each is different.[6]

In 1982, when I saw the Holy Week part of the Easter performance, I observed masks of many kinds: a goat, a sheep, a penis-nosed racoon, a Moor or Arab, a man in a top hat with a black face smoking a fat cigar, a pink-faced bald man, several 'fantasy figures' of yellow, pink, black, and white, a yellow-faced man with Dracula teeth. All had the characteristic jug ears, and most had pointy thin noses.

> It is apparent that the Chapayekas are under the influence of the Soldiers of Rome, having agreed to help them, and they grow more and more intent on their one purposeful activity of tracking down Jesus. This is apparent with each new Friday procession, as they interfere with, almost jostle the faithful, pushing their sticks in front of them and turning over every tiny stone they come to; circle the processional groups; and silently taunt the Maestros [Yaqui priests] by dangling stuffed

> badgers and other animals over the prayer books. [. . .] The Chapayekas in fact go all about the town not only on Fridays but other days as well spying on people and trying to catch children. [. . .] People live in fear of possible punishments, and the tensions heighten as the Chapayekas make their presence increasingly felt.[7]

The Chapayekas are something like Namahage of Ota in Japan, or Halloween maskers in Euro-America: comic and sinister at once; originating in some other world (the north, the mountains, the dead) and making themselves visible and active in the world of humans to which they really don't belong. But finally they are unmasked and revealed as loved relations and trusted neighbours: a fact everyone knew but, according to theatrical and religious convention, agreed to ignore. This 'willing suspension of disbelief' is no trivial thing: it is the very key to worlds of subjunctivity, of 'as if', to what Artaud called the 'theatre and its double'.

The processions around the Way of the Cross take Mary and Jesus and the faithful out into spatial sphere 3, away from the church, out of the plaza, out beyond the foodstalls. It is dangerous out there. Going the Way of the Cross means losing sight of the church. The Crucifixion crosses are set behind the stalls, near the toilets, in the far south and east a direction (from the perspective of Rio Yaqui) from whence came both Jesuits and hated Mexicans; and the direction to which the Yaqui were deported at the end of the nineteenth century. And, importantly, the Yaqui Easter performance is not an uninterrupted tradition dating back centuries. It was stopped during the great diaspora.

> For about twenty years, Yaquis did not carry out Easter Ceremonies anywhere. There was a hiatus in their continuity from about 1886 until I906, when what has become the Old Pascua Ceremony was revived in Arizona. The Easter Ceremonies that we see today in Sonora are also revivals.[8]

Thus when the Yaquis reinstituted their Easter performance they could consciously choose what to include, what to modify. The directional motifs are very particular: written in the geography of the performance is a model of Yaqui experience. Just as directions and movements have deep significance in Ramlila, so they do in Yaqui Easter.

In the interest of brevity (if not wit) I'll skip some important activities of the Chapayekas and get to the Crucifixion. I note only that the Chapayekas capture Jesus in Gethsemane and take him to the church where they guard him throughout Thursday night of Holy Week. For the second time—now with a definite purpose, an evil purpose—the Chapayekas have penetrated the church itself.

There are actually two simultaneous processions around the Way of the Cross on Good Friday. One group, the largest, is led by a man who carries a large cross. This group proceeds in a counterclockwise direction—the 'correct' direction if the Crucifixion is to take place at the 11th cross. The other group, mostly of women, bearing with them the effigies of the Three Marys, move clockwise—but only for five stops, from Cross I back to Cross 11. Actually there are three crosses there, for three people are to be crucified: Jesus and the two thieves. The representation of the Crucifixion itself, out of sight of the church, in the south to southeast in relation to the church, is done by having a man hit the wooden cross with a wooden mallet. There is no body, not even an effigy. But the sound of the wooden mallet striking the wooden cross is a version of the Chapayeka wooden stick music.

Once the Crucifixion has happened the Chapayekas 'swarm all through the church and out into the plaza. They uproot every cross of the Way, throwing each in the dust. They then play games and chase each other in a spirit of complete abandonment during the rest of Good Friday.'[9] By contrast the rest of the town, the women especially, are solemn and in mourning for the crucified Jesus.

> There is a constant stream of mourners. One household has dedicated itself to provide a flower-bedecked bier in which to place the body of Christ. The decoration is elaborate, the highest effort of a whole large family. The bier is blessed and borne to the church by a contingent of the Soldiers of Rome. The Adoration by the townspeople goes on all day and into the early night and creates a mood of deep sadness.[10]

The bier is inside the church. And in the bier is a small statue of Jesus. The feeling I got, in New Pascua 1982, was of a combination bier-crèche. For the colours of the bier were bright, the effigy small, the feel of the cloth material within that of a crib.

The action of the Passion Play has now moved to the centre of sphere 1: inside the church. The next morning, near noon, the Soldiers of Rome and the Chapayekas storm the church. It is not clear exactly why: they have already won their victory. But they have not really occupied the church. Their 'camp' is next to the church, and they have entered the church on several occasions, but it is still not their territory. They march in formation, clicking their sticks, and then they charge the church. But they are driven back by the Little Angels who throw flowers at them. After three attempts the Chapayekas are defeated, their masks are taken off and burned, and they enter the church as supplicants. The Matachin dancers begin their dancing, as do the Pascolas and Deer. At this point the whole space of spheres 1 and 2 are operating, and sphere 3—the outer world, the space of the Way, the route of great agony—is ignored. At this moment one can sense the theatrical and metaphysical function of the foodstalls and parked cars: they block out the space of sphere 3 as the whole town celebrates in various ways in spheres I and 2: in the church, the Ramada, the plaza: they eat, dance, socialize and worship. And it is not easy, nor is it necessary, to make sharp distinctions among these activities.

What is clear from even this brief description of Ramlila and the Yaqui Easter is that these performances knit aesthetic, social, religious, and mythic themes together; and that the actual physical space and mise-en-scène of the performances are in important ways meaningful assertions of these themes. That is to say that although the Ramlila and Yaqui performances follow certain aesthetic conventions with regard to dance steps, costumes, dialogue delivery, and so on, in the matter of over-all scenic arrangement—the use of the town as stage—a mythic-religious model has been constructed. In this large mise-en-scène sense aesthetics is less important than to provide an actual geography in which to act out very important material that seems to find its most powerful form not as literature but as theatre. And it is precisely this kind of meta-aesthetic sense—an aesthetics that goes beyond aesthetics—that Western contemporary theatre lacks.

Experimentalists have felt this lack and have, in their own ways, tried to remedy it. Again many of these experiments over the past 30 years have taken the pathway of exploring new kinds of theatrical space. Experiments in environmental theatre, and in audience participation (even to the dissolution of the audience altogether by Grotowski), have been the major avenues of meta-aesthetics in Euro-American theatre. I want now, very briefly, to give a few examples of these experiments concerned with performance space. They are individualistic and modest, but clearly connections can be seen between them and Ramlila and Yaqui Easter.

Of course at least since the Bauhaus designs of 'total theatre' an active campaign has been waged demanding new theatre space—something different than the proscenium. But it was not until the 1950s and 60s that ideas were translated in a large way into theatrical practice. Some of the theoretical basis for this is outlined in my 1968 article, 'Six Axioms for Environmental Theatre.' The first axiom is that 'the theatrical event is a set of related transactions'. This relocates theatre away from the enactment of a set literary text to what goes on in the performance space—between performers and spectators, events and space, production elements and texts (not necessarily written texts). The second axiom is that 'all the space is used for performance; all the space is used for audience'.

> Once one gives up fixed seating and the bifurcation of space, entirely new relationships are possible. Body contact can naturally occur between performers and audience; voice levels and acting intensities can be widely varied; a sense of shared experience can be engendered. Most important each scene can create its own space, either contracting to a central or a remote area expanding to fill all available space. The action 'breathes' and the audience itself becomes a major scenic element.[11]

What we get is a 'global sense' of theatrical space rather than a 'stage sense' of simulated actuality or contrived artificiality. The third axiom said that 'the theatrical event can take place either in a totally transformed space or in "found space"'. Thus Allan Kaprow in 1964 staged *Eat*, an event in a cave in the Bronx. And he played with the relationship between time and space by building a large monolith of ice in a hot Los Angeles street in 1967. Artists worked inside galleries not designed as theatres, such as Meredith Monk's *Juice* in 1969 at the Guggenheim Museum in New York, Trisha Brown's outdoor dance with spectators on the roof and dancers crouched behind barriers on the Lower East Side of New York; or more bucolically, on the beaches of California, or on a mountainside near Shiraz, Iran, where Robert Wilson staged his week-long *Ka Mountain* in 1972.

The Living Theatre in 1975 staged an outdoor performance on the campus of the University of Michigan that used the buildings as architectural markers of 'death', 'the state', 'money', 'property', 'war', and 'love'. The work premiered in Pittsburgh—so the job of the Living was to find on the University of Michigan campus, or wherever *Six Public Acts* was performed, the necessary 'houses'. The Living wanted to use architecture, and the uses to which certain buildings were put, in roughly the same way that space is used at Ramlila and Yaqui Easter. They wanted to make geography 'speak' the way it speaks in Ramnagar and New Pascua. I saw the performance. The difficulty with it, as with so much political theatre, was an ambivalence on the part of the audience which reflects an analogous ambivalence among the performers. The Living assumed that the audience shared political values with the theatre. But everyone also knows this is not true. Not only does a distance open between what is performed and the audience, but a definite hostility erupts on both sides. It is precisely this hostility that is missing in Ramlila and Yaqui. There certain figures—demons and Chapayekas—are permitted aggressive, even sacrilegious acts; but these are played out within the context of ultimate reconciliation. Ravana's final surrender to Ram—an exact parallel to Yaqui Easter—is to remove his mask and touch the feet of Ram.

I want to end here, abruptly. That is because I've come to the place where divergent societies, and cultural values, make comparisons difficult. Experimenters in Euro-America, and in modern Japan too, have tried to include their audiences by creating special spaces and ritual-aesthetic actions. Have they succeeded in their primary aim, not of creating beauty or impressive entertainment, but of somehow ending, or at least diminishing, the alienation among audiences, and reducing the distance—actual and psychic and ontological—between the performance, the performers, and the spectators?

Notes

1. Edward H. Spicer, *The Yaquis: A Cultural History* (Tucson: University of Arizona Press, 1980), pp. 69–70.
2. Edward H. Spicer, 'The Context of the Yaquis Easter Ceremony', in Tamara Comstock ed., *CORD Research Annual VI: New Dimensions in Dance Research: Anthropology and Dance—The American Indian* (N.Y.: Committee on Research in Dance, New York University, 1974), p. 322.
3. Spicer, *The Yaquis*, p. 76.
4. Ibid., p. 77.
5. Ibid.
6. Ibid., p. 78.
7. Ibid.
8. Spicer, 'The Context . . .', p. 313.
9. Spicer, *The Yaquis*, p. 80.
10. Ibid.
11. Richard Schechner, 'Six Axioms for Environmental Theatre', in *TDR*, (Spring 1968), vol. 12, no. 3, p. 49.

The Performance Group in India

FEBRUARY–APRIL 1976

THERE IS A LIFE RHYTHM to any group that presumes to the status of ensemble. At intervals it re-creates itself, or ends. The Performance Group (TPG) began in 1967, re-created itself in 1970, again in 1972, and again at this moment (summer-fall 1976). Re-creation isn't simply about people coming and going: people leave for reasons and join because they feel their careers and the Group's trajectory are moving in the same direction. In the winter of 1975 Timothy Shelton who played Eilif left TPG because he wanted to test himself in commercial theatre and because TPG didn't offer him the range of roles or the position within the Group that he needed. At the end of the India tour James Griffiths (the Cook) left because he wanted to work in a 'directorless' group in San Francisco. But even more basic shifts are taking place as long-time members of TPG create their own works separate from me, and we all re-construct relationships to each other. There is a long history of working together: MacIntosh and I have been at TPG since 1967; Borst joined in 1969 summer and Gray later that year; LeCompte and Griffiths joined in 1970, Clayburgh in 1972, Sack in

1973, and Vawter in 1974. Rayvid has worked with TPG since 1973 but became a 'provisional member' in 1975. Charney was taken on specifically for the India tour when Alexandra Ivanoff said she didn't want to make the trip.

The changes within TPG reached a critical stage during our India tour. Two rhythms interacted: *(i)* as individuals and as a theatre we met audiences, sponsors, and the multiplicity called India, itself undergoing stress and change during the Emergency; *(ii)* within each of us and as TPG we began to work through—by means of two sets of talks, one in Calcutta in March and one at Juhu Beach near Bombay right after the tour's end in April—our past relationships, present circumstances, future arrangements. There's no doubt that the high of the tour—we were praised even when our work fell short—mixed with its difficulties to bring on the crisis within TPG. It's hard to adjust to a strange culture when you're running around the country on a breakneck schedule needing to perform artistically and socially at every stop. More so when, as we wanted, we didn't get transplanted from one Western style hotel to another—but lived with families, in Indian style tourist bungalows and, as much as time allowed, interacted through workshops and meetings with Indian theatre people. So I'm writing not only a travel journal but an exposition of the group-making process as I see it manifesting itself under stress. I'll probe as deeply as I can how the tour worked on TPG: I'll make suggestions for future tours. But first I must review how *Mother Courage (MC)* was developed in New York, and how its preparation relates to TPG's over-all work.

WORK ON *MC* IN NEW YORK

We began in April 1974, the same time we decided to come to India. All roles are cast from inside TPG. This in-looking leads to 'role clusters,' a chorus-like effect as different characters are played by the same performers and costumes carry over from one role to another. For example, Borst and Griffiths play Recruiter and Sergeant in scene 1 and Lieutenant and Sergeant in scene 11; Gray and LeCompte play the peasants in scenes 5, 10, 11, 12; Gray and Shelton play Swiss Cheese and Eilif and the two soldiers in scene 6. The blue officer's coat is worn by Recruiter Poldi in scene 3, Clerk in scene 6, and

Lieutenant; the khaki soldier's coat is worn by Sergeant in scene 1, Soldier in scenes 3 and 6, and Sergeant in scene 11. But necessity and chance also operate: only the Chaplain and Cook aren't in scene 1; when Shelton left TPG, Rayvid took the roles of soldier and peasant son, while Clayburgh took Eilif. Desire also counts: LeCompte wanted to play the General in scene 2 and this meshed with my wanting to show a woman in a role traditionally linked to male power. In costume she looked like South Vietnamese dictator Ki; this added parody to the role. Also everyone was musician, stagehand, supper-server, and reader of the introductions to scenes. Seeing the performer playing Eilif adjust the ropes, hearing the one playing (mute) Kattrin read the introduction to scene 2, or getting supper served by the person playing the Chaplain all help open conceptual spaces between performers and roles, dramatic narrative and theatrical environment. These methods, long a part of TPG'S work, agree well with Brecht's *verfrumsdungeffekt*.

From April through June 1974 we worked upstairs at the Performing Garage in a space 40 ft by 25 ft. Our main theatre was full of the environment for Sam Shepard's *The Tooth of Crime* which we were performing four times a week. We worked on *MC* about five hours a day, four days a week. *Tooth* closed in June and we began teaching days at NYU—rehearsals of *MC* shifted to the 50 ft by 35 ft by 18 ft (height) main theatre, and we worked four nights a week from 7 to 11 during July and half of August. Then we left on a tour of Europe with *Tooth*. (The summer was very full: part of the NYU work was developing the script of David Gaard's *The Marilyn Project* which opened 18 months later in December 1975.) During the six weeks' work on *MC*, Clayburgh and Jerry Rojo set up the basic environment: a 'wagonstore' area against the west wall, a bridge across the centre of the room (later demolished), galleries at two levels all around (adapted from *Tooth*), an open pit 6 ft by 25 ft by 8 ft deep along the north wall. We decided to play several scenes outdoors on Wooster Street which runs along the east side of our theatre building [Photograph 9, 11]. It wasn't until November 1974 that we rehearsed *MC* full time, five days a week, six or seven hours a day. It opened in February 1975.

After one read-through the performers were on their feet wrestling with the physical problems: what should the wagon be? how does Courage move? what props were essential? what sounds does Kattrin make? etc. etc. I don't believe in 'work around the table' or talk-analysis of characters: it all happens up against the problems of staging, and in constructing not just characterization but the entire world of the performance, including the roles of the spectators. I get the performers moving around, with someone feeding lines so the words are learned through the ear, as speech. I've seen the same technique used in jatra rehearsals. Performers work from the situations of the play, improvising, testing moves, gestures, arrangements, readings. I select blocking and line-readings from what's offered—my job is like that of a sculptor building up and whittling down material already there. Everything is kept fluid for many weeks. But it's not a question of vagueness: one concrete solution yields to another in an exploratory sequence of experiments.

For example, at first the wagon was a costume trunk on wheels to which we attached ropes. After a week this was rejected, and with it the whole idea of a rolling wagon. Any wagon of appropriate size would dominate our theatre as a centre-piece environment like the one we already had for *Tooth*. A rolling wagon automatically referred us to Brecht's (and every other) *MC* production making it impossible to investigate the play in a totally new American way. Soon we began to use the idea of a 'store' anchored against the west end of our theatre. But then the problem was how to physicalize pulling, trekking the roads, back-bending labour; how to show one person exploiting another through oppressive labour and the transformation of human beings into animals dragging a load. Rojo, Clayburgh, and I discussed pulleys, ropes, blocks-and-tackle. One afternoon in May, Clayburgh arrived with this stuff—and immediately the performers tested it. Shelton ran his feet bloody trying to pull free from MacIntosh's hold— but the pulley system gave her a three-to-one advantage: here was the physical expression of exploitation and one person's control over another. Clayburgh hitched the tackle to the wall and put Borst on the hook. The visual-sonic effect was stunning: leaning out at a 45 degree angle, running with all his might but getting nowhere, the tackle jangling behind him, the ropes rising and falling in rhythm with his strides: scene 7 was born. The equipment was flexible: ropes could divide the space any way; they could be strung at any angle; they could hoist, drop, pull, and hold. From that afternoon Clayburgh began working out in detail how the rope-and-pulley system would be used in each scene. With only slight modification this system was used in India exactly as in New York. And from the beginning of 1974 it was clear that everyone would help in scene shifts—these were to be an integral part of the performance.

Paul Dessau's music was from the very start of rehearsals another backbone of the production. If the text and actions were experimented with freely, we applied ourselves with rigour to the Dessau score. Thus a dialectic operated at the centre of the rehearsal process. Richard Fire worked with us through June. Thereafter Ivanoff, a classical singer, became TPG's musical director. Her work went beyond teaching the Dessau score. She trained people in singing, combined traditional musical discipline with an appetite for new ways to make sound. Both these trends are heard in *MC*. They also reach back to TPG work in *Tooth*, *Concert* (1971), *Commune* (1970), and *Makbeth* (1969).

Brecht posits a dialectic between business, war, and dehumanization: the interaction of war and business results in dehumanization. No full-scale war has been fought in America since the Civil War and the wars against the American Indians of the nineteenth century. So I decided to emphasize business and through it to manifest the whole system. All details were organized accordingly. The south wall of the theatre was plastered with a mixture of super-market food ads and armed forces enlistment posters. As spectators enter the theatre they come to me where I sit behind a large cash-register collecting the admissions' charge—no tickets were sold in advance, everyone paid cash at the door. Each time money is taken, exchanged, or mentioned throughout the performance the register bell is rung: from the first spectator in to the moment when Courage gives the Peasant Woman some dollars to bury Kattrin, the register bell itemizes each transaction. Vawter counts the night's receipts at his desk near his drum-set;

real cash is used as props and about $50 is in circulation; a 'gold brick' monoprop is used to ikonize the valuable items Courage accumulates and sells, and as Swiss Cheese's cash box. In scene 6 Kattrin saves the 'gold brick' even at the cost of being raped. Courage curses the war and throws the brick down at the end of scene 6—but then she changes her mind and clutches the brick to her breast. Yvette takes cash from the soldiers who patronize her prostitute's business; and it is Poldi's money that Yvette loans to Courage to ransom Swiss Cheese. But Courage gets the money only when she mortgages the store-wagon, and her haggling costs Swiss Cheese his life. Courage is always doing business—yet the more business she does the poorer she gets.

In TPG performers develop roles on their own. As director I'm concerned with the continuity of training and, for each production, with the visual and sonic scores. Directing is mostly watching and selecting. I comment on rhythms, balance between silence and sound, gestures, groupings. I find in what the performers do things to be retained and things to be eliminated. I make suggestions—but my inventions are based on theirs. I move around to all the places where the audience will be: I'm not interested in a single-perspective picture but a whole environment. I don't talk much about the psychology of characters, feelings, motivations, or objectives. First of all, my colleagues are better trained and more competent in these matters than I; secondly, as Stanislavski showed in his 'method of physical actions', affects will arise on their own if the physical score is precise. What we do discuss is the physical score, the technical aspects—how everything is to be integrated, and the meaning of the play in social terms as it is worked out concretely in the production through the fundamental interaction between performers and spectators. I've given examples in the uses of ropes and money; but every aspect is worked through in meticulous detail. Improvisation is a valuable training and rehearsal tool, but in performance it is unreliable. Of course, performers working so close to spectators deal with contingencies—but these are best described as permutations on the score, not improvisations.

Triumphs of acting arise from patience, repetition, and the ability to re-do scenes that've been unchanged for months. In TPG we have no fear of developing idiosyncratic, divergent, or even contradictory interpretations if these are—or lead to—meeting places of an individual performer's impulses and the production's logic. So much fails, one or the other, and great performing happens only when the two meet. This method pulls us off-course for weeks as when we tried again and again to find a balance between Gray's one-syllable-at-a-time Swiss Cheese and Brecht's simpleton Christ. Once an action is accepted it is rehearsed ruthlessly. It took many hours to score Kattrin's death fall in scene 11 with the heel of her red boot caught on the edge of the ladder; or Yvette's sexual poses during the intercourse section of scene 3 so that the transfer of money from the soldiers to Yvette is visually prominent; or the cracked-voice lullaby Courage sings to Kattrin's corpse in scene 12 followed by her hyena-like stripping of the corpse of its resellable clothes. At the end of the play Courage is hitched to every rope in the theatre: she is enmeshed in her own web, she carries the audience with her, the whole space seems to be moving. To stage this Clayburgh worked backwards from scene 12 to scene 5 figuring how each rope had to be set so that all could be finally gathered at a single terminus. It was only after five months' work that scenes were run through without stopping—to run through too soon freezes work, reducing its experimental potential. Even after *MC* opened we met three hours before each performance for warmups, notes on the previous performance with suggestions for the show at hand, rehearsals of scenes and music. Months before *MC* opened—while it was very rough—spectators came to open rehearsals. In July these spectators were students from our NYU workshops; in November colleagues from other theatres and friends came; the general public was invited through newspaper ads in December. Thus *MC* developed under the public eye and retains the style of a tribunal. But also there is a sense of celebration—heightened by the full supper served after scene 3. In India this supper was more of a snack—but in America it is a full meal at a cheap price. Audiences at open rehearsals, and during the run too (performers talk to the spectators during the supper), share their reactions, make suggestions, and through their very behaviour help test the production as it develops.

The spectator isn't a numb consumer welcome only after the creative work is done, but part of the process from its most formative stages. And the creative work is never ended—even during the fall of 1975—while TPG was preparing four new works—changes were made in *MC*. And in India too changes were made.

THE SCHEDULE, THE PEOPLE

We arrived in Delhi on the morning of 3 February, 12 of us on the Air-India weekly charter from Amsterdam. Joan and I have been to India before, in 1971. At the airport were Suresh Awasthi who originated the idea of TPG coming to India, Rajinder Nath of Abhiyan our Delhi sponsors, and V. Ramamurthy (Murti), our Indian tech director. An immediate plunge into work: we accept the old gym at the Modern School as the place to build the environment; Clayburgh negotiates with Amrit Lal Nayar, a contractor, to supply us with 'slotted angles' and plywood and we decide to haul the environment around India rather than build from scratch at each site. The expense of acquiring the stuff and trucking it was not expected. Also we learned that our Delhi budget was to be met from box office—thus ticket prices would be at Rs 10, very high, and still there'd be a big loss. In fact, the same box office arrangement was made at Lucknow, while at Calcutta, Bhopal, and Bombay our sponsors took responsibility for meeting living and production costs. But everywhere the tickets ranged up to Rs 10. We had a grant of $21,000 from the JDR 3rd Fund—and with this we paid international and India travel, salaries, per diem allowances, and costs in Delhi and Lucknow. The grant didn't cover all these expenses, nor was it meant to; TPG's savings and other contributions added $13,000 to the kitty. The tour was very expensive, possibly too much so. In the future we ought to develop a simple, easily transportable or, even better, duplicatable environment. But nothing can save on the biggest expense, international air travel, which came to over $11,000.

With a hired crew of labourers, help from E. Alkazi and students of the National School of Drama (NSD) and volunteers from different Delhi theatres, work on the environment went well. Alkazi arranges for us to borrow lights not only for Delhi but for the whole tour. Then a big snag: Customs won't release our costumes, props, ropes and pulleys until we put up a Rs 81,000 bond. After two days of negotiations I personally guarantee the money underwriting a Letter of Credit TPG brought to India to cover expenses; my guarantee is in turn guaranteed by the United States Educational Foundation in India (I'm a Fulbright scholar this year); and, finally, Grindlay's Bank puts up the Rs 81,000 bond and our stuff is liberated. Waiting for hours at the Palam customs shed I stare at a sign over the officer's desk: 'I am not interested in excuses for delay. I am interested only in a thing done'—Jawaharlal Nehru. We get our equipment on 7 February, two days before dress rehearsal.

On 10 February *MC* opens to a full house; but by the end about one-third had gone. Possibly they didn't expect a four-hour performance during which they sat on hard wood planks, on the floor, or moved about. My immediate reactions as recorded in my notebook:

> Environment too long for its width. Acoustics bad. One-third of the audience left at intermission; one-third very appreciative. They rushed up to the performers and me after the show and showered us with congratulations. Mostly authentic, some just being polite. The show itself was slow and ragged . . . Mistakes last night: Joan dropped her 'pulpit' speech in scene 3; I got the ropes wrong in scene 2; Griffiths went dry for lines in scene 9; the rope got stuck and Kattrin's ladder wouldn't go up for scene 11—we had to stop the show, fix it, and then go on. It was very hard to hear. People strained their voices. In the other places we should make the environment better proportioned. The theatre is filthy—the dirt road outside means dirt gets tracked in and the place gets suffocatingly dusty so it's hard to speak.
>
> *February 11*

And Joan said in her notebook:

> I was rolling in dirt. I breathed dirt, dry earth dirt. I strained my voice between a dirt-clogged throat and bad acoustics. I felt like I could have been anywhere on tour doing *MC* not in

> India . . . I was exhausted, hungry, sick to my stomach. The wheelbarrow—used as a market basket—didn't work. I slipped and fell on the wagon steps. I spilled a bucket of water on an audience member in scene 3. And yet the Indians loved it. One man squeezed my hand so hard I thought he had broken my knuckles. Scene 12 took on a special meaning to me here of an Indian peasant woman beggar tromping through the dusty countryside, stumbling, enduring . . . During the show I was not at all nervous, only angry or concentrated on what needed to be done: keeping the story clear. The audience's reaction was pleasing, but being a perfectionist I wasn't satisfied. It could've been better.
>
> *February 11*

It got better. The best performance in Delhi—and one of the best of the tour—occurred on 13 February, Friday night. It takes a great audience to make a great performance. They kept pushing in until there were too many of them, probably about 350. The performers bitched—but again and again I've seen that when something unexpected and hard happens—too big a house, a sudden error, a part of the environment that fails, etc.—the performance either collapses or overcomes the challenge luminously: through all the work the clarity of the play's themes and the skill of the performers, the sheer beauty of the event, comes through as it does in athletics.

At the same time that the performances were bringing TPG together, long-range problems troubled us all. On 11 February I wrote:

> New rhythms are needed: a theatre with (1) strong leadership working for (2) continuous training and opening up (3) doing performances in many places before different kinds of people (4) alternating between commercial and non-commercial work . . . TPG is no longer the arena, if it ever was, where people (all, including me) can go beyond.

Instead of feeling encouraged-liberated by the group structure, I felt suffocated. I wasn't alone in thinking this way. Steve, Liz and Spalding wanted to direct and/or compose their own work; Joan wanted to find autonomy as a performer similar to what the others sought as directors and composers; Leeny wasn't sure what she wanted to do; etc. At the same time we didn't want to bust TPG up. We were looking for new arrangements. As often happens in our Group people began talking informally with each other about these feelings—and pressure built to have formal meetings.

In Delhi too the first inklings of the 'sex problem' appeared. In scene 3, Yvette and three soldiers perform a stylized mimicry of copulation while on the other side of the space Courage smears Kattrin's face with mud in order to make her unattractive to rapacious soldiers. The meaning is clear: in war a safe face is one smeared with filth, and love is mostly a business transaction. Two days after we opened Principal M. N. Kapur of the Modern School told me that this scene had repercussions among the governing board of the school. He also felt that it distorted our production—some people came to *MC* just to see it, others stayed away because of it. I discussed the issue with the Group. They argued that TPG hadn't come to India to show how Indians would stage *MC* but how Americans did. I felt torn because Kapur had been of great help to us, exceedingly generous. Just before a performance, as I was about to insist on some modifications in the scene, Kapur came up to me and said: 'No, don't change anything. Do what is right for your work.' My respect for him is deep.

The performances in Chandigarh were cancelled for lack of a suitable space. The Group went on to Lucknow while Steve and I went to Chandigarh to run a workshop. This and other workshops will be discussed later. When we got to Lucknow people were settled at the Government Tourist Bungalow only three blocks from the motor garage where the environment was being set up. Murti tells of delays up to six hours trucking the environment down from Delhi through octroi posts. Experience is teaching us about the local, regional, cultural, religious, political, and linguistic rivalries that both enrich and debilitate India. These rivalries shadowed us in Delhi and Calcutta, and affect us directly in Lucknow. Originally our Lucknow sponsors were Darpan, and the contact Awasthi gave me was Kunwar Narain. On 10 October 1975 I wrote a detailed letter to all our sponsors outlining exactly what TPG needed to stage *MC*. The three page single-spaced letter emphasized the following:

> 1. TPG does not perform in a proscenium theatre or in any way separate the audience from the performers. As the enclosed photographs show, the audience sits among the performers, or stands around them . . . Thus instead of a regular theatre we need a large room for our performance . . . When we do perform on a proscenium stage we put the entire audience on the stage—no one sits in the house, the curtain remains closed. Thus we can perform on a very large proscenium stage. Also we can perform in a gymnasium or a large banquet hall. In every case we need large quantities of scaffolding to build up the theatre.
>
> 2. The performance of *MC* takes nearly 4 hours. After scene 3 we serve a supper to the audience . . . This meal is not 'entertainment' but still it is very much part of the performance; it is important to the themes of the play.

Incidentally, the supper did not work well at all in India. It was more an interval snack than a continuation of Courage's business. Indians don't eat at 7.30; they like to sit down; they eat in family groupings. Also all we could arrange to serve were snacks. In America the meal is actually a good bargain of bread, cheese, soup with meat and/or vegetables, fruit, and beverage. The performers assist in serving the meal. It was cooked by people from our workshops (who were paid for the job) upstairs at our theatre.

> 3. One of the scenes is played in the street outside the theatre. In New York a big door opens and the audience remains inside looking through the door at the performers who are standing in the street. On tour we are sometimes able to play this scene as in New York—but we can also play it indoors if necessary.

In Delhi this scene worked well because the Modern School Gymnasium had a door that could be used like the one in New York. And in Bhopal where we performed on the large proscenium stage of the Kala Parishad's Ravindra Bhawan this scene was played in a field behind the theatre using an ox cart as *MC*'s wagon. A special platform was constructed in Calcutta because the stage door was 12 feet above the street level. In Bombay the whole play was outdoors in the Cathedral and John Connon School courtyard and scene 9 was played within the regular performing space. In Lucknow the scene was played at the entrance to the motor garage, but not actually in the street. Nowhere did the scene work as well as in New York where Wooster Street carries light traffic and the scene gathers a small crowd of passersby. Also during winter the weather enters the theatre, spectators wrap themselves in their coats, the feeling of the final scenes (9 through 12) is very bleak. Courage's talk about winter is actualized.

On 29 October I had a long letter from Narain. 'I could not write to you immediately,' he said, 'as I waited for a confirmation from Darpan who wanted a little time to consider all your requirements and discuss them with their members so that they could make a definite commitment to you. They now assure me that adequate arrangements can be made.' I heard nothing from Darpan until 13 November when B. C. Gupta wrote agreeing to my proposed schedule and other details. That same day Gupta wrote Murti saying, 'the whole Darpan team will be at your disposal'. So I was surprised when I arrived in Lucknow to find out that Darpan wasn't sponsoring TPG at all. At the last minute Raj Bisaria and his Theatre Arts Workshop had taken over. I never found out what happened—only that no love was lost between the rival groups. Everywhere the Indian theatre is plagued by factionalism. But the modern theatre—particularly that wing that wants to do new work, experimental work—is not strong enough to afford factionalism. Throughout my week in Lucknow I split my time between Narain—who I found to be intelligent and perceptive—and Bisaria who worked day and night with his crew to get *MC* up and going. Things were tense all around.

The environment was extraordinary, a motor garage, where amid piles of tyres, broken down cars, and steel girders we set up *MC*. We didn't use the whole 100 x 200 ft space but lashed slotted angles to girders. *MC* looked beautiful but the Lucknow audience was confused;

they lay back from the production. Bisaria explained that relatively few people in Lucknow know English, especially the American dialect TPG speaks. And environmental theatre was new for Lucknow—though I never tired of explaining the structural and conceptual links between it and traditional Indian theatre like jatra, kathakali, Ramlila. But a gap has opened between modern Indian theatre and traditional forms. The issue is complex because the traditional forms are exciting theatrically but ideologically and socially they are often reactionary; or, as in jatra, commercial melodramas. Modern theatre's problem is how to use the staging and direct relation to the audience of the folk forms without at the same time falling into their reactionary *mythopoesis*. The answer is not in imitation or adaptation. Rather I suggest that writers, designers, and actors fully experience the folk forms, and get training in these forms—and then 'forget' what they've learned; fully digesting the techniques so that these become part of the muscle of their own work. It is at the level of body consciousness, integration of music and rhythmic movement, environmental staging, and direct contact with the audience that modern groups can use traditional theatre.

One of the best things at Lucknow was how about 75 poor people came to the show. At first they stood outside—they could see in because one side of the building had no wall. Not all the tickets were sold and during a scene change I gestured for the poor to come in. Most of the adults held back but the kids came. They found places on the floor and in the corners of the environment: they were skilled at fitting into crevices, spaces in the social structure rejected by richer people. And about 50 people scampered across the roof, peering down through the opening between the peaked roof and the horizontal walls. Paying spectators ignored this new group, or moved away slightly. I remembered my nine years in the deep South of the USA where blacks were legislatively 'part of' and 'equal to' whites but actually kept 'apart from' in a conceptual if not physical sense.

By Lucknow TPG had come down from the high of first arrival in India. Almost everyone was sick. And problems that troubled us in America, but were put aside for the tour, reasserted themselves. These boiled down to the fact that TPG is nine years old, its members are entering or are in their 30s (and I'm 42). People want 'autonomy' and their own 'artistic identities'. They don't want to be known as 'members of Richard Schechner's Performance Group'. At the same time I want my leadership acknowledged within the Group. By the end of our stay in Lucknow everyone knew that we needed some full group discussions and these were set for Calcutta.

The Abhinav Bharati theatre off Shakespeare Sarani in Calcutta wasn't finished when we set up there. The audience entered through piles of junk, scraps from sets, hardware—and passed over a plank-boardwalk to the stage where we'd set up *MC*. The environment combined folk and modern elements—the grid was of bamboo, and bamboo railings lined the galleries. Everything went smoothly in Calcutta because of the superb organization led by Shyamanand Jalan and Bishu Sureka. They were of great help on the rest of the tour too. Also in Calcutta we picked up our relationship with Badal Sircar who'd come to North America and worked with TPG in 1971. Space limitations prevent me from discussing Sircar's newest work—done outdoors, in villages, in environmental spaces—*Spartacus*, *Michhil*, *Bhoma*. I say only that of the modern theatre I've seen in India Sircar's Satabdi and the Repertory Company of the NSD are doing the most important work. Performances in Calcutta went smoothly except for the 'sex issue' which came to a head after an unsigned review in the Hindi paper, *Vishvamitra*, proclaimed: 'The most daring use of this environment is made when the actors, both male and female, in full view of the audience and in full illumination strip down completely and change their costumes. In this manner they educate the audience—acting out everything, even the way a woman is disgraced as the soldiers fornicate with her.' The day this review appeared we were besieged by men who offered me up to Rs 100 for a ticket; women with tickets stayed away; men fought on the street in front of the theatre. At interval I said, 'The sex scene is over, so if that's what you came for, eat your supper and go.' Many left, maybe forty men.

The 'sex issue' exploded in Calcutta but it was there in Delhi and Bhopal too. Granted that standards vary greatly from USA to India, *MC* is not a sex show. Costume changes are done in the Green

Room–dressing room which is intentionally visible for the same reason that we show every technical aspect of the production; but no one is naked—and there's absolutely no connection between the Yvette part of scene 3 and the costume changes. The scene itself balances Yvette's business of prostitution with Courage's smearing mud on Kattrin's face so that she'll appear unattractive to the sex-starved soldiers. Ironically, the males who stormed the Abhinav Bharati were like the soldiers of scene 3—and at root neither soldiers nor spectators are to be blamed. The fault lies with a repressive sexual censorship.

On 18 March, under arrangements made by Sircar and Barin Saha, we performed *MC* in Singjole, a village about 3 hours outside of Calcutta. In fact, however, one of our Calcutta sponsors (not Jalan or Sureka) opposed this performance. Shortly before leaving for India I got a letter from Calcutta dated 5 January 1976:

> I would strongly suggest, after consulting people in the theatre field, not to produce the play in any village as it will not only cost a huge amount of money and hard work, but also it will be very difficult to attract the required audience, as the atmosphere in our villages has not yet reached the standard to appreciate productions like yours. Please clarify the situation immediately.

I wrote back on 16 January:

> It is very important to us to be able to play in villages—we want our work to reach the people who live in the villages, no matter how difficult that may be. We are willing to adjust our staging to suit village conditions: outdoors spaces, courtyards, bad lighting or no stage lighting at all . . . It is most important to us that we perform for a cross-section of the Indian public. This is the other reason why we insist on trying to perform, for no charge, in a village near Calcutta.

The production cost almost nothing because we set up under two large trees using them as the grid for our rope system; a trench was dug that came very close to the pit we have in New York; we lit the show with petromax lanterns; a harmonium substituted for the piano; the audience sat on the ground all around; there was no interval and no supper.

Instead of the 800 people we'd expected—two times the most we'd ever played *MC* for—about 2,000 people came [Photograph 9]. As elsewhere in folk theatre the women and young children sat on one side and the men and older boys on the other. The audience stayed for about 3 of the 4 hours (we began at 7.30); at the end there were maybe 750 people left. Sircar introduced the play and before each scene he outlined its action in Bengali. But we weren't skilled at projecting our voices to such a large crowd; and *MC* isn't the kind of play that can be suddenly shouted. I wrote in my notebook:

> Aesthetics went out the window . . .We adjusted our staging and made it broad: telling the story through big actions . . . We didn't contact this audience so much through our work as simply by our presence. It was a Fair and we were entertainment.

We cut large sections of scenes 6 and 8, and all of 9 and 10. The morning after the performance I went around Singjole with Saha talking to people. They liked the performance though they didn't understand its language or anything except the barest story outline. 'What did you like?' 'The songs, the falling, the fighting, the killing. The way Mother tried to save her children. The girl who couldn't talk.' But a Bengali director who saw the performance said, 'They were being polite. The only reason they didn't bust up the show was because you are white.'

Group members found the performance 'liberating'—they were free from the restraint that comes when an audience listens closely—they could go as far as possible in physicalizing their roles, and playing with words as sounds rather than as cognitive speech. As I've seen elsewhere spectators felt free to talk among themselves, wander to and from the performance, and pay attention only to what interested them. Peter Brook and Robert Wilson, among others, have experimented with this kind of rhythm—and I've seen it at performances of chhau, kathakali, and Ramlila. The performance at Singjole pinpointed the biggest shortcomings of the tour: *(i)* we didn't play to ordinary people in the cities; *(ii)* the one time we had a popular audience they couldn't follow the play.

My suggestions for future tours: *(i)* make tickets available free to theatre workers and students training for theatre. These people should see two or more performances so that they grasp the production at the professional level of techniques. After this close viewing, discussions are held between the visiting artists and the local people; these discussions are followed by workshops; *(ii)* either by extending the run or by direct subsidy at least one-third of the tickets are allocated for poor people at a cost no more than that of a front stall at the movies. Because TPG doesn't use fixed seating the poor, middle classes, and rich will either mix or segregate themselves; *(iii)* TPG must make productions that work visually if we are going to play for non-English speakers. And if we are going to play outdoors to large crowds then either microphones or clear loud speaking must be used. These suggestions are based on the fact that groups like TPG rarely visit India and the exchange must be managed so that both sides get the most out of it.

Before the meetings in Calcutta I made some notes about what kind of theatre I wanted, and my place in it:

> Problems: (1) How to make a theatre for the poor, the workers, the office people and still survive and still do theatre that is important personally. (2) How to involve the audience at every level and still keep professional standards . . . I want to get to these things: (1) Performances for 'people' on subjects or themes of importance to society—to do these shows free, where 'people' are. (2) Experiment with the whole range of what performance is—getting to, doing, going from—and to have performers and audience conscious of and participating in this whole range. It means opening not only rehearsals but pre-show notes and warm-ups and post-show discussions and parties to the audience. (3) Find or invent new kinds of psychophysical, psychosocial, and sociophysical exercises. To advance the knowledge of training—especially breathing and making sound.
>
> These meetings are good because they open the possibility for change—even total liberation. For me the liberation can come

> in two ways: Control over TPG so it is an instrument of mine; or freedom from the Group so I can pursue these experiments on my own. In either case I can get free of the ego struggles. I no longer think the Group must reflect what I hope the coming society should be. I now think the instrument must be sharp and held in strong hands—and when it cuts it ought not cut into itself but into the world around it. Otherwise people will mostly subjectivize their lives, turn on or into each other, fail to do anything more than 'express' themselves—while not relating either to the society or to theoretical problems of performance theory, the art. It's the intersection of these two that interests me—not 'holding together' a group (whatever its reputation). Reputations come and go, even art passes. But certain theories and social systems abide, if not for all time, for a long time. I want to teach, change the order of society, and have-make fun.

The meetings took place on 16 and 17 March. The formality of a closed meeting extending over two days guarantees that everyone has a chance to say their say. When the Calcutta meetings were over we knew two things: people other than me would direct and in other ways seek their autonomy (this process began in 1973 with Borst directing *The Beard*), and more meetings were necessary after the tour to find out whether or not TPG should continue as a group and if so, how.

After Calcutta, Bhopal was like emptiness itself. It reminded me of the American southwest and the dry mountains of Mexico. But amid the feeling of newness was the sense that the trees had been cut down, erosion was clawing the land, gutting it. The organizing for TPG by Ashok Bajpeyi and Satyen Kumar was a model of efficiency. Kumar visited Delhi on I4 February, saw a performance, met with me, Murti, Nath and Awasthi; he filed a report on I6 February that formed the basis of our Bhopal programme. Everything was covered, including TPG eating habits. Kumar estimated that our performances would cost Rs 10,000 of which Rs 6,000 could be earned at the box office if tickets were pegged at Rs 10. We set up at the Ravindra Bhawan. To encourage a breeze we left the auditorium open but permitted no one to sit there; we used the outdoor theatre and sloping lawn for scenes 9 through 12. The work at Bhopal went so efficiently that we invited Benu Ganguly, technical director, to come with us to Bombay.

If Calcutta is India's New York, then Bombay is her Los Angeles. All of TPG just slid into Bombay's luxury like falling into velvet. Except for one night at a Tamasha I saw nothing of Bombay's other side. In its segregation of the poor Bombay is very like American cities with their ghettoes and 'ethnic' neighbourhoods. The space for *MC* at the CJC School was a magnificent courtyard surrounded on three sides by galleried buildings. We adapted our environment to the large space making room for 500 spectators, and another 150 (at reduced prices) up in the galleries. I watched some of each show from up top: it was like looking at a terrain map on which figures made dance patterns, the sound rose splendidly so all the dialogue was heard. Everything arranged for us by Narayana Menon and K. K. Suvarna of the National Centre for the Performing Arts was first-rate. The shows were near perfect—we'd learned from Singjole to physicalize a bit more than in America, to speak a little slower, and to eliminate extraneous gestures. The audience understood English and knew Brecht.

On the last night's performance in Calcutta signs appeared in the theatre: 'Schechner Has No Right To Destroy Brecht's Epic Theatre.' 'We Want Brecht Not Environmental Theatre.' 'Environmental Theatre Is A Deliberate Distortion Of Brecht's Philosophy Of Theatre.' 'Long Live Bertolt Brecht, The Dramatist Of The People.' 'Brecht Dealt With War, Schechner Deals With Orgasm.' 'Schechner Preaches Community Involvement By Making You Pay For It.' 'Brecht Spoke of Reality And Struggle, Schechner Deals With Gags, Stunts And Sexual Perversion.' And on 5 April a review appeared in the (Bombay) *Times of India* that praised the production: 'Fantastic! Never before has a Bombay audience been exposed to such an enriching theatrical experience . . . A summative statement on drama; an unforgettable event. Thrice tears welled up in my eyes . . .Through it all, through the words and the action and the noise and the novelty and the enormous planning and intellection behind it Brecht's deep humanism emerges . . . Mother Courage is Man [sic] confronting the absurd. As performed she is vigorous, harsh, pragmatic, tender, defiant, raw as a scoop of earth, ineluctably human.' These contradictory estimates of the production raise the same question: Is TPG true to Brecht, and if not, does it matter?

I don't think fidelity matters much, though I do think TPG's *MC* is true to Brecht. Most of the time the author's intentions aren't known. Who's to say what Sophocles, Kalidasa, or Shakespeare intended? Should Greek tragedies be performed only outdoors in semicircular theatres seating 17,000 spectators who attend as part of yearly civic celebrations? And should these plays be offered up as three tragedies followed by one satyr play? If so, the academies had better instruct us on how to recreate the Athenian city-state. And so on for every past epoch. And if fidelity means the 'interior meaning' of a text, then that is obviously a question of interpretation. Even garrulous Shaw didn't say everything about his plays; and most writers are mum. Fidelity is even less important with Brecht because he staged his plays as he saw fit, and left his 'model books' as evidence—while urging that these should not be slavishly followed. Of *MC* a film exists of the Brecht–Weigel production.

I have long taken the position, and hold it now, that a text is a skeleton, an outline, a plan, a map—but that the body, picture, structure, and territory of a play can be actualized only in performance, at the immediate and unique encounter of performers and spectators; and that rehearsal is a research process for unfolding and discovering what the performance will be. As for 'changing the text,' there are times when that's good and times when it's bad. A classic text that is in no danger of being forgotten is open to retelling, especially if it is to be translated anyway; also neglected plays that will rarely be done in their pristine form. Actually some of the great plays—Shakespeare's *Hamlet*, many of Moliere's plays, Tulsidas' *Ramacharitmanas* (as chanted in Ramlila), not to mention Brecht's *Threepenny Opera*—are versions of older dramas or oral recitations. On the other hand, if a play is new I think the author's words should be respected—he has the right to see his play reach the public first as he wrote it. As a matter of fact, we made no text changes in *MC* except to cut all of scene 4 up to the 'Song of the Great Capitulation'.

But the objections, and praise, are based not on textual changes but on tone—on a sense that TPG didn't do Brecht as Brecht would have done it; and therefore we did it wrong. *MC* is not one of Brecht's hardline plays like *The Measures Taken*. It belongs to a later period along with *The Caucasian Chalk Circle* and the *Good Woman of Setzuan*. Written in 1938, premiered in 1939 in Zurich, *MC* is as much an anti-war play as a condemnation of capitalist greed. In the character of Courage, Brecht internalizes the dialectical conflict which breaks Shen Te and Shui Ta into two persons: Courage is both loving and cruel, generous and stingy, wise and stupid, the best humanity has to offer and an animal. At the end she is neither a hero nor a hyena, but both. Brecht's own *MC* production (I've studied the model book and seen the movie) is, if anything, more sentimental than TPG's: *(i)* the famous open-mouth silent scream of Weigel–Courage when she hears the rifle shots that kill Swiss Cheese but can't express (out loud) her grief; *(ii)* her mourning-lullaby sung over Kattrin's corpse: in Brecht's production Courage allows Kattrin to be buried fully clothed although her clothes are of market-value—in TPG's production we followed the logic of 'hyena of the battlefield' (Brecht's description of Courage) to its extreme by having Courage strip the outer garments off Kattrin; *(iii)* the final action of Brecht's production: on a gray, large, empty stage Courage alone lifts the heavy yoke of her wagon, hitches herself to it, and draws the vehicle two full times around the floor of the revolving stage. I don't criticize Brecht for these choices which point up Courage's humanity, grief, and (pardon) courage; the actions are balanced by others that show her bitterness, contempt, cynicism, and brutality. But I point out that Brecht the director knew different than Brecht the author. Whether different equals better I will not say.

At another level altogether, TPG has been 'true' to Brecht the author even when we've differed with Brecht the director. There is no rolling wagon, but instead a store which is more in the American tradition; we serve supper; the final scenes are played outdoors or with the theatre open to the street. We didn't set the play in seventeenth century Europe in a war between Protestants and Catholics; we use modern costumes and no make-up. We have no separate orchestra playing offstage or from the pit—the performers play the music and all technical people play dramatic roles too. In these ways we out Brechted Brecht: not only is the work of the theatre shown but theatre workers perform roles; and what is a better *verfrumsdungeffekt* than seeing the performer playing Mother Courage play the flute, or the man playing the Chaplain set the ropes between scenes? These choices were made on the basis of how best to get the play across to our audience, and in terms of an environmental theatre we advocate as thoroughly as Brecht advocated his Epic Theatre. The underlying idea of TPG's production—the actualization of the play's inscape—is the same in TPG as with Brecht: a good woman who, in identifying herself with the industrialists, the capitalists, makes choices against her own class interest (which is lower middle, not rich as she gives herself airs of being). Therefore she is systematically—not accidentally—ground down, defeated, and transformed into an animal pulling her own wagon. She is also a hyena of the battlefield, plundering corpses, selling to both sides, cheating, haggling, saving her own skin at the cost of her children's lives. But through all this, and Brecht knew it, she shows grit, a sense of humour with her wise-cracks aimed unfailingly at the generals, priests, kings, and popes. She has a sense of values consistent with Brecht's: she is cynical about religion and politics; she survives. As in *Circle* and *Good Woman* Brecht shows that the only good person in bad times is a bad person (Azdak); good people must act bad to survive in bad times. What the audience experiences is not a bad person getting worse—there's no educative value in that, and Brecht is fundamentally optimistic—but a good person forced to act bad in order to survive. What the audience learns to condemn is the (capitalist and war-making) system that makes Courage choose between her livelihood and a bribe to ransom her son Swiss Cheese.

THE WORKSHOPS, THE AFTERMATH

Under USIS auspices TPG ran workshops in Calcutta and Bombay; we also did workshops on our own in Delhi and in collaboration with our sponsors in Bhopal and Chandigarh. Also I gave slide lectures about our work and the films of *Dionysus in 69* and *The Tooth of Crime* were shown. Workshop is the best introduction to TPG—but unfortunately an introduction that can be given to only a few people. There are other difficulties too. Our work is physical but Indian modern theatre workers are not familiar with—and often are put off by—physical work. I mean simple exertion, as well as self-expression through movement, singing, unstructured sound-making, and touching. Exercises function as vessels—traditions actually—that contain and channel energies, often sexual and aggressive energies (which are normally repressed or redirected). A jumping kick may metaphorize hurting, a deep release of sound and a pelvic thrust may metaphorize sexual intercourse. Unlike traditional forms that already have a grammar (either abstract or mimetic), I try to help performers find in workshop their own mode of expression; later some of these image-actions are used in performance. The workshop is a kind of group socio-psychoanalysis translated into theatrical terms: the space where the personal and the public intersect. I was afraid to go far with this kind of work in India: I didn't want to accept the responsibility of inviting the release of so much repressed energy when I was moving on in a matter of hours. Usually we taught breathing, panting, sound-making, a few of the psychophysical exercises (taken from kathakali via Grotowski), and played theatre games and/or improvisations. Also a lot of discussion went on during the workshops—it was a healthy place to expound on TPG's work, demonstrate some of it, and invite participation. The deepest workshops took place after the tour when Joan and I could spend more time. In July we worked several times with Sircar's Satabdi. I watched and then participated in Debesh Chakravarty's work with his Epic Theatre. Joan and I exchanged work with The Puppets, directed by Raghunath Goswami in Calcutta. In September we did a five day (6 hours per day) workshop with the NSD Repertory in Delhi. This was very satisfying because the Rep people know each other well, are professionals, and wanted to go as far as they could. In October Joan worked more with them, as well as with students at the NSD.

One of the strangest workshops took place in Chandigarh on 23-4 February. Borst and I went there on the invitation of Balwant Gargi after *MC* performances were cancelled. Gargi had gathered theatre scholars and workers from India, Sri Lanka, Nepal, Afghanistan and other places to 'experiment with the translation of the folk ballad Mirza Sahiban into performing arts terms and the resultant production will be performed in a natural rural setting'. The time allotted was 23 February to 20 March. I don't know how it turned out, but it began like Alice's teaparty. Some of the visitors weren't performers; mixed in with them were Punjabi musicians who kept up a steady drumming and chanting behind many of the meetings. Gargi turned over the opening sessions to Steve and me, but I didn't have the foggiest idea what to do. We did standard voice work, warm-ups, and 'line exercises' where people face each other and exchange gestures, sounds, ways of walking, etc. What bothered me was that on paper Gargi's programme read splendidly, but the participants didn't know how to break down the barriers between them—it wasn't their fault, there was no crucible prepared to melt down the divisions. And if Steve and I were supposed to provide the heat we found ourselves as disoriented as the others.

In my letter of 1 August 1974 to the JDR 3rd Fund's Porter McCray applying for the money to take TPG to India I outlined my aims:

> The entire Performance Group will participate in this tour. The tour will involve performing in Delhi, Calcutta, Madras and Bombay; studying at the Kathakali Kalamandalam in Kerala; observing traditional and ritual performances in various places in India; direct contact with Indian theatre and dance people; workshops and lecture-demonstrations at theatre centres. Along with Group projects several individual projects will also be worked out, including the possibility of a joint TPG–Indian production; various study projects in Indian arts.

Except for Joan and me the last TPG member left India on 21 June. Most of my programme beyond the performances, workshops, and lectures didn't happen. After the tour Clayburgh, Kas Self, Joan, and I saw Mayurbhanj, Purulia, and Seraikella chhau, and studied Seraikella chhau; later I studied kathakali, Joan studied Hindustani singing, and we both studied yoga. Clayburgh was going to design a production in Delhi but the project collapsed. Discussions are going on that will bring me back to India to direct in Indian languages with Indian performers. Many Group members thought of staying in India till August, some even longer—so what happened? The meetings at Juhu actually stirred many people to go back to America and begin projects of their own. With me out of the USA until February 1977, time and facilities were available without danger of competition. Then during the tour there wasn't enough time at each centre to see Indian theatre or to follow-up initial contacts with Indian theatre workers. We nearly doubled our planned number of performances in order to earn more money and to respond to the great popularity of *MC*. Our sponsors concentrated on making *MC* a success and few arrangements were made for us to see modern, traditional, folk, or ritual performances. The tour got to be a grind, and at the end of it people were sick, exhausted, and worn out. Actually I didn't anticipate how hard being in India would be for some people—at the level of different food, living conditions, lack of family, friends, and familiar diversions. Maybe I expected too much when I outlined my aims; or maybe those aims were mine and not TPG's. But the 'corollary items' are in the long run as important as the impact of our performing. I consider this tour a success but for next time I want to guarantee those items the joint productions, intensive workshops, experience of Indian theatre, studies—that make a tour more than hit-and-run.

PROGRAMME

Tour funded by JDR 3rd Fund, New York, who paid for overseas transportation, and contributed towards production and TPG living and travel expenses in India. Local sponsors in India paid for most of the local production costs and provided most of the living accommodation for TPG members. Local sponsors also donated in-kind work on publicity, the environments, and day-to-day running of the shows. United States Information Service paid for much of the advertising in India; also USIS paid TPG members for leading workshops in Calcutta and Bombay. TPG contributed money toward salaries while on tour and production expenses.

The Company, in order of speaking:

STEPHEN BORST as Recruiter, Chaplain, Lieutenant

JAMES GRIFFITHS as Sergeant, Cook, Poldi, Soldier

JOAN MACINTOSH as Mother Courage (Anna Fierling)

JAMES CLAYBURGH as Eilif, Man With A Patch Over His Eye, Clerk, Soldier

SPALDING GRAY as Swiss Cheese, Soldier, Peasant

ELIZABETH LECOMPTE as General, Yvette, Peasant

RON VAWTER as Ordnance Ollicer, Townspeople

BRUCE RAYVID as Soldier, Another Sergeant, Peasant

LEENY SACK as Kattrin

Environment designed by JAMES CLAYBURGH

Musical director and pianist, MIRIAM CHARNEY

Technical director, BRUCE RAYVID

Costumes, THEODORA SKIPITARES

Technical director in India, V. RAMAMURTHY

Associate technical director for Bhopal and Bombay, BENU GANGULY

Technical assistants KAS SELF, MUNIERA CHRISTIANSEN

General Manager and drummer RON VAWTER

Director RICHARD SCHECHNER

Music by PAUL DESSAU

Translated from the German by RALPH MANNHEIM

Mother Courage and Her Children by BERTOLT BRECHT

(Written 1938; World Premiere, Zurich, 1939)

Tour Outline: 6 Localities, 23 Performances, 56 Days

Place	*Dates*	*Sponsors*
NEW DELHI Modern School Gymnasium	February 10, 11, 12, 13, 14, 18, 19, 20, 21: 9 performances	Abhiyan Rajinder Nath Som Nath Sapru M. N. Kapur, Principal of Modern School
LUCKNOW A private motor garage	February 27, 28: 2 performances	Theatre Arts Workshop Raj Bisaria
CALCUTTA Abhinav Bharati Theatre	March 9, 10, 12, 13, 14: 5 performances	Anamika Kala Sangam Shyamanand Jalan Bishwambhar Sureka Naveen Kishore
SINGJOLE Under two trees	March 18: 1 performance	Tagore Society Barin Saha Badal Sircar
BHOPAL Ravindra Bhawan	March 26, 27: 2 performances	Madhya Pradesh Kala Parishad Ashok Bajpeyi Satyen Kumar Benu Ganguly
BOMBAY Cathedral and John Connon School courtyard	April 3, 4, 5, 6: 4 performances	National Centre for the Performing Arts Narayana Menon K. K. Suvarna K. Kuruvila Jacob, Principal of Cathedral and John Connon School

Restoration of Behaviour

Restored behaviour is living behaviour treated as a film director treats a strip of film. These strips can be rearranged, reconstructed; they are independent of the causal systems (social, psychological, technological) that brought them into existence: they have a life of their own. The original 'truth' or 'motivation' of the behaviour may be lost, ignored, or contradicted. How the strip of behaviour was made, found, developed may be unknown or covered over, elaborated, distorted by myth. Originating as a process, used in the process of rehearsal to make a new process—a performance—the strips of behaviour are not themselves process but things, items, 'material'. The strips can be of long duration as in some rituals, or of short duration as in some gestures, dance movements, or *mantras*.

Restored behaviour is used in all kinds of performances from shamanism, exorcism, and trance to ritual theatre and aesthetic theatre, from initiation rites to social dramas, from psychoanalysis to newer therapies such as psychodrama, transactional analysis, and primal. In fact, the use of restored behaviour is the main characteristic of performance. The practitioners of all these arts, rites, and healings assumed that some kinds of behaviour—organized sequences of events, scripted actions, known texts, scored movements, exist separately from the performers who 'do' these behaviours. Because the behaviour is separate from those who are behaving, the behaviour can be stored, transmitted, manipulated, transformed. The performers get in touch with, recover, remember, or even invent these strips of behaviour and then rebehave according to these strips, either by being absorbed into them (playing the role, going into trance) or by existing side-by-side with them (Brecht's *Verfremdungeffekt*). The work of restoration is carried on in rehearsals and/or in the transmission of behaviour from master performer to novice. Understanding the work of rehearsals, and the subjunctive mood used there, is the surest way to link ritual process to aesthetic process.

Restored behaviour is 'out there', distant from me in time as in the psychoanalytic abreaction, or in sphere of reality as in the encounter between Rangda and Barong in Balinese dance-drama, or by aesthetic convention as when Hamlet rejects his mother, Gertrude, or by tradition as in the brave way a Gahuku boy during his initiation accepts the ordeal of having sharp, jagged leaves slice the inside of his nostrils bringing much blood, or the shy way a New Jersey 'blushing bride' behaves at her wedding even though she and her groom have lived together for three years.

Restored behaviour is symbolic and reflexive. These difficult terms are reducible to the same principle of self-in/as-other: the social or transindividual self. Symbolic and reflexive behaviour is the hardening into theatre of social, religious, medical, educational, and aesthetic process. Performance means: never for the first time; it means: for the second to the nth time. Reflexive means to see the self in the self-and-other.

Neither painting nor sculpting, nor even writing, uses behaviour in actual flow. But thousands of years before movies, rituals were made from strips of restored behaviour so that action and stasis could coexist in the same act. Great comfort flowed from ritual: the deeds of people, gods, ancestors participated simultaneously in being and becoming, in having been, are, and will be. These strips of behaviour were replayed many times. Mnemonic devices ensured that the performance was 'right' as rehearsed or as received—and some performances have been transmitted across many generations with few accidental variations. Even now the terror of the first night is not the presence of the public but that mistakes are no longer forgiven.

This constancy of transmission is all the more astonishing when you realize that restored behaviour involves choice. Animals repeat themselves, and so do the cycles of the moon, but only when the actor can say 'no' to an action is there the possibility of restored behaviour. Even the shaman who is called—the trancer falling into trance—gives over or resists; and there is general suspicion of he who too easily says yes. There is a continuum from the not-much-choice of ritual to the lots-of-choice of aesthetic theatre. But in aesthetic theatre this freedom is narrowed during rehearsals. Rehearsals function to build a score, and this score is a 'ritual by contract' limited to the duration of the run.

Restored behaviour can be put on as a mask or costume is put on. Its shape can be seen from the outside, and changed. That's what theatre directors, councils of bishops, master performers, and great shamans do: change the performance score. The performance can change because it is not a 'natural event' but one, as Turner says, in the subjunctive mood, in what Stanislavski called the 'as if'. Existing as second nature, restored behaviour is always subject to revision. Its 'secondness' is also its negativity, subjectivity, 'anti-ness'.

II

PUT IN PERSONAL TERMS, restored behaviour is 'me behaving as if I am someone else'. But this someone else may also be 'me in another state of feeling/being'. Performing my dream, re-experiencing my childhood trauma, showing you what I did yesterday. Also social actions: the enactment of events whose origins can't be located in individuals, if they can be located at all. Sometimes these events are attributed to collective individuals like the Books of Moses, the *Iliad* of Homer, the Mahabharata of Vyas; sometimes they belong anonymously to folklore, legend, myth. Restored behaviour offers to both individuals and groups the chance to become someone else 'for the time being', or the chance to become what they once were. Or even, and most often, to rebecome what they never were.

Three performative systems are shown in Fig. 1. In 1 ⟶2, I become someone else, or myself in another state of being. There is only moderate displacement—a few rehearsals, sometimes none—and my performance is a solo. Two or more individuals can perform 1⟶2 simultaneously, as when several people fall into trance together. The astonishing thing about Balinese *sanghyang* is that each dancer has by herself/himself so incarnated the collective score that solo dances cohere into a group performance. Upon recovering from the trance, dancers are often not aware that others were dancing, sometimes they don't remember their own dancing. I've seen similar meshing of solo performing into a group event in a black church in Bedford-Stuyvesant during Easter week, 1978. As the gospel singing reached a climax, more than a dozen women and men 'fell out' into the aisles at the same time. Each was dancing in trance alone—but the whole group was dancing together. The heat of the event was controlled by the singers who definitely were not in trance. Peter Adair's film of a snake-handling sect in West Virginia, *The Holy Ghost People*, shows the same thing.

In 1⟶3 ⟶ 4 a restored event is created from a distant place or an actual past. This is common enough when the action is frozen, as in the dioramas of animal and human habitats at the American Museum of Natural History. Strictly speaking, these are restored environments, not behaviours. But recently, and increasingly, action is being added to the environments. I will have a lot more to say later about 'restored villages' and 'theme parks', where fact and fantasy are freely mixed. Some zoos, reacting to the disappearance of species in the wild, now run 'breeding parks' that replicate the vanishing wilderness. It soon may be that the African veldt is better preserved near San Diego than in Africa. In the breeding park near Front Royal, Virginia, the concern to keep the environment pristine is such that all visitors are excluded. Of course, the breeders, veterinarians, and ethologists are allowed in.

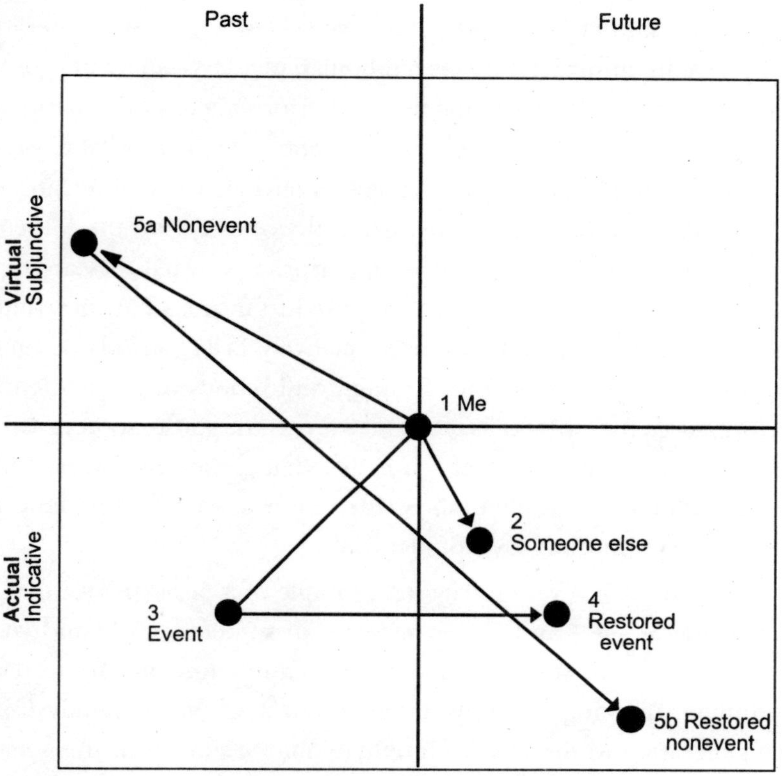

Fig. 1 Restored events are placed in the future because rehearsals are a means of collecting behaviour and 'keeping' it for the performance-to-be. Once performances begin these are, of course, in the present. Presence is an essential quality of live performance. The model is drawn from the perspective of rehearsal or training and practice: whatever goes on 'before' performance makes that performance possible.

Many traditional performances are 1→3→4—or performances that are kept in repertory according to a strict adherence to the original score. When the Moscow Art Theatre visited New York in the mid-1960s they claimed to present Chekhov according to Stanislavski's original mise-en-scène. When I saw several plays of Brecht at the Berliner Ensemble in 1969, I was told that Brecht's *Modelbuchs*—his detailed mise-en-scène instructions were followed to the letter. Certainly classical ballets have been passed on through generations of dancers with minimal change. But even the strictest attempts at 1→3→4 frequently are in fact examples of 1→5a→5b; 1→3→4 is very unstable simply because even if human memory can be improved upon by the use of exact notation, a performance always happens within several contexts, and these are not easily controllable. The social circumstances change, as indeed is obvious when you think of Stanislavski's productions at the turn of the century and the Moscow Art Theatre today. Even the bodies of performers—what they are supposed to look like, how they are supposed to move, what they think and believe—change radically over relatively brief periods of time. Not to mention the reactions, feelings, and moods of the audience. Performances that were once current, even avant garde, soon become period pieces. These kinds of contextual changes are not measurable by labanotation[1] or visible in the written musical score. Even identical performances, in time, are not identical.

Noh drama is a very intriguing example of a performance that is both 1→3→4 and 1→5a → 5b simultaneously and consciously. The whole score of a noh play—its mise-en-scène, music, text, costuming, masking—is transmitted within a school or family from one generation to the next with only minor variations. In this sense, noh, at least since the Meiji Restoration in the nineteenth century, is a clear example of 1→3 →4. During his lifetime a noh *shite*—the main actor, literally the 'doer', the one who wears the mask—moves from one role to another in a progression. He accepts the score of the role he approaches and leaves behind the score of his earlier role which is taken over by another. Only the greatest masters of noh are permitted to change the score, and then these changes become part of the tradition: they are passed on to the next generation. The roles, and their place within the mise-en-scène, and the mise-en-scènes themselves within the progression of noh plays that makes up a lifetime of performing, is a complicated but decipherable system. But each individual noh performance also includes surprises. The groups who come together to do a noh play are made up of representatives of many different families, each with their own traditions, their own 'secrets'. The *shite* and chorus work together; the waki, the kyogen, the flautist, the drummers each work separately. True to its Zen roots, a noh drama staged traditionally occurs only once, finding in the absolute immediacy of the meeting among all its constituent players a unique power. A few days before a scheduled performance the *shite* calls all the participants together and outlines his intentions. The first time the whole thing is done is before the audience during the actual performance. Like the Zen archer, the *shite* hits his mark or he doesn't.

During the performance—through signals coming from the *shite* to the musicians and others—variations occur: routines are repeated or cut, emphases changed, tempos accelerated or slowed. Even the selection of what costume and mask to wear depends on the *shite's* opinion regarding the mood of the audience—an opinion he forms by watching the audience assemble or by gauging their reactions to the first plays of a full noh programme, which may include five noh and four comic *kyogens* and last seven hours or more. Those noh performers, made into a 'company' for foreign tours, where they repeat the same plays over and over, performing with the same people, complain of boredom and the lack of creative opportunity. Traditionally, then, each performance of noh, and every variation during a performance, is the leading edge of a long tradition formed in the thirteenth and fourteenth centuries, almost extinguished by the mid-nineteenth, and flourishing again now. This leading edge is both $1 \longrightarrow 3 \longrightarrow 4$ and $1 \longrightarrow 5a \longrightarrow 5b$.

As interesting as noh, though much more local, is Shaker dancing. Shakers, a religious sect brought from England to America in 1774, are nearly dead now, but about the time of the Civil War numbered about 6000 members. Its ritual included song and dance. Originally these were done for the Shakers themselves. But:

> As Shakerism grew, the religion and the social organization it engendered became less ecstatic and more rigid and institutionalized. The dances and songs, which were the main form of worship, also changed from involuntary ecstatic and convulsive movements with glossolalia occurring during spells of altered states of consciousness to disciplined choreographed marches with symbolic steps, gestures, and floor plans. These rituals became elaborate and fixed dance 'exercises'. A steady

> stream of tourists came to the Shaker communities to watch these spectacles.[2]

The Shakers had stopped dancing by 1931 when Doris Humphrey, one of the pioneers of modern dance in America, choreographed *The Shakers*. I don't have the time to go into the details that Youngerman assembles demonstrating the deep affinities between the Shakers and *The Shakers*. Clearly Humphrey did her research. Youngerman says: 'Humphrey's choreography embodies a wide range of Shaker culture incorporating many direct references to actual Shaker dances.'

Humphrey's dance is still in the repertory of the Jose Limon Dance Company, where I saw it in 1979 and again in 1981. The dance is also labanotated, which means that other companies can dance Humphrey's dance much the way any orchestra can play a Beethoven symphony. In fact, in 1979, the Humphrey dance was performed by the Louisville Ballet at Shakertown, a reconstructed Shaker village at Pleasant Hill, Kentucky. This may not be the only example of an aesthetic dance being a main way of physically re/membering (= putting what has been dis/membered back together) an extinct behaviour. Shakers dancing is 1 ⟶ 3 ⟶ 4; Humphrey's dance is 1 ⟶ 5a ⟶ 5b. The Humphrey dance as a way of finding out what the Shakers did is restored behaviour. The Shaker story goes on. Not only is the Humphrey dance in existence, both through the Limon Company where she danced and through labanotation, but some people have reconstructed the actual Shaker dances from original sources.

Robin Evanchuk visited a few surviving Shakers in 1962 and 1975. They had long since stopped dancing, but by eliciting their memories and those of people who knew Shakers, and by drawing on the research of Edward Deming Andrews,[3] Evanchuk reconstructed the 'authentic' dances. As of 1977 three groups 'have learned and presented this reconstruction', including her own group, the Liberty Assembly. Evanchuk is always bringing new dancers in; she does this by thorough orientation:

> During the teaching sessions, the dancers must overcome their fear of appearing ridiculous due to the strangeness of

> the movements and the intense emotion. In addition to a strong orientation, I find that constant repetition of the movements, which allows the dancers to gradually become comfortable with them, tends to lessen their embarrassment and moves the emphasis from how the dancers feel to concern for how the Shakers themselves felt when they were involved in the exercises.[4]

So we have three different but related performance traditions: the Shakers themselves, an art dance by Humphrey that continues to be performed both by her company and others, and an 'authentic' reconstruction of Shaker dancing by Evanchuk. Of Shaker dancing in the nineteenth century I can say nothing, except to guess that it started as a performance of the 1 ➤ 3 ➤ 4 type but soon became a 1 ➤ 5a ➤ 5b as tourists visited the Shakers to watch them dance. Clearly both Humphrey's *The Shakers* and Evanchuk's reconstructions are performances of the 1 ➤ 5a ➤ 5b type. For these are performances based on performances. One is 'art'; but dance anthropologist Youngerman feels that Humphrey's dance comes close to the heart of the sect, and she reports that

> One of the last two Shaker brothers, Ricardo Belden, then 87 years old, saw the 1955 reconstruction of *The Shakers* at Connecticut College and reportedly was 'enthralled' by the performance. He later wrote to Humphrey offering to come to New London the following summer to teach Shaker dances. What greater tribute could there be?[5]

The notes of this same Ricardo Belden were used by Evanchuk in her work. And it is clear from Evanchuk's writings that her wish is not just to re-create the dances but the feelings: the fervour, ecstasy, and joy that go with the dancing. In a real way she wants to reconstruct not Shaker dancing but the Shakers themselves. Humphrey doesn't call her dance an ethnographic reconstruction, and Evanchuk doesn't call hers artworks; they both fall between these too neat categories. They are both restorations of behaviour of the 1 ➤ 5a ➤ 5b type.

1 ➤ 5a ➤ 5b is a performance based on previous performances—so much so that the totality of all previous performances is

called 'the original'. Just as Evanchuk says she is reconstructing 'authentic' Shaker dances, I can ask: which dances, on which occasions, before what audiences, with whom as dancers? 'The original' is almost always a bundle of performances conventionally represented as 'an' original. Where there is an original, and it has been scored and notated, contextual and historical changes make even the exact replication of the original event different than the original event. Thus technically the Moscow Art Theatre productions, the Brecht productions, the Humphrey *Shakers* danced by the Limon Company are 1➤3➤4 But in practice they are all 1➤5a➤5b. Other examples of 1 ➤ 5a ➤ 5b include theatre when the mise-en-scène is developed during rehearsals; rituals that actualize,[6] commemorate, or summarize myth (though probably it's the other way around: myths are word-versions of rituals); ethnographic films shot in the field and edited at home; versions of ancient forms, neoclassical or other, that purport to recover old works for modern audiences. In 1➤5a➤5b the event restored has been forgotten, never was, or is overlaid with so much secondary stuff that its historicity is lost. History is not what happened (that's its press) but what is encoded and performed.

1➤3➤4 is unstable. Many performances that start out as, or seem to be, 1➤3➤4 are really 1➤5a➤5b. Sometimes masters of an art reconstruct the scores they receive; these changes enter the score and become part of the tradition. This ability to accept change is a characteristic of a living tradition. Noh drama is fixed, but performers who achieve *hana* ('flower' or mastery of their roles) introduce changes some of which are passed on to their successors: noh actors are also noh directors and teachers. But 1➤5a➤5b is not restricted to these kinds of changes.

It's the work of rehearsals to prepare the behaviour of performers so that it seems spontaneous, authentic, unrehearsed. I don't mean only in the psychological way familiar to Western naturalism. Authenticity is a question of harmony/mastery of whatever style is being played, Chekhov or Chikamatsu. For the Brechtian actor to show he is acting is no less difficult than for the Stanislavskian actor not to show he is acting. A story-teller like Bob Carroll plays with his audience—joking, offering them beer, stopping in mid-sentence to welcome a latecomer. Watching Carroll many times, I learned that these gestures, these genuine interactions, are part of a set scheme, strips of behaviour. What Carroll does/says is fixed, the moments where he inserts these strips, the persons he directs them to, change according to circumstances. When planning an open rehearsal, a time when spectators can see the work process in raw form, I discuss with the performers what should and should not be shown. The presence of the public not only changes the way I work but what I work on. If a performer says she's not ready to show something, I don't force the issue, as I might in closed rehearsal.

During rehearsals a past is invented or assembled out of bits of actual experience, fantasies, historical research; or a known score is recalled. Earlier rehearsals and/or performances quickly become the reference points, the building blocks of performances. Useful recollections are not of 'how it was' but of 'how we used to do it'. The 'it' is not of the event but of an earlier rehearsal. Soon reference back to the original, if there is an original, is irrelevant. How Christ offered his disciples wine and matzo at the Last Supper (a seder) is irrelevant to the performance of the Eucharist. The church ceremony has its own history. The language of church ceremony has never been the language Christ spoke, Aramaic-Hebrew. Nor are the gestures or costume of the priest modelled on Christ's. And if the church had chosen another of Christ's gestures as the keystone of the mass—say, the laying-on of hands to heal the sick—this would have developed its own traditional script. Indeed, in some pentacostal churches the laying-on of hands is the key representation of Christ, the demonstration of His presence. Or the taking-up of serpents. And each of these gestures has developed its own way of being performed. What happens over centuries to the various church services, happens much more quickly during rehearsals.

This is not just a thing of the West. John Emigh[7] reports an example of 1 ➤ 5a ➤ 5b from the Sepik River area of Papua-New Guinea. In the village of Magendo, some time before the performance Emigh saw, an uninitiated boy named Wok wandered into the House

Tamboran (men's house, forbidden to the uninitiated) and was killed. The story goes that a bird came to the boy's mother in a dream and told her what had happened and where to find Wok's body. The mother accused her brother of causing Wok's death. She said her brother had painted a dangerous spirit image in the House Tamboran. The brother accepted the blame, the House was torn down, a new one built, and the spirit of Wok resided in the new house. Wok is also credited by the villagers with teaching them how to build better canoes, how to catch fish, and how to plant crops. Emigh goes on:

> Now there are several things about this story and its preparation for the event at hand that I find fascinating. First is the immediate and physical sense of relationship between past and present. The old House Tamboran stood *there* across the swamp. The reeds the child was found in was over *here*—people are very specific about the geography involved, and also about improvements in village life made possible by the intervention of Wok's spirit. Performing the dance at this time would be an act of renewal, of reconnection of past and present.

But what's rehearsal at Magendo like? How does it use the material of Wok's story?

> As the rehearsal proceeded an old man would stop the singing from time to time to make suggestions on style or phrasing, or, just as often, just as much a part of the event being rehearsed, he would comment on the meaning of the song words, on the details of the story. The rehearsal was at once remarkably informal and absolutely effective.

Questions of performing style are combined with interpretations of the story. The historical-legendary Wok is being transformed into his dance. A virtual or nonevent in the past—which, I grant, may have been itself based on something that happened, the death of a child—is made into a concrete, actual present. But this is rehearsal: the present is something being made 'for tomorrow', for the future when the dance will be danced.

> As the rehearsal proceeded men and women would occasionally drift by. The assembled singers, drummers, and witnesses practised the movements of the dance that accompanies the mother's lament. Lawrence, a school-teacher who spoke English, explained that this was an 'imitative' dance, a dance in which both men and women imitated the movements of birds performing activities that loosely correlated to the events described in the mother's lament.

Wok is represented by his mother's lament, and the lament is represented by dancers, both men and women—and they are dancing as birds.

> The dancers imitate birds because the clan the story is significant to is a bird clan, has a bird as its totem. The story is at once distanced—put at an artistic remove—by the translation of the women's lament into gestures performed by both men and women acting as birds and made more immediate in its impact to all the people of the village by this artistic displacement.

More immediate because the bird clan exists now. A woman's lament for a murdered son is transformed into a dance of men and women imitating birds. A nonevent of the past—the killing of Wok (by a spirit?)—is used as the jumping-off place for a theatrical event of the future: a bird dance commemorating a mother's lament. I say 'nonevent' because the killing of Wok, however it happened, even if it happened, is not what makes him significant to Magendo. It's as if the role of hero culture-bearer was there waiting for someone to play it, and Wok was selected. Wok's spirit taught the people how to fish, plant, build ceremonial houses. We don't know whether Wok's murder was the precipitating event or whether his role as culture-bearer meant that he had to be killed. It doesn't much matter. It can't be found out. And the Wok who is the hero bears no necessary relationship to that other Wok who was murdered, except that by now they are both part of the same script, the same strip of behaviour. The important event—the event that Magendo needs—is neither Wok's death, nor his skills, nor his mother's lament: yet the performance of the dance that is none of these brings them all together. The performance is itself the text.

The rehearsal Emigh saw is, like so many performances elsewhere, doubly reflexive. The scheme of time is worked with as a single fabric, to be rewoven according to needs uncovered during rehearsals. And the attention during rehearsal is as much towards the technique of the dance as it is towards what the dance signifies. The rehearsal looks backward to Wok and forward to its finished performance. Rituals disguise themselves as restorations of actual events, when in fact they are restorations of earlier rituals. The ritual process as rehearsal is a shuttling back and forth between the nonevent and the restored event to be performed, between the significance of the event (as story, obligatory act, prayer, etc.) and the details of technique that make up the performance as performance. The rehearsals create the nonevent even as the nonevent is apparently creating the rehearsals. It is not because of Wok that the people of Magendo dance, but because of their dance that Wok (still) exists.

Look again at Figure 1. The fetch, or distance travelled, increases so that the trip 1→5a→5b is greater than either 1→2 or 1→3→4. This increase is in scope of time as well as scope of mood. 1→5a→5b links past, rehearsal time, and performance time both in the subjunctive and indicative moods. (I use '5a→5b' because the nonevent and the restored nonevent are versions of one another, not independent events.) Doing a known score is 1→3→4. But even this known score has behind it a 1→5a→5b: a time when the score was being invented, being put together, in flux.

The model has implications for a unified theory of ritual. The repetition of individual or social facts in the future indicative (1→2) is ritual in the ethological sense. The repetition of a given or traditional performance score (1→3→4) is ritual in the social and religious sense. It is also those aesthetic performances—noh drama, a performance of medieval music on original or facsimile instruments by the Pro Musica Antiqua—that share a necessity for unchangeability. The collective invention of new performances, or the substantial revision of traditional performances, that draws together all times and moods (1→5a→5b) is ritual in the symbolic sense. A particular performance can combine or be between modes—especially between 1→3→4 and 1→5a→5b; that's what noh drama does. The model is meant to provide guideposts in a dynamic system. Performances of the type 1→5a→5b may seem to be recollections of the past, but actually they are conjunctions whose centre cannot be located in any time or mood but only in the whole bundle, the full and complex interrelation among them all. As performances they are played in the indicative mood, but as performances of something they are in the subjunctive mood. The difference between animal ritual and human ritual is that animals are always performing what they are, while humans almost always perform what they are not.

III

A VERY CLEAR EXAMPLE of a restoration of behaviour of the 1→5a→5b type is the *agnicayana* that Frits Staal and Robert Gardner filmed in Panjal, Kerala, India. Staal writes:

> This event, which lasted 12 days, was filmed, photographed, recorded, and extensively documented. From 20 hours of rough footage, Robert Gardner and I produced a 45-minute film, *Altar of Fire*. Two records are planned with selections from the 80 hours of recorded recitation and chant. Photographs of the ceremonies were taken by Adelaide de Menil. In collaboration with the chief Nambudiri ritualists and other scholars, I am preparing a definitive account of the ceremonies, which will appear in two illustrated volumes entitled: *Agni—The Vedic Ritual of the Fire Altar*. . . . Vedic ritual is not only the oldest surviving ritual of mankind; it also provides the best source material for a theory of ritual . . . . Hubert and Mauss . . . used the Vedic animal sacrifice as source material for a construction of a ritual paradigm. However, they did not know that these rituals are still performed, so that many data were inaccessible to them.[8]

This was written in 1978; by now most of Staal's programme has been executed. Note also that he regards the *agnicayana* as a chief source of ritual paradigm: the performance exists to feed scholarship. Indeed, in his work Staal develops a theory of ritual based on the 1975 performance. I am not concerned here with that theory because of an irony: were it not being filmed, photographed, and recorded the *agnicayana* would not have been performed. The impetus for the 1975 *agnicayana* came from America, not India; and most of the funding originated outside India. I doubt that various agencies would have responded with cash to pleas by Nambudiri brahmans for support of a ritual that was too expensive for them to mount unaided. In fact, it was the threat of extinction, the sense that 'this is the last chance to record this event', that created the event.

Yet, accurately, the film's narrator proclaims that the viewer is seeing 'probably the last' of its kind. Actually the 1975 *agnicayana* was either the one after the last of a series or the first of a new series. Before 1975, *agnicayana* was last performed in the 1950s. Behind them is an undocumentable but safely presumed set of performances reaching back maybe the 3000 years Staal and Gardner claim. But maybe not: it's not clear when *agnicayana* was performed before the 1950s. The transmission of the ritual—both its mise-en-scène and its text—was largely oral, from man to boy, older brahman priest to younger, employing a number of mnemonic devices used by Vedic reciters.

The ritual is very expensive by Kerala Indian standards. Many priests are employed, a ritual enclosure has to be built, an altar of fired brick assembled, implements gathered, and so on. The rite itself is archaic: long ago Vedic ritual gave way to later forms of Hinduism; brahman priests had to reconstruct the *agnicayana* from a variety of sources: memory, Sanskrit texts, local opinion. Also, and decisively, the *agnicayana* involves animal sacrifice, now repugnant to many, if not most, Indians in Kerala. A great row erupted over whether or not to include the required sacrifice of fourteen goats. The debate was sharp, often political, with local Marxists being most strongly opposed to blood sacrifice. Finally, the goats were spared, and rice wrapped in leaves was substituted. It's therefore ironic when Staal speaks of 'Vedic animal sacrifice . . . still performed'.

Thus the whole contextual situation of the performance of the *agnicayana* in 1975 is more multiplex than Staal says. For the 1975 performance re-presents the earlier performances while being the single seed of a whole forest of future possibilities. And many of these possibilities are far from Kerala in time, place, and ideational style. This multiplicity is depicted in Fig. 2.

In this figure time is relative to events. The film of the 1975 *agnicayana* becomes the 'now' for all future persons who experience

Time	Original events	in between	Media Events	in between	Scholarship
'Then' 1	Agnicayana, 1950s and earlier: the oral tradition				
'Now' 2		Deciding how to do the ritual: consulting priests, scholars, locals, filmmakers, etc.			
2		The shooting script			
2		Agnicayana, 1975			
2			Rough footage being shot; Still photos being shot; Recording sound		
2		People who came to see the ritual			
			People who came to see the filming		
2		People who came both for ritual and filming			
2		Row over sacrificing the goats			
'Later' 3				Finished film Finished book Finished recording	
'Indefinite future' 4					Theory of Ritual

Fig. 2

the ritual performance through this medium. And, as Staal says, it is likely that most people will experience *agnicayana* this way. Even if a living tradition continues, it is probable that the stagers in Kerala will refer to the film. The filming, as distinct from the film—that is, the process of 'getting the 1975 performance on film'—is in fact a generating event. It generates events behind it: planning, consultations with ritual specialists, assembling people, material, and animals; and it generates events ahead of it: items of Euro-American culture like films, books, cassettes, and items of scholarship, such as theories of ritual shared by Euro-Americans and Indians. The media event—the actual shooting of the film in 1975—attracted locals and internationals, many of whom came as much to see the film being made as the *agnicayana* being performed. The whole bundle in Fig. 2 between original events and scholarship is, in Turner's vocabulary, both liminal (an authentic ritual event) and liminoid (a voluntary performative event). In so far as the 1975 *agnicayana* is liminoid it serves purposes far beyond what the *agnicayana* was when it was solely part of the Kerala oral tradition. Furthermore, in restoring the *agnicayana,* considerations of how best to document the performance were always in the minds of Staal-Gardner; after all, they are as much movie producers as anthropological observers. Their shooting script shows how deeply their instruments intervened in the event. Not that passive recording of events is possible, even with the notebook and pencil; read your Heisenberg. Like many rituals the *agnicayana* involves some very dense hours of theatricality—much simultaneous action occurring over a fairly wide range of spaces. But the camera and microphone are instruments of focus; and certainly finished film and sound cassettes are outcomes of a rigorous selective/editing process. As performed in 1975 the *agnicayana* took 120 hours, plus many more hours of preparations. Staal-Gardner could shoot only 20 hours, and their script says that for 'numerous episodes filming depends on remaining quantity of raw stock'.[9] Exigency *über alles*. The 20 hours of raw footage were edited into a 45-minute film.

As best I can gather—and by analogy with other ritual events I've attended in India—*agnicayana* flows unevenly over its 120 hours. It has the feel often of synchronous not diachronous time; spatially it gathers itself in climaxes and is dispersed among several points: the main altar, the subsidiary altars, the home of the chief sacrificer, the purifying waters, and so on. But filmmaking works by taking bits and then later assembling them, and recombining them, into a diachronous whole. Filmmaking is a Frankenstein process of breakdown and stitched-together assemblage. Staal-Gardner's shooting script is no exception to this process. The 12-day ceremony is broken into episodes convenient to the camera. And the script is very specific about who the main performers are, and what's of interest:

> Advaryu [chief priest]: as stage manager he performs most of the rites and commands the others. He is where the action is. . . .
>
> The final killing of the goat within the Camitra will not be filmed on this occasion [day 1] since this would upset many people; but hopefully on a later occasion. . . .
>
> [For day 2] No more than 30 minutes of filming for the entire day.

These procedures—the media event itself—are only faintly perceived in *Altar of Fire*. Edmund Carpenter, one of the visiting scholars lassoed for the filming, says on camera that three kinds of events are going on simultaneously: the *agnicayana*, the social event surrounding the ritual (common in India), and the media event. *Altar of Fire* spends virtually all its time on the *agnicayana*. There is a saying in India: 'Every *lila* [performance] is surrounded by a *mela* [fair and market]'. Media events are even more rare than *lilas*: so the 1975 *agnicayana* attracted a large number of onlookers, merchants, soothsayers, beggars, entertainers. But *Altar of Fire* is carefully nonreflexive. Except for a few feet here and there, concentrating on the visiting Western scholars, Staal-Gardner used the old fly-on-the-wall technique: 'Gosh, it sure is lucky we got here in time to shoot this.'

No one in the film goes into the controversy surrounding the sacrifice of the fourteen goats. Can there be *agnicayana* without blood sacrifice? How did the priests feel about the issue? What were the political questions surrounding the argument—that is, were 'progressive' Marxists pitted against 'reactionary' ritualists; and did the 'ugly American' come in for a beating? Kerala has long had a Marxist government; Kerala's literacy rate, 80 per cent, is the highest of any Indian state. The issue of the goat sacrifice was debated hotly in the area, and its press, during the filming.

Altar of Fire doesn't hint at any out-of-sequence filming, but as the script indicates the sacrifice was put off from day 1 to a later time; and then effigies were used instead of goats. Was the ceremony using these effigies filmed out of sequence and later edited into sequence? The film is mute on this; everything seems to be 'in place in time'. And, most importantly, except for the shots of the visitors there is no sense that a film is being made. *Altar of Fire* is designed to make the viewer feel 'I am here at the enactment of a rare, ancient ritual'. But after I saw the movie several times, more questions arose. There is an old priest—a Walter Huston of a man, with a scraggly beard and a canny sparkle—a casting director's dream of a 'wise old folksy priest', who explains in English much of what's going on. But he isn't the chief priest, who is much younger and doesn't look the part (to American eyes). Why was the old man chosen? There are other evidences of 'film logic' as understood by American filmmakers taking over.

Such procedures raise important questions. We need no renewed educating to the idea that the instruments and means of observing and recording things so deeply affect what's being observed that a new situation arises, one in which the observer is included in the same bundle as the observed. And we are used to questioning the authenticity of performances like the 1975 *agnicayana*, as Robert A. Paul did and as Staal answered.[10] But if the discussion stops here, we miss a chance to recognize in the Staal-Gardner film another harbinger of an important shift towards the theatricalization of anthropology. I mean this in a double sense.

First, by replacing the notebook with the tape recorder, the still camera with the movie camera, the monograph with the film, a shift occurs whereby we understand social life as narrative, crisis and crisis resolution, drama, person-to-person interaction, display behaviour, and so on. As Staal-Gardner say succinctly in their shooting script: 'the advaryu 1 as stage managers . . . is where the action is.' More than that, media create action.

Second, this shift of paradigm has direct consequences in the world it maps. The shift in anthropology is part of a larger intellectual movement in which understanding of human behaviour is changing from clear differentiation between cause and effect, past and present, form and content—and the literary, linear modes of discovery, analysis, and presentation to the theatrical paradigm. The theatrical paradigm uses editing, rehearsal, deconstruction/reconstruction of actuality: the creation and organization of strips of behaviour. These techniques blur temporal and causal systems, creating in their stead bundles of relations that attain only relative clarity, and only within contexts that themselves need definition. An effect may precede its cause. Something that happened later—in the shooting of a film, in the rehearsal of an event—may be used earlier in the finished performance, as when effigies of goats are edited into the sequence of the *agnicayana* with the result that they appear before it was actually decided to use them at all.

Look at the chart [Fig. 2] mapping the time scheme of the *agnicayana*. The original events—the ritual as performed in the 1950s and earlier—and the scholarship purporting to interpret this ritual are separated by a cluster of performance events. The ritual was not a function of Kerala culture 1975, but of Euro-American culture. Scholars now writing on Vedic ritual, however, will turn to *Altar of Fire*, and the book and recordings. Probably scholars will talk of the *agnicayana*, not of the 'restored *agnicayana*'. Scholars will assume that original events of the class 1➤3➤4are being discussed. But actually the 1975 *agnicayana* is 1➤5a➤5b event. It was restored in order to be filmed. It exists liminally between the original series that ended in the 1950s and the media events of the Staal-Gardner project. *Altar of Fire* ends with the narrator announcing that the viewer has seen what is probably the last performance of *agnicayana*. Not true. The viewer has seen the first of a new series of performances, one in which the event has been restored, compressed, edited; and in which the event will never change because it is 'on film'. When people want to 'see' the *agnicayana*, they will not go to Kerala: they will rent *Altar of Fire*. Scholarship using the *agnicayana* will not be based on the series that ended in the 1950s, about which very little is known, but on the material gathered by Staal-Gardner. And few, if any, scholars will examine the raw footage, the full set of tapes; they will instead look at the movie and listen to the recordings released by Staal-Gardner. Theories will be built on items extrapolated from strips of restored behaviour.

But is this any different than building theories on writings? Writings are more easily recognized as interpretations than restorations of behaviour are. Theories are presented in the same bundle as the data on which these theories rest. References are freely made to earlier interpretations and theories. Often, writing is clearly reflexive. I don't prefer writings to restorations of behaviour as a way of scholarship. But restorations are not yet understood as thoroughly as writing. Therefore, at present restorations leave more mess than writing. People use restorations and consider them 1➛2 or 1➛3➛4 when actually they are 1➛5a➛5b; 1➛5a➛5b is hard to deal with, ambivalent, with no clear temporal sequence, no fixed causal system.

Why not think of Staal-Gardner as film producers-directors? Their work in India is more easily understood when seen in performative terms. An earlier event is 'researched' and/or 'remembered'—actions equivalent to rehearsals. A performance is arranged that presumably duplicates this earlier event. An event created in the future (the film *Altar of Fire*, 5b) is projected backward in time (the 'original' *agnicayana*, 5a) and restored 'now' in order to be filmed (what happened in Kerala in 1975, 1). The items in this bundle cannot be separated; they must be considered as a unit. The so-called prior event—the 'original' *agnicayana* is not strictly prior—certainly did not 'cause' the 1975 performance. The 1975 performance was caused by the project of making a film. So in a sense the future is causing the present which, in turn, makes it necessary to research, remember—rehearse—the past. But this past—what is turned up by the rehearsal process—determines what is done in 1975, and those events are used to make the movie. The movie then replaces the 'original' event; the movie is what we have of the past.

Sometimes the restored event can spark a new series of original performances. Alan Lomax reports the experience of Adrian Gerbrands:

> Gerbrands by chance screened a documentary on Eastern New Guinea mask-making for a native group in New Britain. The audience reacted powerfully during and after the screening. They, too, had once known how to make such masks and should, they felt, try their skill again, especially if their art too would be filmed. After Gerbrands had filmed the group's mask-making, a lone native approached him with the offer to perform a very important and defunct ceremony if he would film it. Naturally again Gerbrands used his camera. On his next trip to New Britain, the other men in the village insisted on seeing the film and were so distressed at the poor quality of the filmed ceremony that they vowed forthwith to re-enact the whole ceremony, masks, costumes, ballet, feasting, and all, but at a length suitable for filming. This event and its resultant film were such a success locally that the ceremony is now being celebrated every year just as in former times.[11]

Ceremonies like this, and like the *agnicayana*, exist between fact and fiction: they are a new class of facts. Simulations, models, and theatricalizations are part of this new class. Their in-betweenness links them to Turner's Talmud on Van Gennep's idea of 'liminality' and to what D. W. Winnicott calls 'transitional objects and phenomena'. More on these later.

Sometimes restorations clash with the very agencies that promote them:

> In an effort to boost tourism, tribesmen in New Guinea have offered to turn cannibal again. They told committee members of the Mt Hagan Show, the big territorial festival, that they were prepared to eat human flesh at the show in August [1975]. The tribesmen added, however, that they did not want to kill any of their enemies and would make do instead with a body from the local hospital morgue. A government officer at the meeting politely but firmly declined the tribesmen's suggestions.

The rhetoric of the Los Angeles *Times* story is the key to the cultural contexts in conflict here. To American readers 'tribesmen' = savages, 'committee members' = Europeanized savages, 'government officer' = the New Civilized Power. The story is full of sly humour, delectably alluding to a taboo appetite. That's why it was picked up by a major American paper. But the locals have logic on their side. If old dances are being restored, why not the cannibal feast? The locals know how far they can go: the body will come from an approved repository of corpses, a hospital, a representation of the New Civilized Power. The Power has its role to play too: it must demonstrate far and wide that, well, New Guinea is and isn't New Guinea anymore. So the story 'gets out', and the sponsors of the Mt Hagan Show have their cake without having to eat it too.

IV

RESTORATIONS NEEDN'T BE EXPLOITATIONS. Sometimes they are arranged with such care that after a while the restored behaviour heals into its presumptive past and its present cultural context like a well-set bone. In these cases a 'tradition' is rapidly established and judgments about authenticity hard to make. Let me give two examples from India.

Bharatanatyam, the classical Indian dance, is traced back not only to the ancient text on theatre, *Natyashastra* (second century BC–second century AD), that describes dance poses but also to temple sculptings that show these poses. The best known of these sculptings is the group at the fourteenth-century temple of Nataraja (Shiva, king of dancers) at Chidambaram, south of Madras. Most writings assume a continuous tradition connecting *Natyashastra*, temple sculptings, and today's dancing. According to Kapila Vatsyayan, India's leading dance theorist and historian:

> Bharatanatyam is perhaps the oldest among the contemporary classical dance forms of India. . . . Whether the dancer was the *devadasi* of the temple or the court-dancer of the Maratha kings of Tanjore, her technique followed strictly the

> patterns which had been used for ages.[12]
>
> Whenever the contemporary forms of Bharatanatyam and Manipuri and Odissi evolved, two things are clear: first, that they were broadly following the tradition of the *Natyasastra* and were practising similar principles of technique from their inception, and, second, that the stylization of movement began as far back as the 8th and 9th century. . . . Some contemporary styles preserve the characteristic features of this tradition more rigorously than others: Bharatanatyam uses the basic adhamadali [postures] most rigorously.[13]

But in fact it's not known when the 'classical' bharatanatyam died out, or even if it ever existed in the form in which it is described by scholars and danced by contemporary dancers. The old texts and the sculptings surely show that there was some kind of dance, but nothing was remembered of this dance, not even its name, when moves were made to 'revive' it at the start of the twentieth century.

There was a temple dance called *sadir nach* danced by women of families hereditarily attached to certain temples. According to Milton Singer:

> The dancing girls, their teachers, and musicians performed not only on the occasion of temple festivals and ceremonies, but also for private parties, particularly weddings, and at palace parties. Special troupes of dancing girls and musicians were sometimes permanently attached to the courts.[14]

Some dancing girls were prostitutes: temple prostitution was widespread. The British and some Indians campaigned from the start of the twentieth century to stop temple dancing. In 1947 Madras State outlawed it. Long before that the number of *devadasis* (dancing girls) dwindled. Connected with the campaign to outlaw *sadir nach* Dr V. Raghavan, scholar and critic, coined the term bharatanatyam to describe the dance he and dancer Rukmini Devi were developing. They wanted to use *sadir nach* but not be identified with its bad reputation. They cleaned up *sadir nach*, brought in gestures based on the *Natyashastra* and temple sculptings, developed standard teaching methods. They claimed that bharatanatyam was very old. And, of course, a conformity to ancient texts and art could be demonstrated: every move in bharatanatyam was measured against the sources of which it presumed to be a living vestige. The differences between *sadir nach* and the old sources were attributed to degeneracy. The new dance, now legitimized by its heritage, not only absorbed *sadir nach*, but attracted the daughters of the most respectable families to practise it. Many study bharatanatyam as a kind of finishing school. It is danced all over India by both amateurs and professionals. It is a major export item.

The 'history' and 'tradition' of bharatanatyam—its roots in the ancient texts and art—is actually a restoration of behaviour of the 1➤5a➤5b type; 5a = the 'ancient classical dance'. But this dance is a construction based on the restoration work of Raghavan, Devi, and others. They used *sadir nach* not as a dance in its own right but as a faint image of some ancient glory. But that 'ancient classical dance' is a projection backward in time: we know what it looks like because we have the bharatanatyam. Soon people believed that the ancient dance led to bharatanatyam when, in fact, the bharatanatyam led to the ancient dance. An original ancient dance is created in the past in order to be restored for the present and future. There is no single source for bharatanatyam, only the whole bundle 1➤5a➤5b.

Purulia chhau, a masked dance of the semi-arid region of rural Bengal adjoining Bihar and Orissa, is an athletic dance-drama of many leaps, somersaults, and stampings. The drummers of the dom caste beat huge kettle drums and long oblong drums, taunting the dancers into frenzied twisting jumps, screams, and mock battles. Rivalry among villages competing at the annual festival at Matha is fierce. According to Asutosh Bhattacharyya, Professor of Bengali Literature at Calcutta University, who has devoted himself entirely to chhau since 1961, the Purulia region is inhabited by many aboriginal tribes whose

> religious customs and social festivals show very little resemblance with those of Hinduism. . . . But, it is also a fact that the Mura of Purulia are very ardent participants in Chhau

> dance. With practically no education and social advancement the members of this community have been performing this art which is based on the episodes of the Ramayana and the Mahabharata and the Indian classical literature most faithfully, in some cases, for generations. . . . Sometimes an entire village, however poor, inhabited exclusively by the Mura, sacrifices its hard-earned resources for the cause of organizing Chhau dance parties.[15]

This presents a problem for Bhattacharyya: 'the system which is followed in chhau dance today could not have been developed by the aboriginal people who practise the dance. It is indeed a contribution of a higher culture keenly conscious of an aesthetic sense.'[16] He guesses that the drummers, the dom, an outcaste group, originated chhau, for the dom were at one time a 'highly sophisticated community . . . brave soldiers in the infantry of the local feudal Chiefs'.[17] Thrown out of work when the British pacified the region in the eighteenth century, failing to farm because of what Bhattacharyya calls the 'vanity of their past tradition of warriors', they were reduced to their present untouchable status: workers of hides, drummers. But their war dance lives on as chhau.

Some interesting prejudices sparkle from Bhattacharyya's story. Aboriginal peoples have no developed aesthetic sense; high-caste dancers are transformed into low-caste drummers because warriors are too proud to farm (how about using their swords to steal land and then becoming landlords, a time-honoured practice?); great amounts are spent on dance parties, but these compete at Matha, the annual festival initiated by Bhattacharyya in 1967, not an ancient tradition at all. As he says:

> In April 1961 I visited an interior village in the Purulia District with a batch of students of the Calcutta University and for the first time observed a regular performance of the Chhau dance. . . . I found that there was a system of this dance and a definitely established method which was well-preserved. But it was on the decline due to lack of patronage from any source whatsoever. I wanted to draw attention of the world outside to this novel form of dance.[18]

And that he did. All-star parties of chhau dancers have toured in Europe in 1972, in Australia and North America in 1975, and in Iran. They have danced in New Delhi, and as Bhattacharyya exults:

> I attracted the notice of Sangeet Natak Akademi, New Delhi [the Government agency established to encourage and preserve traditional performing arts] to this form of dance. It took immediate interest and invited me to give performances of the dance in New Delhi. In June 1969, I visited New Delhi with a batch of 40 village artists for the first time outside their native district. Performances were held there before very distinguished Indian and foreign invitees. . . . Performances were also shown on TV in Delhi. Only three years later it was also shown on BBC television in London and five years later on NBC in New York, USA.[19]

Note how Bhattacharyya refers to the dances as his: 'invited me to give performances of the dance'. This is not bragging but acknowledgment of the circumstances: without a patron the villagers would have got nowhere. And these days a patron needs more than money—or maybe he doesn't need money so much as knowledge, and a wish to devote himself to the form he's restoring. Government comes up with the cash.

Chhau 1961 and after is a creation of the mixture of what Bhattacharyya found and what he invented. But his invention was of the 1 ➤ 5a ➤ 5b type. As a folklorist-anthropologist he dug into the past and constructed a history of chhau, and a technique, that he then proceeded faithfully to restore. His annual festival at Matha coincides with the Chaitra Parvan celebrations common to the area, and the occasion of the annual chhau festivals of Seraikella and Mayurbhanj (related forms of the dance). These festivals, once paid for by maharajas, are now sponsored, less lavishly, by the government. In 1976 I went to Matha, a hill station, not a town, only a few buildings and an open field. The dances go on there all night for two nights. Villagers, arriving from towns as far as a two-day journey, set up camps. Roping together *charpois* (sleeping cots made of wood and twine) a theatre is jerrybuilt. Women and children watch, and sleep, sitting and reclining on the *charpois* elevated to a height of eight feet or more. Men and boys stand on the ground. A narrow passageway leads from the area where performers put on costumes and masks to the roughly circular dancing ground. Parties enter down the passageway, stop, present themselves, then leap into their dancing. All dancing is done with bare feet on bare earth, swept clean of large rocks but still raw, pebbled, with turned-up clods and scrub grass. To me it felt like a rodeo in a backwater town. Torches and petromax lanterns throw shadowy light, the drums bark and roar, the *shehnais* (clarinet-like instruments) shriek, as party after party compete. Most parties consist of five to ninr dancers. Some masks adorned with peacock feathers rise three feet over the dancers' heads. The mask of 10-headed Ravana is more than four feet long. Wearing these masks dancers make full somersaults and twisting leaps. The dances are vigorous, and it's very hot inside the papier-mache masks. Each dance lasts less than 10 minutes. Every village dances twice. There are no prizes but there is competition, and everyone knows who dances well, who poorly.

Just in case there are doubts, on each afternoon following the night's dancing Bhattacharyya critiques the performances. During the dancing he sits behind a desk, two petromax lanterns making him the best-lit figure of the event; and next to him are his university assistants. All night he watches and writes. The next day, one by one the villagers appear before him. I listened to what he said. He warned one party not to use story elements not found in the Hindu classics. He chided another for not wearing the standard basic costume of short skirt over leggings decorated in rings of white, red, and black. Bhattacharyya selected this basic costume from one village and made it general. When I asked him about it he said that the costumes he chose were the most authentic, the least Westernized. In a word, Bhattacharyya oversees every aspect of Purulia chhau; training, dance themes, music, costuming, dance steps. He selects individuals from different villages to make up the all-star teams that tour. He rehearses the touring parties and they, of course, return to their home villages with enhanced reputations. Touring, in fact, has had deep effects on chhau. Three 'foreign parties' came into existence since the first tour in 1972: 19 people went to Europe, 16 to Iran, and 11 to Australia and North America. Because foreigners won't sit through nine hours of dancing, Bhattacharyya made a programme of two-hour duration. And because he didn't think that bare chests looked good on the male dancers he designed a jacket based on an old pattern. Both these changes have become standard back in Purulia. Many of the people who went abroad formed their own groups at home. Each of these groups are called 'foreign parties', and bill themselves as such; this gives them status, drawing power, and the ability to charge more. There is demand now for performances as performances, not as part of the ritual calendar. A performance can be hired for about 1000 rupees—a lot cheaper than jatra, the most popular form of entertainment in rural Bengal. But 1000 rupees is still a lot of money for performers of chhau. In Bhattacharyya's opinion, as the financial opportunities have increased the subtlety of the art has declined. John Emigh spoke to Bhattacharyya in the summer of 1980. In reflecting on the tours, Bhattacharyya told him that he thinks they saved a form otherwise doomed, but at the expense of stirring jealousies and rivalries and generating irreversible changes in the form. Chhau is a masked dance, and one side effect of its popularity abroad has been the demand by tourists for masks. Many masks are shipped that have never been worn by a dancer.

These changes can be traced back to Bhattacharyya. He is the big chhau man, and his authority is rarely questioned, never overturned. He's a professor, a scholar from Calcutta. When he writes about chhau he emphasizes its village base and ancient origins; he even suggests a possible connection between chhau and the dances of Bali. (The Kalinga Empire of Orissa, third century BC, possibly traded across the seas as far as Bali.) But he hardly mentions his own role in restoring the dance. Rather he speaks of himself as 'discovering' it. His 1980 conversation with Emigh is the first acknowledgment of the changes consequent to his discovery.

In 1977, along with Suresh Awasthi, former Secretary of the Sangeet Natak Akademi, the man who introduced me to chhau, and Shyamanand Jalan, a theatre director of modern plays and a Calcutta lawyer, I helped organize a chhau festival in Calcutta. This was the first time ever that all three kinds of chhau were seen on the same programme. And the first time many of the dancers from Purulia, Seraikella, and Mayurbhanj saw each others' dances. Traditionally, chhau is danced only on Chaitra Parvan (in March–April), so all the dancing parties are occupied simultaneously and tied to their home territories. But in 1937–38, when maharajas had plenty of cash, dancers of Seraikella chhau toured to Europe. They also danced for Gandhi in Calcutta. The patron, teacher, and choreographer of the Seraikella troupe was Bijoy Pratap Singh Deo, brother to the maharaja. And the star dancer was Suvendra, the crown prince (he died at age 23). After Independence and the abolition of the Privy Purses the dances declined for lack of patronage. The three forms of chhau are related, though more scholarly work needs to be done to establish exactly what the connections are. Dancing masters from Seraikella were imported into Mayurbhanj by its maharaja early in the century. Both Seraikella and Purulia chhau use masks, though these look very different from each other. Seraikella style is also influenced by Western ballet. Remember that maharajas were often culturally as much European as Indian. At the 1977 Calcutta festival there were three days of dancing, demonstrations of techniques, and talk. A second chhau festival, under government sponsorship, was held in Bhubaneswar, Orissa, in 1978. Festivals such as these are themselves hybrids, crosses between the Indian love of jatra-lila-mela (pilgrimage, performance, and fair-ground) and the Western taste for collecting behaviours as 'items' of culture, then dissecting the collection in a scholarly way at conferences-cum-junkets. Who ever pays his own way to a scholarly meeting? In 1980 Kedar Nath Sahoo, the Seraikella chhau master dancer-teacher, and the last man alive who danced under Bijoy—went to Europe and the United States demonstrating the art and teaching. It's neither possible nor desirable to keep forms 'pure'. The question is to what degree should cross-breeding be managed, and to what degree promiscuous?

Sometimes, actually, changes are insisted upon by insiders and not imposed from without. One of the best-known films concerning non-

Western performance is the Mead-Bateson *Trance and Dance in Bali* (1938). At one of the showings of this film at the American Museum of Natural History in New York, Mead said that in preparing the confrontation between Rangda and Barong for filming, the trance club of Pagutan decided that foreign viewers would rather see young women go into trance and stab at their breasts with krises. Customarily only men and old women perform this. The women often go with their breasts bare—naked breasts do not suggest the same erotic significance in Bali as in New York. But, also I suppose to please, or at least not offend, foreigners, the Balinese women's breasts were covered. Without telling Mead or Bateson, the men of the trance club instructed the young women in the proper techniques for entering trance; the women were also taught how to handle the krises. Then the men of the club proudly announced to the filmmakers the changes made for the special filming. In *Trance and Dance*, as the narrator says, one old woman who 'said she wouldn't go into trance' is unexpectedly deeply possessed. The camera follows her: she is bare-breasted, she is deep in trance, her kris is powerfully turned against her own chest; later, slowly, she is brought out of trance by an old priest. Members of the trance club were angry at this old woman because they felt that her trance disturbed the aesthetic refinements they had rehearsed for foreign eyes.[20] Which is 'authentic'—the young women prepared by the Balinese themselves, or the solitary old woman doing the traditional thing? Cases abound where, as in Pagutan Baji District, local performances are adapted to suit foreign tastes. Hula dancers, for example, are traditionally heavy—that is, powerful and mature—middle-aged women. But tourist hula, now almost traditional in its own right, features slim-hipped young women. It's precisely when changes feed back into the traditional forms, actually becoming these forms, that a restoration of behaviour of the 1 ➤ 5a ➤ 5b type occurs.

Sometimes even, knowing the money that tourists have to spend, performances are invented and foisted upon tourists as traditional when they are not. I was in the Papua-New Guinea Highlands in 1972 where I saw the tourist performance of the famous Mudmen of Asaro, whose story is sad indeed. These white-clay-covered dancers, with their grotesque masks of hardened clay, originally depicted ghosts arising from a stream. Their performance was very effective in scaring away enemies. But when photos of their masks appeared, in the *National Geographic*, I believe, a demand was created for their dancing. The whole performance was dislocated. The dancers danced at midday instead of dawn; they were visible in the centre of the small village instead of lurking in the bush near the stream; they performed twice weekly instead of only when necessary, that is, when threatened by enemies. And, naturally, they were exploited: when I saw them they kept 10 per cent of the tourists' dollars. Because I was photographing the tourists disembarking from their Volkswagen minibus, and because I arrived before the ordinary tourists and remained after, I was approached by a villager. He asked me to come with him to his village, Kenetasarobe, not far from Asaro. Once there he showed me his group of dancers, with their spectacular masks; and he put on a display of fire-making. He made it clear that he had devised this performance and believed that I was a tourist agency booker. I took a few photos, paid some money, accepted a bamboo smoking pipe as a souvenir. Regretfully I told my local choreographer that I could not help him sell his dance.

With both bharatanatyam and Purulia chhau a modern version of an old art is born through the intervention/invention of one or a few dedicated persons from outside the class of those they are leading. This is, maybe, a version of the Moses myth or the Marxist fact; revolution comes to a group from the outside, typically brought in by a lost member of the tribe who rediscovers his origins. As Indians, Raghavan, Devi, and Bhattacharyya are not outsiders the way Staal, Gardner, and Gerbrands are. But Raghavan and Devi were not from *devadasi* families, and Bhattacharyya is no aboriginal tribesman.

I see nothing amiss in the restorations of behaviour called bharatanatyam or Purulia chhau. Artforms and rituals too are always in the process of development. And sometimes the impetus comes by way of restored behaviour. Bharatanatyam and chhau are analogous to the works of the French dramatists of the seventeenth century, who were conforming to what they thought were the rules of Attic tragedy. Or to those of Renaissance architects restoring what they thought were classical styles. These people had at hand Aristotle, the Greek plays, architectural ruins, and Vetruvius. Today we have at hand relics of behaviour, ancient texts, sculptings, and the memories of Hindu priests. We also have ways of getting, transmitting, storing, and broadcasting information that makes a one-world information network a reality. 'Nativistic movements' seek to restore the old ways. I'm talking about something else. There is something postmodern in restoring behaviour. Scholars and specialists fear a disruption of historical variety brought about by world monoculture. Just as physical well-being depends on a varied gene pool, so social well-being depends on a varied culture pool. Restored behaviour is a way of guaranteeing a varied culture pool. It is a strategy that fits within, and yet opposes, world monoculture, It's not the 'natives' who practise restored behaviour. The *devadasis* were content to dance their *sadir nach*, even if it was doomed; the mura and dom danced and drummed their chhau before Bhattacharyya arrived in 1961, even if it was 'in decay'. But the moderns want to bring into the postmodern world 'authentic cultural items'. Within the frame of postmodern information theory—all knowledge is reducible/transformable into bits of information, and therefore potentially reconstructible in new orders, new beings in fact—an illusion of diversity is projected: backward in time to 5a, forward to 5b. This illusion is artful because it is art itself, pure theatre. And the underlying idea that information, not things, is the basic material of nature, not just culture, is at the root of such recent explorations as recombinant DNA, gene-splicing, and cloning. What is created through these experiments is a liminal existence between nature and culture. It suggests that nature and culture might be a false dichotomy, representing not opposing realms but different perceptions of identical processes.

When Bhattacharyya goes to the field and finds chhau 'in decay', or when Raghavan finds 'vestiges' of a classical dance in *sadir nach*, is what they find incomplete? Only with reference to a presumed past and a rehearsed-restored future is it incomplete; only when measured against the whole bundle 1 ➤ 5a ➤ 5b. The restorers view the behaviours they restore through a wider time-lens, a wider conceptual-lens, than the dancers of 'native' *sadir nach* and chhau. Restored behaviour is not a process of scraping away dead layers of paint to reveal the original artwork; it is not discovering an unbroken—dare I say, unconscious?—tradition, but of research and fieldwork, of rehearsals in the deepest sense. There is more of this kind of thing coming. Already the past 70 years are available on film. Waves of styles return regularly because of this availability. We are not going to 'lose' behaviour from the 1920s, for instance, in the same way or to the same extent as we've lost previous epochs. We're in a time when traditions can die in life, be preserved archivally as behaviours, and later be restored.

V

ALTHOUGH RESTORED BEHAVIOUR seems to be founded in the past and follow a linear chronology—'Bharatanatyam is perhaps the oldest among the contemporary dance forms of India', 'Vedic ritual is . . . the oldest surviving ritual of mankind'—it is in fact a synchronic bundle, 1 ➤ 5a ➤ 5b. The past, 5a, is recreated in terms not simply of a present, 1, but of a future, 5b. This future is the performance being rehearsed, the next showing, the 'finished thing'made efficient, graceful, and perfect through rehearsals. Restored behaviour is both teleological and eschatological. It joins original causes and what happens at the end of time. It is a model of destiny.

VI

RESTORATIONS OF BEHAVIOUR are not limited to New Guinea or India, that world of the non-Western other. All over America restorations of behaviour are common, popular, and making money for their owners. Maurice J. Moran, Jr., has written an account of theme parks and restored villages. Their diversity is undeniable: Renaissance Pleasure Fairs in California and New York, restored villages in almost every state, Disneyland and Disneyworld, safari and wildlife parks, amusement parks organized around single themes, Land of Oz in North Carolina, Storyland in New Hampshire, Frontierland, Ghost Town in the Sky, even L'il Abner's Dogpatch. The Marriott Corporation, operators of parks and owners of hotels, describes the parks as 'a family entertainment complex oriented to a particular subject or historical area, combining a continuity of costuming and architecture with entertainment and merchandise to create a fantasy-provoking atmosphere'.[21] These places are large environmental theatres. They are related to get-togethers like the Papua-New Guinea kaiko, the Amerindian powwow, and the Indian Kumbh Mela: pilgrimage centres where performances, goods, services, and ideologies are displayed and exchanged.

In this essay I concentrate on only one kind of theme park, the restored village. As of 1978 there were more than sixty such villages in the United States and Canada, and, it seems, more are coming. Millions of people visit them each year. Typically they restore the Colonial period or the nineteenth century; they reinforce the ideology of rugged individualism as represented by early settlers of the Eastern states (Colonial Williamsburg, Plimoth Plantation), the shoot-'em-up West (BuckskinJoe and Cripple Creek, Colorado, Cowtown, Kansas, Old Tucson, Arizona), or romanticized heroic industries like mining and whaling. Some, like Amish Farms and Homes in Pennsylvania, present a spectacle of people actually living their lives; a few, like Harpers Ferry in West Virginia, commemorate historical confrontations. The scope of the architectural reconstructions and the behaviours of the persons who work in the villages make these restorations more than museums.

At Columbia Historic Park, California,

> the tour of a still functioning gold mine is a major attraction—where would-be spelunkers are warned of the dangers of cave-

> ins and claim jumping. The miners are two retired men who can actually make a living from the little bit of gold left in the vein.[22]

Historic Smithville in New Jersey covers 25 acres on which stand a cluster of 36 buildings including a gristmill, schoolhouse, Quaker meeting-house, cobbler's shop, and firehouse,

> most of which are original structures from the Jersey shore area. 'Residents' of the town are dressed in period costume and work at the tasks of the 18th and 19th century citizens.[23]

Old Sturbridge Village in Massachusetts was started in 1946. By 1978 there were more than 35 buildings on the 200-acre tract. The crafts people are dressed in period costumes. On Sundays

> a Quaker meeting is held. There is village dancing on Wednesday evenings. School is actually taught in the little faded schoolhouse two days a week, and there are presentations of plays from the period (*The Drunkard*, 1840, *Ever So Humble*, 1836). On July 4th the entire village celebrates as it may have been then.[24]

At Louisbourg, Quebec, the employees of the village

> assume the names of people who actually inhabited the village. The visitor is stopped at the gate and instructed to proceed only after an informal search, conducted in French. If you reply in English, a wary eye is kept on you as you proceed.[25]

Given the present temper of relations between English and French speakers in Quebec, this entrance initiation reverberates across several centuries.

> One woman asked this writer if he had met her 'husband'. She was referring in the present tense to the man who had served as the chief engineer in the original Louisbourg. Her 'maid' and 'children' ('I had five, you know, but one died this past winter') cavort in the kitchen, smiling at the strangely clothed visitors with their magic boxes [cameras].[26]

The performance is carried further at Plimoth Plantation in Massachusetts. According to materials sent to me by Judith Ingram, director of marketing at the Plantation, an attempt is made at a total re-creation, including performing actual residents of Plimoth in the seventeenth century:

> Our efforts on this behalf began in the late 1960s. Since that time, visitors to our Pilgrim Village have been afforded the opportunity for total immersion in 17th century life. Staff members are trained in what might be termed 'non-programmatic' interpretation which stresses the ability to converse with visitors naturally while putting in a hard day's work running the community in a holistic way. This approach assures that all the senses are brought to bear in the learning process. . . . No one who has entered the small, cluttered houses in our village in July and had to contend with the flies and dust, who has seen a fire on the hearth on a hot scorching day, or who has observed the difficulties just keeping the food edible, will come away with the traditional stereotype of the starched Pilgrim intact.
>
> In 1978 interpretation in the Pilgrim Village took another important step forward with the introduction of first person interpretation. Within the palisaded walls of the village no trace of the modern world can be found [except for special paths and access to several structures for the handicapped]. Now, we have recreated not only the houses and furnishings, but also the residents of 1627 Plymouth. Great care has been taken in replicating the attire, the personalities, and even regional English dialects of the Pilgrims.[27]

The Plimoth staff are careful to point out that the Plantation is not a 'restoration', but a 're-creation'. 'We have no surviving original houses', says Ingram, 'we do not know the exact design of the houses and must recreate structures typical of the period.'[28] These 're-creations' are built after much research. The same care goes into building roles—and these are modelled not on 'typical' people of the period but on actual residents of the colony.

According to Bob Marten, co-head of the Plantation's Interpretation Department, ads are placed each January to fill about 30 roles to represent the actual 200 persons who lived in the colony in 1627. That is, 30 out of 200 villagers are actually represented by what Marten calls 'cultural informants':

> Marten said the Plantation tries to find people who are similar to the characters they will play. 'We're looking for the 20th century counterparts of 17th-century people. If casting for the part of Elder (William) Brewster, we'll look for someone of approximately the same age with a gracious manner of expression and ready vocabulary. . . . John Billington was a rogue, a con man. So we'll find someone who's capable of being in this role. He's usually played by a character actor who could sell a man his own shoes.'[29]

As in movie acting, a lot of type-casting is done. 'A truck driver makes a better yeoman than a teacher', says Marten.

Interestingly there is little group rehearsal—this is not a play the performers are preparing for, but a more improvisatory world of interaction not only among themselves but with the tourists who visit the Plantation daily. (The Plantation is open seven days a week, nine to five, from 1 April through 30 November.) Each performer is given a 'Documentary Biograph' and a 'Personation Biograph'. The documentary biograph tells what is known about the character to be portrayed: age in 1627, place of origin, parents, social status, and so on. Some of these data are noted as 'current opinion' (rather than established fact), and some as 'learned fabrication'—a category that means invented, but according to probability. The personation biograph includes dialect specimen, signature, names of the character's friends, some suggested readings, and, very importantly, a paragraph or two of 'notes'. For example, Phineas Pratt, we are told, is 34, comes from Buckinghamshire, arrived at Plimoth aboard the Sparrow in 1622, and is a yeoman. The notes on Phineas's personation biograph tell the performer, in part:

> P. Pratt is a man of Character; he cannot Lie, nor swear, nor suffer one heard. Quicker Master P. would unscabbard his temper a' his sword than tolerate a false-hood or an dissembilating man. Nor ought he, by his own Code of Good Word and Valient Deed. One doesn't find him continually Defending his or others verity, however, for the same disposition which causeth him to believe in his own Truth Telling, causeth him to trust the truth of Others—unless he find ample cause to Doubt. . . . He has lived as close to the red men—friends & foes—as anie English Man & accepted—nay, even *adopted* to his open ways, their customs & believs—but his animated telling of the sagacities & civilities of *The Beaver* causes some of the more canny & doubtful of the community to wince at 'Finyuz's' acceptance of what they deem heathan apocrypha.

These notes are written in what I suppose is a seventeenth-century hand, in seventeenth-century grammar. The biograph also has a drawing of Phineas in his clothes—or costume, depending on whether you take his point of view or that of the performer playing him. Along with the biographs a performer is given a cassette tape of someone talking in the proper dialect.

Moran visited Plimoth:

> In each building a member of the household that would have resided there greets you and asks 'How be ye?' Within a few minutes you find yourself responding in a language that was foreign only moments ago. 'I be well, thank ye.' One little girl is asked, 'Where be ye from?' 'New Jersey', she answers. 'I'm afraid I don't know that place.' A parent intervenes. 'You see, Susie, New Jersey isn't invented yet.' . . . As the day proceeds, the villagers go about their work. Food is prepared in black kettles over hot coals, while they explain to their visitors the difference between pottage and ragout. . . . One young lad is helping build Mr. Allerton's house. With Irish brogue he explains, 'I was in a shipwreck on my way to Virginia colony. When I washed ashore the Indians took me here. I was sur-

> prised to find anyone speaking English in these wilds.' . . . One goat insisted on coming into the Standish household, only to be shooed away by the maid. The houses are all hand-constructed, some with wooden floors, some with clay (damp in the spring thaw). The streets are uneven, rocky. . . . Many special events continue the theme of historic reenactment. There is the opening of the Wampanoag Summer Settlement, staffed by native Americans in the style of the 17th century. There is a village barnraising and a reenactment of a typical wedding in the colony and also in the Indian camp. But the classical attraction, and one of the chief fundraisers for the village, is the Harvest Festival in October. . . . Here the villagers renew 17th century harvest customs with cooking and feasting, songs, dances, and a general show of high spirits. Native Americans from the summer settlement join in friendly challenges of skill and chance.[30]

In the information sheet I got from Ingram the 'first person interpretation' technique is celebrated:

> First person interpretation not only encourages the personal involvement of visitors, it also facilitates the discussion of difficult concepts and ideas. Indeed, it has been our experience that since the implementation of this technique in the Pilgrim Village the frequency of questions dealing with matters that can collectively be termed the 7th century world view has risen. There has also been a corresponding decrease in the questions that fall into the 'What is that?' category. By speaking in the first person, our staff can respond to questions in personal rather than abstract terms.[31]

Much effort is made to separate the seventeenth from the twentieth century. 'Unlike places like Sturbridge and Williamsburg', says Ingram, 'no items whatsoever are sold aboard the Mayflower or in the Pilgrim Village. . . . Our programme carefully separates modern element from period element, using the former to prepare the visitor for a suspension of doubt as he steps into the past.'[32] This is somewhat like

Disneyworld, and other theme parks, where a radical separation is attempted between the ordinary world and the world of the park. At Disneyworld the backstage is actually underground, and central control areas are several miles from the part of the park that visitors stroll in. All employees at Disneyworld enter and leave the area underground and out of sight: they are seen in the Magic Kingdom only in costume and in character.

But despite—even because of—these attempts at separating realities, or spheres of experience in time/space, spectators enjoy what can best be described as a postmodern thrill at the mix or close coincidence of contradictory categories. At Plimoth hosts are twentieth-century persons trained in seventeenth-century English (more or less); the visitors are tourists who have paid to be treated as guests dropping in from another century. A brochure emphasizes the reality of the seventeenth-century world, while encouraging the visitors to break that frame:

> The people you will meet in the village portray—through dress, speech, manner and attitudes—known residents of the colony in 1627. Their lives follow the seasonal cycle of all farming communities—planting and harvesting crops, tending animals, preparing meals, preserving food—what you see will depend upon the time of your visit. Busy as they are, the villagers are always eager for conversation. Feel free to ask questions; and remember, the answers you receive will reflect each individual's 17th century identity.

The give-away phrase is 'busy as they are'. It's not true: they are paid to respond to the visitors. I doubt that a villager who refused to talk to the tourists would last long in the seventeeth century, for he will have violated a rule laid down by his twentieth-century employers. The little one-page map and flyer is also full of the contradictions. The Village is entered only after the tourist has gone through a reception centre and an orientation centre. The reception centre is where business is done: restaurant, gift shop, bookstore, tickets for the Village itself; also telephones, toilets, a picnic area. The orientation centre includes a multi-image slide show which is, the flyer tells us, 'an essential part of your visit'. It gives historical background and lays out what's offered. The orientation to the seventeenth century 'lasts about 15 minutes'.

There is some cuteness amidst the insistence on stepping back into the seventeenth century. Spanish and French persons, 'if unarmed', are welcome at the Plantation even though England was at war with Spain and/or France for much of the seventeenth century. The architecture of the Village is totally re-created indoors and out—nothing survives from the original colony. Thus an unusual situation obtains at Plimoth. It is known who was there, and background information has been researched; consequently, the characters have a kind of authenticity that the architecture lacks. The buildings and furnishings are 'typical' of the period, but the people are 'actually from' 1627. At Plimoth restored behaviour is ahead of re-created architecture. And performers who have been at it awhile identify closely with their roles. Marten has played Myles Standish from 1969:

> After living with Myles Standish for all these years, Marten said he's 'more supportive and defensive' in his attitude toward the historical figure than a historian might be. Aside from appreciating Standish's virtues, Marten has gained an understanding of why the soldier committed some of his more controversial acts. 'He killed a number of Indians—not in fair combat, but in ambush', Marten said. 'If he had to knock off a few Indians for the good of the colony, he would do it without question. I don't think I'd have the stomach to do what he did, but in the context of that time, what Myles did made sense.'[33]

What happened to Marten happens to all actors: they build roles, filling in from their own feeling what can't be located in any background study. I don't know Marten's ethnic roots, but Native Americans are hired to portray Indians at Plimoth. And the brochure tells visitors to 'meet the Native American people who lived for centuries along the New England coast'. And an avowed aim of the Plantation is to provide 'the opportunity for members of the Native American community to learn about aspects of their own culture that are in danger of being lost'.[34] I suppose that such authenticity as is needed at Wampanoag is not necessary for the Pilgrim Village. Or is it illegal? Are there any blacks playing pilgrims? And if not do they have the basis for a class-action suit? State health codes prohibit visitors from tasting the ragout boiling in the stew-pots, though one visitor reports that this law is not always observed. The point is that there is no way of avoiding anachronisms at the deepest level: authenticity is a question of stage convention, of respecting the sponsors' implicit request not to question too far, and to enjoy contradictions: real Indians not real British colonists.

Inside the fence a seventeenth-century village atmosphere is kept up. As it is aboard the Mayflower II and in the Indian settlement. But a visit to the whole complex—reception centre, orientation centre, re-created environments alive with restored behaviour—is a thoroughly anachronistic experience, a theatrical experience, made even more sharply so by the use of restored behaviour as the key element. Spectators-participants generally go along with the seventeenth century reality. John S. Boyd plays Stephen Hopkins, assistant to Governor William Bradford. Hopkins is also the Village's first tavern keeper.

> Right now, that is in 1627, Hopkins is a 'husbandman' or farmer who spends much of his time working in the fields around the plantation, when he is not answering the questions of modern tourists. 'You are meeting people from all over the world', Boyd says. 'I have met people from five different countries in one day. . . . Most visitors enter into the spirit of the Plantation', Boyd says, but a few are nonplussed when a plantation resident will claim never to have heard of Pennsylvania or ask visitors if they have a 'good king'. Most of them, though, 'really do accept us as from another century'.[35]

Accept in the same way that Robert De Niro is accepted as Jake La Motta in *Raging Bull*. In fact, in the Pilgrim Village it's the logic of the movies that dominates, not theatre as Artaud, Brecht, or Richard Foreman conceive it.

Looking at the Plantation's programmes over a full year: the meetings held on location by local groups, the films, the winter education programmes, the information distributed explaining how the

Plantation works, the flyers, brochures, even the handsome Annual Report detailing attendance (590,000 in 1979), sales, contributions, and costs (about $1.5 million a year), we have a uniquely late twentieth-century American phenomenon. Everything is as authentic as possible, but the day ends for visitors at five, and the Plantation is closed for the winter. By closed I mean the performers are no longer about their daily chores, no longer living in the seventeenth century. The Plantation is open for special programmes and as a show business gearing up for an early spring opening. Maybe the Village is closed for the winter because those early Pilgrim winters were hard. The ordeals of hunger and cold, of death, can't yet be shown—or, rather, re-created. The limits of theatre end with Thanksgiving. Or maybe it's that outdoor entertainment in Massachusetts would be a loser in the winter. Probably it's both. The contradictions and anachronisms—framed and carefully kept separate (all gifts and books, restaurant and toilets, slide projectors and brochures, are outside the Village proper)—are what gives Plimoth and its sister restored villages their special kick. The contradictions are hidden, almost, and revealed at special times and places: like the magician who shows a little bit of his magic. It keeps the appetite whetted. So inside the Village it is all naturalism; but taken as a whole the Plantation is, after all, somewhat like Brecht and Foreman. The people who make Plimoth are aware that what they're doing isn't 'just' mounting static exhibits a la the dioramas at the American Museum of Natural History. They may not say it in these terms, but Plimoth is restored behaviour mixing 1➔3➔4 and 1➔5a➔5b.

But what of villages that specialize in restoring fantasies? More than one Old West town features regular *High Noon* shootouts or an attack by 'savage' Indians. These events are not taken from history, at least not directly. They are not researched the way data about the early settlement of New England are by people at PIimoth. They are played back from the movies. They are reflexions not reflections of the American experience. Sometimes, curiously, they double-back into movies. Buckskin Joe, Colorado, was created by Malcolm F. Brown, former art director at MGM. The town has been the setting for more than one movie, including *Cat Ballou*, a parody of Westerns. At Buckskin Joe a shootout takes place in front of the saloon, and the spectators, who are actual customers at the bar or other stores, duck for cover. At King's Island in Cincinnati a passenger train is held up, the conductor taken hostage, and passengers asked to intervene to save the day. Audience participation, on the decline in theatre, is increasing at theme parks and restored villages.

Considered theoretically, restored villages, even those built on fantasies and/or movies, raise hard questions. How are they different from the Staal-Gardner *agnicayana*? Staal-Gardner based their Vedic ritual on a reconstruction of an 'old India' as distorted, and as true, as the Old West of America where Amerindians attacked settlers and shootouts occurred in front of saloons. The brahman priests went to texts, their own memories, and what old people could recall of the *agnicayana*, just as architects, performers, and craftspeople of restored villages research their stuff. And as for things taken from pop mythology, as at Buckskin Joe, there are parallels in chhau where the stories re-enacted are from the Ramayana and Mahabharata, sacred in Sanskrit and very popular in numberless other versions including movies and comic books. No, the difference between the American restored villages and the *agnicayana* and chhau is that the performers and spectators in the restored villages know it's all make-believe [Fig. 3].

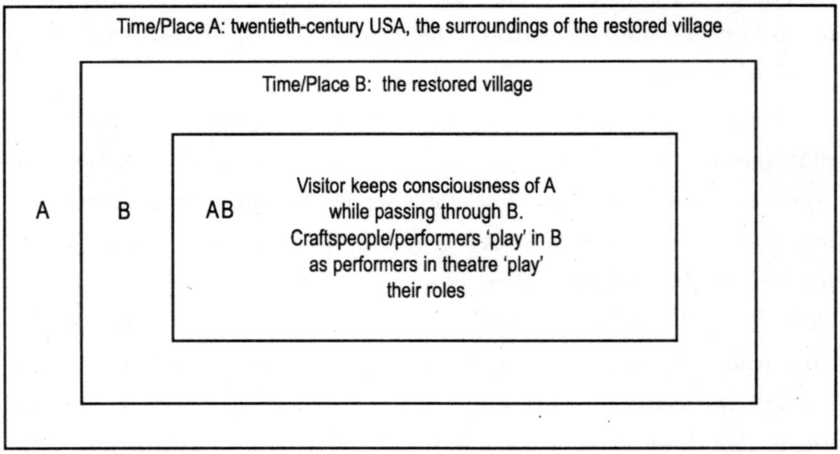

Fig. 3 Restored villages: time/place

There is a move from frame A into frame B resulting in a special consciousness, AB. AB is another way of stating the subjunctive mood of restored behaviour: the overlaying of two frames that cannot coexist in the indicative: 'being in' the nineteenth and twentieth centuries simultaneously, 'being' Ram and Ravana and two village persons, 'doing' a Vedic ritual before cameras and tape recorders. What happens is that the smaller subjunctive frame temporarily and paradoxically expands and contains the indicative frame. Everything is 'for the time being' [Fig. 4].

The indicative world is temporarily isolated, surrounded and penetrated by the subjunctive: on the outside is the environment of the performance; on the inside is the special consciousness of performing and witnessing/participating in a performance. The famous 'suspension of disbelief' is the agreement to let the smaller frame AB become the larger frame AB.

At Plimoth, after a few hours in the village, the visitors leave the seventeenth century; at the end of the day the craftspeople pack up and go home. Even those who make their home in the village keep an awareness of the world outside. But sometimes the anachronistic choice is radical, affecting a person's whole being. I met a number of families living in the mountains surrounding Santa Cruz, California, without electricity and other 'modern conveniences'. But the most studied, most extreme examples of anachronistic living are those done for the media, like the *agnicayana*, or like the Celtic encampment near London:

> Five young couples and their children lived together in a house made of sticks, grass and mud, lighted only by fire and the daylight that came through two low doors.They grew vegetables, raised boars, cows, chickens and goats, and kept a polecat for catching rabbits. They shaped pottery, forged tools, built cartwheels, wove cloth, cured the skins of animals. They sound like the Celtic tribesmen who lived not far from what is now London a 100 years ago; they are actually 20th century Britons who have been living like Iron Age Celts for almost a year. Their experiment was conceived by John

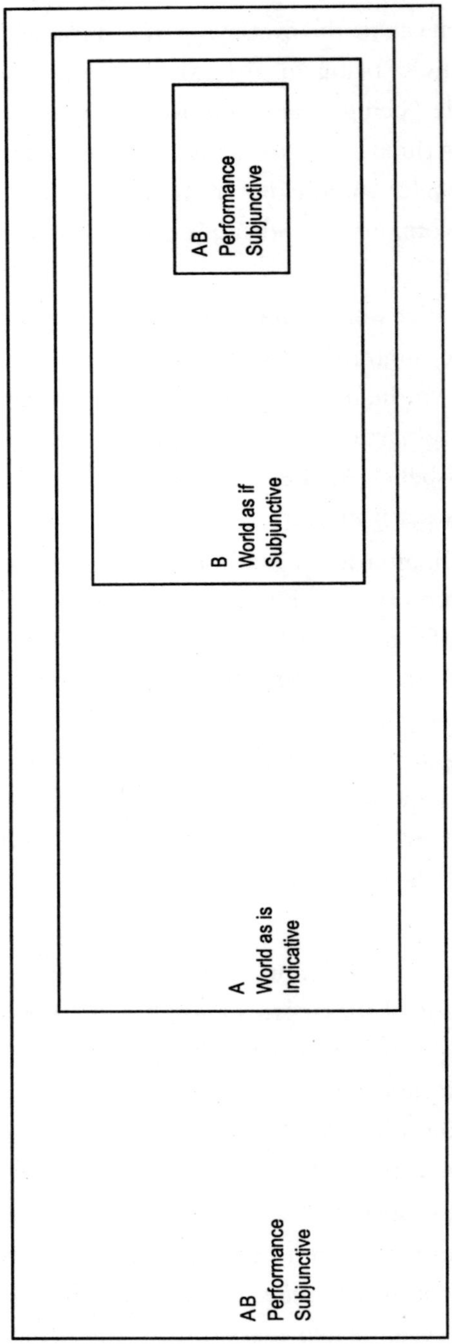

Fig. 4 Subjunctive/indicative

> Percival, a BBC producer, to dramatize archeology for a series of television documentaries. . . . Cameramen arrived at the Wiltshire village southwest of London every week to make films. Otherwise the 'Celts' were well insulated from the modern world. . . . Kate Rossetti, a Bristol teacher, had a long list of what she missed: 'My family and friends, chocolate, comfy shoes, Bach and Bob Dylan, being able to zoom up to Scotland'. But she said she does not think she will ever live in a city again.[36]

This kind of thing is no Arcadian return to nature. Contemporary Arcadians live in the Santa Cruz mountains. The BBC Celts are more like breeding zoos—places where images of bygone life can be bred and recaptured (in this case on film); a convergence of archaeology, anthropology, and media. It stands between the obvious fakery of a restored village and the not so obvious fakery of the 1975 *agnicayana*. By fake I mean something unable to live on its own, something that needs a media push or seems out of joint with contemporary life. Of course theatre is fake, but it celebrates its fakery, while restored villages slyly try to hide theirs. This sly faking is on the increase.

The BBC Celts are close to the brahman priests who restored the *agnicayana* for Staal-Gardner. For the 1975 *agnicayana* there were two audiences: an immediate one of locals, many of whom treated the ritual as a media event (this happens whenever a film is shot on location, even outside my window on Sullivan Street in Manhattan); and an audience of Americans who see *Altar of Fire* mainly as a documentary of an actual ritual. But ritual with a difference—ritual for study, for entertainment: a 'specimen'. The inversion is ironic. The audience in Kerala sees the *agnicayana* as media; the audience in America sees the media (version of *agnicayana*) as ritual. Both audiences are alienated from the 'pure' *agnicayana*. But was there ever a pure *agnicayana*? Isn't every instance of it 1➤5a➤5b? The narrator of *Altar of Fire* tells the audience that the performance they are seeing is probably the last ever of this ritual. This adds a P. T. Barnum flavour. And at Plimoth nothing (new) is going to happen; life there is finished. These examples of restored behaviour are very much like theatre in a theatre: the script is set, the environment is known, the actors play set roles. But bharatanatyam and chhau are different. These restorations have healed seamlessly into their cultural surround: they are living arts. As such these dances will change; their future isn't predictable. Plimoth Plantation either continues as it is or ceases to be what it is: its very existence is knotted into its specific historicity. Each production of aesthetic theatre is like Plimoth, but the theatre as a genre is like bharatanatyam and chhau. The similarities and differences among various performance systems are summarized in Fig. 5.

One of the big differences among performance systems is the physical environment—what contains what. In ordinary theatre the domain of the spectator, the house, is larger than the domain of the performer, the stage, and distinctly separate from it. In environmental theatre there is a shift in that the spectator and performer often share the same space and sometimes exchange spaces, and sometimes the domain of the performer is larger than that of the spectator, enclosing the spectator within the performance. This tendency is taken even further in restored villages and theme parks, where the visitor enters an environment that swallows him. Every effort is made to transform the spectator into a participant. And while the visitor keeps a consciousness of his own time and place, he simultaneously enjoys a temporary surrender of them. The 1975 *agnicayana* combines the qualities of film with those of a restored village. There are two frames working: that of the ritual and that of the film being made of the ritual. The brahman priests are performers of the *agnicayana* and 'visitors' absorbed into it (Vedic ritual being older and different from brahman Hindu ritual); the local people watch both the ritual and the filming of it—neither event is familiar. If the priests had been totally absorbed into the *agnicayana*, they would have insisted on sacrificing the goats, or they would have stopped the performance because in Vedic terms the goat sacrifice is essential. But the priests, too, wanted the film to be made. The priests acted in regard to animal sacrifice not as Vedic priests but as modern Indians. More: they acted as performers in a film with a big stake in seeing that the shooting came off well. Using their authority as priests they devised the substitute effigies as a way of

	A	B
1	Arts Theatre, dance, etc.	Restored Arts Bharatanatyam, Purulia Chhau, etc.

Between these three is little or no phenomonological distinction making it very hard to tell A1 from B1 without doing historical research—B1 heals seamlessly into A1. Both A1 and B1 have a 'life of their own.' In both, performers know why they're 'in a show' and audiences know they're 'watching a show.'

	A	B	C	D
2	Media Fiction Regular movies	Media Simulation Recreated especially for media, as were the BBC Celts	Media 'Push' Without media there would be no event, as the 1975 *agnicayana*	Media 'there' Documentaries, news

A move to the right = decreasing dependence on media to make the event, though news items are edited creating a feedback between what 'is' news and what media 'makes into' news. Also a move to the right = an increase in narration, in suggesting an independent event that needs an observer outside 'objectively' explaining it. B2, C2, and D2 merge into one another. Only in A2 is the performer sure he is 'in a show' and the spectator sure he is 'watching' a show. A recent form, 'docudrama,' combines A2 and D2.

	A	B	C
3	Theme Parks Disneyland, Land of Oz, Dogpatch, etc.	Restored villages made from fantasy and history Buckskin Joe, Frontierland, Columbia Historic Park, etc.	Restored villages made from history Plimoth, Smithville, Louisborg, etc.

In A3 everyone knows they are 'in a show' as spectators-participants or performers. In B3 and C3, even the performers begin to feel they are 'in life.' But, paradoxically, B3 and C3 are very close to A1 and B1 where the event begins to have a 'life of its own.' In A3 most of the machinery—mechanical and human—is hidden from the spectator creating a fictive environment. In B3 and C3 there is an attempt—as at museums—to show as much as possible. But these days even museums are fictionalizing. For example, the Ice Age Art exhibit at the Amercian Museum of Natural History (1978–79) was made mostly from simulated items.

Fig. 5 Performance systems: a comparative chart

making the film, performing the *agnicayana*, and not offending the values of modern Kerala Indians. Thus the priests played three roles: Vedic ritualists, brahman priests arbitrating a living tradition, and film performers. In a way the film performers convinced the brahman priests that it was okay to tamper with the Vedic tradition. Or, as film performers brahman priests were asked to play the role of Vedic ritualists. This double, or triple, life is typically that of theatre actors; it is the theatrical brand of truth. And between the frame of the *agnicayana* and the frame of the filmmaking stood the local audience, enjoying both spectacles.

But is it fair to say that the priests were play-acting? From the perspective of Euro-American conventions, 'acting' means make-believe, illusion, lying. Even Goffman, who has studied acting in ordinary life, identifies it most directly with con men and others who must maintain a 'front' separate from their 'true' selves. This understanding of acting derives from our Platonic view of a hierarchy of realities in which the most real is the most distant from experience and from our Aristotelian view of art, which is an imitation of a reflection. But from the perspective of Indian conventions—and the system of maya/lila underlying them—acting is playful illusion, but so is the world itself, so that in India acting is both false and true. In fact, in Asia the mask is often credited with being closer to the way things are in the world than the face behind the mask can be: acting becomes not a species of lying but a means to the truth. Since Stanislavski at least this has been the ambition of theatre in the West; and it is this ambition—this wish to have art search out and represent truth—that has fired much theatrical experimentation. And driven artists to seek non-Western cultures, Asian especially, ways of making theatre that are not Aristotelian. Brecht, Meyerhold, Grotowski, Artaud, Cage—seminal figures all—used Asian practices as models for their own work.

But back to the priests officiating at the Staal-Gardner *agnicayana*. I might think they were acting, and Kerala villagers might think they were doing what priests always do—mediating between ordinary and non-ordinary experience, both of which need acting. The priests are trained/prepared by birth and education to restore the behaviour of the *agnicayana*. It is not accurate to call them actors and it is not accurate to not call them actors. They were between 'not actors' and 'not not actors'—a realm of double negativity that precisely describes the process of theatrical characterization, a liminal realm. As for American restored villages, anyone with proper training can demonstrate colonial crafts and speak English in a seventeenth-century Yankee dialect. At the end of the workday, craftspeople and performers take off their costumes, put down their tools, and go home. The visitors assume this divestiture of roles is taking place even if they don't see it with their own eyes. At Plimoth some of the conventions ordinarily followed in an American theatre are dropped. The performers are not on a stage, not rewarded by applause, and don't strictly follow a word-by-word script called a drama. In some of the villages the actors interact with spectators, making the visitor enter into the world of the village, thereby further blurring the seam between the performance and its nonacting surround. The performers at Plimoth are acting, but they may not seem to be acting. In America we say someone is 'only acting' when we detect the seams between the performance and the nonacting surround. We also say someone is acting when he or she is performing on a stage. We say someone is not acting when he or she is doing what one ordinarily would do were there no audience. Documentary film imposes an acting frame around a nonacting situation. But documentaries like Curtis's *In the Land of the Head Hunters* or Flaherty's *Nanook of the North* combine people sometimes going about their ordinary tasks, sometimes restoring behaviours of a recent past, and sometimes acting for pay in fictive situations in an 'on location' set wearing costumes and saying lines written for the occasion.

In some cases, in the restored villages, and from the effect of people like Curtis, matters have grown more complicated. Some performers at restored villages have become permanent residents of the village, live off the income from their crafts, eat the food they have cooked that day in the presence of the visitors. Their 'lived lives' mesh with their 'performed lives' in so strong a way that it feeds back into their performances. Their roles become their 'ordinary life', supplying their restored behaviour with a new source of authenticity. When this happens, the residents of the restored villages can no more comfortably be subsumed under the category of 'play actors' than can the Kerala brahman priests.

In T. McLuhan's 1974 film, *The Shadow Catcher*, a few of the original participants in Curtis's 1914 *Head Hunters* explain how Curtis's interest in the 'old ways' rekindled their own interest—and led to their restoring some ceremonies previously abandoned. Thus the value frame of the new dominant culture encouraged the enactment as fiction of what was previously performed in fact; while other actions—masked dancing, shamanic healing—were done in fact but before the rolling camera. Later a new cultural whole emerged combining fiction and fact and including performances invented for tourists. Younger Kwakiutls said Curtis's movie helped them learn about the old life, because seeing something 'really being done' is so much more powerful than just hearing about it. But what was 'really being done' even the old-timers didn't do anymore by the time Curtis arrived. Who knows if they ever did it the way he filmed it. Curtis paid performers 50c an hour—$5 when there was danger, like rowing the huge war canoes or hunting sea lions.

Increasingly, American theatre of all kinds is like *Head Hunters* (whose title was changed to *Land of the Long Canoes* because Curtis thought American audiences would find head-hunting repulsive; the movie failed commercially anyway)—combining documentary, fiction, and history: in other words, restored behaviour, 1→5a→5b. From the 1970s into the 1980s experimental theatre has put acting and non-acting side by side, as in the work of Spalding Gray, Leeny Sack, Robert Wilson-Christopher Knowles, and Squat Theatre. In contrast, such strongholds of 'fact' as network news programmes are anchored by people selected for their ability to perform, not to gather or edit news. A suitable aesthetic theory doesn't exist to handle these crossovers and juxtapositions. They are all 1→5a→5b.

Taken as a whole, the performances I'm discussing belong to the subjunctive, not the indicative, mood. And the spectators, too, by virtue of their being physically inside the action instead of standing outside looking in, give over to the subjunctive—to behaving 'as if' they were really there in that negotiated space-time-event I call restored behaviour. Negotiated because it takes an agreement among all parties to keep the thing up in the air, moving, alive. The restored village and Curtis's half restoring, half inventing for the sake of his feature film are performances intermediate in type between the brahman priest restoring an archaic and nowadays unperformed ritual for the benefit of the cameras and Olivier playing Hamlet on the orthodox Euro-American stage. Intermediate also are performances like those of Wilson-Knowles, Gray, and Squat. The most interesting work of the past ten years is intermediate, liminal: work that illuminates its own ambivalence, that is explicitly reflexive, and that is very difficult to categorize. In orthodox theatre the domain of the spectator ('the house') is larger than and separate from the domain of the drama ('the stage'). This framing helps maintain the objectivity and critical/aesthetic distance of the orthodox theatre-goer. But in restored villages, as in environmental theatre, the domain of the performance surrounds and includes the 'spectator'. Looking at becomes harder; being in, easier. There is no house, and spectators are thrown back on their own resources for whatever assurance they need to maintain who/where they are. How to behave, what to do or not to do, are troubling questions in this situation. Although work like Wilson-Knowles's and Gray's does not include the spectator physically, it undermines his psychic distance by presenting nonacting as performance. The same uneasiness results.

VII

THE THEORY EXPLAINING ALL THIS will come from theatre specialists or from social scientists learned in theatre. Theatre is the art that specializes in the concrete techniques of restoring behaviour. Turner's theory, like Goffman's, is actually a theatrical one generalized to suit social process. Working the same field are Geertz, Rappaport, and Myerhoff. The field is fertile because individual cultures and world monoculture are increasingly theatrical.

Preparing to do theatre includes memorizing a score of gestures, sounds, and movements and/or achieving a mood where apparently 'external' gestures, sounds, and movements 'take over' the performer as in a trance. This basic theatrical process is universal. Whether the performer is in a Broadway musical, an experimental theatre workshop in Soho, a shingeki performance in Tokyo, a noh drama in Kyoto, the Bolshoi ballet, or the Moscow Art Theatre, a Balinese trance drama, Ramlila in India, the dances of the pig *kaiko* of Papua-New Guinea, or Yoruba theatre—anywhere—behaviour that is other is transformed into the performer's alienated or objectified parts of his own self either his private self or his social self—then reintegrated and shown publicly in a total display. The process has two parts and a conclusion; these are strictly analogous to what Van Gennep and Turner describe as the ritual process. First there is the breaking down, where the performer's resistance is overcome, where he is made open and vulnerable, 'ready': then there is the building up, or the filling up, where at first short and then increasingly long and integrated strips of behaviour are added to what the performer can do. At a certain point in the process—a point that differs widely from culture to culture, artistic form to form—a public is required before whom, or in collaboration with whom, the new behaviour is displayed.

This process has been described from the social perspective by Turner and from the individual-psychological perspective by Winnicott. Turner's key idea is his elaboration of Van Gennep's term, liminality:

> Liminal entities are neither here nor there, they are betwixt and between positions assigned and arrayed by law, custom, convention, and ceremonial. As such, their ambiguous and indeterminate attributes are expressed by a rich variety of symbols in the many societies that ritualize social and cultural transitions.[37]
>
> The neophyte in liminality must be a *tabula rasa*, a blank slate, on which is inscribed the knowledge and wisdom of the group, in those respects that pertain to the new status.[38]

Theatre is an 'artificial species' of ritual, a hothouse version often created by individuals or temporary groups. Turner calls the arts and some other leisures of modern society 'liminoid', suggesting that they share some of the functions and processes of liminal acts, but that they are also characterized by a voluntariness—a conscious subjunctivity—that is not present in liminal actions. In theatre the performer induces in himself, or has induced for him, replications/restorations of those life-crises most people avoid or undergo only when pressed by necessity. Comedy as well as tragedy deals with difficult, anxiety-ridden crises. The pleasure comes because of the subjunctive mood of the activity, the learned ability to experience an action without suffering its consequences. Hamlet dies, not Olivier. Of course, as I've noted, contemporary theatre skirts or even crosses the boundaries, and some of our recent Hamlets have suffered a real wound or two.

The workshop-rehearsal phase of performing, the 'preperformance', is designed to make the performer a *tabula rasa* with regard to what is going to be performed. The performer is stripped of his everyday identity or learns how to put it aside then, once cleansed, the performer brings out of himself, or is inscribed upon, or filled up with, Another, a 'character', or some special aspect of himself, his 'persona'. Workshop-rehearsal passes through three distinct steps that coincide with the ritual process: (1) separation or stripping away, reducing, eliminating, or setting aside 'me'; (2) initiation, or revelation, or finding out what's new—in 'me' or in/from Another, or what's essential and necessary, and (3) reintegration, or building up longer and longer meaningful strips of behaviour; making something for the public—preparing to re-enter the social world but as a new and/or different 'self'. The time spent in these three steps, and the place where this work is done, is liminal. Not the finished performances but this multiphasic process of 'making up' performances is what needs to be compared to ritual. Little comparative work of that kind has been done because few anthropologists have participated in, or closely observed, the workshop-rehearsal process.

How do workshop-rehearsals work? There are two basic methods. In the first, actual items of performance are passed on directly from master to neophyte. There is no 'technique' separate from parts of the performance to be learned. I've watched Kakul, the dance guru of

Batuan, Bali, as he stood behind a young girl, maybe eight years old, manipulating her wrists, hands, and shoulders with his hands; her torso with his body; her legs with his knees and feet. He used her as a puppet transferring directly his own body-sense of the dance. She gave her body over to him. Eventually, Kakul says, the dance 'goes into' her body; she learns it in much the same way that spoken language is learned, by being surrounded and immersed in it. She may never know the 'grammar' of her dancing, just as many fine speakers of English never know its grammar. Also this way of training prepares her for trance possession where culturally known beings will go into her body using it in much the way that Kakul used it to train her. In this method of 'direct acquisition' by manipulation, imitation, and repetition there is the paradox that the 'creativity' of the performer comes only after he has mastered a form by rote learning. Kakul, at the end of his career, after he gained a reputation as a great performer, began to improvise and introduce new material; just as a noh performer who has achieved *hana* (flower) can modify what he has learned from his father. Experimentation which literally means 'going outside the boundaries' is reserved for the most experienced, most respected and often the oldest performers. In Euro-American theatre, experimentation is mostly the work of the young. And this is because the initial phases of workshop-rehearsal are the freest; and it is the youthful performer who is encouraged to 'do something new'.

In the method of direct acquisition there is no reference during training to any generative grammar of performance. Nor do training or exercises stimulate 'creativity' or encourage experimentation or the discovery of new material or patterns. I've watched the *vyas* (director) of the Ramnagar Ramlila employ direct acquisition in teaching the texts and gestures to the teen-age boys who perform the *swarupas* (the gods Ram, Bharat, Lakshman, and Shatrughna). Learning the score 'prepares' the boys to be entered by the gods during moments of the actual performance. The last thing a *vyas* wants of such performers is 'creativity'. The *swarupas* must be receptive, even passive. When the boys are not wearing the crowns that signify the activation of the godhead within them, they are just boys, lectured by the *vyas*, scolded by their mothers. At the same time, however, they are fed a special diet of godly foods: pure milk, sweet rice, fruit, nuts, yoghurt. This diet not only gives them strength but makes them feel like gods. Through the method of direct acquisition two tasks are accomplished simultaneously. Performance texts—I mean not only the words but the whole mise-en-scène—are passed on from generation to generation, and particular performances are made ready for the public. There is no way to separate these tasks, for the texts are both written and oral: the libraries where these texts are kept are the bodies of the performers.

The second method of workshop-rehearsal is to teach a grammar, a set of 'basic exercises' out of which, through transformation, the particular, and often very different, mise-en-scènes will come. Some great texts do not exist as performances but only as words. There is no one way to play *Hamlet*, nor even any 250 ways. There is no continuity of performing *Hamlet* from 1604 to now. Not only were the theatres closed during the Cromwell era, but the Euro-American modern tradition locates continuity in the written text and innovation in the performance. Recent 'violations' of this tradition—for example, my collaging and rearranging classic texts, or the attempt to build in theatre 'performance texts' as is seen in the work of Brecht and Mabou Mines—have had tough going. In the 'learn a basic alphabet/grammar' method students learn how to 'use' their mind-bodies in order to invent the particular gestures that will make up this or that production. A radical separation of written text and performance text has occurred. The written text is preserved separately from any of its performances. A large body of criticism dealing with the written text arises, and this criticism tends to dominate the field. There is also a separation between training and rehearsal. Training is generalized, in the sense that techniques are learned that can be applied to any number of performances. Schools brag that their graduates can act in any number of styles. It would be absurd for a noh actor to perform modern naturalism. However, Kanze Hideo, a leading noh actor, has worked with experimental theatre director Tadushi Suzuki, who bases much of his training on noh (as well as martial arts and kabuki). In the 'alphabet method' an actor pants, not so that he may be able to pant in performance, but in order to strengthen his diaphragm, get in touch with the different ways the voice can resonate, control his breathing so that difficult physical exertions can be accomplished without losing breath, and so on. Or scenes from plays are practised in training not because they will be performed soon or in that way, but so that the student can learn to 'build a character', evoke genuine emotions or effectively feign them on stage, or deal with his fellow actors.

But just as there are intermediate or liminal performance styles, so are there some training methods that occupy a position in between these extremes, combining elements of both. Guru Kedar Nath Sahoo, master dancer of masked Seraikella chhau, teaches first a set of sword and shield exercises that will later be transformed into moves used within the dance-drama. These exercises also strengthen the body and familiarize the performers with chhau's martial roots. And in kathakali, the dance-drama of Kerala, training begins with a series of massages administered by the guru's feet to the student's whole body. These massages literally erase old body stances and help bring the student's body to a new alignment. The massage period coincides with a series of rigorous exercises that are later used with some variation in the kathakali itself. Neither in chhau nor in kathakali are the exercises used as the basis for invention; they are there to help the student use his body in the necessary way. Thus the exercises can be looked at as part of the 'breaking down' phase of training. They do not help a student grasp the underlying logic of the performance. That can come only after years of experience as the student deciphers for himself what he is doing. Many excellent performers never come to this kind of theoretical knowledge. But some do, and those are the ones most likely to introduce changes.

In the Euro-American method rehearsal is not a matter of transmitting a known performance text but the invention of a new text. This new text is arrived at during rehearsals. It is necessary to teach performers a generative code. In the method of direct acquisition rehearsals consist not in inventing a new performance text but in mastering a known one. But performance itself can be more flexible. No drama appears very formal and set. But during performance subtle cues pass between the *shite* (principal actor) and musicians, chorus, and *waki* (second actor). These cues tell the others that the *shite* has decided to repeat a section, or will increase the tempo, or slow it down, and so on. If, however, a performer goes beyond what is given him to vary—if he performs publicly without mask or traditional costume—a storm breaks: is this 'new thing' actually noh? In the Euro-American method rehearsals are 'explorations' that lead to a 'fixed score' during performance. Only shows advertised as improvisatory change markedly night to night. And most improvised shows are mere rearrangements of fixed routines. But the physical details of shows can vary greatly as long as the written text is recognizable. Shakespeare has been done in period costume, modern dress, eclectic mixed dress. Yet when I staged plays environmentally, and introduced audience participation, journalists publicly demanded, 'Is this theatre?'

During rehearsals of the Euro-American type the grammar of techniques is used to discover and 'keep' items that will later appear in the performance. That which is already known in the direct acquisition method is discovered or invented. Something happens that is 'right', and the director says 'keep that'. What he means is, not to do it again, but to put it ahead in time—to literally throw it forward in the hope that the item of action will be used later, that it will provide a clue as to what the finished mise-en-scène will look like. During rehearsals the shape and feel of the performance being discovered/invented/restored lies in a liminal area between present and future, and between past, present, and future as personal associations from performers and director are added to the scheme. Thus a 1→5a→5b situation occurs. To the outside observer, the bits of performance being 'thrown forward', being 'kept', may appear haphazard. But sooner or later a pattern emerges as when, through a fog, a coastline is first sensed ('I smell land'), then vaguely discerned as a darkness, then seen as a blurred image, and finally resolved with increasing detail. So too, in this method, depicted in Fig. 6, the performance evolves out of rehearsals. As Brecht said, the performance is the least rejected of all the things tried.

Early rehearsals are not only jerky and disjointed, they are laden with anxiety. The actions of the rehearsal have a high information potential but a very low goal orientation. 'What are we doing?' 'What are we looking for?' 'Why are we doing this?' are the common questions. The director doesn't know; he too is hunting. A director may maintain confidence by imposing order in the guise of known exercises, or he will introduce new basic techniques, expanding the range of the group's generative grammar. But if, by a certain time, a target is not visible (not only a production date but a vision of what's to be produced), if not enough has been thrown forward to provide an outline, a goal, the project falters, then fails. The possibilities for failure are great enough when, as in the case of *Hamlet*, it's a matter of generating a performance text that suits a written one. Where there is no preexisting text whatsoever—as with much contemporary theatre—the likelihood of failure is still greater.

During the past 50 years, since Artaud at least, the two kinds of workshop-rehearsal process—transmission of whole items by direct acquisition and transmission by means of learning a generative grammar—have been linked. This linkage is, in fact, the great work of experimental theatre in this century. Richard Foreman, for example, transmits to relatively passive performers a complete performance text in a method parallel to that used by the Ramlila *vyas*. Foreman

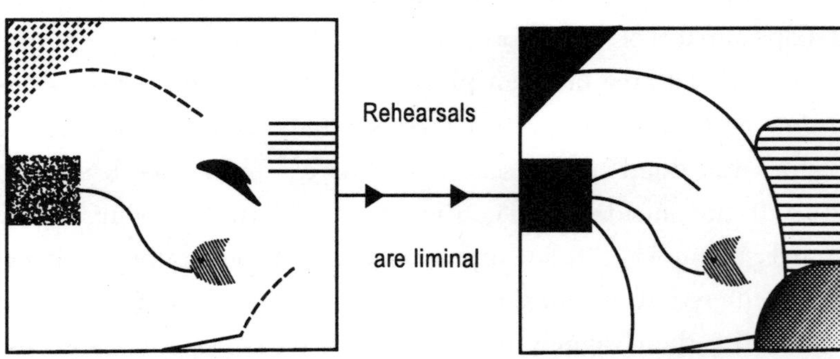

Early rehearsals: fragments thrown forward, 'kept', shape not yet clear. But some details are already 'there.'

Later rehearsals: pattern now discernible; details all connected to make a whole; performance has a 'logic of its own.'

Fig. 6 Rehearsals

writes his plays, makes a schematic of how they are to be staged, designs the setting, and often is present as chief technician at each performance. And the 'grammatical' methods of Guru Sahoo and the teachers at the kathakali may be due to extensive contact with European methods. Also techniques such as yoga, martial arts, and mantra chanting, transmitted as whole texts in their cultures of origin, are now used in the West as training of the generative grammar kind. In 1978, at a meeting outside of Warsaw convened by Grotowski, I saw Kanze Hideo put on a noh mask, crawl on the floor, and improvise actions having nothing to do with classical noh. And his friend, director Suzuki, in a production of Euripides' *Trojan Women*, combined noh, kabuki, martial arts, modern Western experimental theatre, and ancient Greek tragedy. The play was as much about post-atomic-bomb Japan as Troy. Examples multiply, bearing witness to exchanges between, especially, Asian and Euro-American theatre. Three kinds of workshop-rehearsal are now occurring: (1) those based on transmitting a total performance text; (2) those based on generative grammars resulting in new performance texts; and (3) those combining 1 and 2. This last is not a sterile hybrid, but the most fertile of the three.

There is another way of looking at the workshop-rehearsal process connecting Turner's ideas of subjunctivity/liminality to Stanislavski's 'as if'.

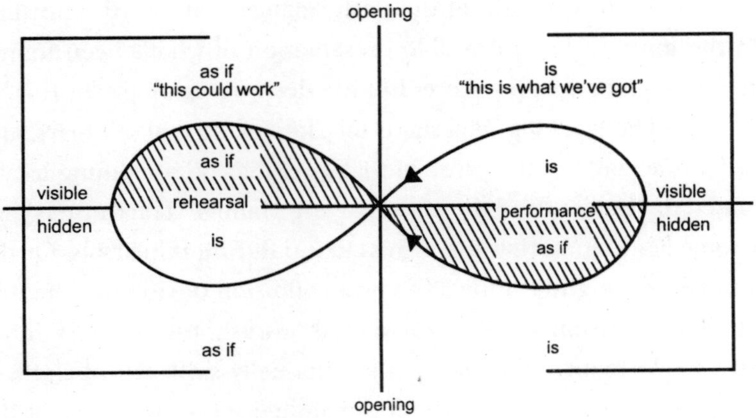

Fig. 7 'As if'

Fig. 7 shows that the deep structure of workshop-rehearsal inverts the deep structure of performance.[39] In workshop-rehearsal real work is being done, work that is serious and problematical. Workshop-rehearsal ironically belongs to the indicative, to the realm of the 'is', but on a deep, hidden level of structure. The visible aspect of workshop-rehearsal, its processual frame, is 'as if', subjunctive, tentative—'let's try that', 'this could work', 'what would happen if?'—play. Techniques of 'as if'—exercises, games, improvisation, therapy—bring up material from within those making the show or from the outside. The work of workshop-rehearsal is to find, reveal, express these deep things, and then to integrate them into a new whole. Even while deep things are 'brought up' the workshop-rehearsal must be kept open—that is, liminal. The 'as if' is a scalpel cutting deep into the actual lives of those making the work. And the most serious crises of performance—the things that can destroy a work most surely—happen during workshop-rehearsals. This is the period during which performers throw tantrums, directors fire persons who disagree, and writers phone their agents in terror. For during this time every small change can have immense consequences on the 'work as a whole'.

The performance is the inverse of the workshop-rehearsal. The show becomes 'real', part of history, when it opens; certain public rituals such as reviewing, attendance by an audience of strangers, an opening night party, mark the transition from rehearsal to performance. The frame and visible structure of the performance is an 'is', the finished show, the more or less invariable presentation of what's been found, kept, and organized into a score. But the deep structure under this 'is' is an 'as if'. The tears Ophelia sheds for Hamlet are real salt tears, and her grief is actual, but the cause of that grief may be something totally unrelated to Hamlet or to the actor playing Hamlet. The cause is possibly some association that the actress found during rehearsals. Or the final scene of slaughter appears to be a confusion of violence when in fact it is a precision of near misses. As workshop-rehearsals move towards performance, the 'as if' is intentionally sunk out of sight. If the performance is a good one, all the audience sees is the 'is' of the show. Of course, there are variations of this classic scheme. The investigation of the rehearsal process by Stanislavski and Brecht made it possible to play around with the process. Brecht wanted actors to be in character ('is') some of the time and to stand beside their characters ('as if'), questioning these very characters, at other times. Thus Brecht introduced a part of the rehearsal process into public performances. And since Brecht many others have staged rehearsals. But this breaking of frames occurs not only in serious drama, but in circus and Broadway musicals as well. There is a scene in *Sugar Babies* where the star, Mickey Rooney, loses his wig. He laughs, his face turns red, he runs to the edge of the stage and shouts something at the audience; he acknowledges that underneath all the puff roles he plays there is the person, the star, Mickey Rooney. Losing the wig looks accidental, but I have confirmed that it happens in each performance in the same scene. Probably Rooney lost his wig 'for real' during one rehearsal, and this nice piece of business was kept. It helps the audience feel good about paying so much money to see the star; for a brief moment they see him as himself, unmasked. Of course this unmasking is a trick, not an unmasking at all. In the 1980 Ringling Brothers Circus a female performer concluding a stunt on the high bar is unable to pull herself up. The orchestra stops, there is silence in the arena. Slowly, inch by precious inch, she hoists herself up until she is able to reach the bar with her hands and regain a safe position. I saw the circus five times and the same 'accident' occurred each time. Paul Bouissac assured me that such tricks are common, especially in acts that need to look more dangerous than they are. I do not criticize the rehearsedness of these scenes. In my own work, whenever I've tried to have 'open rehearsals' where the public was invited to see a work 'in process', or when during finished performances I've tried to include 'raw elements' such as having the green room visible during *Mother Courage*, I learned how quickly the processual or open nature of workshop-rehearsal is lost. The performers in *Mother Courage* soon found a space out of sight of the audience where they went, making that hidden space the genuine green room; what the audience saw was a make-believe green room. The performers even tried to fool me, knowing that I wanted them to 'be really in the green room' in sight of the audience. It was only when I found ashtrays, costumes, and empty soda cans back where the lights were stored did I know what was going on. I shouldn't have been surprised. The 'as if' wants to submerge when the public is present. Only while working with those they can trust, usually a few comrades who have shared a lot of working together, can performers play 'as if' with 'is' material. When working under the eye of a critical public, the performers present only the 'is' of their 'as if'.

The last part of rehearsal is practice. Longer and more complicated units of restored behaviour are organized into the actual performance. Music, costumes, lighting, make-up accumulate. Each of these is blended in with the intention of making an integrated whole. During this final push gestures are edited so that they send the clearest signals, and practised until they become second nature. Pacing, the relation of the rhythm/tempo of each part to that of the whole, becomes all important. This last phase of rehearsal is comparable to the phase of reintegration in a rite of passage. Strangers to the theatre often think only of this last phase when they hear the word 'rehearsal'. But as I have tried to show, reintegration is only the final part of a long process.

Immediately before going on most performers engage in some ritual. The noh actor contemplates his mask; jatra performers in Bengal worship the gods of the performance who manifest themselves in the props assembled on the trunks set up backstage; Stanislavski advised 30 seconds of silent concentration. Warm-ups are universal in experimental theatre. These preparations immediately preceding public performance somehow recapitulate the workshop-rehearsal process and concentrate the performer's attention on the task at hand. It's a little like the moment of prayer or the singing of an anthem before a ballgame or prize fight. But these ceremonies are not holy in the religious sense, even when they include religious ritual. I think, rather, the ritual is a way of focusing the work of workshop-rehearsal and bringing this work across a difficult threshold, limen, that separates rehearsal from public performance. Sometimes these preparatory 'moments' are hours long. Tribesmen in Papua-New Guinea, and performers of yakshagana, kathakali, and Ramlila in India, spend up to four hours putting on make-up and costumes. I always met with The Performance Group two hours or more before a performance to give notes, clean up the space, and do warm-ups. The main function of these preparations—even the putting on of effectively transformative costumes, masks, and make-up—is not merely to make the performer 'look' the role, but to set aside time immediately before the performance for the work of training, workshop, and rehearsal to be awakened and take hold. I've seen Guru Sahoo even without the paraphernalia of chhau, without mask or costume or music, give great performances. But never without a moment of worship.

The three phases—separation, initiation, and reintegration—apply even to performances without audiences, such as Grotowski's paratheatre. Participants in Grotowski's experiments leave the city, travel to remote areas, and there perform actions with and under the supervision of Grotowski's people. These actions vary according to who the participants are and the current interests of the Laboratory Theatre. But the actions always involve discovering and revealing hidden personal themes, finding new ways of behaving, sharing in an I-thou relationship. The physical actions—running through the woods at night, sudden immersion in water, circle dances where fire is passed from dancer to dancer, group chanting, singing, and storytelling are very like those in initiation rites. Maybe these rites served as a model for Grotowski; maybe he came upon these actions independently. When the participants return home after a few days, or weeks, they say that they can't talk about what happened. This isn't due to any vows of secrecy, but to the conviction that words can't do justice to the experience. 'It changed my life' is a frequent summary. So also at the level of action the experience with Grotowski resembles an initiation rite in which a transformation of self, a change of status, is effected. But ex-Grotowski-ites have been mostly unsuccessful in starting their own theatres or feeding what they've done with Grotowski into their own work. They are disabled rather than invigorated. Grotowski has not worked out, nor have his clients been able to supply, phase three of the rehearsal/ritual process: reintegration. There is no reintegration in

Grotowski's paratheatre—no way that the participants can bring it home or do it publicly. Thus participants are left hanging: they have been separated, stripped down, made into *tabulae rasae*; they have had deep experiences, been 'written upon', made new; but they have not been enabled to reintegrate this new self into the social world. Not only does Grotowski's theatre no longer perform publicly, he disavows that his work is religious, and so it does not knit in with any existing system.

The absence of a means of reintegration in Grotowski's paratheatre is related to the intentions of Grotowski's experiments. Theatre has but two stances in relationship to society at large: either to be tightly woven into broader social patterns, as rituals are, or else to serve as an analytical instrument for the dialectical critique of the society which is theatre's backdrop and surround, as Brecht's theatre tried to do. Most theatre people are not conscious of these stances, and their work drifts. But Grotowski is among the most conscious individuals I've ever met, and until recently he has avoided taking either of these stances. That's why his work is intentionally incomplete. His newly proposed 'theatre of sources' will culminate in a 'transcultural village' where masters of performance from different non-Western cultures (a performative theme park/theatre zoo) will meet Grotowski's people and selected individuals from Euro-American culture. It is a move towards integrating his work into larger social patterns. It's also very romantic.

The three-phase process is the basic machine for the restoration of behaviour. It's no accident that this process is the same in theatre as it is in ritual. For the basic function of both theatre and ritual is to restore behaviour—to maintain performances of the 1➤5a➤5b type. The meaning of individual rituals is secondary to this primary function, which is a kind of collective memory-in/or-action. The first phase breaks down the performer's resistance, makes him a *tabula rasa*. To do this most effectively the performer has to be removed from familiar surroundings; hence the need for separation, for 'sacred' or special space, and for a use of time different from that prevailing in the ordinary. The second phase is one of initiation, of developing new or restoring old behaviour. But so-called new behaviour is really the rearrangement of old behaviour, or the enactment of old behaviour in new settings. In the third phase, reintegration, the restored behaviour is practised until it is second nature. The final moment of the third phase is the public performance. Public performances in Euro-American theatre are repeated until there aren't any more customers; theatre 'productions' are treated as commodities. In most cultures performances occur according to schedules that strictly ration their availability. What we call 'new behaviour', as I said, is only short strips of behaviour rearticulated in novel patterns. Experimental theatre thrives on these rearticulations masquerading as novelties. But the ethological repertory of behaviours, even human behaviours, is limited. In rituals, relatively long strips of behaviour are restored, giving the impression of continuity, stasis, tradition: not only the details but the whole thing is recognizable. In creative arts, especially experimental performance, relatively short strips of behaviour are rearranged and the whole thing looks new. Thus the sense of change we get from experiments may be real at the level of recombination but illusory at the basic structural/processual level. Real change is a very slow evolutionary process.

VIII

D. W. WINNICOTT'S IDEAS add an ontogenetic level and a new set of categories to my description of what the performer does. Winnicott, a British psychoanalyst (now dead), was interested in the mother-baby relationship, particularly how the baby discovers the differences between 'me' and 'not me'. Winnicott proposed a mind/body state between 'me' and 'not me'. This third, intermediate state is a double negative very like Bateson's description of the 'play frame' in his 'Theory of Play and Fantasy'. It also is analogous to Turner's concept of the liminal. Winnicott writes:

> I am here staking a claim for an intermediate state between a baby's inability and his growing ability to recognize and accept reality. I am therefore studying the substance of *illusion*, that

> which is allowed to the infant, and which in adult life is inherent in art and religion.[40]
>
> I think there is use for a term for the root of symbolism in time, a term that describes the infant's journey from the purely subjective to objectivity; and it seems that the transitional object (piece of blanket, etc.) is what we see of this journey of progress toward experiencing.[41]
>
> The transitional object and transitional phenomena start each individual off with what will always be important to them, i.e. a neutral area of experience which will not be challenged.[42]
>
> The important part of this concept is that whereas inner psychic reality has a kind of location in the mind or in the belly or in the head or somewhere within the bounds of the individual's personality, and whereas what is called external reality is located outside these bounds, playing and cultural experience can be given a location if one uses the concepts of the potential space between the mother and the baby.[43]

In babies, and in performers (as adults), the movement from 'not me' to 'not not me' is seen in the following objects and situations:

—a security blanket that a child needs to hold in order to feel good

—favourite toys that can't be replaced

—the script—not just words but the whole pattern of words and actions that during the rehearsal become 'mine'

—necessary props, even some that the audience doesn't see

—the gestures of a role as the role becomes 'mine'

—anything a person acquires, needs, and can't throw away even though a replacement is available and/or the item is of no 'use'

In each of these cases a process occurs in which something that is 'not me' becomes 'mine' in a bodily, deeply felt, ingested way. The thing or action is more than 'mine'—it is 'me'. Or, as I have put it, it is 'not me . . . not not me'. Thus the liminality that Turner identifies at the heart of the ritual process is also an essential part of individual development: at the heart of each person's most private growing. The process is two-directional: some things stop being 'me' and become 'not me':

—mother's breasts

—something deeply 'mine' that I slowly begin to share but never can give away

—'my' body as it is caressed by a loved one

—a performance I'm in going stale

—any favourite thing once treasured but now no longer 'right'

This constant movement in the liminal space 'not me . . . not not me' is the matrix of performance. Olivier is not Hamlet, but he's also not not Hamlet; and the reverse is also true: Hamlet is not Olivier but he is also not not Olivier. And over the centuries of its performing Hamlet (both play and character) takes on the qualities of those who have entered this dynamic, precarious, playful relationship with it.

But what is 'it'? It is any of those things and situations I just named: security blankets, toys, favourite places, smells, associations, Hamlet, artworks, lovers, situations that feel 'just right', fantasies, routines, 'rituals' if you will. Hierarchies of all kinds—ontological, social, aesthetic—are dissolved, set aside for the 'time being' so that people can 'make believe'. Thus in theatre we get a very powerful kind of subversion/deconstruction followed by a reconstruction of realities according to new, playful possibilities. Winnicott goes on:

> The essential feature in the concept of transitional objects and phenomena . . . is the paradox, and the acceptance of the paradox: the baby [the performer] creates the object but the object was there waiting to be created [actions in the script] . . . . We will never challenge the baby [the performer] to elicit an answer to the question: did you create that or did you find it?[44]

A restatement in psychoanalytic terms of Turner's notion of liminality (= transitional). Also a version of the old saw about 'willing suspension of disbelief', which can be translated into my double negative as 'not agreeing to not believe'. Winnicott is saying the player playing Hamlet is not to be interrupted in the middle of 'To be or not to be' and asked: Did you think up those words? Nor is Othello to be stopped while smothering Desdemona and interrogated about the authenticity of his passion. Or if the performer is stopped—as Brecht might do, or Pirandello the audience assumes at once that the interruption is itself part of the script. By script I don't mean just the written play, but the whole score of the performance, including what arrangements have been made to deal with hecklers.[45]

Restored behaviour of all kinds—rituals, theatrical performances, restored villages, *agnicayana*—is 'transitional behaviour'. Elements that are 'not me' move towards becoming 'me', and parts of 'me' move towards becoming 'not me'. The whole process is framed in the negative, the subjunctive, the 'as if'. This is the peculiar but necessary double negativity that characterizes symbolic action in general. Performance is where this double negativity is most visible because in performing, the performer, the 'me', does not disappear as the performance takes shape. A painting may be hung without doing the same to the painter, but a play needs players to be played. More: a performer experiences his own self not directly but through the medium of performance, of what happened during rehearsals, or under the aegis of tradition, of experiencing the Others. While performing, he no longer has a 'me' but a 'not me . . . not not me'. In this way restored behaviour is simultaneously private and social: the performer moves between denying himself in favour of the social reality of the script and denying the social reality of the script in favour of himself. A person performing recovers his own self only by going out of himself, by entering the social field: the 'space between'. A performance 'takes place' in the 'not me . . . not not me' area 'between' performers; 'between' performers and script; 'between' performers, script, and environment; 'between' performers, script, environment, and spectators. The larger the field of the 'not me . . . not not me', the more powerful the performance. It is the ambition of every performance to expand this field until it includes all beings and things and relations. But this field is precarious. The larger it gets, the more doubt and anxiety are aroused.

When everything is going well, the 'between' field, the liminal space, is experienced as the 'ensemble feeling' performers enjoy, the sense of being 'touched' or 'moved' spectators talk about: that special absorption the stage engenders in those who enter on it or come close to it.

By integrating the thought of Winnicott, Bateson, and Turner with my own work as a theatre director, I am proposing a theory that includes the ontogenesis of individuals, the social action of ritual, and the symbolic-fictive action of art. Clearly these overlap. That's because their process is identical. It is the process I've called the 'not me . . . not not me'; the restoration of behaviour; the rehearsal process; the deconstruction-reconstruction of experience through workshop-rehearsal-performance; tradition as expressed in ritual; the play frame; the liminal; the transitional.

The field of performance, the liminal time space, is precarious because it rests not on how things are but on how they are not: that is, it rests on mutuality among participants. It's not that the women in Papua–New Guinea don't know who is behind the masks, but that they agree to proclaim that they don't know. As with Londoners enjoying Olivier, these women do not agree to not believe. Why do I insist on a double negative = a positive instead of a simple positive? Because in the direction of negativity lies potentiality. A choice made denies all choices not made; but a choice not made keeps alive every possibility. Thus a double negative has the existential actuality of a doing while maintaining the full potentiality of the suspended choice. The whole performance is 'not real . . . not not real' at the same time/space. Or, to put it another way, the technical mastery of performing is knowing how to do certain things, achieve levels of skills, pull off tricks. But no matter how phony the show, an audience responds to sincerity, and there is as much sincerity involved in tricking as there is in so-called truth-telling. To perform excellently is to master whatever the craft is: telling the truth, telling lies. This amorality is one of the main things that makes theatre dangerous.

In Fig. 8 I have tried to portray this system. This figure is a version of 1➤5a➤5b.

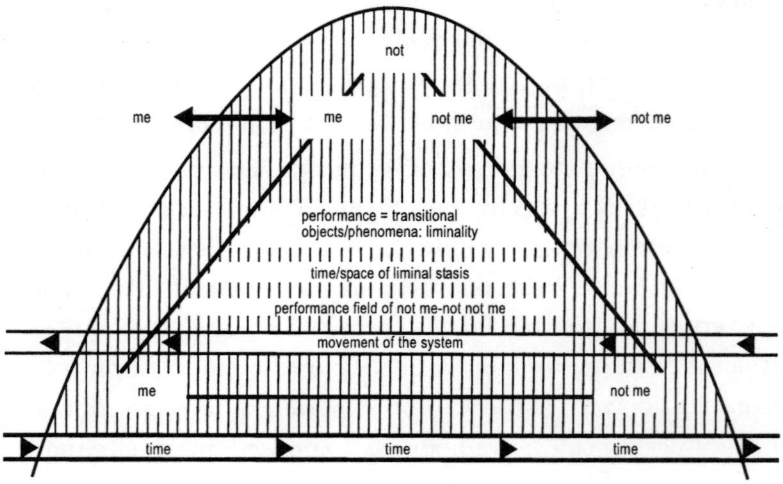

Fig. 8 The me/not me system

Things, actions, people—whatever is being 'worked on' in the performance (and a shaman will work on different orders of being than a stand-up comic, but the process of their working will, I think, be the same)—move from 'not me' towards 'me' and from 'me' towards 'not me'. This constellation of performative elements passes through the time/space of 'not me . . . not not me'. And in this time/space diachronics are abolished. Actions are thrown forward in time— 'keep that', says the director—to be recovered and used later.[46] A show is assembled out of fragments, rehearsed out of order later to be reintegrated into the order, the 'unity', the audience sees; and many details are repeated over and over again. The French word for rehearsal is *répétition* (repetition), and it's apt. Even where there are no rehearsals in this Western sense—as in noh drama—the gestures used have been devised over the centuries and practised in the training for years. It's all restored behaviour. Associations from early in life are juxtaposed with spontaneous interactions happening in the here and now of workshop-rehearsals. Or, as in noh drama and many rituals, in the here and now of performance. The system as a whole moves against the flow of ordinary time. That is, the completed total system is always coming at you from the 'future', where you meet things earlier thrown ahead. During performance, if everything is going well, the experience is of synchronicity, of flow, as ordinary time and performance time eclipse each other.[47] And, as in a solar eclipse, a scintillating corona is briefly visible: a radiance splashing out from the dark core of double negativity. This eclipse/corona is the 'present moment', the 'eternal present', the reactualized *illud tempus*,[48] the ecstasy of trance, liminal stasis, the balancing act of shamans.[49] Great performers are very special because they keep their balance in the presence of onlookers. Not for long.[50]

IX

THE THEATRE OF RICHARD FOREMAN exemplifies this 'liminal-transitional' process. Much in Foreman's work is interesting, but I'll attend to only one thing: the overall arrangement of space and Foreman's place in it. From 1971 to 1979 he wrote, directed, and designed his own productions in his own theatre—a loft about 100 ft deep and 25 ft wide—on lower Broadway. In terms of control Foreman's work belongs more to painting than to theatre: his struggle is with his material, including people, but not against co-creators who might mess up his vision. The audience of 75 sat on steeply rising bleachers facing the long narrow stage area reaching back more than 60. Sometimes this whole tunnel was open to view, and sometimes flats broke or shortened the space [see Fig. 9].

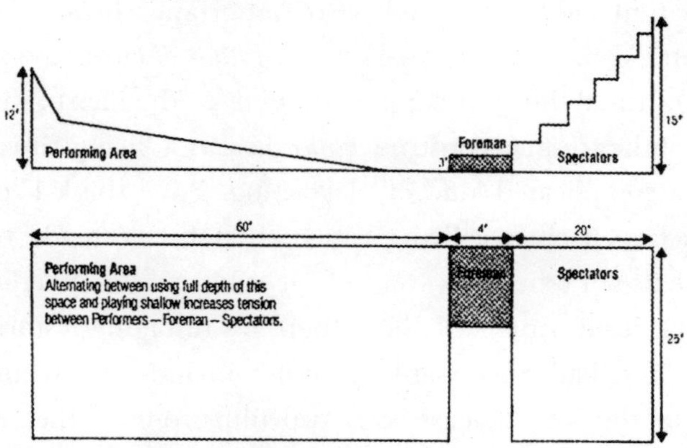

Fig. 9 Performing area in relation to spectators

Foreman himself was located between the performers and the spectators. To the spectators he was a performer, and to the performers he was a spectator. He was 'not a performer. . . not not a performer', 'not a spectator . . . not not a spectator'. Foreman manipulated all the sound, scenic, and light cues himself, and his voice is the one heard on tape giving directions to the performers and making comments on the action. Foreman not only supervised the performance but indirectly entered it. Yet his position is peculiar and precarious. He was 'in transition' and 'liminal' relative to his own work. His actual presence was made ambivalent by his mediated presence as tape-recording, script, director, technician, and designer. In one of his productions he began to resolve this ambivalence by pointing it up. A Sword of Damocles descended from the ceiling and hung inches above his balding skull, at once pointing him out to all in the room and threatening him. In the next production he got up from his seat and entered the stage briefly. Shortly thereafter, he sold his theatre.

X

WHAT ABOUT STAAL AND GARDNER? They entered Kerala as theatrical producers-directors in the guise of anthropological researchers. Not finding a ritual worthy of being filmed, they arranged for one to be performed. They made sure there was enough lead time to get money to make the film and to import a bevy of important scholars. Their lie, if there is one, comes with the marketing of *Altar of Fire* as a document of an ancient ritual they just happened upon. In the nick of time, too. The film's audience may construe *agnicayana* as a 'living ritual' when in fact it's a complicated kind of play-acting. But I think I've shown how play-acting itself is a living ritual, though one made reflexive through the use of rehearsals. *Altar of Fire* is not a film of Vedic ritual. The filming itself ritualizes the action of restaging/restoring the *agnicayana*. Too bad Staal-Gardner didn't include a reflexive consciousness of this—or at least issue two films, one of the ritual 'in itself' and one of their making of the film about it, a kind of Truffautian film of them filming *Altar of Fire*. The same twist is at the heart of restored villages. They aren't a return to earlier centuries but our own epoch's way of ritualizing our daily lives. And like all rituals a visit to a restored village gives one a sense of tradition, of significance, of continuity. And the ritual includes, of course, packing the family into the car and driving off to the village.

Maybe even today most anthropologists would agree with Turner, who said of his own stay with the Ndembu, 'We never asked for a ritual to be performed solely for our own anthropological benefit; we held no brief for such artificial play-acting.'[51] There are two responses to Turner. First, I think the presence of the field worker is an invitation to play-acting. People want their pictures taken, want books written about them, want to show how they are and what they do. Second, what does he propose relative to traditions that are near extinction? Ought we not recognize that in many societies patronage itself has been traditional and has guaranteed the continuation not only of aesthetic but also of ritual forms? How ought we respond to the dooming of many varieties of ritual theatre by modernization? In Karnataka, South India, not too many miles from where Staal-Gardner filmed, Martha Ashton was studying yakshagana, a form of dance-drama hardly ever done according to the old ways. Ashton got a company together drawing on several different groups. She hired actors, singers, musicians. She assisted them in recollecting the old stories: in reconstructing the old steps, music, and training. And she filmed the results of their mutual labours. Was she wrong in doing this? Today there are three styles of yakshagana: the popular version, a style for modern audiences developed by K. S. Karanth, a well-known writer, and the 'classical yakshagana' reassembled by Ashton's troupe. This last style was the one to tour America. Was it the most or the least Indian?

The position of the purists who won't stage the rituals they are studying and recording is not pure but ambivalent. Their position is analogous to that of Foreman, who, in his theatrical productions, sits between his players and his audience, often running a tape recorder that broadcasts his own voice interpreting and asking questions and giving instructions. To the society the field worker temporarily inhabits, he represents his own culture in one of its most inexplicable aspects: why send somebody around the world to observe and record how people live? Why ask all those questions? Why make movies, record songs? What does it mean to embody the contradictory action of a 'participant observer'? But to those who read—or see and hear—the reports of the field worker, he is our big link with both fresh aspects of human nature and the often proposed but never proven thesis that humans comprise one species culturally as well as biologically. As more and more field reports accrue, the exotic annals of human behaviour look less and less exotic: we can detect structural affinities, universal patterns and processes. These are nowhere more apparent than in the arts, which seem to be of a piece from the earliest cave paintings to present-day performances.

The script of the field worker demands a pretended distance, a studied absence: to be present but invisible. Everything is supposed to be as it would if the field worker weren't there. Of course this is a gross fiction, a theatrical convention. The field worker is like the aristocrat preening on the Restoration stage: everyone watches his slightest move, but he's not part of the story. Yes, the field worker's circumstances are theatrical. He exists in a liminal state, a situation in transition. He is not a performer and certainly not a spectator. He's in the middle, like Foreman, between two spheres of actuality, two societies. To each society he represents the other; in each society he is a 'not me . . . not not me'. Foreman put himself precisely where these two actualities press against each other. How can the field worker position himself?

The field worker, like the theatre director, like performers in workshop-rehearsals, goes through the three-phase process Van Gennep mapped out as the preliminal rites of separation, the liminal rites of transition, and the postliminal rites of incorporation.[52] My restatement of this process as it applies to the field worker is:

> 1. The stripping away of his own culture-habits—a brutal *separation* that is the deepest struggle of fieldwork, which is never completed, learning 'to see with a native eye'. The field worker always lives 'in between'. So does the director who is part of the audience to the performers and part of the performers to the audience.

2. The finding out of what's 'new' in the society he is temporarily a part of, or 'partner of'. This is the field worker's *transition*: his new role, identity, position, status in regard to his adoptive culture. The theatre director works in a similar way to understand and then draw from the performer's 'material'.

3. The task of using field-notes, or whatever, to compose an acceptable monograph, film, whatever: something that's 'true to' both his adopted people and his home culture. The director must find a way to make a production 'work'. If successful, the field worker becomes a professor, the director is given new works to direct: their *incorporation* is completed.

The field worker is no novelist freely transforming his own actual or fantasy experiences; nor is he a 'hard scientist' building models strictly fenced off from ordinary life.

More and more—especially as films, photographs, and tape cassettes become his tools—the field worker is like the theatre director—the evoker-observer who participates and keeps a distance at the same time; the collector of items to be 'thrown forward' in time and made into a unified construct that 'comes after' but is not necessarily 'true to' its sources: a restorer of behaviour. The field worker, like the director, is present at the mid-phase of making a production but apparently absent at its inception (script making) and conclusion (performance for a public); he does not author the script but somehow guarantees its realization before an audience. The field worker doesn't create the societies he studies, but his presence gives these cultures a special significance, a reverberation felt both among those he studies and back home where his productions find their niche. The field worker, like the director, is the embodiment of linkage, the essence of in between.

Now theatre directors are leaving the shadowy area out of sight off stage. They are entering the stage, as Foreman did, as Tadeusz Kantor, the director of *The Dead Class*, does when all during the show he talks to, manipulates, and coaches the performers: the play is set, rehearsed, but also taking new shapes right before our noses. This doesn't make the director a performer just like the others, just as the field worker isn't a hard scientist or novelist, but a special kind of performer, a master of liminality, a specialist in reflexivity. He is always working the 1→5a→5b, the 'not me . . . not not me'. Field workers and theatre directors are restorers of behaviour. The time is on us when field workers, like directors, produce for us not only versions of faraway cultures but performative works of our own multiple actualities. In an epoch of hyperconsciousness we are concerned with knowing how we know what we know: restoration of behaviour is the industry of the future. Theatre workers, field workers: we are one with the clowns and jugglers, the double agents and dissimulators, the con men and shamans.

Earlier versions of some parts of this article have appeared in A Crack in the Mirror: Reflexive Perspectives in Anthropology, *Jay Ruby ed. (University of Pennsylvania Press, 1981).*

Notes

1. Labanotation, roughly analogous to musical notation, was developed by Rudolf von Laban in 1928. According to an article in *New York Times* (6 May 1979: 'Arts and Leisure', p. 19) by Jack Anderson: 'The system records dance movement by means of symbols on a page that is read from the bottom up. Three basic vertical lines represent the body's centre, right, and left sides. Where the symbols are placed on the lines indicates the direction of the movement, and their length indicates the movement's duration.'
2. Suzanne Youngerman, 'The Translation of a Culture into Choreography', in *Essays in Dance Research*, ed. Dianne L. Woodruff (Dance Research Annual IX, N.Y.: CORD, 1978), p. 95.

3. Edward Deming Andrews, 'The Dance in Shaker Ritual', in *Chronicles of American Dance*, ed. P. D. Magriel (N.Y.: Henry Holt, 1948); *The People Called Shakers* (N.Y.: Dover, 1963); *The Gift to be Simple: Songs, Dances and Ritual of the American Shakers* (N.Y.: Dover, 1967). Andrews had done more research than anyone on the Shaker rituals.
4. Robin Evanchuk, 'Problems in Reconstructing a Shaker Religious Dance Ritual', in *Journal of the Association of Graduate Dance Ethnologists*, I: Fall–Winter (Los Angeles: UCLA, 1977–78), p. 22.
5. Youngerman, op. cit., p. 106.
6. For my ideas about performances that 'actualize'—and therefore a sense of what I felt 11 years ago about this whole problem—see Schechner, 'Drama, Script, Theatre, and Performance'; and 'Actuals: A Look into Performance Theory', *in Essays on Performance Theory 1970–76* (N.Y.: Drama Book Specialists, 1977).
7. All Emigh citations from a letter he distributed to a few persons concerning his 1975 work in West Irian. Emigh was trying to establish connections relating Balinese performance to West Irian, and other Micronesian performance styles. Most of Emigh's stuff has not yet been published, but I think he is on to establishing a stratum of performance including masks, dance styles, and relationship to sacred geography that was/is present across vast areas of the Pacific. W. H. Rassers, *Panji, The Culture Hero* (The Hague: Martinus Nijhoff, 1959), has shown a definite relationship between Balinese shadow puppetry and Sepik River ceremonies. In performance people tend to be technologically conservative, always maintaining to a degree the ideas that Grotowski gathered under the banner of 'poor theatre'. This keeping out of old ideas of how to do things also preserves, almost in archaeological layers, old belief systems and behaviours too. These are constantly being worn away and then restored.
8. Frits Staal, 'The Meaninglessness of Ritual' (manuscript, 1978). Staal bases much of his argument on the 1975 *agnicayana*.
9. I got the shooting script when I was in Kerala in 1976. The script gives detailed instructions to camera people, technicians, etc. It also provides drawings of the site, altars, and background material.
10. Robert A. Paul, 'Review of *Altar of Fire*', in *American Anthropologist*, 80 (1978), pp. 197–9. Frits Staal, 'Response to Robert A. Paul', in *American Anthropologist*, 81 (1979), pp. 346–7.

11. Alan Lomax, 'Cinema, Science, and Cultural Renewal', in *Current Anthropology*, 14:4 (1973), p. 480.
12. Kapila Vatsyayan, *Indian Classical Dance* (New Delhi: Publications Division, 1974), pp. 15–16.
13. Kapila Vatsyayan, *Classical Indian Dance in Literature and the Arts* (New Delhi: Sangeet Natak Akademi, 1968), pp. 325, 365. Vatsyayan's opinion is universally shared by other dance scholars in India.
14. Milton Singer, *When a Great Tradition Modernizes* (London: Pall Mall Press, 1972), p. 172.
15. Asutosh Bhattacharyya, *Chhau Dance of Purulia* (Calcutta: Rabindra Bharati University Press, 1972), p. 15.
16. Ibid., p. 23.
17. Ibid., p. 24.
18. Ibid., Introduction.
19. Bhattacharyya, 1975 programme used on 22 February, University of Michigan, p. 3
20. Until John Emigh told me about Mead's account I thought *Trance and Dance* wholly 'authentic'. It proves how easily I can fall into the very trap I'm warning others against. To many American students *Trance and Dance* is the most powerful example of what Balinese trance 'really is'.
21. Maurice J. Moran, Jr., 'Living Museums: Coney Islands of the Mind' (Master's thesis, New York University School of Arts, Department of Drama (now Performance Studies), 1978), p. 25.
22. Ibid., p. 31.
23. Ibid., p. 36.
24. Ibid., pp. 40–1.
25. Ibid., p. 50.
26. Ibid., p. 51.
27. From a three-page mimeograph information paper dated '2/80', sent to me by Ingram, pp. 1-2.
28. From a letter sent by Ingram to Jay Ruby, dated 30 April 1981.
29. From a newspaper article by Tim Miller describing how roles are cast

and prepared, in *The Old Colony Memorial* (Plymouth, Massachusetts, 2 April 1981).

30. The repartee between centuries is sometimes seasoned with nice ironies. A visitor at Plimoth apologized for interrupting a craftsperson with questions. 'As many as you like, sir', the performer responded. 'I have a few questions meself about your time period'. For more on restored villages, theme parks, and related entertainment-performance environments see Irwin Haas, *America's Historic Villages and Restorations* (Secaucus: Citadel Press, 1974); Gary Kriazi, *The Great American Amusement Park* (Secaucus: Citadel Press, 1976); and Patricia Mackay, 'Theme Parks', in *Theatre Crafts*, September 1977, pp. 27ff. And James H. Bierman, Department of Theatre Arts, University of California, Santa Cruz, has lots of material on the Disney enterprises.
31. Mimeo paper dated 2/80, p. 2.
32. Ingram letter, 1981.
33. See note 29 (Miller).
34. Mimeo paper dated 2/80, p. 3.
35. From a newspaper article by Tom Reilly in the *Sippican Sentinel* (Marion, Massachusetts, 29 April 1981).
36. *New York Times* (Sunday, 5 March 1978).
37. Victor Turner, *The Ritual Process* (Chicago: Aldine, 1969), p. 95.
38. Ibid., p. 103.
39. I use this same figure in another essay where I consider the relationship between 'social drama' and 'aesthetic drama'. There theatrical techniques are the hidden, implicit underbelly of social and political action—the dramatic ordering of events; and conversely, social and political action underly theatrical works. Thus it is not proper to speak as Aristotle did of 'art imitating life'. But neither is it true that 'all the world's a stage'. Together these statements make up the poles of a dialectical, dynamic process by which artistic action creates possibilities for living and events in ordinary life provide material and models for art. The whole bundle must be looked at as a single system. See my *Essays on Performance Theory 1970–76* (N.Y.: Drama Book

Specialists, 1977) for a discussion of the relationship between social and aesthetic drama. The visual pun with infinity was not at first intended when I drew the figure. Later, becoming aware of it, I was not unpleased.

40. W. D. Winnicott, *Playing and Reality* (London: Tavistock, 1971), p. 3.

4I. Ibid., p.6.

42. Ibid., p. 12.

43. Ibid., p. 53

44. Ibid., p. 89. I thank Cynthia Mintz for pointing out to me the importance of this paradox and how it applies to performing.

45. In 'Drama, Script, Theatre, and Performance', I discuss in detail the relationship among these various magnitudes and dimensions of performance.

46. I discuss the rehearsal process—and compare it to the ritual process as described by Birdwhistel and Lorenz, in 'Towards a Poetics of Performance'.

47. For a detailed discussion of flow, and reports on how it feels to experience flow, see Mihaly Csikszentmihalyi, *Beyond Boredom and Anxiety* (San Francisco: Jossey Bass, 1975). As he says: 'Perhaps the clearest sign of flow is the merging of action and awareness. A person in the flow has no dualistic perspective: he is aware of his actions but not of the awareness itself. . . . Typically, a person can maintain a merged awareness with his or her actions for only short periods' (p. 38).

48. I use the Latin in Mircea Eliade's sense when the mythic or original time is 'reactualized' and made present for the 'time being' of the performance. Among Eliade's many books see especially *Rites and Symbols of Initiation* (N.Y.: Harper, 1965), and *Shamanism: Archaic Techniques of Ecstasy* (Princeton: Princeton University Press, 1970).

49. Barbara Myerhoff, 'Balancing Between Worlds: The Shaman's Calling', in *Parabola*, 1:2 (1976), pp. 6-13.

50. Except for some: At Kumbh mela in Prayag I saw a man who claimed to have stood on one leg for eighteen years. 'The greatest mela of all is the Kumbh mela at Prayag', writes Ved Mehta. This is so because at Prayag (modern Allahabad) the mela takes place at the *sangam*

(Sanskrit 'joining'), the place where the sacred river Jamuna meets the sacred river Ganga. There these rivers are joined by the mythical underground river Saraswati. Kumbh mela at Prayag happens during the dry season, in January, and the rivers are low. A vast city of tents is pitched on the dry river bed. And in 1977, when I was there, between dawn and noon on the most sacred day, some 3 million people bathed from a triangle of sand no larger than a New York City block like the triangle formed at Broadway and 42nd Street, Times Square. Assembled that January, as for every Kumbh mela, were mystics, fakirs, avatars, sadhus, pilgrims, tourists, scholars, performers, merchants, beggars—seekers of every kind. The man standing on one leg was a big draw. Crowds pressed in to see him, his face painted in white and red, his right eye bulging, his whole upper torso twisted to the right, his head askew and looking up over his right shoulder. He supported himself with a staff and leaned against a board. His left leg was tucked behind him, bound to his thigh with cloth. His right leg, from the knee down, and right foot were swollen enormously, the blood and other fluids having drained down to there. The admiring crowd pressed in on him with gazes, small change, and many advanced to offer sweets at his elephant's leg or fed some directly to him as the Hindu gods are offered *prasad*. He talked in a rough voice, coarse and loud, laughed and enjoyed himself. Also he seemed to be in pain. I asked one of his companions-guardians-keepers how he slept, defecated, did the ordinary things of life. 'This way, the way you see him, always, day and night, for so many years, the same.'

51. But now, more than a quarter of a century later, and deep into the practice of what he calls the 'anthropology of experience', Turner himself is helping American students stage some of the rituals he and his wife, Edith Turner, observed among the Ndembu. See Turner, 'Dramatic Ritual/Ritual Drama: Performative and Reflexive Anthropology', in *Kenyon Review*, 1:3 (1979), pp. 80–93.

52. Van Gennep originally published his ideas about liminality in 1908. Particularly through the work of Turner these ideas are still very alive and developing. See Van Gennep, *The Rites of Passage* (Chicago:

University of Chicago Press, 1960). Also Turner, *The Ritual Process* (Chicago: Aldine, 1969); *The Ritual Process: Dramas, Fields, and Metaphors* (Ithaca; Cornell University Press, 1974); 'Dramatic Ritual/Ritual Drama: Performative and Reflexive Anthropology', *in Kenyon Review*, 1:3 (1979), pp. 80-93; and forthcoming *From Ritual to Theatre* (working title, N.Y.: Performing Arts Journal Publications).

Performers and Spectators transported and transformed

By using masks, costumes, and physical actions arranged in a set way, or improvised according to known rules; by performing following a script, scenario, or set of rules; by performing in special places or places made special by performing in them; by performing on holidays or at times set aside 'after work' or at crises in the life cycle such as initiations, weddings, and funerals: by all these means, and more, theatrical reality is marked 'non-ordinary—for special use only'. Furthermore, what is performed is encoded—I want to say nested, trapped, contained, distilled, held, restrained, metaphorized—in one, or more, special kinds of communication: either as a mixture of narrative and Hindu temple service as in Ramlila; or as fixed narrative and individual creativity as in any of the productions of, say, Chekhov's *The Cherry Orchard*; or as a well-known sequence of events better known to connoisseurs than to common spectators as in the *kuse mai* of the noh drama *Yorimasa* as performed by the Kanze school; or as closely guarded secrets revealed to initiates during the performance itself as in the vomiting and bleeding that is part of the initiation of Gahuku boys in Papua–New Guinea; or as a script imposed by a single writer-director-scenographer such as with Richard Foreman's *Pain(t)*; or as words and actions devised collectively as with *Mysteries and Smaller Pieces* of The Living Theatre; or as a scenario sent to hundreds of people, some of them friends, some strangers, to be acted (or discarded) separately, and in many different styles, by recipients of one of Allan Kaprow's happenings. This Homeric list may exhaust you, reader, but not the field. They are mere smatterings of evidence of the incredible diversity of performance events. And I have pointedly omitted events like the Mass, professional football, psychodrama, whirling dervishes in devotion, Sumo wrestling: a wide variety of performative rituals, games, sports, and hard-to-define activities that lie between or outside established genres. After all, 'established genre' indicates a record of what has found its place, while performance activities are fundamentally processual: there will always be a certain proportion of them in the process of transformation, categorically undefinable. But all performances—defined and undefined—-share at least one underlying quality. Performance behaviour isn't free and easy. Performance behaviour is known and/or practised behaviour—or 'twice-behaved behaviour', 'restored behaviour'[1]—either rehearsed, previously known, learned by osmosis since early childhood, revealed during the performance by masters, guides, gurus, or elders, or generated by rules that govern the outcomes as in improvisatory theatre or sports.

Because performance behaviour isn't free and easy it never wholly 'belongs to' the performer. In Euro-American theatre (Stanislavski and after) much of the work of training and rehearsal makes performance behaviour seem 'as if' it belongs to the performer.

> Because the very best that can happen is to have the actor completely carried away by the play. Then regardless of his own will he lives the part, not noticing *how* he feels, not thinking about *what* he does, and it all moves of its own accord, subconsciously and intuitively.[2]

But Stanislavski well knew that this kind of intuitive flow is unreliable. Thus the 'Stanislavski system' is largely devoted to training the actor so that flow can be generated through a conscious process. But such a seamless knitting of the 'life of' the character and that of the actor is not the goal of all theatre everywhere. In the West, Brecht distrusted it, but Brecht himself modelled his ideal actor—one who alternated between flow and reflexivity, between 'being the character' and speaking about the character—after what he had learned of Asian theatre, especially Chinese theatre. And in the Ramlila of Ramnagar, India's best-known Ramlila, the directors of the spectacle, the *vyases*, stand behind the performers, open regiebuchs in hand, correcting words and actions: making certain that everything happens according to the book. Interestingly, the crowds at Ramlila are not troubled into supposing that the actions of Ram or Hanuman are any less 'real' due to the presence of the *vyases*, or even their intervention. But clearly the 'life of' Ram and Hanuman intersect but are not identical to the 'life of' the actors. Like the presence of director-author T. Kantor during the performances of his *The Dead Class*—where Kantor makes slight adjustments in the performance by lowering a performer's hand, or whispering to another to speed up the delivery of some lines—the corrections of the performance become part of the performance. The stage—and I don't mean only the physical place, but the time/space/spectator/performer aggregate—generates a centripetal field that gobbles up whatever happens on it or near it. This absorption into the centre is the chief parallel between performance process and ritual process; it's what Kafka meant when he wrote the mini-parable:

> Leopards break into the temple and drink to the dregs what is in the sacrificial pitchers; this is repeated over and over again; finally it can be calculated in advance, and it becomes part of the ceremony.[3]

After some performances Kantor's corrections became predictable; people who saw *The Dead Class* many times say that Kantor's gestures are no longer free but part of the performance score. But even the intervening-when-needed, and therefore unpredictable, actions of the *vyases* at Ramlila are part of the performance score—just as the officials moving in and out of a football game intervene only when there is an infraction but still play decisive and well-defined roles in the game.

As Kafka says, accidents become part of the ceremony, even adding a special thrill. During the 1980 Ringling Brothers Circus at Madison Square Garden, a trapeze artist attempts to rise from a position where she is hanging by her ankles. She starts, hesitates, reaches, almost falls. The music stops, the crowd gasps—if she cannot reach the bar she will drop 40 feet. Finally, inching her way up, grabbing her left forearm with her right hand, she reaches the bar. The music crescendos, the crowd sighs in relief and then cheers. The whole bit is repeated each show. It doesn't matter whether this bit actually happened once and then was kept as business, or whether it was invented wholesale. It is now 'calculated in advance': part of the show. And each show—of theatre, sports, ritual—is a palimpsest collecting, or stacking, and displaying whatever is, as Brecht says, 'the least rejected of all the things tried'. But the performance process is a continuous rejecting and replacing. Long-running shows—and certainly rituals are these—are not dead repetitions but continuous erasings and superimposings. The overall shape of the show stays the same, but pieces of business are always coming and going. This process of collecting and discarding, of selecting, organizing, and showing, is what rehearsals are all about. And it's not such a rational, logical-linear process as writing about it makes it seem. It's not so much a thought-out system of trial and error as it is a playing around with themes, actions, gestures, fantasies, words: whatever's being worked on. From all the doing, some things are done again and again; they are perceived in retrospect as 'working', and they are 'kept'. They are, as it were, thrown forward in time to be used in the 'finished performance'. The performance 'takes shape' little bit by little bit, building from the fragments of 'kept business' so that often the final scene of a show will be clear before its first scene—or specific bits will be perfected before a sense of the overall production is known. That is why the text of a play will tell you so little about how a production might look. The production doesn't 'come out' of the text, but is generated in rehearsal in an effort to 'meet' the text. And when you see a play and recognize it as familiar you are referring back to earlier productions, not to the playscript. An unproduced play is not a homunculus but a shard of an as yet unassembled whole.

During the run of a play—or over the calendrically fixed course of the performances of a ritual—even in the most traditional genres (I've seen noh, Ramlila, kathakali, and Balinese dance-drama do this) new business is accumulated and stale business eliminated. A person going to a particular performance only once, as is the habit in our culture, can't notice the process of continuous change. Sometimes, where a performance is frozen tight, it takes great effort, and ceremony, to update the show: as when a Pope summons a Council to revise the Mass. But on the local level, the Mass is always being adjusted to suit the living relationship between priest and parishioners. This relationship is as much one between performer and participating spectators as between religious leader and faithful. Individual performative variation will be appreciated even more when you recognize that a performance of the Mass far transcends the recitation of a set text: it involves the particular and peculiar styles of the performers. And as with the Mass, so with all ceremonies/rituals everywhere.

I wrote before that performing isn't free and easy: it is behaviour that is 'put on'. This is what gives theatre its bad name. Theatre is that art where the master teacher says, 'Truth is what acting is all about; once you can fake truth you've got it made.' This is not a wholly cynical statement, as can be seen in the story Lévi-Strauss tells of Quesalid, a Kwakiutl who wanted to expose the quackery of the shamans.[4] 'Driven by curiosity about their tricks and by the desire to expose them, he began to associate with the shamans until one of them offered to make him a member of their group. Quesalid did not wait to be asked twice.' He was thoroughly trained in acting, magic, singing; he learned how to fake fainting and fits, how to induce vomiting and to employ spies who would tell him about the lives of his patients. He learned how to hide a wad of down in the corner of his mouth and then, biting his tongue or making his gums bleed, to produce this bloody evidence before patient and spectators as 'the pathological foreign body extracted as a result of his sucking and manipulations'. Quesalid mastered the art so well that he not only exposed the other shamans as quacks but built a powerful reputation for himself as a true shaman. Over the years he began to believe in his cures, even though he always knew that they were based on tricks. But he reasoned that the ill got better because they believed in him, and they believed in him because he knew his art so well and performed it so stunningly. Finally he thought of the bloody down and all his other tricks as manifestations of his own authentic powers. As Lévi-Strauss says: 'Quesalid did not become a great shaman because he cured his patients; he cured his patients because he had become a great shaman.' Quesalid, like the leopards in Kafka's parable, was absorbed into the field of his own performing. He was transformed into what he had set out to expose.[5]

At the Ramlila of Ramnagar, India, one of the best actors is the man who plays the semi-divine sage, Narad-muni. When Narad-muni speaks or sings the audience—sometimes of more than 25,000—listens with special care; many believe the performer playing Narad-muni has powers linking him to the sage/character he plays. This man is no longer called by his born name, not even by himself. Over the 35 years he has performed Narad-muni he has increasingly been identified with the legendary sage. Because he is a brahman, and any brahman can perform priestly ceremonies, Narad began some years ago to practise priestcraft. Now he is the *mahant*—owner and chief priest—of two temples in Mirzapur, a city about 40 miles from Ramnagar. He is rich. People come from far away to his temples because they know Narad-muni speaks through Narad-priest. Narad never claims to be an incarnation of Narad-muni. But each year at Ramlila his connection to Narad-muni is renewed, displayed, deepened, and ritualized before an audience of thousands. This man is not Narad-muni, but also he is not not Narad-muni: he performs in the field between a negative and a double negative, a field of limitless potential, free as it is from both the person (not) and the person impersonated (not not). All effective performances share this 'not—not not' quality: Olivier is not Hamlet, but also he is not not Hamlet: his performance is between a denial of being another (= I am me) and a denial of not being another (= I am Hamlet). Performer training focuses its techniques not on making one person into another, but in permitting the performer to act in-between identities; in this sense performing is a paradigm of liminality.

Indian culture with its tradition of reincarnation encourages this kind of multiplication of impersonations. When the beautiful black god Krishna was desired by all of the *gopis*, he multiplied himself so that each woman had Krishna with her: this theme is a favourite of Indian artists, both visual and performative, and forms the praxiscore of many kinds of Krishna worship.[6] And who is the 'genuine' Hamlet? Olivier? Burton? Bernhardt? Or Burbage, who played it first in 1603? Or a nameless English actor who toured France even earlier in a lost play now known only as the *ur-Hamlet*? This question of multiple realities, each the negativity of all the others, does not merely point to a peculiarity of the stage, but rather locates the essence of performance: at once the most concrete and evanescent of the arts. And in so far as performance is a main model for human behaviour in general, this liminal, processual, multi-real quality reveals both the glory and the abyss of human freedom.

Few are the performers who have experienced Narad's transformation. Even at Ramlila most performers don't get absorbed into their roles. This is not to say the roles don't deeply affect the performer's lives. In approaching the village where the family who have played the demon-king Ravana lives, I was told that 'Ravan-raj [King Ravana] lives over there'. Everyone knows Ravana: he is royalty among peasants. The family has grown rich since the time in the 1860s that a forefather was picked through audition by the Maharaja of Benares to play Ravana. And over the years the situation of that family has become more and more a structural antithesis to that of the boys who play Ram and his brothers, the protagonists of the Ramlila and arch-enemies of Ravana, whose role is roughly analogous to that of Satan in *Paradise Lost*. The boys are picked by audition yearly; they mostly come from city families and are educated; after their stint in Ramlila most enter professions ranging from the priesthood to journalism and acting. During the 31 days of the cycle play the boys playing Ram and his brothers live in seclusion in three different dharamsalas in Ramnagar—moving along with the play itself to different locations;

Ravana returns each night the several miles to his native place: like his mythic Lanka he lives away from Ram, Hanuman, Sugriva, or any of their party. But at the climax of the cycle, when Ravana is killed in battle by Ram, the performer signifies this moment by taking off his ten-headed mask and prostrating himself before Ram, kissing his feet. But again, I ask, who is doing the kissing? The actor without his mask is doing devotion to the boy who, with his sacred crown, is Ram-incarnate. Both man and boy are 'between personae', in that liminal, double-negative field where they are neither themselves nor their roles. And if few performers have experienced Narad's transformation, most have felt Ravan-raj's and Ram's doubling: the sense of being taken over by a role, of being possessed by it—in its 'flow', or in the flow of the audience's appetite for illusion: *ludus*, lila: play.

This surrender to the flow of action is the ritual process. Here it is that the two root meanings of *ri* converge: the action is orderly, even numerical—'play it by the numbers'—but the sense of being in it is, as Csikszentmihalyi says, 'the merging of action and awareness. A person in flow has no dualistic perspective: he is aware of his actions but not of the awareness itself.'[7] 'The steps for experiencing flow . . . involve the . . . process of delimiting reality, controlling some aspect of it, and responding to the feedback with a concentration that excludes anything else as irrelevant.'[8] Or as Ryczard Cieslak, the great actor who performed in many of Grotowski's works, told me:

> The score is like a glass inside which a candle is burning. The glass is solid; it is there, you can depend on it. It contains and guides the flame. But it is not the flame. The flame is my inner process each night. The flame is what illuminates the score, what the spectators see through the score. The flame is alive. Just as the flame in the glass moves, flutters, rises, falls, almost goes out, suddenly glows brightly, responds to each breath of wind—so my inner life varies from night to night, from moment to moment . . . I begin each night without anticipations. This is the hardest thing to learn. I do not prepare

> myself to feel anything. I do not say, 'Last night, this scene was extraordinary, I will try to do that again.' I want only to be receptive to what will happen. And I am ready to take what happens if I am secure in my score, knowing that, even if I feel a minimum, the glass will not break, the objective structure worked out over the months will help me through. But when a night comes that I can glow, shine, live, reveal—I am ready for it by not anticipating it. The score remains the same, but everything is different because I am different.[9]

Cieslak is the Zen master for whom the moment of action is when all the preparation falls away: what remains is readiness. As Shakespeare says, 'ripeness is all'.

When the performance is over Cieslak 'cools down'. Often he drinks vodka, talks, smokes a lot of cigarettes. Getting out of the role is sometimes harder than getting into it. Little work has been done on the 'cool-down', at least in the Euro-American tradition. Here the emphasis is on training, rehearsal, and warm-up. In Bali, by contrast, there are rituals for cooling down including sprinkling with holy water, inhalation of incense, massage, and even sacrifice of animals and blood sprinkling. What the cool-down does is return the performer to an ordinary sphere of existence: to transport him back to where he began. Acting, in most cases, is the art of temporary transformation: not only the journey out but also the return. Quesalid and Narad both, over the long run, gave in to their roles; Cieslak knows how to prepare and be ready to flow with his role. But he has hardly an inkling of what to do afterwards. And some roles effect a swift and permanent transformation, as in initiation rites and other 'rites of passage'. I am interested in these different kinds of changes that occur within performers—and the concomitant changes that happen in an audience — not from a psychological point of view, but as a baseline from which to project several stops along a continuum of performance types. This continuum will tell something about performance in a number of cultures, and also interculturally. The continuum runs from those performances where the performer is changed through the 'work' of the performance to those in which he is transported and returned to his starting place. A vertical axis of this continuum would show whether transformation occurs gradually, as with Quesalid and Narad, or suddenly, as when a Gahuku boy is changed into a man through the work of a single set of initiatory performances. And also I will show how often these two kinds of performances—transportative and transformative—occur together, working together.

I call performances where performers are changed 'transformations' and those where performers are returned to their starting places 'transportations'. 'Transportation' because during the performance the performers are 'taken somewhere' but at the end, often assisted by others, they are 'cooled down' and re-enter ordinary life just about where they went in [Fig. 1].

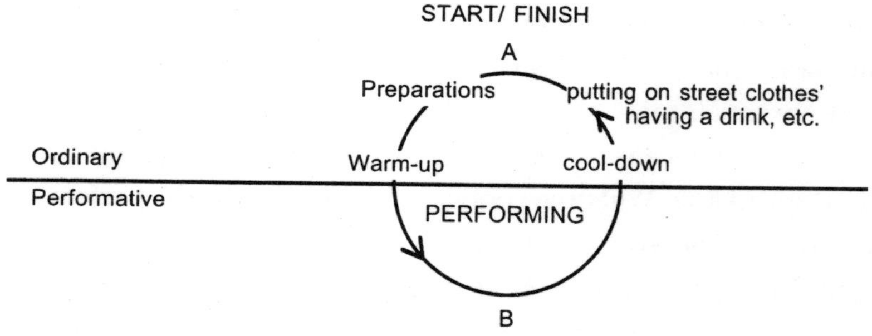

Fig. 1

The performer goes from the 'ordinary world' to the 'performative world' from one time/space reference to another, from one personality to one or more others. He plays a character, battles demons, goes into a trance, travels to the sky or under the sea or earth: he is transformed, enabled to do things 'in performance' he cannot ordinarily. But when the performance is over, or even as a final phase of the performance, he returns to where he started. Otherwise he is left hanging—as some movie actors, not all happily, have found out. If John Wayne was satisfied in becoming (like Narad) what he portrayed, Bela Lugosi was not. I do want to point out that if a change occurs within the performer, or in his status, it happens only over a long series of performances, each of which moves the performer slightly [Fig. 2].

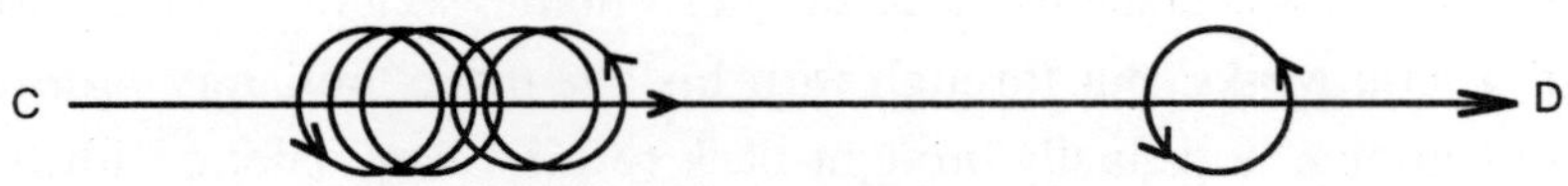

Fig. 2

This is what happened to Narad and John Wayne. Thus each separate performance is a transportation, ending about where it began, while a series of transportation performances can achieve a transformation. It's not my task here to describe the ways the ordinary world is different from the performative world. In some kinds of performances—trance dancing, for example—extreme care is exercised in bringing the performer out of trance. This is so because trance exhibits both a quality of personality change and involuntariness: the trancer clearly needs help 'coming back', while the character actor appears to be in control of himself. We might even say that there are two kinds of transportations—the voluntary and the involuntary—and that character acting belongs to the first category and trance to the second. However, in watching trance—and seeing many films depicting it—I suspect that the difference between these kinds of transportations has been overemphasized. The character actor is self-starting (at least if he has orthodox Euro-American training), but once warmed-up and in the flow of things he is quite deeply involved in what Keats called the 'negative capability' and what I've schemed out as the 'not me—not not me'. The character actor in flow is not himself but he is not not himself at the same time. Also, trance performers are frequently very conscious of their actions even while performing them; and they too undergo training and warm-up. The difference between these kinds of performance may be more in labelling and cultural expectations than in their performance processes.

Transformation performances are clearly evidenced in initiation rites, whose very purpose it is to transform people from one status or social identity to another. An initiation not only marks a change but is itself the means by which persons achieve their new selves: no performance, no change. Kenneth E. Read tells how a Papua-New Guinea boy, Asemo, was taken from his mother's home, secluded in the bush for several weeks, put through with his age-mates initiatory ordeals and training, and finally brought back to his village (along with his age-mates) transformed into a man. Read lets us know that the underlying action of the initiation is performative. To give but two examples, after two weeks of seclusion the boys are brought back to Susuroka, their village:

> The noise and movement were overwhelming. Behind us, the shrill voices of women rose in keening, ritual, stylized cries informed by genuine emotion that were like a sharp instrument stabbing into the din around me. The ululating notes of male voices locked with thumping shouts, deep drumbeats expelled from distended chests counterpointed the crash of bare feet on the ground, and, rising above it all, came the cries of the flutes.[10]
>
> Asemo and his age-mates were somewhere in the middle of the throng, almost certainly blinded by the dust, carried along by the press of stronger bodies . . . Other youths had told me, laughing, of their panic during these opening minutes of their day-long ordeal.[11]

This ordeal included forced vomiting and nosebleeding. Read describes how Asemo and the other boys were 'sadly bedraggled' and 'dejected' and 'limp'. Literally exhausted, the boys were carried, dragged, and pushed into running a gauntlet where Gahuku women attacked the men and boys with 'stones and lethal pieces of wood, an occasional axe, and even a few bows and arrows'. The men picked the boys up and put them on their shoulders and together they ran through no-man's-land.

> The men had bunched together as they ran, so closely packed that they struck each other with their legs and arms. In the centre of the throng the initiates, riding the shoulders of their

> escorts, swayed precariously from side to side, their fingers clutching the feathered hair of the head between their legs.[12]

Read says 'there was no mistaking the venom in the assault' of the women; and the men didn't think of the attack as a 'ceremonial charade' but recognized that it 'teetered on the edge of virtual disaster'. On the edge, but not over: the attack was contained within its performative boundaries much the way a bloody hockey game barely but reliably remains a game. The ordeal, the gauntlet, the attack: these are all 'twice-behaved behaviours'—scored, expected, performed.

Six weeks later the 'final act was played out in the . . . village'. Asemo spent those weeks absorbing training. The day of his coming out—a day of feasting and dancing—culminated in the presentation of the initiates to the whole village. This time the women didn't assault the men but greeted them with a 'rising chorus of welcoming calls'. Then the initiates danced as a group, without the assistance or protection of the older men.

> They moved unsteadily under the ungainly decorations, and I failed to see the splendid stirring change that had been apparent to their elders' eyes. But dignity touched them when they began to dance, a slow measure based on the assertive stepping of the men but held to a restrained, promenading pace by the weight [of the headdresses] they carried on their heads. For a moment I was one with the crowd of admirers.[13]

Asemo and his age-mates had become men in the Gahuku scheme of things. During and after his day of dancing Asemo was a male Gahuku with the responsibilities and privileges of that status. Abolition of the initiation rites—and Read thought when he wrote *The High Valley* in 1965 that they would not be performed again—signals a shift in the whole basis of Gahuku society. That is because the initiation doesn't merely mark a change that has occurred elsewhere in the social scheme—as bar-mitzvah, graduation, or entrance into a professional association usually do in the Euro-American context—but is in its whole duration the machine that works the changes transforming boys into men. Without this machine Gahuku boys will be different kinds of men. To be taken from Susuroka, to undergo the ordeals, to be trained in lore and dancing, to return and dance: that process equals becoming a Gahuku man. This status—whatever its personal meanings and effects, whatever private styles it accommodates—is fundamentally social, public, and objective. It does not determine what kind of Gahuku man Asemo will be, or even how he feels about it, any more than a wedding ceremony determines what kind of husband the groom will be. But definite acts have been performed. These acts accomplish a transformation.

People are accustomed to calling transportation performances 'theatre' and transformation performances 'ritual'. But this neat separation doesn't hold up. Mostly the two kinds of performances coexist in the same event. Just as Asemo and his age-mates were being transformed, the Gahuku men who vomited and bled with them, who carried them on their shoulders through the attack by the women, who trained them to dance—these men were transported, not transformed. They were trainers, guides, and co-performers. Those who no longer change—or who do not change 'this time', through the work of this performance—effect the changes wrought in the transformed. This relationship can be figured this way [Fig. 3].

The experienced performers enter the performance and share in its actions of bleeding, vomiting, gauntlet-running. But when the performance is over, the already-initiated Gahuku men re-enter ordinary life approximately where they left it. If any change among them

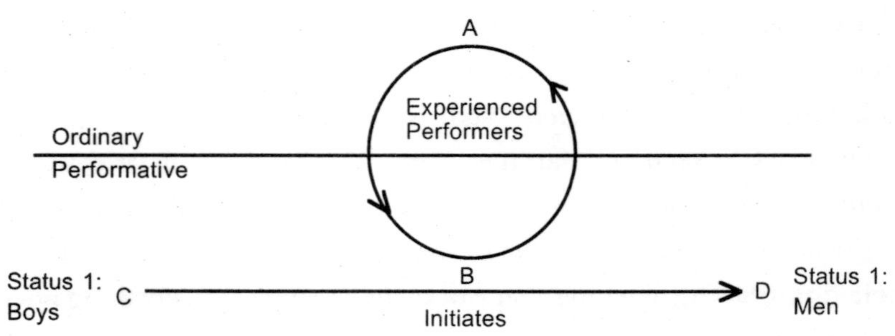

Fig. 3

occurs, it is subtle: the way persons achieve more respect, or lose it, through doing what is necessary in their social lives. When the performance is over the transported have been returned to their place of entry and the transformed have been changed. The system is analogous to a printing press, where information is imprinted upon a piece of paper as it is fed through. The performance—and the training leading up to it—are points of contact between the 'press' (transported) and the 'paper' (transformed). Point B—the performance witnessed by spectators who are far from casual seekers of entertainment—is the decisive contact between transported and transformed. What the transported imprint upon the transformed at that point of contact is there to stay: circumcision, scarring, tattooing, and so on; or the giving of special clothes, ornaments, and artifacts, such as wedding bands, the sacred four-strand thread of Hindu initiation, the *teffilin* to be bound and unbound daily by Jewish males, and so on. Or something is taken from the transformed: the bloody down Quesalid displays, the foreskin taken from the circumcised, a ceremonial haircut, or, as in the Gahuku case, blood and vomit. These markings, additions, and subtractions are not mere arrows pointing to deeper significance; they are themselves loaded with power: they bind a person to his community, anchor him to a social identity; they are at once intimate and public. Theatre people especially ought to be sensitive to the force of the surface. The surface of the social being is like the surface of the sun: always seething, throwing up from the depths material heretofore hidden, and sucking down into the depths what just now was surface.

For the system to work the transported must be as unchanged as the transformed is permanently changed. The work of the transported is to enter the performance, play his role, wear his mask—usually acting as the agent for larger forces, or possessed directly by them—and leave. In this process the transported is identical to the actor. Or to put it another way, the actor in Euro-American theatre is an example of a transported performer. For reasons that will be made clear later, the Euro-American theatre is one of transportation without transformation. Much activity from 1960 onwards has sought to introduce into Euro-American theatre the process of transformation.

And the audience? Spectators at transformation performances usually have a stake in seeing that the performance succeeds. They are relatives of the performers, part of the same community. Thus in transformation performances the attention of the transported and the spectators converges on the transformed [Fig. 4].

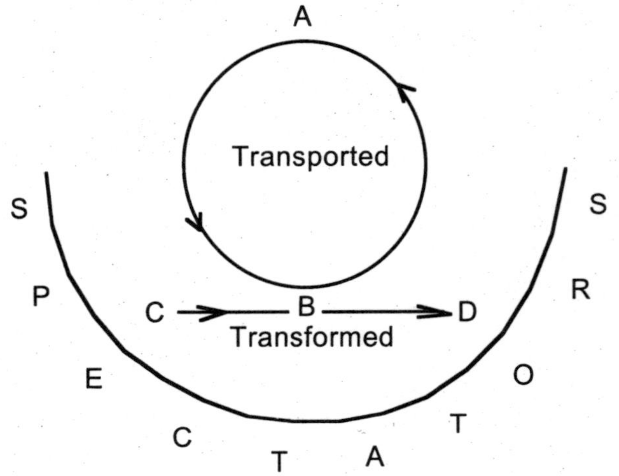

Fig. 4

This convergence of attention, and direct stake in the performance, is why so many transformation performances use audience participation. All of Susuroka gathered for the final day of dancing as Asemo and his age-mates made their debut as men. At first only the boys-now-men dance, but then everyone joins in a general celebration. So it is also with bar mitzvahs, weddings, and even funerals.

In a transformation performance the stars of the show may not be the best performers, technically speaking. Asemo and his agemates can't dance as well as the older men, any more than a bar mitzvah boy sings his part from the Torah as well as the *chazan*. Throughout the initiation process the older men have concentrated on getting the boys through—doing what must be done for the initiation to be completed, for it to work. And on that last day, the concentration of the village is on what has been made: new men, the work done. Interestingly, the word 'drama' derives from the Greek root *dra*: to do, to make. Similarly, at a wedding the attention is on the marrying couple, at a bar mitzvah it's on the bar mitzvah boy, and so on. This isn't to say that the transported need not be skilled performers. Everywhere the pleasure an audience gets from a transformation performance depends greatly on the skills of the elders and/or professionals who train, guide, officiate, and often co-perform with the transformed. The bar mitzvah boy is praised for his singing, but the *chazan* better sing better; ditto for the dancing of Asemo's father and uncles.

It would be easy if it ended here. But the status of the transported can be more important than their skills as performers—even if, as in Quesalid's case, this status derived from performative skill. Think what would happen if the Pope played Christ at Oberammergau. As it is, Pope John Paul II cooing to an audience/congregation of 17,000 teenagers bussed into Madison Square Garden is flashed on national TV. John Paul's performance is 'out of character' for a Pope, but mushy evidence of his 'humanness'. John Paul's 'human image' often makes people forget about his conservative theology. And Polish John Paul is an unusual bit of casting for a role usually reserved for an Italian. But what would happen to a common parish priest if, on national TV, he cooed to a big bunch of teenagers brought before him? An absurd question, because why would the networks broadcast the doings of an ordinary priest? And yet this same parish priest celebrating Mass is more powerful, in the Church's view, than an actor playing the Pope in *The Deputy*. And how about the unlikely possibility that a priest (or the Pope himself) play the role of Pope in a play? However unlikely these combinations are, they point to the four variables operating in every performance: (1) whether the performance is efficacious, directly making changes in ordinary life (initiations, weddings, and so on), or whether it is fictive, even about 'real events' (*The Deputy*, ordinary plays, documentaries); (2) the status of the roles *within* a performance; (3) the status of the persons playing the roles—whether they are playing themselves (as in initiations), are possessed by others, or have, in the Stanislavskian sense, 'built a role'. (Remember that Quesalid started by playing the role of unmasker/investigator and ended behind the mask he wanted to rip off others, and that Carnival and other celebrations pivot upon the inversion of roles where fools play the king and the king is required to act foolishly.) And, finally, (4) the quality of the performance measured by the mastery performers have over whatever skills are demanded (and these vary from society to society, occasion to occasion)—even, sometimes, the skill to feign a lack of skill as in many con games. None of these four variables is absent from any performance, transformative or transportational.

My model of transportation/transformation performance is open. It can be applied across cultures and genres. I have already applied it to the initiation rites of Gahuku boys in Papua–New Guinea. And presently I will apply it to a few more kinds of performances selected not only to be representative but also because I have had some personal experience with most of them. In the Greek case, obviously I wasn't around in the fifth century BC, but I have directed versions of Euripides' *The Bacchae* and Sophocles/Seneca's *Oedipus*. I will also look at theatre according to the Indian treatise *Natyashastra* (fourth century BC–second century AD), the noh drama according to the writings of Zeami (thirteenth century), and as practised today in Japan; the *Elephant Man* currently on Broadway; and my own production of *Dionysus in 69* as an example of environmental theatre and audience participation.

First let me show how the model looks when applied to that period of Athenian theatre when writers alone received prizes [Fig. 5].

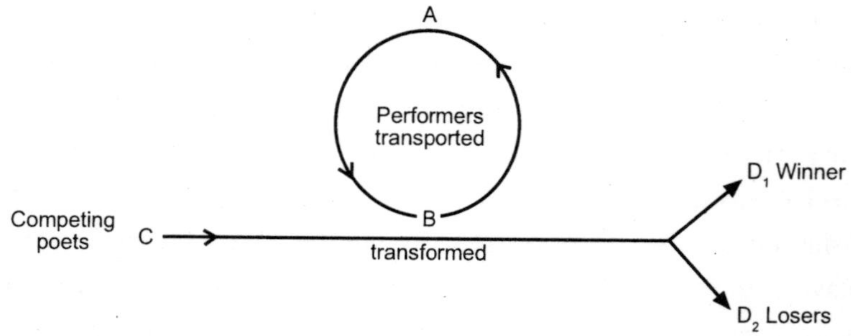

Fig. 5

This is the opposite of what happened in the village of Susuroka. There people of different statuses were transformed by the initiation performance into people of the same status: boys + men became all men. Here people of the same status, poets competing, are transformed by the performance into unequals: a winner + losers. This competitive differentiation is of course that of the *agon*: the core action of each Greek tragedy is identical to that of the City Dionysia as a whole. The revelation through direct competition among agonists (pro- and ant-) of who wins and who loses is deep not only in Greek tragedy but, by derivation, in Euro-American theatre, whose narratives until very recently always involved conflict and resolution into winners and losers.

The Greeks so loved competition that they preferred it over aesthetics. At first, prizes were given only to the writers, and each formed an ensemble of who he thought could best present his play. Aeschylus was noted for training his own chorus. But commencing in 449 BC, prizes were also given for the best actor. From then on writers were not allowed to select their own protagonists—these were assigned by lot and paid by the archon out of public funds. This lessened the possibility that writers and actors would form teams—certainly a strange regulation from the modern viewpoint because it foreclosed one of the ambitions of twentieth-century theatre: to form an aesthetically balanced company. But the Greeks wanted to reduce the possibility that the two competitions—one in writing, the other in acting—although they occurred at the same time and used the same medium, and clearly affected one another, would in practice be reduced to one. What happened was that writers were transporters for actors and actors for writers: each was the means the other used to achieve victory. The model thus could be drawn twice: once with the writers as the 'straight line' and once with the protagonists.

In Susuroka the men compete with each other. But even as they do they collaborate to help the boys through. The object of the performance is to eliminate winners and losers—the boys helped the most are those least able to do what's needed. Ultimately, all the boys are initiated, all win, all dance together on the village ground. This isn't saying that among the Gahuku there aren't better or worse dancers; but these differences, during the initiation, are effaced as much as possible, or at least not made a formal part of the ceremonies. With the Greeks the differences are displayed as much as possible—though even they made mistakes: Sophocles lost the year he entered with *Oedipus*.

I said that among the Greeks competition was preferred over aesthetics. That may be hard to swallow because Euro-American aesthetics, thanks to the Greeks, is a function of competition. If aesthetics is a concern for how well (= how beautifully) a thing is done, it developed among the Greeks when they ceased looking at a group in the process of being transported—as in the dithyrambic dances—and began selecting from the group individuals who 'do better' than others [Fig. 6].

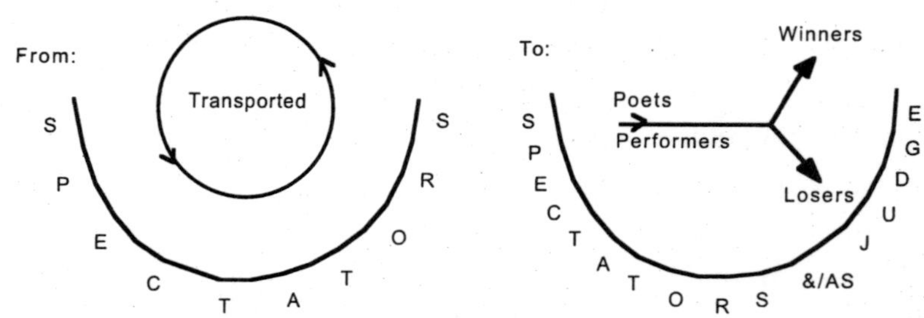

Fig. 6

Only by observing the details of performance—the what and how—could the Greeks, and any who follow the Greek model, discern winning poets and actors from losers. This process of differentiation is even more demanding when it's possible for a winning actor to perform in a losing play and a losing actor in a winning one. Spectators and judges—who actively claim to represent the 'whole city', just as the judges who award Obies and Tonys claim to represent the 'theatrical community'—confront the artists directly; they are neither absorbed into the performance as participators nor simply 'enjoying' it. Critics must, and spectators often do, rank performances in relation to other performances, even separating out within a given performance the 'good' from the 'bad'. And writers and players—knowing they are being judged, that something important is at stake—react by playing up to the audience or intentionally scorning it. Rare is the performance, especially on opening night when the critics are there, in which performers feel the audience working with them, mutually absorbed in the task of making the show go. Instead, the mutuality is of confrontation—the radical separation of audience and judges/critics on one side and performers, playwrights, and other theatre people on the other. This basic confrontation leads to the accumulation of 'values' by which artists are transformed into winners and losers. Again, much of the experimental work during the last twenty years has been directed—through devices of audience participation, environmental staging, and collective creativity—at abolishing this agony.

Aesthetics need not be built from competition—-as is clear when you look at theatre according to the *Natyashastra*. This book, called the 'Fifth Veda', was compiled between the fourth century BC and the second century AD It is almost certainly not the work of a single person. And the details it contains describing theatre architecture, staging, exact gestures of the body, limbs, face; its discussion of emotions, of acting styles, of the different types of plays; and its mythical frame of a theatrical performance decreed by the gods and later brought down to earth for people all point to a flourishing theatre-dance tradition long preceding extant Sanskrit drama. Unlike Aristotle, who wrote from a philosophical-literary perspective, the author(s) of the *Natyashastra* write of a complicated, sophisticated living performance genre. The book is so full of details, of exact descriptions and specifications, that it can be nothing else than a manual, a how-to-do-it text. Out of all this I want to look very closely at the relationship between the means of theatrical production—gestures, dance steps, mode of dialogue delivery, costumes, make-up, masks, theatre architecture and stage design, and so on—and the particular kind of 'entertainment' enjoyed by the spectators.

This relationship is epitomized in the Sanskrit notion of rasa. Rasa literally means 'flavour' or 'taste', and Indian theatre—like the Indian painting and sculpting of roughly the same period, especially the caves at Ajanta and the sculptural group at Mahabalipuram—is, in Richard Lannoy's McLuhanesque term, 'synaesthesic'. As Lannoy says:

> The Ajanta style approaches as near as it is likely for an artist to get to a felicitous rendering of tactile sensations normally experienced subconsciously. These are felt rather than seen when the eye is subordinate to a total receptivity of all the senses . . . The seated queen with the floating hand is drawn so that we obtain information which cannot be had by looking at her from a single, fixed viewpoint . . . The logic of this style demands that movements and gestures can only be described in terms of the area or space in which they occur; we cannot identify a figure except by comparing its position with others around it . . . It could be said that the Ajanta artist is concerned with the order of sensuousness, as distinct from the order of reason.[14]

Lannoy shows how the Sanskrit drama, based on the *Natyashastra* (or probably vice versa), is analogous—especially in its synaesthesic technique—to the cave art and even to the caves themselves. 'The structure and ornamentation of the caves were deliberately designed to induce total participation during ritual circumambulation. The acoustics of one Ajanta *vihara*, or assembly hall (Cave VI), are such that any sound long continues to echo round the walls. The whole structure seems to have been tuned like a drum.'[15] This tuning was not fortuitous—these caves are human-made, excavated and carved out of a solid mountain wall.

> In both cases [the caves, the theatre] total participation of the viewer was ensured by a skilful combination of sensory experience. The 'wrap-around' effect [of] the caves was conveyed on the stage by adapting the technically brilliant virtuosity of Vedic incantation and phonetic science to the needs of the world's most richly textured style of poetic drama.[16]

What the *Natyashastra* supplies are the concrete details of that style which is not at its core literary but theatrical. Even today in such popular forms as Ramlila, Raslila, and the Krishna bhajans, there is circumambulation, trance dancing, sharing of food, open or cyclical rather than confrontational narrative, wrap-around environmental theatre type staging, processions; phases of the performance where the spectators watch and phases where they participate: a total blending of theatre, dance, music, food-sharing, religious ceremony, and a resulting sensuous overload that convinces me that the *Natyashastra* informs not only the classical Sanskrit drama, extinct for 1200 years, but also dozens of living forms beloved by the Indian people.

I said that rasa is the essence of the performance theory of the *Natyashastra*. And that rasa means taste or flavour: a sensuous essence that enters through the snout—nose, mouth, tongue—and engages the eyes and ears the way a sumptuous meal does, ultimately satisfying the belly which, to minds conditioned by yoga, is the seat of breath. Thus rasa is neither gross nor leaden, but highly sophisticated and subtle. Food-sharing symbolism is a paradigm of more than Indian theatre. Food, with accompanying oblations of ghee (clarified butter), water, flowers, bells, fire: these are the integers linking Indian theatre and puja, the basic Hindu ceremony whose roots reach down to pre-Aryan Harappa. At the core of puja is the offering of prasad, food, to the gods. This food is sanctified by the gods and returned to the people. The food makes a circular journey but is transformed in the process from human offering to divine gift. Different foods—different flavours and textures, different references and associations—have different functions and meanings; fruits, sweets, rice, and so on, prepared in various ways, constitute a language of food. Indian theatre, derived from the entertainments among the gods (according to the *Natyashastra*), also is an offering to the gods: a food for the gods, which the gods return to people for their enjoyment. And the gods are frequent characters in the plays, as well as spectators of the human show. In Ramlila at Ramnagar long poles topped by effigies represent the gods on high looking down at the performance. This appearance of the gods as performers and spectators is natural and easy among a people who believe in reincarnation and whose basic religious texts, the Vedas, depict gods modelled on 'primal man' and not the other way round. Also, the occasion for theatre in India is not, nor was it ever, a competition among poets and actors. Performances occur for any number of reasons ranging from the celebrations of fixed annual events like Ramlila, Raslila, and chhau to pure enjoyment at commercial theatres like jatra and tamasha to the marking of auspicious events like marriages, the visit of a dignitary, or recovery from an illness. The performance is sometimes thought of as an offering. Need I add that these occasions and functions overlap? At the Ramlila of Ramnagar the outskirts of the performing area are occupied by sellers of food, trinkets, clothes and the operators of games of skill and chance. Everyone attends the Ramlila, from the nursing infant to the highest god. On one night, from a tower later to be occupied by the Maharaja of Benares's family, performers representing Vishnu and Lakshmi watch as Ram and Sita are displayed; these are all manifestations of the same deity, scattered abundantly in time and space like flower petals or tossed rice and saying the same thing: This is an auspicious event.

Rasa is the flavour of the performance—how it tastes, how it appeals to the tastes of people from different *jati*, 'castes', and experience; and Indians use the word 'taste' with a great deal more subtlety and range of socio-aesthetic signification than we do. If some theatres need an audience to hear it, and some need spectators to see it, Indian theatre needs partakers to savour it. I don't have the time here to discuss exactly how rasa is used. What I do want to point out is that according to the *Natyashastra*—and in many Indian performances of today—the enjoyment of the performance is shared between the performers and the spectators, or as I shall say from this point, between the preparers and the partakers. Rasa happens where the experience of the preparers and partakers meet. Each, using skills that have to be learned and that are not easy, moves towards the other. The experience of the performance is like that of a banquet where the cooks and servers must know how to prepare and serve, but the diners must know how to eat. And, as in Asian banquets in general, there is more food than can possibly be consumed: a great part of the skill is in

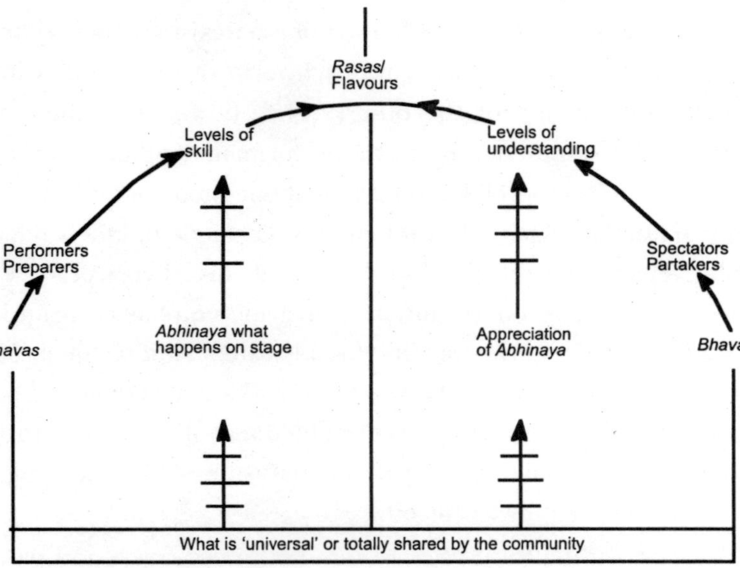

Fig. 7

knowing how and what to select for any given occasion. This relationship can be depicted as in Fig. 7.

A successful performance is one where both the levels of skill (preparers) and understanding (partakers) are high and equal. If the partaker expects more than the preparer can deliver, the performance is inadequate; if the preparer does more than the partaker can savour, the performance is wasted. Low skill matched by low understanding is preferable to an imbalance. Perfect rasa is a meeting at a very high level of preparer and partaker. Noh drama in Japan works in a similar way, except that the root metaphor is gardening and what is shared is *hana*, 'flower'. More on that later.

This Indian system of participant enjoyment—a system exported to Southeast Asia, China, and Japan—is one of the main things that attracted Brecht to Asian theatre. This system involves the audience in a very active way while at the same time enhancing its enjoyment. The system works with relations among four variables:

1	2		3	4
performer/preparer	performed ⟶	RASA	⟵ savoured	spectator/partaker

Rasa is the interface of 1/2 : : 4/3. Rasa doesn't exist independently: it is a function of the interface. And each term of the system can be varied independently of the others. That is, for example, some spectators can savour one part of a performance, others another; a performer can be absorbed into his role at one moment and detached from it at another. Again, Brecht took this technique of independently variable elements and developed from it his theory/practice of *Verfremdung*—'alienation' or 'distance'. Let me emphasize again how close this system is to the way fine food is eaten. At a banquet, feast, or fine restaurant—and this is even more striking at ceremonial occasions and ritual observances—it is presumed that all the food is superb or sanctified, but only some of it is eaten: one of the meanings of 'taste' is to sample only a little bit.

Thus, according to the *Natyashastra* both performers and partakers are transported, and no one is transformed [Fig. 8].

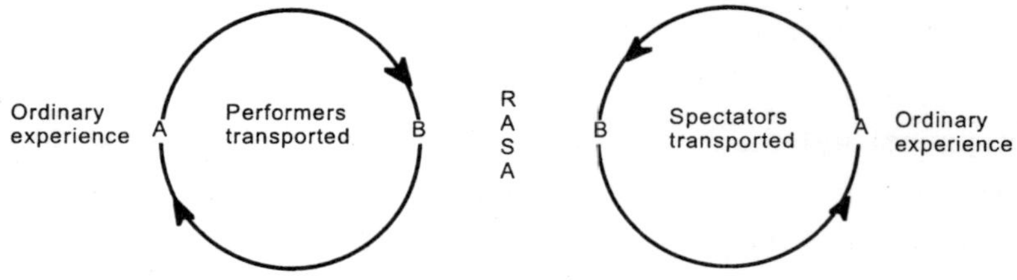

Fig. 8

Rasa is the mutuality, the sharing, the co-creation of preparers and partakers. Every detail of the presentation is worked out, but variable: theatre architecture, mise-en-scène, gestures, music, types of plays, spectator comportment, the proper occasions for theatre, et cetera, et cetera, et cetera. If Aristotle's *Poetics* is so laconic as to be considered only notes towards a text, the *Natyashastra* is so detailed as to be thought collectively authored, compiled over four or five centuries, a collective lore-book of performance. But while the details are worked out to a degree unknown in the West, there is much liberty within the scheme because the parts are variable.

For example, how much should be presented at one time? There is a 'start' and 'finish' to each night's performance—and many plays in the Sanskrit and folk traditions extend over a number of days and/or nights—but there isn't any definite 'beginning' or 'end' as there is in Greek drama. Where to stop in a given series again depends on circumstances. At Ramlila the size of the crowds, the weather, the energy of the performers, and the wishes of the Maharaja all can determine how much is done on a given day. Like post-modern performance in Europe and America, the Indian system is a braid of several strands of activities and demands that performer and partaker attend together

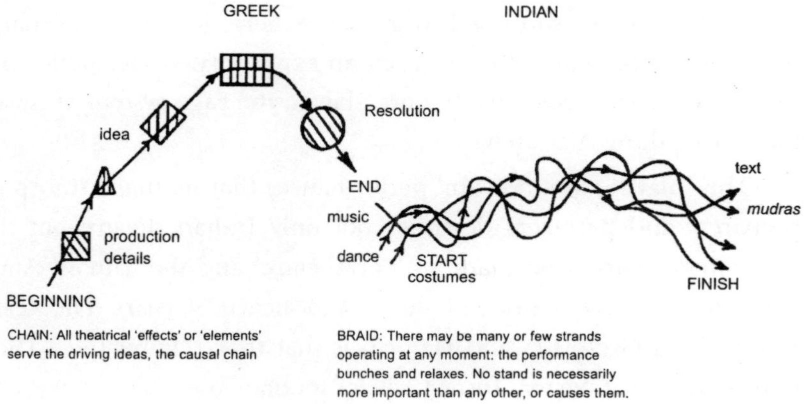

Fig. 9

to the here and now of the ever-changing relations among the strands. The two systems, Greek and Indian, can be diagrammed as in Fig. 9. This difference affects not only the performance but training, rehearsals, and the means of transmitting performance knowledge. Paradoxically, the Greek system—as it has worked itself out in Western theatre historically—is freer than the Indian in training and rehearsal but more fixed in performance. Through training and rehearsal the 'idea' or 'action' of the performance is 'discovered', and this takes searching; in performance this idea is 'shown', and this takes a fixed score. In the Indian system training and rehearsal are fixed because what is being transmitted is not a means of discovery but the performance elements themselves broken into learnable segments. The performance, however, is truly contingent. The more experienced and respected the performer, the more he is permitted to vary elements of the show during performance. The performance is truly contingent, an ever-changing *lila* ('play', 'sport', 'illusion') created between preparer and partaker. But these days, as even classical and folk arts are restored according to Westernized training methods, Indian theatre is losing its quality of contingency.

This view of the difference between causal chains and braided relations also helps explain why Western theatre develops from crises that it is then the business of the performance to resolve, while Sanskrit drama, and much contemporary Indian theatre, 'doesn't go anywhere'. It's not supposed to go somewhere, it's not a 'development–resolution' kind of drama, but an expository, synaesthetic, and playful set of variations much more akin to the raga system of music than to anything Aristotelian.

This 'playing around with' performances that mutually transport preparers and partakers describes not only Indian theatre but the experiments Grotowski made in 'paratheatre' and the 'rituals' Anne Halprin has been devising in California for nearly 30 years. The weakness of both Grotowski and Halprin is that they rely on the I-Thou immediacy, what Victor Turner labels 'spontaneous communitas', to generate the rules of the game, and they depend on 'group creativity' to come up with the elements to be bunched and braided. Without the benefit of a worked-out, culturally elaborate theatrical system (which the *Natyashastra* both describes and provides, and which is ever-present in the Indian oral tradition) the participants are thrown back on their own 'sincerity', their own 'personal truth'. This truth is but a version of that radical individualism so rampant in twilight capitalist culture: all too often a combination of clichés of intimacy, unexamined cultural fact, and romantic distortions of pre-industrial religious experience. The results—as I've witnessed them and heard them described—are actions like staring deeply into your partner's eyes, swaying or moving in circles in 'ritualistic' dances, passing fire, telling personal stories during long hours spent quietly in candlelight, running through the woods at night, and so on.[17] Yet the underlying tendency of this kind of experiment is, I think, valid: to restore to performance, or invent anew, that quality of mutuality so powerfully present in rasa.

Nothing could be further from the narcissistic experiments of today's theatre than Japanese noh—a form that is describable by the figures I devised for the *Natyashastra*. In noh there is a close relationship between highly skilled performers—many of them apprenticed in the art from early childhood by their fathers, uncles, and grandfathers—and an audience of connoisseurs. Zeami and his father, Kannami, gave noh its definitive shape in the fourteenth and fifteenth centuries. Zeami, in a series of monographs, is very specific about how noh performers are to be trained, how noh is to be performed, and what the underlying theory of the art is. I can, in this essay, only touch on this rich literature—one of the most detailed accounts ever written by an individual on theatre. And Zeami was not only a director and actor of great force, but the author of the largest number of noh plays still in the repertory. His output and range is roughly that of Brecht and Stanislavski combined.

Zeami is specific about how a performance of noh is to be adjusted according to a number of circumstances outside the mise-en-scène: the season, weather, quality and comportment of the audience. For example:

> When Noh is performed in a shrine or in the presence of a noble, there are many people assembled, and it is very noisy with the buzz and murmur of their voices. In that case, the performer better wait until they become calm and quiet and all their eyes are concentrated on the entrance . . . If he begins to sing *issei* [entrance music] immediately, the atmosphere of the theatre will take on the tone of the performance, the attention of the audience will be concentrated on the movements of the *shite* [main actor] and the noisy voices will become quiet . . . But as one of the principles of Noh is that it should be performed in front of nobles, if the noble arrives at his box earlier than usual, the *shite* might begin the play as soon as possible. In this case, the audience has not yet become quiet, or latecomers are entering the boxes, and everyone's

> mind is not yet prepared to see the Noh, some standing, others sitting in their boxes. In this case, one will not have a sufficiently calm atmosphere in which to perform. At such a time . . . the player had better be clad in more ornamental dress than usual, sing more strongly, step more loudly on the floor, and his carriage should be much more vivid and attractive. This will calm down the atmosphere of the theatre . . . So to judge whether the audience is ready for the play to begin, or whether their minds are not yet concentrated on it, is very difficult. Only the experienced *shite* can do it.[18]
>
> The audience whose eyes are not sharply appreciative will not praise the talented *shite*, and, on the other hand, the audience who can really appreciate Noh cannot endure to see an immature *shite* performing. It is natural that the unskilled *shite* is never admired by a cultivated audience; but that the real master sometimes cannot hold the attention of an unappreciative audience is partly because these people do not have enough taste to recognize the master's talent.[19]
>
> The purpose of this art is to pacify and give pleasure to the minds of the audience and to move them, both nobles and the common people, and this will also assure prosperity and long life [for the actor].[20]

So close and immediate is the relationship between performers and spectators that if the audience is noisy the costumes are changed at the last minute, a kind of homoeopathy is tried where brighter costuming is used to calm a too-flashy audience. Noh's apparent solemnity and fixity are deceptive. At its core is a set of contingencies unmatched elsewhere in world theatre. The *shite* rehearses only with the chorus The *waki* (second character), *kyogen* (comic actor), flautist, and drummers are each from different families, and rehearse separately from each other. The whole group of actors, chorus, musicians meets only once or twice before a public performance. The *shite* outlines his plans. Rehearsals as such are rarely held. The performance itself is the meeting place of the strands—singing, chanting, dancing, reciting, music-making—that are braided into the public noh. And the performance is variable not only in the ways Zeami describes but also because the *shite* can signal the musicians to indicate that a dance will be repeated or shortened. Again, like Indian raga music, noh takes advantage of the immediacy of the encounter among artists and between the ensemble and the audience. An audience of connoisseurs is aware of, and delights in, these contingencies. Noh—the very word means 'skill'—is like a sport, and the spectator's enjoyment is increased if, like the baseball fan who can read the third-base coach's signs to batter and runners, he knows the details of the interplay on stage. Today many spectators of noh also study its chanting or dancing, and are attached to one school or other. For their part, noh performers complain of boredom when, for tours, a company is assembled to repeat a fixed repertory. The onceness of Zen—a meditation and a martial art—is the heart of noh.

Not rasa, flavour, but *hana*, flower, is the root metaphor of noh. To understand *hana* you must see many *sumi-i* paintings, where each stroke of the brush is allowed just once, there are no corrections, so that a great work, when it occurs, is what happens when all training drops away in an unrevised meeting of artist and medium. Zeami speaks of *hana* often, but at no time more cogently than here.

> My father Kannami died on the nineteenth of May [1384] at the age of fifty-two. On the fourth day of the same month he gave a dedicatory performance in front of Segen Shrine in the province of Suruga. His own performance on this programme was especially brilliant, and the audence, both high and low, all applauded. He had ceded many showy plays to uninitiated *shite*, and he himself performed easy ones, in a subdued way; but, with this additional colour to it, his flower looked better than ever. As his was *shin-no-hana* [*hana* acquired through training, literally 'true flower'] it survived until he became old without leaving him, like an old leafless tree which still blossoms.[21]

Pure Beckett: an art of distilled discipline. Not only *sumi-i*, but Zen rock gardens and bonsai trees are analogues to noh. *Hana* exists between performers and spectators; when it is there both performers and spectators are transported [Fig. 10].

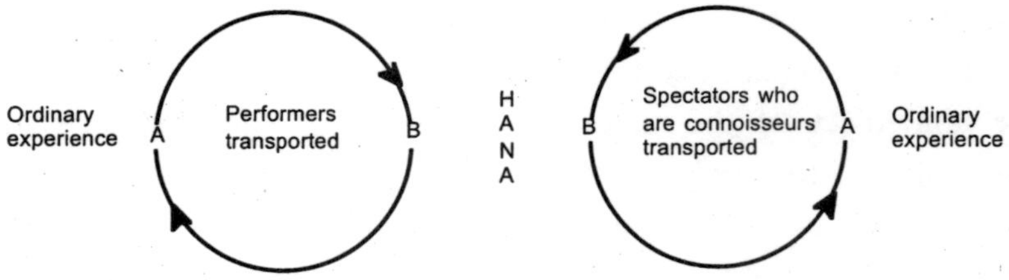

Fig. 10

But unless the spectators know what's going on through specific instruction in noh the *hana* is missing. As in the Tea Ceremony the ability to appreciate the service and the objects shown is directly proportional to what the guests know. This is different from the Indian situation where mutuality but not special knowledge is required. Living in a north Indian village will give a person by the age of five all that he needs to participate in Ramlila; from then on the experience will deepen year by year. But the noh spectator must become a connoisseur or he will fail the performance. And that is why so many newcomers to noh find it impenetrable.

It doesn't take special training to like Broadway theatre, or to dislike it. But in this trait Broadway is like experimental theatre. Almost all Euro-American theatre prides itself on its popularity: what it asks of its audience is not special knowledge but responsivity. The historic sources of this theatre are not so much religious ritual or initiatory ordeals but popular entertainments. I saw *The Elephant Man* on Broadway in 1979. Philip Anglim's portrayal of the title role was a model of professionalism as understood in the American theatre: physical, restrained, precise, and according to the conventions of a stylized naturalism. By holding his right arm extended and twisted from the shoulder and again at the wrist, by dropping his right shoulder and turning his neck to the left, by rotating his left wrist and clenching his fist—and then keeping this excruciating position for more than two hours (except when off-stage)—Anglim gave the impression of deformity without help from the costumer or makeup artist. This is in contrast, say, to Lon Chaney's *Hunchback of Notre Dame* in the movies—or dozens of other films—where the actor is an armature for a construction. But Anglim's work on himself serves another purpose too. It allows individual spectators to sympathize with the character Anglim is playing and not be repulsed. In admiring Anglim's skill, and in recognizing his discomfort, a spectator is relieved from confronting directly the Elephant Man's look and stink. A spectator can congratulate herself: 'I saw Anglim/Elephant Man, and I was not disgusted. I saw that he was a human being, just like me.' This kind of sentimental empathy, earned by acting skill, is what got the production its great success critically and commercially. The performer is transported while individual spectators experience their own reactions at the level of private responses. Some, like me, may simply respond to Anglim's skill. There is no collective work set out for the audience to do or participate in [Fig. 11].

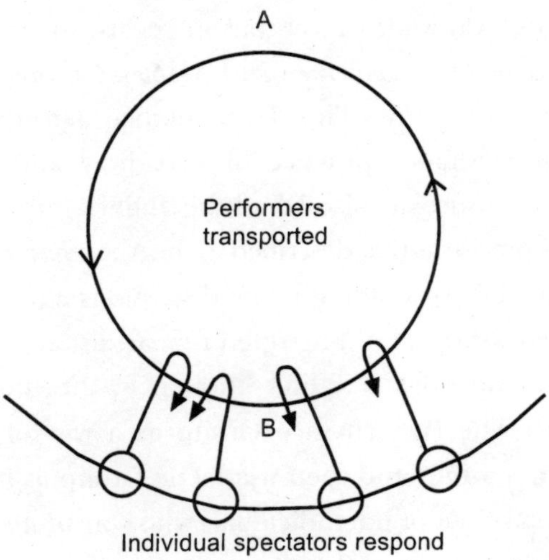

Fig. 11

The difference (can I say emptiness?) between this experience, these sets of individual experiences—parallel but not collective—and Asemo's initiation, Greek theatre, *Natyashastra*, and noh is clear. In each of the others the audience has a definite collective role to play. The tie-ins do not stop with responsivity but go on to include consciously articulated and practised interactions. Asemo and his agemates exist as initiates between the men and the rest of Susuroka, somewhat the way rasa and *hana* are co-created by audience and performers in Indian and Japanese theatre. And in the Greek theatre, a particular performance determined who won the prize. The only thing close to this kind of celebratory play/work in our culture is what fans do at football, baseball, boxing, or other sports events.

Brecht knew this and wanted people to attend theatre with the same critical/supportive mind they take to sports. It was this lack of mutuality, a symptom of the audience's lack of power, and the performances' lack of transformative potential, that led to the experiments of the 1960s and 70s. These involved audience participation, creation of new kinds of spaces for theatre, a widespread interest in shamanism: performances that heal, transport, transform. And conscious links were forged between theatre and religion. I do not have space to investigate these experiments here. I have written extensively about them elsewhere.[22] But I do want to say that in regard to some of my own work—*Dionysus in 69*, *Commune*, and *Mother Courage* especially—I positioned my company, The Performance Group, somewhere between the individualist practice of Broadway and the collective social process of Susuroka. Also I had the ambition to develop a performing style as precise as that described in the *Natyashastra*. I even sought to train the audience by holding many discussions after performances, giving public workshops, holding open rehearsals, and lecturing/writing a lot about the work. I didn't know it at the time, but I used workshops with The Performance Group as a way of transforming individuals into a group and then used The Group as transporters in an attempt to make out of the individuals who constitute an audience a collective, if only a temporary collective—a community for the time being [Fig. 12].

I treated the members of the audience as if they were joining a workshop, and I tried to condense the workshop into a single performance. Grotowski, recognizing as early as 1967 that this couldn't be done, did away with the audience altogether. In his paratheatrical work he has broken his acting company into subgroups who lead people in attempts to generate 'spontaneous communitas'. Eugenio Barba started in 1980 the International School of Theatre

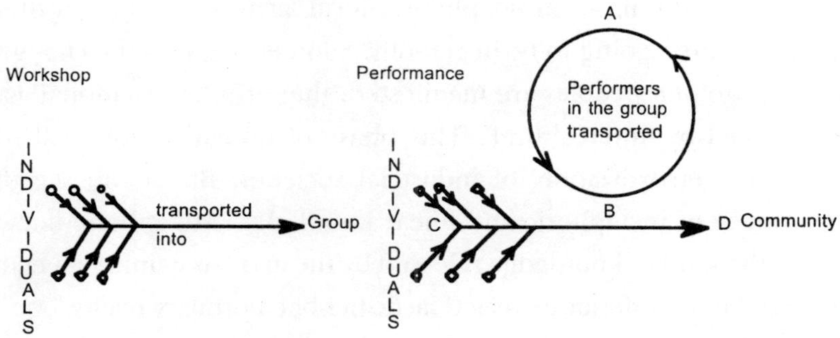

Fig. 12

Anthropology to bring together master teachers from Asia and students from Europe and America. He doesn't want to teach oriental techniques but get at 'certain laws that determine organic tensions in the actor's organism . . . The study and understanding of these laws, going beyond the styles and conventions of their theatrical forms, can, for the European actor, facilitate an awareness of his own energy processes.'[23] Barba says that 'theatre anthropology is the study of the biological and cultural behaviour of man in a theatrical situation, that is to say, of man presenting and using his physical and mental presence in accordance with laws differing from those of daily life.' My own attention has turned, temporarily I think, from actually making performances to the writing of 'performance theory'.

Today there is a quiet in the American theatre. But the surface calm lies. Tectonically there is movement bringing a collision of cultures. And where traditions collide—or separate radically—up bursts creative magma. If this is not happening right now on the 'art front', it is happening in the social sciences—disciplines undergoing transformation. In the Spring 1980 issue of *The American Scholar*, Clifford Geertz writes about 'blurred genres'—his attempt to catch up to, and criticize, movements in social thought dealing with cultures in terms of games, dramas, and texts. Geertz, a pioneer of these processes (they are not yet frozen into 'methods'), recognizes them as ways of handling the new world that has borne itself since World War II: a world of colliding cultures no longer dominated by Europeans and Americans, and no longer dominable by anyone. Dominance, of course, can be political, economic, cultural, scientific, philosophical, artistic. In none of these spheres is there going to be hegemony. Soon enough, as the changed relations among peoples are manifested, the term 'international' will be replaced by 'intercultural'. This phase of human history will not bring the 'retribalization' of industrial societies. But it will see the coexistence of metaphoric and linear knowledge. Metaphoric knowledge—the kind of knowledge released by the arts—is gaining an equal footing: it is not inferior to 'realer' facticities but a primary reality, one of several that braid into the human helix. And theatrical metaphor—restored and reactualized behaviour—is the root metaphor. It is the root because theatre = action = transportation/ transformation. Chased from Plato's republic as nonrational and subversive, but existing always, sometimes marginally, theatre is now showing itself everywhere: in social dramas, personal experience, public displays, political and economic interaction, art. So now: on with the show.

Notes

1. I discuss this idea of 'twice-behaved behaviour' extensively in 'Restored Behaviour' in this volume. I see in the rehearsal process itself the paradigm of ritual, and in 'restored behaviour' the operation linking such diverse activities as ritual, theatre, psychotherapy, shamanism, and reflexivity.
2. From K. Stanislavski, *An Actor Prepares* (N.Y.: Theatre Arts, 1946), p. 13. This sense of being 'carried away' is what M. Csikszentmihalyi calls 'flow', and it characterizes a number of activities, such as sports, mountain climbing, chess, surgery (for the surgeon), theatre, dance. It is the opposite of reflexivity. Probably many human activities are dialectical, depending on a wavelike alternation of flow and reflexivity. It may also be that some activities—theatre being among them—have a reflexive rehearsal phase followed by a flowing performance. For

more on flow, see Csikszentmihalyi's *Beyond Boredom and Anxiety* (San Francisco: Jossey-Bass, 1975).

3. F. Kafka, *Wedding Preparations in the Country and Other Posthumous Prose Writings* (London: Secker and Warburg, 1954), p. 40.
4. C. Lévi-Strauss, 'The Sorcerer and His Magic', in *Structural Anthropology* (N.Y.: Basic Books, 1963), pp. 167–85.
5. It is another example of the peculiar power of performance to invert causal progressions so that effects precede causes. That is, the 'power' of a performer is both cause and effect of his performance. Performance—and its effect on the audience—and feedback comprise a synchronic bundle that, paradoxically, unfolds during the performance according to a diachronic progression.
6. The best discussions I know of are of M. Singer's 'The Radha-Krishna *Bhajanas* of Madras City', in *When A Great Tradition Modernizes* (London: Pall Mall Press, 1972), pp. 199–244, and N. Hein, *The Miracle Plays of Mathura* (New Haven: Yale University Press, 1972).
7. Csikszentmihalyi, *Beyond Boredom*, p. 38.
8. Ibid., pp. 53–4.
9. Quoted in R. Schechner, *Environmental Theater* (N.Y.: Hawthorn, 1973), p. 295.
10. K. E. Read, *The High Valley* (N.Y.: Charles Scribner's Sons, 1965), p. 159.
11. Read, *High Valley*, p. 160.
12. Ibid., p. 172.
13. Ibid., p. 177.
14. R. Lannoy, *The Speaking Tree* (London: Oxford University Press, 1971), pp. 48–9.
15. Ibid., p. 43.
16. Ibid., p. 54.
17. Grotowski's work is complicated—combining as it does elements of old-fashioned Polish Catholicism with the new religions of California. Also Grotowski's own position inside communist Poland is not easily defined. He is, or was, a member of the Party; and he is, or was, an avant-garde theatre director. His work is not anti-government in any sense, concentrating as it does on the inner life of his followers. Grotowski's work can be divided into two parts: up until 1967, when he concentrated on presenting public performances according to a

technique described in his book, *Towards a Poor Theatre*; and from 1967 to the present, when he has experimented in paratheatrical activity, some of which is described in a pamphlet, 'On the Road to Active Culture', ed. Leszek Kolankiewicz, trans. Boleslaw Taborski (unpublished manuscript; Wroclaw, Poland, 1978).

18. Zeami, *Kadensho*, trans. Chuichi Sakurai, Shuseki Hayashi, Rokuro Satoi, and Bin Miyai (Kyoto: Sumiya-Shinobe Publishing Institute, 1969), pp. 36–9.
19. Ibid., p. 63.
20. Ibid., pp. 64-5.
21. Ibid., pp. 23-4
22. See especially R. Schechner, *Environmental Theater* (1973) and *Essays on Performance Theory* (N.Y.: Drama Books Specialists, 1977).
23. From a three-page announcement of the first session of the International School of Theatre Anthropology, held in Bonn, West Germany; Holstebro, Denmark; and Stockholm, Sweden from 1 October through 30 November 1980. Barba's school is only the most recent of a very extensive set of exchanges among the world's theatres, both ritual and aesthetic. Peter Brook has run his International Centre for Theatre Research in Paris for more than 10 years, using performers from Africa, Asia, Europe, and America and experimenting with forms as diverse as Shinto worship and African storytelling, and texts ranging from the Mahabharata to the *Ik*, adapted from Colin Turnbull's *The Mountain People*. Ellen Stewart at La Mama ETC in New York sponsors the Third World Institute of Theatre Arts Studies which, for example, in October 1980 ran performances and workshops of traditional theatre and rituals from Nigeria, Japan, the Dominican Republic, the Philippines, Korea, Indonesia, India, and Haiti. This work, and much more like it, is laying the foundation for an extensive reconstruction of theatricality—what it means, how it works—on a world-wide basis. The exchange is not one-way: a Nigerian explained how TV is used to reawaken among children interest in traditional games and ceremonies. The Performance Group's tour of India in 1976 had an effect on directors, actors, and writers in India.

From Ritual to Theatre and Back: the Structure/Process of the Efficacy-Entertainment Dyad

THE *KAIKO* CELEBRATION of the Tsembaga of Highlands New Guinea is a year-long festival culminating in the *konj kaiko*—pig *kaiko*. *Kaiko* means dancing, and the chief entertainments of the celebrations are dances. During 1962 the Tsembaga entertained 13 other local groups on 15 occasions.[1] To make sure that the *kaiko* was successful young Tsembaga men were sent to neighbouring areas to announce the shows—and to send back messages of delay should a visiting group be late: in that case the entertainments were postponed. The day of dancing begins with the dancers—all men—bathing and adorning themselves. Putting on costumes takes hours. It is an exacting, precise and delicate process. When dressed the dancers assemble on the flattened, stamped-down grounds where they dance both for their own pleasure and as rehearsal in advance of the arrival of their guests. The visitors announce their arrival by singing—they can be heard before they are seen. By this time many spectators have gathered, including both men and women from neighbouring villages. These spectators come to watch, and to trade goods. Finally,

> the local dancers retire to a vantage point just above the dance ground, where their view of the visitors is unimpeded and where they continue singing. The visitors approach the gate silently, led by men carrying fight packages,[2] swinging their axes as they run back and forth in front of their procession in the peculiar crouched fighting prance. Just before they reach the gate they are met by one or two of those locals who have invited them and who now escort them over the gate. Visiting women and children follow behind the dancers and join the other spectators on the sidelines. There is much embracing as the local women and children greet visiting kinfolk. The dancing procession charges to the centre of the dance ground shouting the long, low battle cry and stamping their feet, magically treated before their arrival . . . to enable them to dance strongly. After they charge back and forth across the dance ground several times, repeating the stamping in several locations while the crowd cheers in admiration of their numbers, their style and the richness of their finery, they begin to sing.[3]

The performance is a transformation of combat techniques into entertainment. All the basic moves and sounds—even the charge into the central space—are adaptations and direct lifts from battle. But the Tsembaga dance is a dance, and clearly so to everyone present at it. The dancing is not an isolated phenomenon—as theatre-going in America still is usually—but a behaviour nested in supportive actions. The entry described takes place late in the afternoon, and just before dusk the dancing stops and the food which has been piled in the centre of the dancing ground is distributed and eaten. It might be said, literally, that the dancing is *about the food*, for the whole *kaiko* cycle is about acquiring enough pigs-for-meat to afford the festival.

> The visitors are asked to stop dancing and gather around while a presentation speech is made by one of the men responsible for the invitation. As he slowly walks around and around the food that has been laid out in a number of piles, the speechmaker recounts the relations of the two groups:

> their mutual assistance in fighting, their exchange of women and wealth, their hospitality to each other in times of defeat . . . When the speech of presentation is finished they gather their portions and distribute them to those men who came to help them dance, and to their women.[4]

After supper the dancing resumes and goes on all night. By dawn almost everyone has danced with everyone else: and this communality is a sign of a strong alliance.

With dawn the dancing ground is converted into a market place. Ornaments, pigs, furs, axes, knives, shells, pigments, tobacco are all traded or sold (money has come into the Tsembaga's economy).

> The transactions that take place on the dance ground are completed on the spot; a man both gives and receives at the same time . . . At the men's houses, however, a different kind of exchange takes place. Here men from other places give to their kinsmen or trading partners in the local group valuables for which they do not receive immediate return.[5]

This orchestrated indebtedness is at the heart of the *kaiko*. At the start of the celebration the hosts owe meat to the guests and guests owe items of trade to the hosts. In the first part of the *kaiko* the hosts pay meat to the guests; in the second part of the *kaiko* the guests pay the hosts trade items. But neither payment ends in a balance. When the *kaiko* is over the guests owe the hosts meat, and the hosts owe the guests trade items. This symmetrical imbalance guarantees further *kaikos*—continued exchanges between groups. Often trade items are not given back directly, but traded back through third or fourth parties. After the public trading and the gift-giving, some dancing resumes which ends by midmorning. Then everyone goes home.

The *kaiko* entertainments are a ritual display, not simply a doing but a *showing of a doing*. Furthermore, this showing is both actual (= the trading and giving of goods resulting in a new imbalance) and symbolic (= the reaffirmation of alliances made concrete in the debtor-creditor relationship). The entertainment itself is a vehicle for debtors and creditors to exchange places; it is also the occasion for a market; and it is fun. The *kaiko* depends on the accumulation of pigs and goods, and on a willingness to dress up and dance; neither by itself is enough. The dancing is a performance—and appreciated as such, with the audience serving as frequently acerbic critics—but it's also a way of facilitating trade, finding mates, cementing military alliances and reaffirming tribal hierarchies.

> The Tsembaga say that 'those who come to our *kaiko* will also come to our fights'. This native interpretation of *kaiko* attendance is also given expression by an invited group. Preparations for departure to a *kaiko* at another place include ritual performances similar to those that precede a fight. Fight packages are applied to the heads and hearts of the dancers and *gir* to their feet so that they will dance strongly, just as, during warfare, they are applied so that they will fight strongly . . . Dancing is like fighting. The visitors' procession is led by men carrying fight packages, and their entrance upon the dance ground of their hosts is martial. To join a group in dancing is the symbolic expression of willingness to join them in fighting.[6]

The *kaiko* dance display is a cultural version of territorial and status displays in animals; the rituals of the Tsembaga are ethological as well as sociological. They are also ecological: the *kaiko* is a means of organizing the Tsembaga's relationships to their neighbours, to their lands and goods, to their gardens and hunting ranges.

A *kaiko* culminates in the *konj kaiko*. The *kaiko* lasts a year, the *konj kaiko* a few days, usually two. *Kaiko* years are rare. During the 50 to 60 years ending in 1963 the Tsembaga staged four *kaikos*, with an average of 12 to 15 years between festivals.[7] The whole cycle is tied to the war/peace rhythm which, in turn, is tied to the fortunes of the pig population. After the *konj kaiko*—whose major event is a mass slaughter of pigs and distribution of meat—a short peace is followed by war, which continues until another *kaiko* cycle begins. The cycle itself lasts for enough years to allow the raising of sufficient pigs to stage a *konj kaiko*. The *konj kaiko* of 7 and 8 November 1963 saw the slaughter of 96 pigs with a total live weight of 15,000 pounds, yielding around 7,500 pounds of meat; eventually about 3,000 people got shares of the kill.[8] What starts in dancing ends in eating; or, to put it in artistic-religious terms, what starts as theatre ends as communion. *Perhaps not since classical Athenian festivals and medieval pageants have we in the West used performances as the pivots in systems involving economic, social, political and religious transactions*. With the re-advent of holism in contemporary society at least a discussion of such performances becomes practical. It is clear that the *kaiko* dances are not ornaments or pastimes or even 'part of the means' of effecting the transactions among the Tsembaga. The dances both symbolize and participate in the process of exchange.

The dances are pivots in a *system of transformations which change destructive behaviour into constructive alliances*. It is no accident that every move, chant and costume of the *kaiko* dances are adapted from combat: a new use is found for this behaviour. Quite unconsciously a positive feedback begins: the more splendid the displays of dancing, the stronger the alliances; the stronger the alliances, the more splendid the dancing. Between *kaikos*—but only between them—war is waged; during the cycles there is peace. The exact transformation of combat behaviour into performance is at the heart of the *kaiko*. This transformation is identical in structure to that at the heart of Greek theatre (and from the Greeks down throughout all of Western theatre history). Namely, characterization and the presentation of real or possible events—the story, plot or dramatic action worked out among human figures (whether they be called men or gods)—is a transformation of real behaviour into symbolic behaviour. In fact, *transformation is the heart of theatre, and there appear to be only two fundamental kinds of theatrical transformation*: (1) the displacement of anti-social, injurious, disruptive behaviour by ritualized gesture and display, and (2) the invention of characters who act out fictional events or real events fictionalized by virtue of their being acted out (as in documentary theatre or Roman gladiatorial games.) These two kinds of transformation occur together, but in the mix usually one is dominant. Western theatre emphasizes characterization and the enactment of fictions; Melanesian, African and Australian (aborigine) theatre emphasize the displacement of hostile behaviour. Forms which balance the two tendencies—noh, kathakali, the Balinese ketchak, medieval moralities, some contemporary avant garde performances—offer, I think, the best models for the future of the theatre.

Much performing among communal peoples is, like the *kaiko*, part of the overall ecology of a society. The *Engwura* cycle of the Arunta of Australia, as described by Spencer and Gillen in the late nineteenth century,[9] is an elegant example of how a complicated series of performances expressed and participated in a people's ecology. The fact that the *Engwura* is no longer performed—that the Arunta, culturally speaking, have been exterminated—indicates the incompatibility of wholeness as I am describing it and Western society as it is presently constituted. In so far as performing groups adapt techniques from the *kaiko* or *Engwura* they are bound to remain outside the 'mainstream'. But the chief function of the avant garde is to propose models for change: to remain 'in advance'. The *Engwura* was an initiation cycle that spanned several years; the last phase consisted of performances staged sporadically over a three-to-four-month period. Each phase of the *Engwura* took place only when several conditions meshed: enough young men of a certain age gathered in one place to be initiated; enough older men willing to lead the ceremonies (particularly important in a non-literate culture); enough food to support celebration. Then the sacred implements and sacred grounds were prepared painstakingly and according to tradition. Finally, there had to be peace among neighbouring tribes—but the announcement of a forthcoming *Engwura* was sometimes enough to guarantee a peace.

The daily rhythm recapitulated the monthly rhythm: performance spaces were cleared, implements repaired and laid out, body decorations applied, food cooked. Each performance day saw not one but several performances, with rest and preparations between each. Each performance lasted on an average ten minutes, and was characteristically a dance accompanied by drumming and chanting. Then the performers rested for about two hours; then preparations for the next performance began, and these preparations took about two hours.[10] The whole cycle recapitulates the life cycle of the Arunta male; and during his life he could expect to play roles co-existent with his status in society: initiate, participant, leader or onlooker. Thus on each day performers enacted condensed and concentrated versions of their lives; and the three-to-four-month culminating series of performances also replicated the life cycle. The whole cycle was, in fact, an important—perhaps the most important—set of events in an Arunta life.[11] Each phase of the cycle was a replication (either an extension or a concentration) of every other phase.

The subject matter of each brief dance-drama was life events of mythical Dreamtime beings who populated the world 'in the beginning'.[12] These mythic events were very important to the Arunta and constituted for them a history and, since each Dreamtime event was connected to specific places and landmarks, a geography.[13] The rituals are a concrete symbolization and re-enactment of Dreamtime events, and to this extent the *Engwura* is familiar to us: it is not unlike our own drama except that we accept the reactualization of past events only as a convention. The Arunta, like the orthodox Catholic taking the Eucharist, accepted the manifestation of Dreamtime events as actual [Fig. 1].

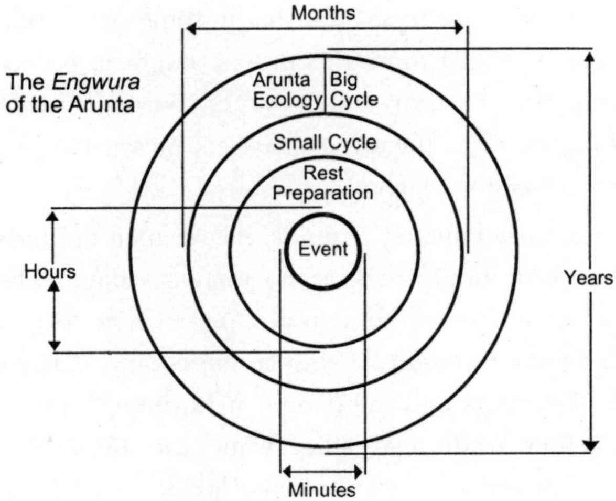

Fig. 1

The overall structure of the *Engwura* is analogic, while its interior structure is dramatic. The two structures are integrated because the

Arunta believed concretely in the Dreamtime and experienced their own lives as divided between 'ordinary' and 'super-ordinary' realities. They experienced an interaction between these realities, and *Engwura* performers were the navel, or link, or point-of-time-and-place where the two realities meshed.

I saw an ecological ritual similar to the *konj kaiko* (but much less inclusive than the *Engwura*) in March 1972, at Kurumugl in the Eastern Highlands of New Guinea.[14] Surrounding the performance of the *kaiko* is no special self-conciousness—that is, the ritual functions without the Tsembaga being explicitly aware of its functions; and aside from commendatory or critical comments on the dancing no aesthetic judgments are passed. In other words there are neither performance theorists nor critics among the Tsembaga. At Kurumugl the people know what the ritual does and why it was established—to inhibit warfare among feuding groups. The ritual at Kurumugl is already travelling along the continuum towards theatre in the modern sense. Knowing what the ritual does is a very important step in the development of theatre from ritual.

It's my purpose to outline a process through which theatre develops from ritual; and also to suggest that in some circumstances ritual develops from theatre. I think this process ought to be documented from contemporary or near-contemporary sources because so often the jump from ritual to theatre is assumed, or attributed to ancient events the evidence for which is suspect.[15]

Unlike the *kaiko* dancing grounds, the 'council grounds' (as they are called) at Kurumugl are near no regular village. The colonial Australian government set them up as a place where former enemies assemble to *sing-sing* (pidgin for drama-music-dance). The difference between the Tsembaga and the people at Kurumugl is that the *kaiko* brought together traditional allies while the Kurumugl *sing-sing* assembles traditional enemies. The performances at Kurumugl are always in danger of tipping over into actual combat, even though the performances are very much like those of the *konj kaiko*: dance movements adapted from combat, war chants, the arrival of a guest group at a dance ground piled high with freshly slaughtered, cooked pork.

The celebration at Kurumugl that I saw took two days. The first consisted of arriving, setting up temporary house inside long rectangular huts, digging cooking ovens. All the people gathered—about 350—were of one tribal group. They awaited the arrival of their guests, a group comparable in size, but recently their enemies. The second day began with the slaughter of about two hundred pigs. These are clubbed on the snouts and heads. As each owner kills his animal he recites—sings—a speech telling how difficult it was to raise the pig, who it is promised to, what a fine animal it is, etc. The *proforma recitatives* are applauded with laughs and roars, as they often contain jokes and obscene invective. The orations are accompanied by the death squeals of the pigs. Then the animals are gutted, butchered and lowered in halves and quarters into earth ovens to cook. Their guts are hung in nets over the ovens and steamed. Their bladders are blown into balloons and given to the children. The sight and smell of so much meat and blood excites the people, including me. No special clothes are worn for the killing. The only ritual element I detected was the careful display of pig jawbones on a circular altar-like structure in the middle of the dance grounds. From each jaw flowers were hung.

As the cooking starts, the men retire to the huts to begin adorning themselves. From time to time a man emerges to try on a towering head-dress of cassowary and peacock feathers. The women cook and tend to the children. After about four hours the meat, still nearly raw, is taken from the ovens and displayed in long rows. Each family lays out its own meat—the women doing most of the work—like so much money in the bank: pork is wealth in the Highlands. As more and more men finish dressing they emerge from the huts to show off and admire each other in a grudging way—the adorning is very competitive. Some women also adorned themselves, dressing much like the men. I couldn't determine if this was traditional or an innovation. A man invited Joan MacIntosh[16] and me into his hut to watch him put on his makeup. He set out a mirror and tins of pigment (bought from a Japanese trading store) and then applied blue, red and black to his torso, shoulders, arms and face. He painted half his nose red and the other half, blue. I asked him what the patterns meant. He said he chose them because he liked the way they looked. The Australian aborigines, by contrast, adorn their bodies with patterns each detail of which is linked to ancestral beings, sexual magic or recent events. Aborigine body painting is mapmaking and myth-telling.

Our performer showed us his headdress of four-foot-long feathers, and stepped outside to try it on. As he emerged from the hut his casual air dropped and he literally thrust his chest forward, gave a long whooping call, put on his headdress and displayed himself. He was costumed for a social not a dramatic role—that is, not to present a fictional character whose life was separable from his own, but to show himself in a special way: to display his strength, his power, his wealth, his authority. It is not easy to distinguish between these kinds of roles, except that in drama the script is already fixed in its details, the precise gestures of the role are rehearsed for a particular occasion (and other occasions, other 'productions', might eventuate in different gestures), while 'in life' the script is 'replaced by an ongoing process, this process is set in motion by the objective demands of the role, and the subjective motives and goals of the actor'.[17] An awareness that social and dramatic roles are indeed closely related to each other, and locating their points of convergence in the mise-en-scène rather than in the mind of the playwright, has been one of the major developments in contemporary theatre. This development has been helped by film and television—by film because it presents dramatic actions on location, as if in 'real life', and by TV because all so-called news is staged. It is staged not only by the obvious editing of raw footage to suit TV format and the need to sell time (that is, to hold the viewer's attention), but also as it is actually made. Many guerrilla activities, terrorist raids, kidnappings, assassinations and street demonstrations are theatricalized events performed by groups of people in order to catch the attention of larger masses of people by means of TV. This is the main way today in which powerless groups get a hearing. In response, the authorities stage their repressive raids, their assaults and their reprisals: to show the world how the insurgents will be dealt with, to display the power of authority and to terrorize the viewer. Thus an apparent two-person exchange between activist and authority is actually a three-person arrangement with the spectator supplying the vital link. Thus are we continually being educated to the histrionic structure of communication.[18]

The seeds of this histrionic sense are at Kurumugl. As these people are 'technified' (already they have planes before cars, TV before newspapers) they will leap not into the twentieth century but beyond, going directly from pre-industrial tribalism to automation-age tribalism. The big difference between the two is that pre-industrial tribalism scatters power among a large number of local leaders, there being no way for people to maintain themselves in large masses; automation-age tribalism is a way of controlling megalopolitic masses. I mean by tribalism the shaping of social roles not through individual choice but by collective formation; the substitution of histrionic-ritualized events for ordinary events; the sacralization or increasingly closely codified definition of all experience; and the disappearance of solitude and one-to-one intimacy as we have developed it since the Renaissance. Automation-age tribalism is medievalism under the auspices of technology. Such tribalism is good for the theatre if by good one means that most social situations will be governed by conventional, external gestures loaded with metaphorical symbolic significances. Anomie and identity crisis are eliminated and in their places are fixed roles and rites of passage transporting persons not only from one status to another but from one identity to another. These transportations are achieved by means of performances. I call these kinds of performances 'transformances' because the performances are the means of transformation from one status, identity or situation to another.

When the performer at Kurumugl stepped outside his hut he joined a group of envious males whose costumes were, like his, peculiar amalgams of traditional and imported stuff: sunglasses and bones stuck through the septum; cigarette holders and homemade tobacco pipes; khaki shorts and grass skirts. But despite the breakdown in traditional costume an old pattern was being worked out. An ecological ritual where the pig meat was a 'payback' (pigdin for fulfilling a ritual obligation) from the hosts to the guests. As among the Tsembaga every adult male at Kurumugl was in a debtor relationship to persons arriving in the afternoon of the second day. The nature of the payback is such that what is given back must exceed what is owed. (This is true even of war, where a perpetual imbalance in casualties must be maintained.) The payback ceremony involves an exchange of roles in which creditors become debtors and debtors become creditors. This insures that more ceremonies will follow when the new debtors accumulate enough pigs. Never is a balance struck, because a balance would threaten an end to the obligations, and this would lead to war. As long as the obligations are intact the social web transmits continuous waves of paybacks back and forth. The visitors approaching Kurumugl came not as friends but as invaders. The afternoon's performance was not a party but a ritual combat with the guests assaulting Kurumugl in a modified war dance, armed with fighting spears, and the campers at Kurumugl defending their ground and the immense pile of meat piled in the centre of it. Instead of a secret raiding party there were dancers; instead of taking human victims, they took meat. And instead of doubt about the outcome everyone knew what was going to happen. Thus a ritualized social drama (as war in the Highlands often is) moves toward becoming an aesthetic drama in which a script of actions is adhered to—the script being known in advance and carefully prepared for.

Again, differences between social and aesthetic drama are not easy to specify. Social drama has more variables, the outcome is in doubt—it is more like a game or sporting context. Aesthetic drama is almost totally arranged in advance, and the participants can concentrate not on strategies of achieving their goals—at Kurumugl, to penetrate to where the meat was, or to defend the meat pile—but on displays; aesthetic drama is less instrumental and more ornamental than social drama. Also, it can use symbolic time and place, and so become entirely fictionalized.

Early in the afternoon of the second day I heard from outside the camp the chanting and shouting of the invaders. The people in camp returned these shouts so that an antiphonal chorus arose. Then the men in camp—and a contingent of about twenty women who were fully armed—rushed to the edges of Kurumugl and the ritual combat began. Both sides were armed with bows and arrows, spears, sticks and axes. They chanted in a rhythm common to the Highlands—a leader sings a phrase and is overlapped by the unison response of many followers. This call-and-response is in loud nasal tones, a progression of quarter and half notes. Such chants alternate with ketchak-like staccato grunts-pants-shouts. From about one to five in the afternoon the two groups engaged in fierce ritual combat. Each cycle of singing and dancing climaxed when parties of warriors rushed forward from both sides, spears ready for throwing, and, at apparently the last second, did a rapid kick-from-the-knee step instead of throwing their weapons. The weapons became props in a performance of aggression displaced, if not into friendship, at least into a non-deadly confrontation.

The assaults of the invaders were repeated dozens of times; a lush and valuable peanut field was trampled to muck; each assault was met by determined counterattack. But foot by foot the invaders penetrated to the heart of the camp ground—to the pile of meat and the altar of jaw bones and flowers. All the meat previously laid out in rows was now piled three feet deep—a huge heap of legs, snouts, ribs and flanks all tangled together. Three live white goats were tethered to a pole at the edge of the meat pile. Once the invaders reached the meat they merged with their hosts in one large, whooping, chanting, dancing doughnut of warriors. Around and around the meat they danced, for nearly an hour. I was pinned up against a tree, between the armed dancers and the meat. Then, suddenly, the dancing stopped and orators plunged into the meat, pulling a leg, or a flank, or a side of ribs, and shouted-sung-declaimed things like:

> This pig I give you in payment for the pig you gave my father three years ago! Your pig was scrawny, no fat on it at all, but my pig is huge, with lots of fat, much good meat—much better than the one my father got! And my whole family, especially my brothers, will remember that we are giving you today better than what we got, so that you owe us, and will help us if we need you beside us in a fight!

Sometimes the speechifying rises to song; sometimes insults are hurled back and forth. The fun in the orating, and the joking, stands on a very serious foundation: the participants do not forget that not so long ago they were blood enemies. After more than an hour of orating, the meat is distributed. Sleds are made to carry it shoulder high and whole families, with much singing, leave with their share of meat.

The performance at Kurumugl consists of displaying the meat, ritual combat, the merging of the two groups into one, orating and carrying the meat away. Preparations for this performance are both immediate, the day before at the camp (and at the visitors' residence), and long-range: raising the pigs, acquiring costumes and ornaments. After the performance comes the cleanup, the travel home, the distribution of the meat, feasting and stories about the *sing-sing*. By means of the performance the basic relationship—one might say the fundamental relationship—between the invading and the host groups is inverted.

ACTUALITY 1 ⟶	TRANSFORMANCE ⟶	ACTUALITY 2
Group A is debtor to Group B		Group B is debtor to Group A

As in all rites of passage something has happened during the performance; *the performance both symbolizes and actualizes the change in status*. The dancing at Kurumugl is the process by which change happens and it is the only process (other than war) recognized by all the parties assembled at Kurumugl. Giving and taking the meat not only symbolizes the changed relationship between Group A and B, it is the change itself. This convergence of symbolic and actual event is missing from aesthetic theatre. We have sought for it by trying to make the performer 'responsible' or 'visible' in and for his performance—either through psychodramatic techniques or other psychological means. This use of psychology is a reflection of our preoccupation with the individual. Where performances have been sociologically or politically motivated—such as happenings and guerrilla theatre—the authenticating techniques have included emphasis on the event in and for itself, the development of group consciousness and appeals to the public at large. But a fundamental contradiction undermines these efforts. At Kurumugl enough actual wealth and people could be assembled in one place so that what was done in the performance focused actual economic, political and social power. In our society only a charade of power is displayed at theatrical performances. When this is recognized, authenticating theatres preoccupy themselves with symbolic activities, feeling helpless in the face of the hollowness of the authenticating tasks they set up for themselves. So-called real events are revealed as metaphors. In a society as large and wealthy as ours only aesthetic theatre is possible. Or authenticating theatres must seek a basis other than economics; or fully ally themselves with established authority. None of these options is as easy as it sounds.

At Kurumugl the change between Group A and B is not simply the occasion for a celebratory performance (as a birthday party celebrates but does not effect a change in age). The performance effects what it celebrates. It opens up enough time in the right place for the exchange to be made: it is liminal: a fluid mid-point between two fixed structures. Only for a brief time do the two groups merge into one dancing circle; during this liminal time/place *communitas* is possible—that levelling of all differences in an ecstasy that so often characterizes performing.[19] Then, and only then, the exchange takes place.

war parties	transformed into	dancing groups
human victims		pig meat
battle dress		costumes
combat		dancing
debtors		creditors
creditors		debtors
two groups		one group

The transformations above the line convert actualities into aesthetic realities. Those below the line effect a change from one actuality into another. It is only because the transformations above the line happen that those below the line can take place in peace. All the transformations—aesthetic as well as actual—are temporary: the meat will be eaten, the costumes doffed, the dance ended; the single group will divide again according to known divisions; today's debtors will be next year's creditors, etc. The celebration at Kurumugl managed a complicated and potentially dangerous exchange with a minimum of danger and a maximum of pleasure. The mode of achieving 'real results'—paying debts, incurring new obligations—was performing; the dancing does not celebrate achieving results, it does not precede or follow the exchange, it is the means of making the transformations; the performance is effective.

The Tsembaga, Arunta and Kurumugl performances are ecological rituals. Whatever enjoyment the participants take in the dancing, and however carefully they prepare themselves for dancing, the dances are danced to achieve results. In religious rituals results are achieved by appealing to a transcendent Other (who puts in an appearance either in person or by surrogate). In ecological rituals the other group, or the status to be achieved, or some other clearly human arrangement is the object of the performance. An ecological ritual with no results to show 'below the line' would soon cease. The 'above the line' transformations change aggressive actions into harmless and pleasure-giving performances (in the cases cited). One is struck by the analogy to certain biological adaptations among animals.[20]

In the New Guinea Highlands, at first under the pressure of the colonial police, later under its own momentum, warfare is transformed into dancing. As above-the-line activities grow in importance, entertainment as such takes over from efficacy as the reason for the performance. It is not only that creditors and debtors need to exchange roles, but also that people want to show off; it is not only to get results that the dances are staged, but also because people like dancing for its own sake. Efficacy and entertainment are opposed to each other, but they form a binary system, a continuum.

EFFICACY ⟵⟶	ENTERTAINMENT
(Ritual)	(Theatre)
results	fun
link to an absent Other	only for those here
symbolic time	emphasizes now

brings Other here	audience is the Other
performer possessed, in trance	performer knows what s/he's doing
audience participates	audience watches
audience believes	audience appreciates
criticism is discouraged	criticism is encouraged
collective creativity	individual creativity

The basic opposition is between efficacy and entertainment, not between ritual and theatre. Whether one calls a specific performance ritual or theatre depends on the degree to which the performance tends towards efficacy or entertainment. No performance is pure efficacy or pure entertainment. The matter is complicated because one can look at specific performances from several vantages; changing perspective changes classification. For example, a Broadway musical is entertainment if one concentrates on what happens onstage and in the house. But if the point of view expands—to include rehearsals, backstage life before, during and after the show, the function of the roles in the careers of each performer, the money invested by backers, the arrival of the audience, their social status, how they paid for their tickets (as individuals, expense accounts, theatre parties, etc.) and how this indicates the use they're making of the performance (as entertainment, to advance their careers, to support a charity, etc.)—then the Broadway musical is more than entertainment; it reveals many ritual elements.

Recently, more performances have been emphasizing the rehearsal and backstage procedures. At first this was as simple as showing the lighting instruments and using a half-curtain, as Brecht did. But within the last fifteen years the process of mounting the performance the workshops that lead up to the performance, the means by which an audience is brought into the space and led from the space and many other previously automatic procedures, have become the subjects of theatrical manipulations. These procedures have to do with the theatre-in-itself and they are, as regards the theatre, efficacious: that is, these procedures are what makes a theatre into a theatre regardless of themes, plot or the usual 'elements of drama'. *The attention paid to the procedures of making theatre are, I think, attempts at ritualizing performance, of finding in the theatre itself authenticating acts*. In a period when authenticity is increasingly rare in public life the performer has been asked to surrender his traditional masks and be himself; or at least to show how the masks are put on and taken off. Instead of mirroring his times the performer is asked to remedy them. The professions taken as models for theatre are medicine and the church. No wonder shamanism is popular among theatre people: shamanism is that branch of doctoring that is religious, and that kind of religion that is full of ironies and tricks.[21]

At present efficacy is ascending to a dominant position over entertainment. It is my belief that theatre history can be given an overall shape as a development along a core which is a *braided structure* constantly interrelating efficacy and entertainment. At each period in each culture one or the other is dominant—one is ascending while the other is descending. Naturally, these changes are part of changes in the overall social structure; yet performance is not a passive mirror of these social changes but a part of the complicated feedback process that brings about change. At all times a dialectical tension exists between efficacious and entertainment tendencies. For Western theatre, at least, I think it can be shown that when the braid is tight—that is, when efficacy and entertainment are both present in nearly equal degrees—theatre flourishes. During these brief historical moments the theatre answers needs that are both ritualistic and pleasure-giving. Fifth-century Athenian theatre, Elizabethan theatre, and possibly the theatre of the late nineteenth century and/or of our own times show the kind of convergence I'm talking about. When efficacy dominates, performances are universalistic, allegorical, ritualized, tied to a stable established order; this kind of theatre persists for a relatively long time. When entertainment dominates, performances are class-oriented, individualized, show business, constantly adjusted to suit the tastes of a fickle audience. The two most recent convergences—the rise of entertainment before the Elizabethan period and the rise of efficacy during the modern period—are necessarily opposites of each other.

The model that I offer is of course a simplification. I present it as a help in conceptualizing my view of the progression of theatre history, which I think has its own logic and internal force. The late medieval period was dominated by efficacious performances: church services, court ceremonies, moralities, pageants. In the early Renaissance these began to decline and popular entertainments, always present, gained, finally becoming dominant in the form of the public theatres of the Elizabethan period. The private and court theatres developed alongside the public theatres. The private theatres were for the upper classes. Although some professionals worked in both public and private theatres, and some spectators attended both, these entertainments were fundamentally opposed to each other. The conflicts between the public and private theatres never worked themselves out because all the theatres were closed in 1642. When theatres reopened at the Restoration the Elizabethan public theatre was gone and all the theatres resembled the private theatres and masques, the property of the upper classes. During the eighteenth and nineteenth centuries this aristocratic theatre developed into the bourgeois theatre, as that class rose to displace the aristocracy. The dominant efficacious mode of the medieval centuries went underground to re-emerge in the guise of social and political drama during the last third of the nineteenth century. This new naturalistic theatre opposed the commercialism and pomposity of the boulevards and allied itself to scientific theatrical styles and techniques. The avant garde identified itself both with Bohemianism—the outcasts of bourgeois society—and science, the source of power. Avant garde artists used terms like 'experimental' and 'research' to characterize their work, which took place in 'laboratories'. Efficacy lies at the ideological heart of all aspects of this new theatre [Fig. 2].

During the last third of the twentieth century, in America at least, the entertainment theatre, threatened by irrelevance or extinction, broke into two parts: an increasingly outmoded commercial theatre typified by Broadway and a subsidized subscription-based 'regional theatre' existing in many mid to large sized cities across the nation. The 1974 First American Congress of Theatre (and, as it turned out, the last) was an attempt by New York commercial producers to ally

Efficacy/Entertainment Braid:
Fifteenth to Twenty-First Centuries
in the English and American Theatres

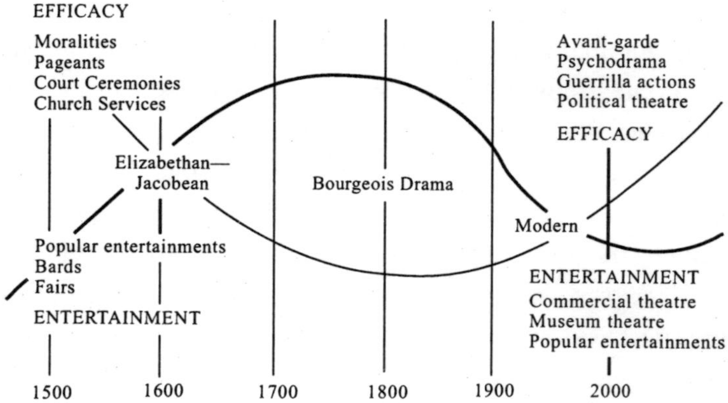

Fig. 2

themselves with the regional theatres.[23] Although such an alliance is inevitable—many Broadway plays now originate at regional theatres—it's most likely ultimately that the regional theatres will absorb Broadway. Or, as is happening increasingly, film interests such as Disney will use Broadway as a profitable market for film-to-stage productions such as *The Lion King* or *Beauty and the Beast*. In the meanwhile, the efficacious performing arts—political theatre, therapeutic performance, theatre for development and education—continued to expand and flourish. At the same time, the braid is tightening with regard to the relationship between entertainment performance and avant garde performance genres (experimental theatre, certain kinds of dance, performance art). Many practitioners of these arts desire a successful commercial career—on Broadway, in films or TV. In the early 1970s, I thought that by the turn of the twenty-first century efficacious performance would dominate. Instead, all kinds of performance types are existing side by side. The notable fact is that the efficacity in performance is here to stay for the foreseeable future.

Up to here I've said this: (1) in some social settings ritual performances are part of ecosystems and mediate political relations, group hierarchy and economics; (2) in other settings ritual performances begin to take on qualities of show business; (3) there is a dialectical-dyadic continuum linking efficacy to entertainment—both are present in all performances, but in each performance one or the other is dominant; (4) in different societies, at different times, either efficacy or entertainment dominates, the two being in a braided relationship to each other.

O. B. Hardison quotes Honorius of Autun's twelfth-century view of the Mass as evidence that people at the time saw this ceremony as drama:

> It is known that those who recited tragedies in theatres presented the actions of opponents by gestures before the people. In the same way our tragic author [i.e. the celebrant] represents by his gestures in the theatre of the Church before the Christian people the struggle of Christ and teaches to them the victory of his redemption. [Honorius then compares each movement of the Mass to an equivalent movement of tragic drama.] . . . When the sacrifice has been completed, peace and Communion are given by the celebrant to the people. . . . Then, by the *Ite, missa est,* they are ordered to return to their homes with rejoicing. They shout *Deo gratias* and return home rejoicing.[24]

What is extraordinary about Honorius' description is that it is a medieval view, not a backwards glance by a modernist. Honorius' Mass is more familiar to those who have attended avant garde performances than to those whose experience is limited to orthodox theatre. The twelfth-century Mass employed many avant garde techniques: it was allegorical, it used audience participation, it treated time teleologically, it extended the scope of the performance from the church to the roadways to the homes. But for all this I still think it is fair to call this Mass a ritual rather than theatre. My opinion is founded on the almost totally efficacious nature of the Mass. As Hardison says, 'The service . . . has a very important aesthetic dimension, but it is essentially not a matter of appreciation but of passionate affirmation.'[25] The Mass was a closed circle which included only the congregation and the officiants; there was literally and figuratively no room for appreciators. The Mass was an obligatory action entered into either joyfully or sullenly, through which members of the congregation signalled to each other and to the hierarchy their continued participation in the congregation. What I say of the twelfth-century Mass, Rappaport has said of the Tsembaga:

> While the scope of the social unity is frequently not made explicit, it would seem that in some studies it is what Durkheim called a 'church', that is, 'a society whose members are united by the fact that they think in the same way in regard to the sacred world and its relations with the profane world, and by the fact that they translate these common ideas into common practices.' . . . Such units, composed of aggregates of individuals who regard their collective well-being to be dependent upon a common body of ritual performances, might be called 'congregations'.[26]

Because of its all-inclusive hold on its congregation the Mass was not theatre in the classical or modern sense. Theatre comes into existence when a separation occurs between audience and performers. The paradigmatic theatrical situation is a group of performers soliciting an audience who may or may not respond by attending. The audience is free to attend or stay away—and if they stay away it is the theatre that suffers, not its would-be audience. In ritual, staying away means rejecting the congregation—or being rejected by it, as in excommunication, ostracism or exile. If only a few stay away, it is those who are absent who suffer; if many stay away, the congregation is in danger of schism or extinction. To put it another way: *ritual is an event upon which its participants depend; theatre is an event which depends on its participants*. The process is not cut-and-dry. But evidence of the transformational steps by which theatre emerges from ritual—by which an efficacious event in which the participants depend on the performance is transformed into an entertainment in which the entertainers depend on an audience—is not locked in ancient or medieval documents. The transformation of ritual into theatre is occurring today.

Asaro is a village about seventy miles east of Kurumugl. There the famous dance of the Mudmen is performed as a tourist entertainment three times a week. It was not always so. The villagers originally performed only when they felt threatened by attack. Before dawn village men went to a local creek, rubbed their bodies with white mud (the colour of death) and constructed grotesque masks of wood frames covered by mud and vegetation. Emerging from the creek at dawn, possessed by the spirits of the dead, the dancers moved in an eerie, slow, crouching step. Sometimes they went to the village of their enemies and frightened them, thus preventing attack; sometimes they danced in their own village. The dances took less than ten minutes; preparations took most of the previous night. (This ratio of preparation to performance is not unusual; it is present even in modern Western theatre in the rehearsal-performance ratio.) The dance of the Mudmen was performed occasionally, when needed. After pacification by Australian authorities there was less need for the Mudmen. However, in the mid-sixties a photographer from the *National Geographic Magazine* paid the villagers to stage the dance for him. These photos became world famous—and it was not long before tourists demanded to see the Mudmen. (Even the name 'Mudmen' is an invention for tourists; I don't know the original name of the ceremony.) Because Asaro is near the Mount Hagan-Goroka road it was easy to arrange for minibuses to bring spectators to the village. Tourists pay up to $20 each to see the short dances; of this sum the Asaroans get 10 per cent. Because the 10-minute dance is not a long enough show by Western standards, the dancing has been augmented by a display of bow-and-arrow marksmanship, a photo session and a 'market'. But Asaro is not (yet) a craft village, and the few necklaces and string bags I saw for sale were pathetic—the day I was there no one bought anything.

The people of Asaro don't know what their dance is any more. Surely it's not to frighten enemies—it attracts tourists. It has no relationship to the spirits of the dead who appear only before dawn, and the tourists come a little after midday. The social fabric of Asaro has been torn to shreds, but the changes required of the Mudmen dance are a result of the deeper disruptions of Highlands life and only in a minor way a cause of these disruptions. In fact, despite the exploitation of the village by the tourist agencies, the meagre sums paid the Asaroans are needed desperately during a period when the barter economy has fallen apart. I expect future changes in the dance will make it longer, more visually complicated, possibly adding musical accompaniment; the craft skills of the villagers will improve, or they will import stuff to sell; their percentage of the take will rise. In short, the dance will approach those Western standards of entertainment represented by the tastes of the audience, and the benefits will rise accordingly. Presently, the Asaroans perform a traditional ritual emptied of its efficacy but not yet regarded as a theatrical entertainment.

Joan MacIntosh and I arrived before the tourists and stayed after they left. The villagers looked at us curiously—we were taking pictures of the tourists as well as of the dancers. After the other whites left, a man came up to us and in pidgin asked us to come with him. We walked four miles along a ridge until we got to Kenetisarobe. There we met Asuwe Yamuruhu, the headman. He wanted us to go to Goroka and tell the tourists about his dancers; he wanted tourists to come and watch a show which, he assured us, was much better than the Mudmen. It began to rain very hard as we squatted in the entrance to a round hut—around us, in the rain, a few villagers watched. We agreed on a price—$4 a person—and a time, the next afternoon; not only would we see dances but we could tape-record songs too.

The next afternoon we arrived with two friends, paid our $16, and saw a dance consisting of very slow steps, as if the dancers were moving through deep mud, their fingers splayed and their faces masked or tied into grotesque shapes. (Peter Thoady, headmaster of the Goroka Teachers' College, told us that the distortion of the faces probably was in imitation of yaws, a disfiguring disease common in the area.) The dancers moved in a half-crouch and occasionally shouted phrases and expletives. The Grassmen of Kenetisarobe were very like the Mudmen of Asaro. After the dancing we spent about an hour recording music, talking and smoking.

The Kenetisarobe dance was adapted from ceremonial farces of the region. Asuwe staged them for us—he knew that Asaro was making money from its dance, and the Kenetisarobe show was modelled on the Asaro formula: slow dance, grotesque masks, plenty of opportunity for photographs and a follow-up after the dance. What the people of Asaro did with a minimum of self-awareness, Asuwe did with a keen sense of theatre business. Examples of the same pattern abound. In Bali tourist versions of barong and ketchak are everywhere—along the Denpasar to Ubud road signs advertising these performances are as frequent as movie marquees in America. Signs, in English, often read: 'Traditional Ketchak—Holy Monkey Dance Theatre—Tonight at 8', or 'Barong—Each Wednesday at 8 on the Temple Steps'. The Balinese, with characteristic sophistication, make separate tourist shows and keep authentic performances secret—and, more important, far from the main road. Tourists want to drive to their entertainments; they want a dependable schedule; and they want a way to leave conveniently if they choose to go early. Most authentic performances—of ketchak and of other actual ritual performances—are accessible only on foot, through rather thick jungle and only with the permission of the village giving the performance. During my two weeks in Bali I saw two such performances. We stumbled on a ketchak while walking through the monkey forest near Ubud—we followed some women carrying offerings of food. Once we entered Tigal we stayed there for ten hours before the ketchak began a little after 9 pm. At Tenganan we saw the final two days of the annual Abuang. Some of the ceremony was public and about fifty tourists joined the villagers to enjoy the afternoon dancing. These people were asked to leave by 5 pm. We were quietly told to remain in the town office. Then, after dark, we were taken to different compounds in the village for different aspects of the ceremony. We were also allowed to listen to special gamelon music played before dawn. We weren't allowed to photograph, and only a limited amount of tape recording was allowed. The daytime ceremonies definitely had the feel of an entertainment: outsiders came in, shops were open and doing a brisk business, the dances were carefully choreographed to the gamelon music. At night the operation was different: each aspect of the ceremony was privatized and done not with an eye to its prettiness but to its correctness; time gaps between elements were longer and more irregular; many discussions concerning how to do certain things were held, and this delayed the ceremonies. The subject matter of the Abuang—if I can use that phrase—is the presentation of all the unmarried males to all the unmarried females. The daytime dances showed everyone off; the night-time ceremonies concerned actual betrothal.

Surely the tourist trade has influenced so-called 'genuine' performances in Bali and elsewhere. I have no contempt for these changes. Changes in conventions, themes, methods and styles occur because of opportunism, audience pressures, professionalism (itself often a new concept) and new technology. Tourism has been really important and worldwide only since the advent of cheap air travel. Theatre historians will regard tourism as of as much importance to twentieth-century theatre as the exchange between England and the Continent was in the sixteenth and seventeenth centuries. Theatre people imitate popular imported modes, and the locals respond to the demands of rich visitors—or local audiences demand changes because they've absorbed the tastes of alien cultures. From one point of view these changes are corruptions—a clamour is raised to establish cultural zoos in which the original versions of age-old rituals can be preserved. But even traditional performances vary greatly from generation to generation—an oral tradition is flexible, able to absorb many personal variations within set parameters. And the cultural-zoo approach is itself the most pernicious aspect of tourism. I hate the genocide that has eradicated such cultures as that of the Australian Aborigines. But I see nothing wrong with what's happening in Bali and New Guinea, where two systems of theatre exist. The relationship between these is not a simple division between tourist and authentic. More studies are needed on the exchange between what's left of traditional performances and emerging tourist shows. And at what moment does a tourist show become itself an authentic theatrical art?

Tourism is a two-way street: travellers bring back experiences, expectations, and, if the tourists are practitioners, techniques, scenes and even entire forms. The birth ritual of *Dionysus in 69* was adapted from the Asmat of West Irian; several sequences in the Living Theatre's *Mysteries* and *Paradise Now* were taken from yoga and Indian theatre; Phillip Glass's music draws on gamelon and Indian raga; Imamu Baraka's writing is deeply influenced by African modes of storytelling and drama. The list could be extended, and to all the arts. Many innovators since World War II (a great war for travel) have been decisively influenced by work from cultures other than their own; this means, for Western artists, Asia, Africa and Oceania. The impact of communal-collective forms on contemporary Western theatre is like that of classical forms on the Renaissance. The differences, however, are also important: in the Renaissance all that remained of classical culture were architectural ruins, old texts and relics of the plastic arts. This material was frequently fragmented and corrupt. Also, Renaissance scholars looked with universal respect, even awe, at what they found of classical Greece and Rome. Today's cross-cultural feed is mainly in the area of performances; the shows have been seen intact; the originators of the performances are former colonial peoples, or peoples who were considered inferior by populations around the north Atlantic basin. In other words, it is logical that today's influences should be felt first in the avant garde.

A very clear and provable Asian influence on contemporary Western theatre is seen in Grotowski's work, particularly its 'poor theatre' phase, from around 1964 to around 1971. This period includes several versions of *Akropolis*, *The Constant Prince* and the first versions of *Apocalypsis Cum Figuris*. The foundation of this work is the psychophysical/plastique exercises which Grotowski and Ryszard Cieslak taught in many of their workshops in Poland and abroad. Ever since I learned some of these exercises in 1967, I felt they were influenced not only by yoga, which Grotowski acknowledges, but by the south Indian dance-theatre form, kathakali. In 1972, while visiting the Kathakali Kalamandalam in Kerala, I asked about Grotowski's visits to the school. No one remembered him, but Eugenio Barba was remembered, and in the school's visitors' book I found the following entry:

> The Secretary
> Kalamandalam
> Cheruthuruthy
>
> Dear Sir:
>
> I had not the occasion, last night at the performance to thank you for all the kind help you have given me during my stay here. To you, and to the Superintendent, and to all the boys who were so willing to be of service, I would like to express my gratitude and sincerest thanks.
>
> My visit to Kalamandalam has greatly helped me in my studies and the research material I have collected will surely be of the greatest assistance to those people working at the Theatre Laboratory in Poland.
>
> Many thanks once again,
>
> Yours sincerely,
> Eugenio Barba [signed]

Barba brought kathakali exercises to Grotowski in Poland—they form the core of the plastique and psychophysical exercises. When Barba founded his Odin Teatret he used these exercises—as modified by the Polish Lab—as the basis of his own work. Grotowski has visited India on several occasions, the first in 1956–57, when he also travelled to China and Japan.

Peter Brook's three-month trip in 1972–73 with a troupe of 30 persons through Algeria, Mali, Niger, Dahomey and Nigeria is another version of the 'trading partner' idea. Brook, even more consciously and fully than Grotowski-through-Barba, went to Africa to trade techniques, perform, observe performances. In Brook's words:

Once we sat in Agades in a small hut all afternoon, singing. We and the African group sang, and suddenly we found that we were hitting exactly the same language of sound. Well, we understood theirs and they understood ours, and something quite electrifying happened because, out of all sorts of different songs, one suddenly came upon this common area.

Another experience of that same sort occurred one night when we were camping in a forest. We thought there was no one around for miles, but as always, suddenly, children appeared from nowhere and beckoned. We were just sitting and doing some improvised song, and the children asked us to come down to their village, only a couple of miles away, because there was going to be some singing and dancing later in the night and everyone would be very pleased if we could come.

So we said 'sure'. We walked down through the forest, found this village and found that, indeed, there was a ceremony going on. Somebody had just died and it was a funeral ceremony. We were made very welcome and we sat there, in total darkness under the trees, just seeing these moving shadows dancing and singing. And after a couple of hours they suddenly said to us: the boys say that this is what you do, too. Now you must sing for us.

So we had to improvise a song for them. And this was perhaps one of the best works of the entire journey. Because the song that was produced for the occasion was extraordinarily moving, right and satisfying, and made a real coming together of the people and ourselves. It is impossible to say what produced it, because it was produced as much by the group that was working together in a certain way, with all the work that has gone into that, and as much by all the conditions of the moment that bore their influence: the place, the night, the feeling for the other people, so that we were actually making something for them in exchange for what they had offered us.[27]

Throughout Asia, MacIntosh and I found this same 'exchange policy'. We were invited to stay at Tenganan because the people knew we performed, and at the main public performance the chief insisted that I do a dance.[28] At Karamui in New Guinea—far from any road (we flew in)—we were shown funeral ceremonies (a villager, with much laughter, played the role of the corpse), but we were expected to sing songs in exchange. In the Sepik River village of Kamanabit the headman insisted that MacIntosh be awakened and brought to his house to sing even though she was exhausted from a day's travel; his demand came after I'd been listening to village women singing.

The kind of influence through observation and trading reflected in Barba's letter, Brook's trip and my own experiences is different from Artaud's reaction to Balinese theatre. Artaud was influenced, but the Balinese didn't care; there was no exchange. In the more recent examples work was consciously traded, professionals sought to expand their knowledge.

Whatever the ritual functions of kathakali within the context of Kerala village life, the Kalamandalam is a professional training school and its troupe performs for pay in India and overseas. Foreigners come to study at the Kalamandalam (while I was there about five Westerners were studying). This training does not eventuate in the establishment of kathakali troupes outside India—rather the work is integrated into existing styles. It remains to be seen how the presence of outsiders at the Kalamandalam, and the frequent tours of the troupe, affect the work in Kerala. The situation with Brook is different. The African villagers were in the midst of a religious ritual (a funeral ceremony) but they were also eager to share their entertainment (trading songs) to use their ritual as an item of trade. That the exchange was mutually moving is no surprise—entertainment and ritual co-exist comfortably.

Touring ritual performances around the world—and thereby converting them into entertainments—is nothing new: the Romans were fond of importing exotic entertainments, the more authentic the better. Every colonial or conquering power has done the same. In 1972, at the Brooklyn Academy of Music the following show took place (I quote from the programme):

THE BROOKLYN ACADEMY OF MUSIC
in association with
Mel Howard Productions, Inc.
and
Ninon Tallon-Karlweis
in cooperation with
The Turkish Ministry of Tourism and Information
Present
THE WHIRLING DERVISHES OF TURKEY
(THE PROGRAMME IS A RELIGIOUS CEREMONY. YOU ARE KINDLY REQUESTED TO REFRAIN FROM APPLAUSE.)

The audience had to be told that what they paid money to see as an entertainment retained enough of its ritual basis to require a change in conventional theatrical behaviour. The performance was simple and moving. I suppose a fairly accurate presentation of the dervish ritual. I know that several theatre groups in New York were influenced by it. Both Robert Wilson's Byrd Hoffman group and The Performance Group have used whirling.

In October 1973, the Shingon Buddhist monks came to the Brooklyn Academy of Music with 'ceremonies, music and epics of ancient Japan'. The dervishes whirled on a stage facing the 2,000-seat opera house. The monks performed in a room designed for Brook's appearance after his African trip—a space 75 ft x 40 ft, with a height of about 30 ft. The audience numbered around 200, seated on cushions scattered on the floor, and on bleachers. As at Asaro and Kenetisarobe the Buddhist rituals were not long enough to constitute an entertainment by Western standards. So the programme was augmented by performers of Japanese contemporary music and a recitation of Japanese war tales from the twelfth to fourteenth centuries. Only after the intermission did the monks perform their temple service. The programme described in detail what the monks were doing, what it meant and how the ceremony is used in Japan. Thus the audience was treated as if it were attending Grand Opera, where the libretto is summarized, or a new kind of sport in which the rules, equipment and structure are explained. It seemed to me that the monks, like the dervishes, were deeply into what they were doing. They were 'in character'—and it was impossible to distinguish what they were doing from what Stanislavski required of actors. I was convinced: these dervishes were Dervishes, these monks were Monks. A defined interface between spectators and performers existed; on one side was authenticity, efficacy and ritual, on the other side was entertainment and theatre.

Any ritual can be lifted from its original setting and performed as theatre—just as any everyday event can be.[29] This is possible because context, not fundamental structure, distinguishes ritual, entertainment and ordinary life from each other. The differences among them arise from the agreement (conscious or unexpressed) between performers and spectators. Entertainment/theatre emerges from ritual out of a complex consisting of an audience separate from the performers, the development of professional performers and economic needs imposing a situation in which performances are made to please the audience rather than according to a fixed code or dogma. It is also possible for ritual to arise out of theatre by reversing the process just described. This move from theatre to ritual marks Grotowski's work and that of the Living Theatre. But the rituals created were unstable because they were not attached to actual social structures outside theatre. Also, the difference between ritual, theatre and ordinary life depends on the degree spectators and performers attend to efficacy, pleasure or routine; and how symbolic meaning and effect are infused and attached to performed events. In all entertainment there is some efficacy and in all ritual there is some theatre.[30]

The entire binary 'efficacy/ritual—entertainment/theatre' is performance: performance includes the impulse to be serious and to entertain; to collect meanings and to pass the time; to display symbolic behaviour that actualizes 'there and then' and to exist only 'here and now'; to be oneself and to play at being others; to be in a trance and to be conscious; to get results and to fool around; to focus the action on and for a select group sharing a hermetic language and to broadcast to the largest possible audiences of strangers who buy tickets.

At this moment The Performance Group is working on Brecht's *Mother Courage and Her Children*. Most of our rehearsals have been open—when weather permits, the big overhead front garage door of our theatre has been raised and people off the street, students and friends have come in to watch us work. Every rehearsal has had from five to forty people watching. The rehearsals have a feeling of stop and go, with nothing special planned to accommodate the spectators. Yet their presence makes a deep difference: work on the play now includes a public social core; and the work is about showing-a-way-of-working. This theme will be worked into the formal performances. The space for *Courage*—designed by Jerry N. Rojo and James Clayburgh, collaborating with all the other members of the Group—expresses the interplay between Brecht's drama and the larger performance in which it takes place. A part of the room has been made into a Green Room wholly visible to the audience. When a performer is not in a scene he or she goes into the Green Room, gets some coffee, reads, relaxes. The rest of the theatre is divided into three main spaces: an empty cube 30 ft x 30 ft x 20 ft (including an open pit 20 ft x 8 ft x 7 ft); a 20 ft x 20 ft x 20 ft cube filled with irregular scaffolding, platforms, and ropes; galleries, walkways and a bridge about 11 ft off the ground. The audience can move freely through the entire space, continually changing perspective and mood. It is possible to see everything from a single vantage, but only if one looks through other structures. Scene 9 takes place outside the theatre in Wooster Street, with the large garage door open. The door stays open for the final three scenes—in winter this means that the temperature in the theatre plunges.

Our production has one intermission, after Scene 5. During intermission supper is sold, and the performers mix with the audience. During supper the 'Song of the Great Capitulation' (Scene 4) is sung, as in a cabaret, without insistence that people pay attention. When the drama resumes after supper I think it is experienced differently because of the hour of mingling, talking and sharing of food and drink.[31] Another shift in the mode of experiencing the play comes when the performance moves outside, and the theatre takes on the feeling of the outside. *Mother Courage* is treated as a drama nested in a larger performance event. The ideas behind The Performance Group's production of *Courage* are common to ritual performances: *to control or manipulate the whole world of the performance, not just present the drama at its centre*. In this way a theatrical event in Soho, New York City, is nudged a little way from the entertainment end of the continuum towards efficacy. Without diminishing its theatricality, I hope to enhance its ritual aspects.

Orthodox theories say that ritual precedes theatre, just as efficacy and monism ('primitive oneness') precede entertainment. It is a cliché of interpretations of Paleolithic cave art that some kind of 'ritual' generated the art—and by ritual is meant a serious, efficacious, result-oriented performance either to insure fertility, to placate the powers who control the hunt, to maintain a balance between male and female or something. These things, or some of them, may be true; but they are not the whole truth: entertainment, passing time in play and fun (not the passive and cut-off feeling of 'art for art's sake', but an active involvement with the process of making art) are interwoven with and inseparable from any efficacious aspects of the earliest art. The idea of a primitive oneness is a combination of Edenic fantasy and the Protestant work ethic supported by the projections of early ethnographers too many of whom were missionaries. Accumulating evidence from Paleolithic, early historical, classical, Asian, African and contemporary communal peoples suggest that a complicated social life and rich, symbolic art are co-existent with the human condition. The idea of the 'simple primitive' either noble or savage—has been killed by Lévi-Strauss, La Barre and others. Shamans were artists and performers and doctors and trance-possessed (temporary) psychotics and priests and entertainers. To argue that because several roles are played simultaneously by one person (or class of people), or that because a single performance expresses many contradictory impulses that the art of such people (and their societies) is simple is to look at things upside down.

Industrial societies separate/standardize functions/expressions; communal societies combine many functions/expressions in single , often extended, complicated events. The experience of urban life is to move from one 'pure' event to another—only over time and by means of a synthesis managed by each individual (and many people can't manage it) is there a sense of unity emerging from the multiplicity and pluralism. I personally enjoy this pluralism, but it can go too far and fragment people, not cut them off so much as cut them up. Communal life, on the other hand, includes in each event—even a ceremony as short as the ten-minute Arunta dance a bundle of meanings/functions/expressions. These are not implicit: each participant knows the connections, and the initiate is taught them. The leader of the dance is also the leader of his band, is also a skilled hunter, is also related to the boys being initiated, etc. And, as I've shown, the dance is nested in a complex of ceremonies where each part is a synecdoche. Much of the post-war avant garde is an attempt to overcome fragmentation by approaching performance as a part of rather than apart from the community. Sometimes this community is the community of the artists making the work; this has been the pattern in New York, London, Paris and other Western cities. Sometimes—as in the general uprisings of 1968 the art is joined to large political movements. Sometimes, as in black and Chicano theatre, and more recently in other 'special interest' theatres, the artists identify with—even help to form—a sense of ethnic, racial or political identity. This community-related avant garde is not only a phenomenon of the industrialized West, but also of countries that are industrializing or undergoing great changes in social organization. In Eastern Europe, Japan and in the work of people like Rendra in Indonesia, Soyinka in Nigeria, Boal in Brazil and Argentina we see the same process.

This work is not simple atavism, it is not a wild attempt to dismantle industrialism, or to halt its spread. It is an active seeking to find places within industrial societies—even within the industrial process itself—for communities to exist; and to demand a restructuring of the social order in terms of community, collectively and person-to-person interaction, or 'meetings', as Grotowski says. The problems of industrialization and fragmentation are clearly not problems of capitalism alone. Experiments of the kind I've been talking about are taking place in socialist states too. These experiments still relatively scattered and tentative, and always facing a hostile establishment, are showing signs of taking root; they address themselves to the audience not as a collection of money-paying individual strangers, or forced participants in a show of solidarity (as in mass rallies or coercive church-going), but as a community, even as a congregation, as Turner calls them. And the object of such performances is both to entertain—to have fun—and to create *communities*: a sense of collective celebration. This contemporary movement originated in the avant garde theatre and is moving towards ritual.

Performance doesn't originate in ritual any more than it originates in entertainment. It originates in the binary system: efficacy–entertainment which includes the subset ritual-theatre. From the beginning—logically as well as historically—both terms of the binary are present, are required. At any historical moment there is movement from one pole towards the other. This oscillation is continuous—performance is in an active steady-state.

The whole binary system efficacy/ritual—entertainment/theatre is what I call 'performance'. Performance originates in impulses to make things happen and to entertain; to collect meanings and to pass the time; to be transformed into another and to be oneself; to disappear and to show off; to bring into a celebratory space a transcendent Other who exists then-and-now and later-and-now and to celebrate here-and-now only us who are present; to get things done and to play around; to focus inward on a select initiated group sharing a hermetic language and to broadcast out to the largest possible collection of strangers. These oppositions—and all the others generated by them—comprise performance: it is an active situation, a steady process of transformation. The move from ritual to theatre happens when a participating audience fragments into a collection of people who pay, who come because the show is advertised, who evaluate what they are going to see before they see it; the move from theatre to ritual happens when the audience as a collection of separate people is dissolved into the performance as participants. These opposing tendencies are present in all performances. Brecht, and Meyerhold before him, worked to keep the tension between these extremes working throughout each performance by moving an audience back and forth moment to moment. The deep effect of Brecht's *verfremdung* is to unexpectedly shift modes, styles, rhythms, perspectives; and at the moment of change, when the affective part of a scene abruptly stops, or when a distanced beat suddenly becomes moving—the dramaturgic structure allows the writer/director/performer to make a 'statement', to insert an ironic comment, to encourage the spectator to think about what he's seen and/or felt. The structure of the performance is obliterated by its anti-structure and in the liminal moment a direct communication, a deep contact, with the audience is made. Of all the experiments with theatrical structure over the past century this one is most likely to stick. It resonates back to medieval theatre, and to many folk theatres existing now.

I can best summarize by drawing four models, explaining each as I go.

Actuality 1 ⟵—— ENCOUNTER/EXCHANGE ——⟶ Actuality 2

A meeting takes place at a market or on a battlefield. Goods are traded, money is earned, territory taken, a group routed. The encounter is intended to be entirely efficacious—even though sometimes nothing is traded or battles end in stand-offs. The rituals in this kind of activity are ethological and/or sociological. That is they are based on 'fixed-action patterns', and they are intended to regulate human interaction so that what is supposed to happen, or be determined, by the meeting of individuals and/or groups actually happens. The entertainment/theatrical elements in these kinds of meetings are reduced to a minimum, though they are present. The job is to get through the encounter/exchange as efficiently as possible and arrive at Actuality 2. But even this model doesn't show all that really happens. Markets are places of display, joking, gossiping, singing; they often attract mountebanks and other popular entertainments. Battlefields are places to show the colours, parade strength and in general scare your opponent off the field. Guerrilla war and mass combat work against these theatrical qualities. Thus even at this level the ethological and sociological rituals are embroidered with entertainment. There is a tendency towards:

This is the case with ecological rituals such as those among the Arunta and Tsembaga. Their performances effect changes both in the status of some people participating (through initiation, marriage and other rites of passage) and in economic matters (pigs, sago, trade items). In fact, how good a performance is can be an important element in determining social status. The Greeks offered prizes to their tragedians; our society offers wealth and fame. Among Aborigines and New Guinea people high status is conferred on the better performers. A shaman among the American Indians or in Siberia is honoured for his or her tricks and style.

This process can itself become highly advanced resulting in:

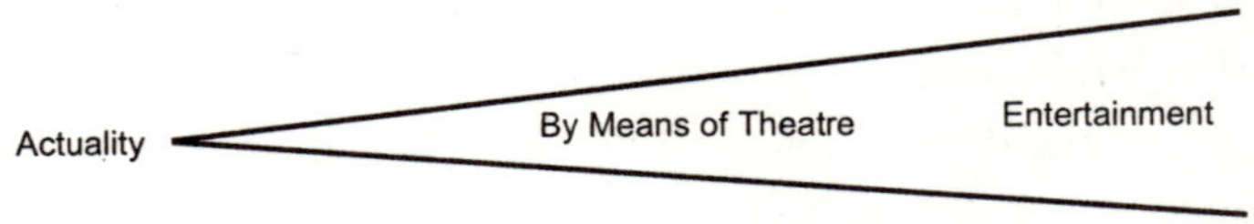

This is what happened when the Dervishes or the Monks performed at the Brooklyn Academy. Rituals which have efficacy in a defined setting become entertainments in another setting. *The Yoshi Show*, presented at the Public Theatre in New York in 1975, included a Buddhist monk, a Shinto priest, a martial arts expert and a Tibetan monk performing along with Yoshi, a Japanese actor who had studied extensively with Peter Brook. The show combined elements of different religious ceremonies with theatrical performing. The event was very confusing because it was neither the presentation of a ritual as theatre nor an entertainment. On the other hand this ambiguity gave it a special power, almost as sacrilege because of the clash of different kinds of worship. In shows of this kind money is exchanged for a peek at ritual. And 'new rituals' are synthesized for the sake of entertainment.

Another example of this model is its reverse:

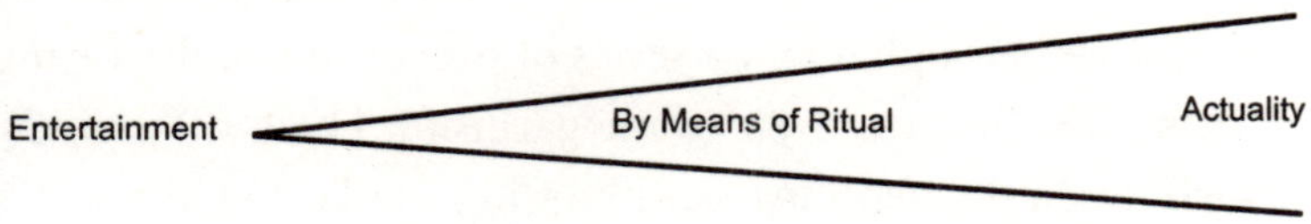

This is what Grotowski is doing. This tendency has been present in his work for the last 10 years. He sets many of his performances in churches, selecting audiences either on an individual basis, or by some means (including very high prices) that limit the number of people, making audiences into elites. In *Fire on the Mountain* each *ul* was peopled by invited participants only. And the nature of the work in the *uls* was to bring about a kind of intimacy and quasi-religious solidarity by means of performance exercises, group encounter/therapy techniques and submission to the will of a strong leader.[32] Grotowski's experiments are like EST in America where groups of people are 'broken down' over a weekend's experience of extreme intensity, often an ordeal of shouting, physical work and direct confrontation. Although this subject won't be explored here the means of encounter therapy are very close to traditional initiation rites where the young boy is broken down and re-made in a short period of time through a series of instructions and ordeals.

During the appearance in Philadelphia in 1973 of the Polish Laboratory Theatre the performances of *Apocalypsis cum Figuris* were only the first step in a more elaborate ceremony. During the performances Grotowski literally 'tapped' five to ten students and asked them to remain after the performance. They were then invited to go with Grotowski and his company to a retreat in the hills not far from Philadelphia where the students and the performers would meet 'on a one-to-one basis'. Clearly the performance of *Apocalypsis* was an entry into some other kind of experience, one which can't be called theatre in the usual sense.

In *Paradise Now* the Living Theatre attempted a similar transformation of entertainment into actuality—in their case a political rather than religious actuality. By challenging the audience where they sit, by inviting them onto the stage, by not presenting a drama or even a set of incidents but rather a plan and a series of provocations, the Living undercut orthodox theatre, even avant gardism. Then, after many spectators left, often the majority—a winnowing similar to Grotowski's but carried out in a different way: where Grotowski selected who was to go with him, the Living allowed the spectators to individually select themselves—the performers led some of the remaining spectators into the streets. An actual political event arose out of the entertainment event by means of a theatrical confrontation. In the streets the performers and spectators were often met by the police. While Grotowski's work eventuates in religious meetings the Living's eventuates in public acts.

The origins of theatre—considered since Aristotle's day to be found in ritual—look different when seen from the perspective of popular entertainment. E. T. Kirby sees theatre beginning in shamanism, certainly a ritual system. But shamanism itself—as Kirby notes—is closely connected to magic acts, acrobatics, puppetry and other popular entertainments. La Barre points out that the Asiatic-American Trickster—a figure that can be traced back to Paleolithic times—is a 'mixture of clown, culture hero and demigod'. La Barre reminds us of the connections between the Trickster and the Greek origins of theatre:

> The great antiquity of the trickster should be suggested first of all by his being much the same in both Paleosiberian and American hunting tribes; and again by the fact that the more a tribe has been influenced by agriculture in America, the less important he becomes in the total tribal mythology as compared with his pre-eminence among both Siberian and

> American hunters. [. . .] We must not forget the element of *entertainment* in Old World shamanism: were tales of the erotic escapades of eagle-Zeus once told in the same tone of voice as those of Sibero-American Raven? And did not shamanistic rivalry develop into both the Dionysian bard-contests of Greek drama in the Old World and into *midewewin* medicine-shows in the New? As for that, have modern medicine-men entirely lost the old shamanic self-dramatization?[33]

So wherever we look, and no matter how far back, theatre is a mixture, a braid, of entertainment and ritual. At one moment ritual seems to be the source, at another it is entertainment that claims primacy. They are a twin-system, tumbling over each other, and vitally interconnected.

Even at this more or less quiet moment, 1976, it's clear that the orthodox dramaturgy—the theatre of plays done in fixed settings for a settled audience relating stories as if they were happening to others—is finished. At least, this kind of theatre doesn't meet the needs of many people—needs as old as theatre itself, combining ritual and entertainment. These needs also include actual group interaction as a remedy for a runaway technology. I am not reacting against technology—I have not bought a cabin in Vermont yet. But I know an authentic need exists for encounters that are neither just informal person-to-person gatherings like parties nor formal, mediated, programmed routines like office or factory work—or watching television and films, for that matter. Theatre is a middle world where actual group interaction can happen—not only through audience participation but by subtler means of audience inclusion and environmental staging; theatre combines artistic-composed behaviour with everyday-spontaneous behaviour. Theatre people are moving into areas once solely occupied by religion and politics. Priests and politicians will doubtlessly pick up new techniques from theatre. But whether they will be able to restore public confidence in their professions is questionable. Will theatre then become a big avenue rather than the sideroad it's been for the past 300 years?

Notes

1. In describing the *kaiko* I followed the account in Roy A. Rappaport's *Pigs for the Ancestors* (New Haven: Yale University Press, 1968). His study is a paradigm of how to examine ritual performances within an ecological context.
2. A fight package is a small bundle containing 'the thorny leaves of the males of a rare, unidentified tree growing in the *kamunga*, called the "fight tree" and personal material belonging to the enemy, such as hair, fragments of leaves worn over the buttocks, and dirt scraped from the skin' (Rappaport, op. cit. p. 120). It is said that pressing the packages to the heart and head will give a man courage and improve his chances of killing an enemy. Materials used in fight packages are acquired from neutrals who have relatives among the enemy; fight packages are items of trade. Their use in peaceful dancing shows the relationship between the dancing and combat; in many parts of Asia performance forms have arisen from martial arts.
3. Rappaport, op. cit. p. 187.
4. Ibid., p. 188.
5. Ibid., p. 189.
6. Ibid., p. 195–6.
7. Ibid., p. 156.
8. Ibid., p. 214.
9. B. Spencer and F. J. Gillen, *The Native Tribes of Central Australia* (N.Y.: Dover Publications, 1968, reprinted from 1899). This study has the advantage over later ones that the tribes described were relatively intact, having just been contacted by the invading Europeans. In Australia contact meant extermination both demographically and culturally.
10. This rhythm of relatively long preparations followed by a brief performance, with a series of performances given on a single day, is common in Australia. See also A. P. Elkin and Catherine and Ronald Berndt, *Art in Arnhem Land* (Chicago: University of Chicago Press, 1950); and Ronald and Catherine Berndt, *The World of the First Australians* (Chicago: University of Chicago Press, 1964). Although we accept this rhythm in dance and music, it has not yet found acceptance in theatre. Still dominated by Aristotelian injunctions we act as if a work has to be of a certain length to acquire seriousness.

11. In Oceania it is not unusual—or was not until the eradication of traditional ways—for ritual performances to form the core of a person's life. Van Gennep's classic analysis of rituals into crisis moments preceded and followed by long periods of relative calm is not wholly descriptive of the situation in New Guinea and Australia. Although the performances are peak experiences, preparations for them continuing over months and years dominate the lives of the people. See F. E. Williams, *The Drama of the Orokolo* (London: OUP, 1940), and Richard Schechner, 'Actuals: A Look into Performance Theory', *in Essays on Performance Theory* 1970–76 (N.Y.: Drama Books Specialists, 1977). See also V. W. Turner, *The Ritual Process* (Chicago: Aldine Publishing Company, 1969); and V. W. Turner, *Dramas, Fields and Metaphors* (Ithaca: Cornell University Press, 1974).
12. See the discussion of 'reactualization' and its relation to the Dreamtime in Mircea Eliade, *Rites and Symbols of Initiation* (N.Y.: Harper Torchbooks, 1965).
13. An excellent account of the intimate association among events, landmarks, and body decorations is given in Richard A. Gould, *Yiwara: Foragers of the Australian Desert* (N.Y.: Charles Scribner's Sons, 1969). See also Geza Roheim, *The Eternal Ones of the Dream* (N.Y.: International Universities Press, 1969; reprinted from 1945).
14. The Highlands consist of a central valley, and many spur valleys, surrounded by mountains rising to 15,000 ft. The whole area is about 300 miles long and 150 miles wide. It is sparsely populated, by less than three million; villages average 400 inhabitants. Because of the terrain many local groups have little contact with each other—and there is much local warfare and feuding. There are about 500 languages, most of them mutually unintelligible, and the largest of them spoken by only 130,000 people. English and pidgin are the basic *linguae francae*.
15. By now criticism of the Cambridge Anthropologists' thesis concerning the ritual origins and structure of Greek theatre is well known. See, for example, E. R. Dodds, *The Greeks and the Irrational* (Berkeley: University of California Press, 1951).
16. Joan MacIntosh, a performer with The Performance Group and my wife, was my partner on the trip to Asia in 1971–72 which forms the experiential background to this piece.

17. Elizabeth Burns, *Theatricality* (N.Y.: Harper and Row, 1972), p. 132. This way of looking at ordinary experiences as theatre has roots, of course, in literature. But its systematic application has only recently begun. The key observations have been made by Erving Goffman, *The Presentation of Self in Everyday Life* (Garden City: Doubleday Anchor Books, 1959), and *Relations in Public* (N.Y.: Basic Books, 1971).

18. According to Robert Brustein, 'News Theatre', in *The New York Times Magazine*, 16 June, 1974, pp. 7ff., news theatre is 'any histrionic proceeding that results from a collaboration between newsworthy personalities, vast public, and the visual or print media (television, films, book publishing, magazines and newspapers). News theatre, in other words, is any event that confuses news with theatre and theatre with news.' I think Brustein's description is accurate, but that he is wrong when he says that 'news' and 'theatre' should be kept distinct. Certainly there are areas of independence, but the two are inherently interdependent. Both are public, action-centred, and crisis-dominated. Furthermore, as the means of news transmission abandons print and uses visual media they approximate the means of theatre. The problems stirred up are not solved by bemoaning the inevitable. Only in finding ways of controlling what's happening will a satisfactory process occur. Take one limited, but decisive, area—the ethics of news reporting. I refer to the ways in which reporting shapes people's responses to events. We all know that so-called 'objective' reporting is anything but objective. But is it distorted simply through the evil designs of the news managers, or is there at work a deep structure which makes even attempts at objectivity impossible? Drama has long had an ethical purpose which is expressed not only overtly but in dramatic structure. News broadcasting used the same structures but without consciousness of the ethics inherent in them. And it is axiomatic that an unconscious ethic will automatically reinforce the *status quo*; or, as Brecht put it, to remain neutral is to support the stronger side. The need then is to make the structures of news reporting—especially its dramatic structures—more conscious; this will lead to greater control over what is being said. Whether these new powers will be used to advance the causes of the people or to repress them remains in doubt.

19. For extended discussions of the concepts of liminality and *communitas* see Turner, *The Ritual Process* and *Dramas, Fields and Metaphors*.

20. Konrad Lorenz, *On Aggression* (N.Y.: Bantam Books, 1967), discusses at some length the development of 'appeasement ceremonies' in animals. More technical descriptions are offered by Irenaus Eibl-Eibesfeldt, *Ethology: The Biology of Behaviour* (N.Y.: Holt, Rinehart and Winston, 1970). Lorenz's description of a special kind of ceremony is almost exactly what I saw in New Guinea, and what so many others have described. 'Of all the various appeasement ceremonies, with their many different roots, the most important for our theme are those appearing or greeting rites which have arisen from redirected aggression movements. They differ from all the already described appeasement ceremonies in that they do not put aggression under inhibition but divert it from certain members of the species and canalize it in the direction of others. This new orientation of aggressive behaviour is one of the most ingenious inventions of evolution, but it is even more than that: wherever redirected rituals of appeasement are observed, the ceremony is bound to the individuality of the participating partners. The aggression of a particular individual is diverted from a second, equally particular individual, while its discharge against all other, anonymous members of the species is not inhibited. Thus discrimination between friend and stranger arises, and for the first time in the world personal bonds between individuals come into being' (pp. 131-2). Or, as the Tsembaga say, 'those who come to our *Kaiko* will also come to our fights'. It is also important to note that the ceremonies Lorenz focused on were greeting ceremonies; the dances in the Highlands may correctly be called greeting dances.
21. E. T. Kirby, 'The Shamanistic Origins of Popular Entertainments', in *TDR*, (March 1974), vol. 18. Kirby sees shamanism as 'The "great unitarian artwork" that fragmented into a number of performance arts' (p. 6). See also E. T. Kirby, 'The Origin of Noh Drama', in *Educational Theatre Journal*, 25: October (1973) and Schechner, *Environmental Theatre* (N.Y.: Hawthorn Books, 1973), the chapter 'Shaman'.
22. George J. Becker, ed., *Documents of Modern Literary Realism* (Princeton: Princeton University Press, 1963). See especially Emile Zola's 'Naturalism in Theatre' and Strindberg's 'Naturalism in Theatre'.
23. The First American Congress of Theatre met in Princeton, 2-6 June 1974. It brought together more than 200 leaders of the American

theatre—very heavily weighted towards producers, managers of regional theatres, and professional administrators. Also the conference was weighted towards New York, organized as it was by Alexander H. Cohen, the New York producer. Eleven panels discussed various problems confronting the theatre, but the real action was in the interaction among individuals and interest groups. It seems likely that a second Congress will be held, one which is less New York dominated. However, it does not appear as if theatre artists will be given any more prominence—that is, writers, directors, actors, and designers will still be under-represented in relationship to the overall number of delegates. The fundamental theme of the Congress—and future Congresses as well—is a growing recognition of a contradictory reality: theatre is marginal, economically speaking, but it seems also to have enduring roots in society. Means are therefore necessary to bring the disparate wings of the theatre together for a common rumination of basically economic issues. Whether politics can, or should, be kept out of these meetings is another question. As for aesthetics, forget it.

24. O. B. Hardison, *Christian Rite and Christian Drama in the Middle Ages* (Baltimore: University of Maryland Press, 1965), p. 40.

25. Ibid., p. 77.

26. Rappaport, *Pigs for Ancestors*, p. 1.

27. Peter Brook, 'On Africa', in *TDR* (September 1973), vol. 17, pp. 45-6. Brook's anecdote is a fine example of what I mean by 'preparations' rather than rehearsals. Rehearsal is a way of setting an exact sequence of events. Preparations are a constant state of training so that when a situation arises one will be ready to 'do something appropriate' to the moment. Preparations are what a good athletic team does. Too often those interested in improvisation feel that it can arise spontaneously, out of the moment. Nothing is further from the truth. What arises spontaneously is the moment itself, the response is selected from a known repertory and joins with the moment to give the impression of total spontaneity. Most performances among communal peoples are not rehearsed, they are prepared.

28. His invitation was based on my reputation on the island. Although I was there for only two weeks I used to play games with children in which I would imitate animals. I did one act that especially amused the children: making my hands into horns I would charge at them as if I were an enraged bull. On several occasions while riding a bus to

a remote village some children would spot me and make the horn gesture. At Tenganan the dance I did at the public performance was a variation on the animal game. MacIntosh's singing was appreciated everywhere, and people would actually get very angry if she refused to sing. In New Guinea especially, almost anything—an object, a relationship, an event, a performance—is made into an item of trade; there are no neutral or valueless events.

29. The late sixties and early seventies saw a number of performances based on this premise. A family in Greenwich Village sold admission to their apartment where spectators watched them in their daily lives. Of course the Loud Family epic on television carried this style of documentary drama to its logical end: The feedback from the weekly series actually affected the lives the Louds lived, and so we watched the family change under the impact of their knowledge that they were being watched. The theoretical foundations of this kind of art lie in Cage's assertion that theatre is actually an attitude on the part of the spectator—to set up a chair in the street and to watch what happens is to transform the streets into a theatre. These ideas are still very much with us in Process Art.

30. The kind of classification I'm indicating for performance is one which is being increasingly used in the sciences, and is replacing older forms of classification where one class of events excludes another. 'Classifications need not be hierarchies and the clusters may overlap (intersect). The whole idea of hierarchic, non-overlapping (mutually exclusive) classifications which is so attractive to the human mind is currently undergoing re-examination. From studies in a variety of fields the representation of taxonomic structure as overlapping clusters or as ordinations appears far preferable.' (Robert R. Sokal, 'Classification: Purposes, Principles, Progress, Prospects', *Science*, 27 September 1974, p. 1121). One 'locates' a performance by using the coordinates of efficacy and entertainment.

31. In *Commune*, there was one night an interruption of more than three hours. During that time the spectators and performers came to know each other in a way much more intimate and actual than is usually possible in a theatre. When the play resumed there was a feeling surrounding the performance that added power to it. The supper sequence in *Mother Courage* is an attempt at building-in the kind of relationship between performers and the spectators that accidentally occurred that night at *Commune*. See Schechner, *Environmental Theatre*,

pp. 49-56.

32. This experiment, now called 'Mountain Project', has been revised and is still going on. It is part of Grotowski's 'paratheatrical phase' which began in 1969. In the paratheatrical work there are no spectators, the form is not fixed, the process is what emerges from each participant. Members of the Polish Lab working alone or in teams lead this work. Each project has its own title, such as: *Acting Therapy*, *Vigil*, *Meditations*, *Aloud*, *Soundings*, etc. The events take from a few hours to several weeks, and use all kinds of space from rooms to large sections of the countryside (pilgrimages).

33. Weston La Barre, *The Ghost Dance* (N.Y.: Dell Publishing Company, 1972), pp. 195–6.

Dixi, Namahage, and the Question of 'Folk Performance'

ALMOST EVERYWHERE IN THE WORLD what was 'folk performance' has become, or is becoming, 'tourist performance.' If an event is in any way out of the ordinary, distinctly local, colourful (that is, different); and if it has a definable schedule and reasonably limited place of performance it becomes fair game for the tourist industry. This industry does not, as some fear, simply prey on local events, corrupting and transforming them forever. Often local people are involved in the tourist promotion. This is because in even the remotest areas of the world, a structural and apparently irreversible trend is occurring. Namely the drastic reduction of the number of people who earn money off the land. Dwarfing the migrations across borders by boat people, refugees, or others seeking a new place to live, are the internal migrations drawing people from the countryside, from farming villages and communities, to large cities and vast urban sprawls. Much has been written about these conglomerations of humanity, but less attention is paid to those left behind. As farming becomes less and less of an occupation of families and more an agro-industry (and this is true not only in the so-called industrialized nations but increasingly within the third world also), the question arises: on what economic base will the former farming communities stand? Tourism, for some, is the answer.

And as tourist performance becomes its own genre, the whole category 'folk performance' is thrown into doubt. If by 'folk performance' is meant events that originate within and are controlled by local people, expressing their beliefs and practices, then a diminishing number of these exist each year. And those that continue to exist become raw material for the tourist industry, local, national, and international.

What I am focusing on in this paper are two folk performances, one Chinese and still relatively in the hands of farmers (but, I predict, not for very long); the other Japanese and cut loose from its folk and ritual moorings and more and more surviving as a tourist performance. I am also going to suggest a new paradigm for the study of so-called folk performance, a reasonably simple phenomenology or 'thick description' approach so named by Clifford Geertz.[1] I urge this on folklorists, anthropologists, and performance theorists alike because although I do not know of any satisfactory new paradigm to theorize the dynamics of the folk-tourist dyad, I am certain that older theories of folk culture and folk performance do not fit the emerging circumstances.

Dixi of south central China and namahage of the Oga Peninsula of Japan, two kinds of masked performance, are regarded as 'folk theatre.' But what does this mean? To call something 'folk' is already to deny its historicity and its connection to contemporary or progressive culture. Such an approach is that of Chinese scholar Yu Quiyu who says that dixi and like forms are 'ancient forms closely connected with religious ritual that have been preserved in certain remote regions as living fossils, essentially unchanged by modern civilization'.[2] Namahage also has changed considerably during the 200 years for which historical information on namahage exists.[3] What does it mean to call a performance a 'living fossil' or, for that matter, a 'folk art'? Using such nomenclature is a way of asserting an urban or academic hegemony over the performance in question. And it is also a way of

1 TOP LEFT. Children watching the dixi performance.

2 TOP RIGHT. A child dixi warrior.

3 BOTTOM LEFT. A 'angry' dixi warrior.

4. BOTTOM RIGHT. A woman dixi warrior.

All photos by Richard Schechner.

5 TOP. Woman warrior in battle

6 BOTTOM. Welcoming Schechner after the performance.

All photos by Richard Schechner

7 TOP LEFT. Elders watching the dixi performance. Photo by Cao Lusheng.

8 TOP RIGHT. Putting on the namahage costume.

9 BOTTOM LEFT. A dressed namahage.

10. BOTTOM RIGHT. Namahages frightening/amusing people.

Photos 8-10 by Richard Schechner.

11 TOP. A namahage being greeted by a family, and offered some sake and snacks. Photo by Richard Schechner.

confessing ignorance about the genre's detailed historical development. 'Folk' has the additional onus of meaning without a codified, closely scripted, professional, or theorized practice. A folk performance is practiced by amateurs whose sincerity and depth of belief are more in evidence than their artistic skills. Folk forms are thought to be of interest mostly as evidence of how things used to be or as precedents of classical genres (kagura to noh, for example) or as repositories of ritual practices, a kind of rural bank of where ancient beliefs and practices have been deposited and can now be withdrawn by properly trained scholars. And, as I have noted, the newest use of folk performance is as an economic resource for the tourist industry.

Dixi as I saw it in 1988 is performed as part of the Spring celebrations (February/March) in Guizhou province, south central China. This mountainous region is among China's least developed from the perspective of industry, transport, housing, per-capita income, and other indices of modern life. Farmers long ago stripped the trees from the hills in order to establish terraced paddies. Aside from the provincial capital, Guiyang, and a few large towns, the people live on the land, in small villages.

Dixi means 'theatre performed on the ground.' The dixi I saw in Qilungtun in south central Guizhou near to the town of Anshun was played by a group of farmers who supplemented their income by performing each Spring. Some of their splendidly carved, brightly painted wood masks dated from the 1920s, but most were carved recently by local maskmakers. The four-hour performance, observed by more than 500 villagers, and by visiting scholars Cao Lusheng, Huangpu Chongqing, and me took place midday in the main open spot of the village. Huangpu, who has spent years studying dixi, said that usually a performance 'can last 10 to 20 days or more—until a complete story is told'.[4] I have not been able to determine if dixi was more usually performed in the farm fields before planting, as might be appropriate for what scholars call a 'fertility' performance. If indeed playing inside the village in the central open space is a recent development, then dixi has taken a decisive step towards making itself available for tourist exploitation.

Our party arrived too late to witness any preliminary religious rituals, which are supposed to be performed the day before the cycle begins and on the last day. Whether or not they were performed at all remains an open question. Communist rule since the 1940s and Cultural Revolution of the 1960s–70s have effectively stifled, if not wholly eradicated, visible religious practice in much of China. The style of performance is simple and direct. Surrounded by an appreciative audience of villagers, actors declaimed their speeches loudly, giving their brightly painted wooden masks different expressions by tilting or rotating their heads. The actors' mouths are hidden by black cloth attached to and descending from the masks allowing for the dialogue to be shouted with clarity. Dixi masks are worn at a 45 degree angle atop the head. Thus when two characters face off the performers actually bend their heads forward in almost a butting position. Despite the difficulty of maintaining this posture for long periods of time, the performers were able to manipulate their masks in ways that made the characters' faces extremely expressive. On the other hand, there was not much 'body work' to the performance. Basically the actors faced off or circled each other. Their costumes, though colourful and effective, did not have the fine quality of detailed workmanship seen in the masks.

The *lianzi* (masks) are of mytho-historical figures who were deified after death. The masks are carefully wrapped in white cotton paper and kept in a special wood box. The masks cannot be handled casually. Opening the box lets the deities onto the stage. More research needs to be done to determine the origin and diffusion of the masks. Some of the dixi masks were similar to Tibetan masks. One possibility is that they came into China from India via the overland trade route or along with the spread of Buddhism.

It is not necessary here to discuss in detail the narrative of the performance I saw. Enough to note that it was part of a very popular tale from the Han dynasty (202 BCE-220 CE), *Xue Ding Shan Conquering the West* which depicts the victory of a woman warrior over her male adversaries. All roles are performed by men. The village spectators enjoyed the performance immensely. They laughed at the sexual theme enacted, and the reversal of everyday life apparent in the victory of the woman over the man. There is general delight in the ultimate life-affirming outcome. Huangpu nicely summarizes dixi's functions: 'A dixi performance educates and gives enjoyment. It is a prayer for a good harvest, an exorcism of what might hurt the crops; it propagates '*Hong, Ex, Jib, Y*' (loyalty, filial piety, integrity, fairness). It celebrates military prowess.[5]

According to Yu, and I agree with him, the ritual and the entertainment qualities of dixi cannot be separated.

> Ancient Chinese ritual performances—or theatrical rites—therefore formed a broad, loose, elastic system which was easily adapted to new situations. Lacking any canonical form, they could adapt and absorb in the face of new customs and aesthetics. [. . .] Today, adaptation has meant allowing entertainment to take precedence over worship, but the basic structure of the shamanistic rite remains.[6]

It is this very adaptability that makes dixi ripe for tourist exploitation. What presently protects it is the remoteness of Guizhou.

Oga Peninsula is also remote, if such a word can be used with reference to Japan. But what concerns me here is not so much the similarities between dixi and namahage, but the differences. These differences are both of a practical and theoretical nature. The modernity of the Japanese transportation system means that tourists can and do come to Oga in the winter to enjoy the hot springs and to view namahage. Flyers depicting the namahage masked performers advertise the January *matsuri*, drawing people in for the festivities.

Namahage is a 'visitor performance,' one in which young men, costumed in straw and wearing large, grotesque masks representing *marebito* (foreign visitors) or *oni* (demons), beings from 'elsewhere,' make selected stops in the village demanding food and *sake*, frightening children, and teasing girls and young women. As Yamamoto points out in her excellent study, based on fieldwork done during the 1960s (and therefore a good basis for comparison regarding changes in namahage over the past quarter century), across the arc of north west

Honshu facing the Sea of Japan there are, or were, many varieties of namahage-like festivals, with different names, different classes of participants (ranging from teenage males only to boys and girls under 14 to men, women, and children).

I saw namahage in 1980 in the village of Iinomori just after 1 January. The participants were all young men, ranging from their late teens to their mid-20s. Although the 'game' of namahage is based on the belief that the monsters are from 'elsewhere,' everyone except very young children knows the namahage really are villagers. Preparations for the visit of the namahage are made both by the *oni* and the welcoming households. While preparing the masks and costumes are traditionally said to be 'secret,' my wife and I were welcome at about 9 pm the night of the festival in the small community centre where the masks were given their final touches and the *kende*, the straw costumes were being fitted. We did not just wander in, however, but were brought by Kobayashi Susumu, a theatre scholar who had made prior arrangements for our presence. The chill in the room was dispelled only by a single wood-burning stove. Outside the snow was deep, the wind blowing. Even as final touches of paint made the large, wooden masks brighter—frightening or cheery, depending on one's attitude—the men were knocking down *sake* and joking, clearly excited about the events to come.

Yamamoto describes the preparations in some detail,[6] so I shall not repeat. Suffice it to say that a little after 9 pm the young men were in costume, ready to 'invade' the village. A small pickup truck came to fetch the *oni*, transporting them from the community centre to the Inari shrine, from whence they would descend into the village. Which homes to visit had all been pre-arranged. Families decorated the rooms of their homes near the front entrance with scrolls, plates of rice cakes and other foods, and especially *sake*. Small amounts of money were also set aside to give to the namahage. At the shrine, the namahage, in full costume and masks, roared as they rushed down the hillside into the town.

When a namahage knocks, the male head-of-house is waiting to greet him and his fellow *oni*. Children and unmarried girls were nowhere to be seen. A wife may be next to her husband or out of sight in the kitchen. The visit of the namahage is a mixture of precise formal gestures of hospitality made by the host answered by the namahage with roaring and generally boisterous behavior. *Sake* is downed in quantity. The namahage shouts short sentences only, such as: 'Are there any bad kids in this house?! Does the new bride get up early to do her work?! Where did you hide Yukiko [unmarried girl]?!' Because the namahage are from the community, their improvised remarks are based on gossip; because they were once children, they know where to look for hidden children, several of whom I saw flee in terror of the *oni*. As the night goes on, the young-men-namahages get drunker, their behavior rowdier. The adults treat the namahage with respect, even as they joke with them. The villagers know that the namahage are their own young men, even as the *oni* are supposed to be Yamabushi. As the namahage leave, residents grab a stalk or two of straw from the *kendes*. It is said that these straws bring good health. The straws swept up after the namahage visit are kept. When the festival is over, the *kende* are tied in front of the shrine gate and around the shrine building where they are left until the Spring Hamlet Festival. Yamamoto details how the normative namahage festival works. Things were somewhat different in 1980, when I attended.

The Namahage I followed worked their way through the village toward a youth hostel where they knew a number of young women were staying. The hostel-owner had prepared the traditional offerings for the *oni*, but his was no ordinary household. There were no young children, but a plentiful supply of 18-to-20-year-old women. The namahage stayed an extra-long time drinking, joking, chasing, and pinching. The women played 'frightened,' even as they pulled vigorously to obtain lucky straws. The namahage knew they ought to make their stay brief, but could not find the will to leave. The women were not members of the community, but out on a holiday possibly to enjoy the hot springs for which Oga is famous. After about 20 minutes, the namahage left the youth hostel, hopped into their truck and headed to the community centre where they took off their costumes, joked with each other, sang, drank, and generally caroused.

Dixi is a farmer's theatre performed in farming communities by farmers and for farmers. Dixi is also somewhat a 'professional' theatre because troupes charge for their performances and the money earned is a significant fraction of the performers' incomes. At the same time, dixi troupes do not advertise their work by means other than word of mouth. However, the attention paid to dixi by Chinese scholars signals the beginning of a long road that has already led to appearances at international art festivals, workshops in 'dixi training,' and which will sooner or later result in tourist exploitation of dixi, with predictable changes in the genre itself.

My own account of dixi was published in March, 1989 in a popular American theatre magazine, *American Theater*;[7] Huangpu's article appeared in the scholarly *TDR* in 1992; other articles have appeared in *Asian Theatre Journal* and in several European journals. The foot work and gestural language of dixi is well-enough formed that in 1988 Shen Fu Xing, dixi artist and researcher, and Ma Guo Cheng, dixi performer and farmer, led a two week workshop on 'dixi training' in London. The dixi artists were in London because in 1986 they were among those who played at the Festival d'Automne in Paris, 'the only dixi troupe to perform outside China'.[8] Dixi can therefore be regarded as an 'aesthetic entity' as well as a ritual; a performance that can be taken from its original context and displayed elsewhere 'as art.' However, the art of dixi is regarded, by Europeans and Chinese, as fundamentally different from, say, the art of jingju. Relative to codified genres, dixi is regarded as quaint, primitive, and naive; it is not given the same respect as jingju and other classical genres. As a 'living fossil,' dixi is believed to be an example of what culture was, not what it is. This attitude will foster tourist exploitation along lines parallel to visiting a game reserve: dixi is among those performances felt to be like 'endangered species,' worthy of study and observation but not thought able to fully be integrated into mainstream cultural activities.

Of course, a real and difficult problem exists. Dixi is not codified as jingju or noh are; its traditions are embedded in rural areas far from urban capitals. Dixi training cannot be presented as the equivalent of training in the codified forms. And once removed from its rural setting, dixi will change drastically—in the direction of either imitating the codified forms or of becoming a representative 'folk performance,' reinterpreted by professional dancers hoping to 'capture' what dixi is and present it to a large, urban, and international audience. This kind of reduction, transformation, and radical interpretation of indigenous performances is what is practised by such groups as Mexico's Ballet Folklorico.

Namahage is both more and less 'advanced' than dixi; and the problems surrounding its performances are somewhat different than those facing dixi. At present, namahage maintains its amateur qualities, its indissoluble links to a particular community and its aesthetic-ritual practices. At the same time, advertising distributed by Oga authorities, show namahage processions in torchlight that are, actually, staged intensifications of the actual festival. The advertisements also give maps and information helpful to tourists coming from the outside who wish to view namahage. A namahage-like figure has become the emblem of the Oga area. Although I do not expect that the house-to-house processional qualities of namahage will be much changed, there will be more visits of the kind I saw at the youth hostel. Oga hotels will include a namahage performance along with other attractions. These kinds of performances introduce a self doubt about who the figures represented and what the meaning of their presence signify.

What does the future hold for dixi and namahage? Dixi will probably be absorbed into the 'culture industry,' perhaps functioning for a time as both what it was in Guizhou and as an item for display and export, not only to foreign destinations but to the great urban centres of China itself. Namahage will probably continue its slow transformation from a serious local celebration to a practice enthusiastically performed but less fully believed-in. And although it will not be exported, it will serve as a tourist attraction, doing its share to keep Oga in business. For both dixi and namahage, the global net of scholarship, information, curiosity, tourism, and appetite for 'cultural adventure' indicates that their isolation is yielding to a situation where these, and forms like them, develop as part of, rather than apart from, the general cultural-economic situation of the larger urban centres.

At present, dixi and namahage are 'amateur' in both their execution and reception. Their connection is much more to audiences of ordinary people, not connoisseurs. Dixi and namahage are propelled forward in history through the agency of those who perform them, not by means of government subsidy. Of course, scholarly and touristic interest may lead to intervention ostensibly to preserve forms and/or to show them outside of their accustomed communities. This is what has happened to kagura in Japan and chhau in India—and what seems to be happening to dixi. But the current state of dixi is much different from that of namahage. Dixi continues to be practised by poor farmers still working the soil in a rural area of Guizhou province. Dixi feels still connected to the beliefs and people who brought it into existence. By contrast, in a totally modernized Japan, namahage is now treated as a combination tourist event (aimed at Japanese visiting Oga to enjoy bathing in the hot mineral springs) and for local residents as a reminiscence of the 'old days.' The youth practicing namahage give the appearance of middle class culture, with belief systems far removed from those that brought namahage into existence. This is not 'bad,' but it ought to warn officials and scholars alike concerning the price paid for preservation. 'Living fossils' are not possible; once 'discovered,' genres change—and it is questionable if they ever were static. Often enough 'development' means total change, even extinction. Everyone involved ought to ask what will be preserved and for what purpose. The analogy between culture and nature, between endangered species and endangered genres, can be carried only so far.

Finally, to return to the questions I raised at the start of this essay, what does the whole category 'folk performance' or 'folk art' signify? What is meant when these categories are invoked? Several kinds of limitations and exclusions are implied. First, 'folk art' is usually associated with rural areas or places far away, both physically and culturally, from the centres of power and the arbiters of taste. A folk art can be practised in the city, but only under a situation where either the artist is 'imported' and exhibited almost as an animal, a vanishing species, or as a rare natural resource; or the art is made over for city use, as a recreation or as an antidote to an urban culture that is thought to lack the 'old values.' Secondly, folk arts are considered 'natural,' without single authors who sign their work, passed down relatively unchanged from generation to generation with few if any written rules. That is, folk performance is practised, not codified or theorized. Many argue, in fact, that codified forms 'come from,' evolve out of, folk performances (as noh came from dengaku and saragaku). Thus a kind of Darwinism is applied to folk arts, assigning the 'folk' to societies, cultures, and groups considered earlier, prior, simpler, more primitive.

But more primitive than whom? Than the people writing the theories, studying the folk arts, setting the standards. I believe all these categories need to be re-examined. Those who practice namahage and dixi live far from the urban centres where dominant cultural values are debated and fixed. Their 'primitivism' is more a result of their being excluded from setting cultural values than anything categorical or generally identifiable in the so-called folk performances themselves. Social Darwinism has been discredited as an explanation of historical processes; why is it still so widely adhered to as an explanation of aesthetic processes? I believe there are specific differences in performance practices and genres. But these differences are not explained by the categories 'folk' and 'classical'. We might better investigate—in forms like dixi and namahage, as well as in kabuki or jingju, precisely what the performance practices are, how performance knowledge is transmitted, what the relationships between performers and spectators are, and so on. It would be better to leave nineteenth-century notions of 'folk' and 'classical' out of the discussion altogether.

Notes

1 Clifford Geertz, *The Interpretation of Cultures* (New York: Basic Books, 1973).

2 Quiyu Yu, 'Some Observations on the Aesthetics of Primitive Chinese Theatre,' *Asian Theatre Journal* 1989, vol. 6, no. 1, p. 12.

3 Yoshiko Yamamoto, *The Namahage* (Philadelphia: Institute for the Study of Human Issues, 1978), p. 129.

4 Huangpu Chongqing, 'Dixi: Chinese Farmer's Theatre,' *TDR* (1992), vol. 36, no. 2, p. 110.

5 Ibid., p. 107.

6 Quiyu, op. cit., p. 16.

6 Yamamoto, op. cit., pp.104-8.

7 Richard Schechner, 'Notes from Abroad: On Chinese Theatre,' *American Theatre* 1989, vol. 12, 55ff.

8 Franc Chamberlain, 'Fragments of a Dixi Training,' *TDR* (1992), vol. 36, no. 2, pp. 118-25.

Believed-in Theatre

Believed-in *performances*—where real people really act out their lives—have long been with us. Courtroom trials, sacred and secular rituals, protest demonstrations, Gofmanian performances in everyday, and so on. In believed-in performances people are who they perform, playing their social and/or personal identities: judges, accused, rabbis, lawyers, doctors, teachers, activists, bus drivers, lovers, whoever. Judith Butler argues that even 'gender proves to be performative—that is, constituting the identity it is purported to be'.[1] She comes to this conclusion by joining feminist/poststructuralist theory to the ideas of J. L. Austin. Believed-in performances have been theorized over the years by Erving Goffman, Milton Singer, Victor Turner, Barbara Myerhoff, Eve Kosofsky Sedgwick, myself, and others.

Believed-in *theatre* is related but different. Orthodox theatre is not believed-in, in the sense I am using the phrase. Watching or being in plays such as *Inherit the Wind* or *The Investigation* does not mean one sees or becomes the real Scopes, Bryant, or Nazi war criminals. The mimetic theory of theatre demands a prior or at least a separate actuality which the theatre 'reflects' or 'interprets,' but which it is not. Some theatre simulates the original, such as the Soviet 1920 *The*

Storming of the Winter Palace, directed by Nikolai Evreinov, with its cast of 8000 soldiers. But *Storming*'s 8000 actor-soldiers, many of whom took part in the actual event, and the 100,000 spectators, knew they were not doing or seeing the real thing, but participating in an onsite re-enactment.[2]

Onsite re-enactments, that's what many living history museums and restored villages are. Sites such as Plimoth Plantation or Colonial Williamsburg combine environmental theatre, popular entertainment, and educational instruction.[3] Plimoth Plantation is an unscripted ensemble performance. Improvisational and environmental, it aligns itself with environmental theatre. The display of history of the site reveals a shift from ceremony to virtuality, from commemoration to exploration, from authoritative narrative to ongoing conversation, from discrete moments, objects, and scenes [the usual fare at museums] to the waking dream of a virtual Pilgrim world. Much of the site's appeal derives from its failure as a perfect time machine. It promises an experience of transport to the year 1627. But what the visitor experiences is the juxtaposition of 1627 and 1995 and the willful forgetting by the Pilgrims in the village today of all that occurred after 1627. The visitor has the uncanny sense of seeing into a future that those locked into an eternity of 1627 are not supposed to know. Actors and visitors collaborate in a jumbling of time by sustaining one small slice of it indefinitely, even while abutting it with the present moment.[4]

Evreinov restaged recent history, giving a Soviet jolt to events. Living history museums celebrate mainstream American 'values' such as the nuclear family, capitalist enterprise, courage, and perseverance. Colonial Williamsburg is ambivalent about a 'way of life' many Americans despise while others yearn for: racism and segregation, not to mention slavery. At Plimoth the Pilgrims are given top billing, while the Native Americans, without whose assistance the English settlers would have perished, are located literally off the beaten path at the bottom of a not well-trodden trail. All living history museums enact a reductive, simplified American past. Some do it convincingly, in the first person, in carefully researched behaviour, dialect, costume, and events. The historical presence surrounds the visitors. Being there, talking to persons from another historical era, watching them tend to crops and farm animals, prepare food, interact with each other and with the visitors, using the language and tools of the past, actually going through the routine of some specific day in eighteenth or seventeenth century American history sure beats looking through glass at a diorama. But as in the Soviet spectacles and orthodox theatre, the spectators, even young children, know it's just a game, that these 'Pilgrims,' 'Colonials,' 'Native Americans,' or whoever, are 'actors.'[5] The producers of living museums recognize that 'acting' taints their projects. At Plimoth and elsewhere, the actors are called 'interpreters.' But whatever the jargon, living museums fictionalize, making history into make-believe.

A more ambivalent experience is the Israeli Akko Theatre Center's *Arbeit Macht Frei vom Toitland Europa*,[6] ostensibly a drama, with paid admissions, a theatre address, and a clearly defined schedule. The production is well described by Dan Urian and Rebecca Rovit.[7] Urian, an Israeli theatre professor, writes:

> *Arbeit Macht Frei* is a play about memories of the Holocaust and their place in Israeli reality. Its materials are the collective biography of its actors and their spectators, the majority of whom are second generation Holocaust survivors. [. . .] The spectator at *Arbeit Macht Frei* is deluged by words, music and song, gestures, costume changes, props, changing locations and scenery. Many spectators have the impression that the text and the actors' actions are to a great extent improvised. This impression is enhanced by the constant tension between the actor's own identity, which is preserved during the performance, and the role or roles he or she plays. [. . .] The actors in *Arbeit Macht Frei* wrote the text employing only such facts as they had read, or heard, or experienced themselves from sources such as documents, films, interviews with Holocaust survivors, musical excerpts, and visits to Holocaust memorials and museums. The process of writing the text took three years, during which the montage was created by David Ma'ayan, Smadar Yaron-Ma'ayan, and Moni Yosef. The rest of

the work was also carried out as teamwork, including building the set.[8]

Arbeit is a site-specific performance for an audience of about 50. The performance in Akko begins in a parking lot where spectators were loaded into a bus guarded by actors/Israeli soldiers and driven across town to the Akko Holocaust Museum. So many Israelis are in the armed forces reserve I wondered if they were wearing their actual uniforms. At the museum, Smadar Yaron Ma'ayan introduced herself as Zelma, a Holocaust survivor and tour guide. Again, was she telling the truth? She explained some exhibits, then took us to the museum auditorium for a movie depicting the SS shoving children into a windowless truck with Red Cross markings whose exhaust feeds back into the cabin. This mobile gas chamber was a prototype for the gas chambers at Auschwitz and elsewhere. Was I alone in recalling the bus ride we had just taken? Watching *Ambulans* I did not know it was Polish (Janusz Morgenstern, director) and not, as it seemed, a Nazi instruction film. After the movie, Zelma turned the group over to Khaled Abu Ali (his real name), who said he was an Israeli Arab whose job at the museum was to explain to Arab school children what happened to the Jews of Europe. Again, was he telling the truth? Only later, when Zelma and Khaled appeared in the rest of *Arbeit*, do we learn that these people are not who we thought they were . . . maybe. Members of the Akko Theatre Center, is the Arab an Arab, the Polish-Israeli woman—is she too young to be a survivor?

We left the Museum not knowing who was what. Back at the Akko Theatre we were ushered—herded is more like it—into a small room with a ceiling so low we had to stoop; we were packed onto hard narrow benches, the actors inches away. At our backs were small windows blocked by barbed wire. We were in a house, in a concentration camp, in a bunker, in a theatre. At a grand piano bizarrely outsized in this cramped space, Zelma sang a medley honoring Israeli heroes plus sentimental love songs. She argued with a neighbour about who suffered most during the Holocaust. Suddenly, the ceiling crashed down inches away from our knees and noses: behold, a fully-laden table, a kind of seder. 'Instead of a tablecloth, documents and photographs referring to the Holocaust completely cover the table. [. . .] We pass around kosher dishes of cholent, hummus, eggs, and matzo'.[9] Zelma's husband Menash (Yosef) brags how the Israeli war machine is capable of crushing any Arab resistance. Obsequiously, Khaled dusts everything in sight, including Zelma as he serves snacks and schnapps to the family and spectator-guests, while singing/explaining his plight as an Israeli Arab. When *Arbeit* was performed in Berlin in 1992, spectators were asked about the treatment of Turks. In Israel, the questions were about the treatment of Arabs. The performance drove home analogies between the Holocaust and the displacements caused by Zionism, the treatment of the Arabs, the wars for Palestine/Israel. Everything was designed to make the mostly Jewish-Israeli audience uncomfortable.

When the sardonic feast ended, we were moved to an upper level.

> The naked actors are scattered in the room. Miri Tsemach sits naked in an iron bathtub threshing about in a heap of food remains, eating and spitting them out. Na'ama Manbar is in a glass tank, swimming in a pile of papers, evidence of Holocaust survivors, and Moni Yosef is hanging from one of the walls. Smadar Ya'aron Ma'ayan, a naked living skeleton is dancing a sort of dance of death, almost like a circus acrobat. Khaled Abu Ali, the naked Arab, runs about scourging himself and offering his whip to the spectators to lash him.[10]

Khaled was acting the part of a Shi'a Muslim during t'aziyeh, a cycle play depicting the martyrdom of Mohammed's nephew, Hussein. Laughing, crying, Khaled offered spectators the whip and bottles of beer. Sometimes, Khaled later told me, persons accept both. On the night I attended, Khaled whipped himself until there were welts on his back and buttocks. Finally, a spectator took the whip away. But this intervention did not 'end the violence.' Khaled subverted the attempt to save him by reaching into his store of whips: As soon as one was taken away he grabbed another. The Akko Theatre Center refused giving spectators a comfortable way out.[11] Finally, 'Smadar approaches and embraces him, and with this tableau of the *Pieta*, in which the flagellated Arab rests in the arms of the Jewish deathlike figure, a refugee from the Holocaust, the play ends'.[12] Not the night I saw it. Khaled kept whipping himself until the last spectator, me in this case, left.

Arbeit spectators were not asked to intervene, and if they did, the intervention was exposed as ineffective. *Arbeit*'s effect emerged from the movement from site to site, the claustrophobic environment, the shared food, the intensity of direct address, the raising of historical/ethical questions and analogies. *Arbeit* inhabited a conceptual and actual space between what is usually thought of as theatrical—symbolic, not-for-real—and what is actual: the Holocaust museum, actors whose identities slip from 'self' to 'character.' A meal was served and eaten, Khaled's body bled, the welts were real. As at a seder or t'aziyeh, the actions were real and symbolic simultaneously. The theatrical signs were surpassed by the actuality of the actions, the doubleness of the performers. *Arbeit*'s peculiar flavour was in its address to a specific community-within-a-community: Holocaust survivors and children of survivors who are Israelis. When *Arbeit* played in Berlin, ghosts haunted the performance: the six million Jews slaughtered by the Nazis. *Arbeit* is believed-in theatre not only or even mostly because it is a documentary or because it draws a parallel between the Holocaust and how Israelis oppress Arabs, but because, using experimental theatre techniques, its creators explore and express feelings and ideas at the precise point where the personal, the historical, and the political intersect. Only by means of the presence of Khaled Abu Ali could *Arbeit* dare to speak directly of Israeli and Palestinian Arab experiences; only because of who the rest of the company are, could *Arbeit* examine with such acerbity Jewish-Israeli attitudes.

The actors and spectators in *Arbeit* co-performed a shared history, problematizing their roles in creating that history. Sardonic, angry, accusatory, bitter *Arbeit* lets neither actor nor spectators off easy. Across America today community-based theatres, celebrating rather than excoriating, engage history and memory as these shape social and personal relations. 'Community theatre' used to mean local amateurs staging Broadway hits and/or popular classics. Using playtexts issued by Samuel French or the Dramatist Play Service, community theatres had written out for them detailed blocking, sets, costumes, and props.

This was 'mail order theatre,' like ordering a dress pattern. Community-based theatre is the very opposite of community theatre. Community-based theatres perform local materials. There is one similarity however. Some community-based theatres import professional directors and writers to lead or give shape to local resources. Appalshop, Alternate ROOTS, and Swamp Gravy, for examples, are the tip of a huge movement including theatre, storytelling, poetry readings, folk music, and so on. The feelings among participants in the community-based theatre movement are a combination of several very American phenomena: a belief in the 'truths' of ordinary people, the 'democratic spirit', the 'new age' practice of sharing the 'present moment' in a kind of populist Zen open to all, and the fervency of an old-fashioned American Christian 'revival' where people are 'born again'.

Carson is the playwright-in-residence of the Colquitt, Georgia Swamp Gravy project, about which I will write later. Raphael's rhetoric in describing what he experienced is decisive: 'zen,' 'spiritual,' 'common agenda,' 'beautiful harmony,' 'sharing,' and so on. This is the vocabulary both of the 'new age' and of an old-fashioned American 'revival.' This mix is characteristic of community-based theatre.

Swamp Gravy is an example of community-based theatre linked to the construction and expression of both individual and collective identity. It is connected to the work of Augusto Boal, Grotowski, and performance art. Using materials contributed by local people of different ages, races, ethnicities, political outlook, genders, economic station, and sexual orientations, Tennessee playwright Jo Carson stitched the texts for the *Swamp Gravy* series: *Sketches* (1993), *The Blue Doctor* (1994), and *The Gospel Truth* (1995). In a way these plays were the opposite of the Akko Theatre's *Arbeit,* also based on community experience, but presented in an ironic, cutting, bitter, and painful way—keeping old and new wounds open. Swamp Gravy is about celebrating the community, even when painful. 'The people that have a part in this production, which numbers in the hundreds, have a respect for each other that was not possible before this started,' wrote Terry Toole, publisher of the Miller County *Liberal.*[14] Where 'difficult' subjects are touched on, such as violence against women and race relations, there are limits beyond which the community is not willing to go yet. Those limits are decided by the people making the *Swamp Gravy* plays.

> 'It isn't about theatre,' said lighting designer Brackley Frayer opening night of the first play. 'It's about something else. It takes some getting used to.' It's anthropology, theater, drama therapy, and missionary work, I thought. It's not about the play, it's about the stories; it's not about the acting, it's about the communal agon.[15]

Geer's mentors include Augusto Boal, Victor Turner, Ann Jellicoe, Maryat Lee, and me. The believed-in core of community-based theatre is in the fact that people are enacting their own stories and performing mostly for people of their own communities. Playwright Carson comments:

> Almost all of the material in the four shows I have written for Colquitt is direct address, because we have people as performers who live with storytelling (the old sense), and are extraordinary storytellers/ performers of the sort the deep South grows, but who don't have much sense of themselves as actors. [. . .] But most don't need to 'act,' if I can write the work right. So the cast is onstage in a very Brechtian construct: they are themselves, in costumes that suggest an older time, telling stories that come from other people—sometimes, when I can do it, a person kin to them—and they have, in their choice of attitude and presentation, a comment on the story. [. . .] And it is moving, right up close to a religious experience—a community experience with real roots in it—when stories have this kind of reality for the players and the audience.[16]

When Carson speaks of a 'religious experience,' she is describing believed-in theatre: a theatre where conviction and sincerity, 'direct address' or 'testimony,' depending on your frame of reference, are more important than professional acting skills. Ironically, though millions of evangelical Americans subscribe to the public expression of religious belief—speaking in tongues, being possessed by the Holy Spirit, trance dancing, laying on of hands, healing through prayer and touch, rib-rocking preaching—the theatre as such has long been associated with untruth: the anti-theatrical prejudice is strong. Swamp Gravy is exactly the kind of theatre that can flourish in this environment—it is 'truthful' rather than 'theatrical.' At the same time, of course, the outsiders, Geer especially, but also lighting and scenic designers, and to some degree Carson (a southerner, but not a Colquitter), are prized because of their theatre skills. These skills are governed by the community, used as the community sees fit. Geer tells of the time when he overstepped his authority, cursing the cast because they were late for rehearsals. What happened next came more from American evangelical Christianity than from theatre, as told by Geer:

> I have offended everybody. [. . .] Charlotte said that more offensive than swearing was the fact that I lost my temper. [. . .] Harold Burrell, the Baptist minister, has come to see me, said he is my friend and will stand with me. Joy Jinks told me she loves me and doesn't understand what has happened. [. . .] Don Chandler told me the only way the project could be salvaged was if I got on a plane and went home. He would not speak to me and wanted to hit me for swearing in front of women and children. Tammy Spooner said I was just doing what I've been doing since I got here: pushing ideas that I wanted regardless of what other people said. [. . .] Harold made me feel better, he told me the story of Peter who said, 'to Hell with the Lord,' and then was forgiven. Harold put his arms around me and Joy and prayed, he said, 'Father, I know you don't approve of the words that Richard used, but I know that you forgive him. He is repentant.' [. . .] After much discussion, a special meeting was called, and I was allowed to apologize to the cast and families. Then I stepped outside while they put my fate to a vote. Annette Miller, an African American woman who had argued for Christian forgiveness,

> moved that I be retained, and Don Chandler, who had wanted me gone, seconded; the vote was unanimous.[17]

As Geer comments, 'For an outside director, learning the local mores is a task comparable to mastering the region's dialect. No one ever questioned my theater knowledge to my face, but what did get questioned, and often, was my ability to direct in a manner appropriate to the people of Miller County'.[18]

If Swamp Gravy, and any of the other projects in five states modelled on it, perform outside of their homebase (as at the 1996 Cultural Olympiad), there is the chance that the work will become 'generalized,' 'aestheticized'—be made into 'better theatre' in some abstract normative way. Playing before strangers, the Swamp Gravy actors would have to get 'better,' even as they lose direct touch with their audience. In this, Swamp Gravy and the like would become somewhat akin to Roadside Theater, whose 'local knowledge' is professionalized, like many fine blue grass musicians. This traffic between the different genres of theatre—commercial, community-based, experimental, local, regional, educational—is complicated.

An example of community-based theatre actively seeking intercultural contact is Appalshop, started in 1969, producing work that 'reflects the diversity of experience in the Appalachian mountains and rural America'.[19] Projects include broadcast TV, videotapes, media production education, sound recordings, WMMT-FM radio, the Roadside Theater, and the American Festival Project (AFP), 'a national coalition of artists working together with presenters and community co-sponsors. AFP develops arts-based community collaborations that actively involve people who have little access to the arts and confront pressing issues such as race, poverty, and intolerance'.[20]

Roadside's *Corn Mountain/Pine Mountain* (1996) is:

> a cultural exchange between Roadside Theater and Idiwanan An Chawe, a group of Native American artists of the Pueblo of Zuni in New Mexico. [. . .] The seeds of the collaboration were sown 10 years ago [1986] when Zuni artists and Roadside Theater began visiting each others' homes, getting to know

> each other, performing and conducting workshops in schools and senior citizens' centers, and having conversations about issues facing both cultures. Two years ago, seven Zuni artists and students culminated their visit to Central Appalachia with a performance at the Appalshop Theater [in Whiteside, Kentucky]. This performance was well received, and Zuni and Roadside decided that the next phase of the continuing exchange would be the scripting and production of a collaborative performance that would demonstrate the cultural strengths of the two separate cultures and address contemporary concerns. Zuni stories and songs would be presented in the Zuni language and Appalachian stories and songs in English.[21]

Traditional cultures and mutual respect, a hybrid show that ordinary persons can understand and enjoy. The Roadside-Zuni exchange is viewed as long term, a kind of extended 'barter' along the lines that Eugenio Barba has for many years advocated and practised.[22]

At another level of belief, but drawing also on traditional cultures, is the work of Jerzy Grotowski, who after nearly 20 years of secrecy reemerged in the 1990s with two theatre pieces, *Downstairs Action* and *Action*.[23] These have been seen at the Grotowski Workcenter near Pontedera, Italy, or by means of film elsewhere, by hundreds of people. The work has a history: In 1969 Grotowski 'left the theatre' for Paratheatre and, successively, Theatre of Sources, Objective Drama, and Art as Vehicle.[24] The conceptual roots of this work include both Martin Buber's *ich und du*[25] and the 'cultural performance knowledge' of a number of 'masters.' Grotowski's work in this regard is postmodern: a hybrid or hypertext stitched from many disparate pieces. Grotowski's genius, of course, is to make a seamless performance text from the pieces. In 'Art as Vehicle,' Grotowski both distances himself from the avant garde he was such a defining part of in the 1960s, and makes clear his strong links to it:

> When I speak of 'theatre company,' I mean the theatre of ensemble, the long-term work of a group. Work which is not linked in any particular way to the concepts of the avant-garde

> and which constitutes the basis for professional theatre of our century. [. . .] In 'Art as Vehicle,' from the point of view of technical elements, everything is almost like in the performing arts; we work on song, on impulses, on forms of movement, even textual motifs appear. And all is reduced to the strictly necessary, until a structure appears, a structure as precise and worked out as in a performance: the *Action*. [. . .] What then is the difference between this objectivity of ritual and a [regular theatre] performance? Is the difference only in the fact that the public is not invited?[26]

The difference, according to Grotowski, is that in ordinary theatre, the 'seat of the montage' rests with the spectator, while in *Action* it is with the performer.'

> [. . .] when I speak of Art as vehicle, I refer to a montage whose seat is *not in the perception of the spectator but in the doers*.[27] It is not that the doers agree between themselves about what the common montage will be, it is not that they share some common definition about what they will do. No, no verbal agreement, no spoken definition: It is necessary, through the very actions themselves to discover how to approach—step by step—toward the essential.[28]

Flying against the trend toward cultural specificity, the denial of 'universal' or 'archetypal' human cultural traits, Grotowski's method has been to sift through practices from different cultures for what is similar among them, searching for the 'first,' the 'original,' the 'essential.' During Objective Drama, Grotowski worked with masters of traditional and ritual performance from Haiti, Bali, Korea, and Taiwan, as well as brief visits by Sufis, Japanese martial artists, and others. From these masters, and from 'work on the self' Grotowski's group formed precise, repeatable elements of song, chant, gesture, and movement. Grotowski said his goals is, 'To re-evoke a very ancient form of art where ritual and artistic creation were seamless. Where poetry was song, song was incantation, movement was dance'.[29]

So what is *Action*? To those who know earlier Grotowski works such as *The Constant Prince*, *Akropolis*, and *Apocalypsis cum Figuris*, *Action* will come as no surprise. There is song, dance, chant; intensity bottled into a tightly confined space admitting only a few spectators; no stage as such, but movement throughout the space; the spectators-witnesses are 'confronted' but not asked to participate; the performers are highly disciplined in body and voice and, even more impressive, in some kind of extremely intense 'spiritual' discipline. *Action* does not tell a story, so much as evoke a mood. The performers play with such concentration, that they seem to have entered a believed-in reality far beyond Stanislavsky's 'as if.' And yet these performers are not in trance, not possessed by 'another.' Quite the opposite, they have found 'themselves.' Wolford was hard pressed to go beyond a detailed physical description.

> I cannot say in language what is *Action*; I think it would be monumental hubris to pretend that I could grasp in a matter of days, of hours seated in this room, the mystery that these people have discovered/created, some of them over a span of many years. In the text 'Performer,' written during the earliest phase of his current research, Grotowski asserts that 'knowledge is a matter of doing'.[30] In no instance is this more clear or more important to remember than in relation to the process of energy transformation that constitutes the essential aspect of Art as vehicle. It is a knowledge born in and through the body, pervading the cells, an *active becoming* that I as a passive witness cannot fully share. [. . .] The song is a seed of light that finds its rootedness in the heart of the doer, radiating outward, upward, burning away the dead matter and leaving behind it a visible trace—in the body, yes, but not only and not even primarily in the body. To some extent I perceive and respond to the presence of the song-as-force, the song-as-living-entity, but my perception is not the same as that of the doer who takes the song into himself and allows it to rise through his body, voice, and being.[31]

Rapture, religious as much as aesthetic, St. Sebastian pierced by arrows, happy in union with his God. Wolford insists that *Action* is 'non-mimetic, non-representational',[32] even if a 'proto-narrative' exists. Although one might think that *Action* is better called a dance than theatre, neither orthodox genre-word applies. What marks *Action* is the intensity and totality of belief-in-the-doing-of-it of the doers, a belief that is felt by spectators, as one feels the heat of a fire when one draws close.

What Grotowski seeks from traditional sources are do-able acts of the body. These are learned separate from the ideologies they express or represent. But how can actions exist outside of—or behind, before, separate from—cultures and genres? Quests for the universal too often cover up a desire to own powers thought to reside in exotic (for Westerners) others. Who benefits from the harvest of the world's cultures? Only those who can pay, travel, run centres, publish?

Augusto Boal's Theatre of the Oppressed (TO) takes the side of the down-trodden even as it shares qualities with community-based theatre. TO, modelled on fellow Brazilian Paulo Freire's 'pedagogy of the oppressed,' starts with the assumption that 'all theater is necessarily political, because all the activities of man are political and theater is one of them'.[33] Over the quarter century since he began developing TO in the early 1970s in Argentina after he was forced to flee Brazil, the emphasis has shifted from hard-edged intervention towards something between political action and psycho-social therapy. If Boal has Brecht standing on his left, Jacob Moreno (founder of psychodrama) is on his right.

In TO, what Boal calls 'spect-actors' construct, with the help of Boal-trained facilitators, alternatives to known local examples of 'oppression.' Boal described how it works:

> First, participants are asked to tell a story containing a political or social problem of difficult solution. Then a ten- or fifteen-minute skit portraying that problem and the solution intended for discussion is improvised or rehearsed, and subsequently presented. When the skit is over, the participants are asked if they agree with the solution presented. At least some will say no. At this point it is explained that the scene will be performed once more, exactly as it was the first time. But now any

> participant in the audience has the right to replace any actor and lead the action in the direction that seems to him most appropriate. The displaced actor steps aside, but remains ready to resume action the moment the participant considers his own intervention to be terminated. The other actors have to face the newly created situation, responding instantly to all the possibilities it may present. [. . .] Anyone may propose any solution, but it must be done on the stage, working, acting, doing things, and not from the comfort of his [sic] seat.[34]

> Forum theatre is not propaganda theatre, it is not the old didactic theatre. It is pedagogical in the sense that we all learn together, actors and audience. The play—or 'model' [shades of Brecht]—must present a mistake, a failure, so that the spect-actors will be spurred into finding solutions and inventing new ways of confronting oppression.[35]

What TO offers is not theatre productions, but the acting out of concrete alternatives to oppressive situations. Boal points out that talking change is easy, but doing it—even in play, on stage, in front of a crowd—is not. In terms of believed-in theatre, TO is complex. Spect-actors are led to play out what oppresses them and the means to alleviate the oppression. But to propose in theatre is not to accomplish in life. Boal recognizes that. 'It is not the place of the theater to show the correct path, but only to offer the means by which all possible paths may be examined'.[36] Boal's critics point out that TO mostly lets people blow off steam. Boal spoke about this in 1989.

> When I do Theatre of the Oppressed there is a catharsis. But which? Not the catharsis of the dynamic factor [Aristotle's catharsis] but the catharsis of the blockage. I want to purge myself of what blocks me.[37]

To accomplish this, Boal needs those taking part in TO to believe in what is going on. The spect-actors cannot think they are just doing make-believe as in orthodox theatre. They must consider themselves the vanguard of imagining and performing new social and personal relations, a utopia.

Recognizing this, Boal took the next logical step, devising what he called 'legislative theatre.' From the early-1990s until his defeat for re-election in 1996, Boal sat on the Rio City Council. From the more than 30 active TO theatres in Rio—partly supported by Rio municipal funds—spect-actors proposed laws to alleviate their wretched conditions of life. Now that he no longer sits on the Council, the future of legislative theatre is in doubt.

Very different from utopia, closer to hell, is the believed-in theatre of the AIDS epidemic. This theatre usually takes one of two forms. AIDS sufferers perform documentaries of their lives, a touching theatrical realism, touching because spectators know that the actors are condemned persons, infected and dying. The second kind of AIDS theatre draws on the tradition of performance art. Performance art emerged in the late 60s from dada and fluxus, experiments with 'projective verse,' Happenings, Cage's and Kaprow's Zen-influenced theories of non-judgment and present-centredness, street demonstrations, politicized art, and feminists who insisted that the 'personal is the political.'[38] A current example of AIDS performance art believed-in theatre is Ron Athey's *Martyrs and Saints* as it was performed in 1993 at New York's PS 122. This kind of specificity is necessary because Athey's theatre, like so much performance art, varies over time and venue.

Athey, HIV positive, carries the virus that causes AIDS. As John McGrath describes a scene near the start of *M&S*:

> Women enter. One of them begins to run needles through Athey's scalp. We realize that this is really happening, that blood is running down Athey's face. The needles form a crown of thorns. The women whip Athey, they make him dance. Finally, Athey is tied to a pole, standing on a plastic sheet. A woman pushes darts into his body, slowly, agonizingly. The program tells us to remember St. Sebastian, but we forget St. Sebastian, we see only Athey's skin being pierced, his blood running down his body and onto the plastic. The panic of his blood, the breaking of his skin's barrier, destroys the theater of the moment, allows no metaphors of mysticism or s/m to insert meaning into the spectacle.[39]

Shades of Chris Burden, Stellarc, and other pierced, wounded, mutilated performance artists. The difference is that they were hurting only themselves, Athey's blood could kill us. But, as McGrath makes clear, Athey takes great pains to set up barriers—plastic, rubber—between his infected body fluids and the not-wanting-to-be-infected audience.

For the most part, 'Athey's theatricality is blatantly badly done and cliched [. . .] and not even in some campy fun way; this is just bad theatre'.[40] But intentionally so. If Swamp Gravy presents one alternative to professionalism, Athey and other performance artists show another. These carry the same message: Something is going on here that is more actual, more true, more sincere, and more meaningful than what you get in ordinary theatre. This something is often testimony: a town's history, a personal story, a bleeding to show one's deadly existential situation. And the players, far from being ordinary actors playing characters, incorporate in their very bodies the meanings they represent. Athey's performance oversteps aesthetics and directly addresses both the AIDS community and we who have fetishized it:

> Occupying a status that has been mythologized by our society's relation to death—the HIV-positive person—Athey throws all of the Western imagery for that status into the trash heap of bad theatre. Sitting in the trash heap, we then watch as he carefully constructs experience from the manipulation of the boundaries that are supposed to maintain a separation between us and him (skin and latex). His performance is both the destruction and fetishization of these boundaries. It is the deconstruction of the space between us. [. . .] In Athey's performances there is a multiple inscription of the religious into the sexual, from the Christian iconography of sadomasochism to the personae of Christ and St. Sebastian to the invocations of Indian mysticism in the piercing rituals.[41]

Although Athey's use of religious iconography troubled McGrath, the next time he saw *M&S* he was overcome. 'It was a hot day and the club was overcrowded, but the experience was not of nausea. It was more like a kind of religious possession. As though this time Athey's performance had circumvented my skepticism about his iconography and taught me a direct lesson in the power that his references carry'.[42] When McGrath saw Athey a third time, 'his images were composed and beautiful. Lights and sound were carefully modulated. Theatre was on his side. [. . .] I felt distant and the audience seemed like voyeurs'.[43] So here is the paradox, and not Athey's alone: the 'better' the theatre the 'worse' the experience, the more abstracted, irrelevant, and distanced (and not in a Brechtian way). Or, as in Grotowski's *Action* where the skills of the doers are obvious, other means are used to separate the performance from ordinary theatre. Believed-in theatre wants to distance itself from pretend-theatre.

AIDS performances are just one kind of believed-in theatre associated with performance art. The genre specializes in performing the self, identity performance, work on the edge of 'decency,' and pushing the art/life boundary. Performance artists such as Spalding Gray, Suzanne Lacy, Judy Chicago, Karen Finley, Linda Montano, Annie Sprinkle, Lin Hixon, Tommy Eddy, and Bobby Baker are exemplars from a very long list. Ironically, even as academic performance theorists argue against 'authenticity,' performance artists win audiences by showing stuff that 'is really happening to me' or that 'is really what I feel and experience' or that 'are really my fantasies.' In orthodox theatre, one would be surprised to discover that the actors were the characters; in performance art spectators would feel cheated to discover that the performers are not who they say they are. The sources for this kind of believed-in theatre are many: Dada actions/events, Happenings, audience participation, emotional recall as interpreted by Lee Strassberg, various media-conscious 'movements' that swept America from the 1960s onward, identity politics.

The impact of TV demands an extra comment. With roving cameras and satellite hookups, real events from almost anywhere are broadcast everywhere within hours or minutes of their occurrence. These are accompanied by two kinds of commentary. The opinion of experts who interpret events; the reactions of ordinary people on the site, the 'human interest' angle. The events and the human interest sideshows appear to be authentic, real, the thing-itself and its effects.

But performance theory teaches that even 'real events' are mediatized. If they are not staged (who stages a war, but the USA in Iraq; or a plane crash, but terrorists?), what gets broadcast is edited—usually in the direction of drama and a morality play: good guys/bad guys, lessons to be learned. The victims, their relations, the bystanders—these do not argue events as Brecht wished they would in his 'Street Scene' (1964:121–29)—but emote on camera, or are edited to bring forth the greatest pathos. In other words, people have long since learned to receive events-as-TV-drama; and many people are even prepared to perform-for-the-camera if given the opportunity.

These habits and expectations spill over from TV-land to live theatre. Paradoxically, along with the expectation that events will entertain there is the demand that theatre 'actually accomplish something,' be useful. Puritans reject a theatre emanating from the body, enjoying the body, offering only entertainment, beauty, and pleasure. Athey's show, for all its shock and pathos, underwrites this Puritan value as he punctures and scourges his infected body. Much performance art is didactic. Annie Sprinkle does not show her vagina or simulate pornographic film-shoots to excite or give pleasure but to demystify, educate, and oppose sexploitation. From Piscator, Brecht, and Meyerhold to El Teatro Campesino, the San Francisco Mime Troupe, and Augusto Boal, ideologues have demanded of theatre more than pleasure. Theatre needs to serve the people, unmask and humiliate their oppressors, lead to a better life. And entertain.

The convergence of performance art and community-based theatre was never more transparent than when *High Performance*, performance art's premier journal, changed its address and focus. Leaving Santa Monica, California for Saxapahaw, North Carolina, *HP* wasn't sold or taken over by new editors—Linda Fry Burnham and Steven Durland, the founders, are still at the helm. In 1996 they introduced the new *HP* this way:

> What's that community about? For 18 years, *High Performance* has long been devoted to progressive thinking in the arts. We have done our best to support art that reflects not only a commitment to quality but a concern for the culture in which that

> work appears. We see the arts as an integral part of a healthy society in which the artist provides both intellectual nourishment and social benefit. Over the past five years we have come to identify a large number of individuals and organizations with those same goals—people working both within and outside of the traditional arts community. [. . .] Together they are creating art in the public interest: projects and programs that actively promote the arts as part of education, political life, health recovery, prisoner rehabilitation, environmental protection, community regeneration, electronic communication, and more. We have tried to provide this broad and rich field with a quarterly magazine that tells their stories. That's why so many of our writers are artists, and why so many of our stories are in the first person.[44]

HP has a homepage—

(http://artswire.org/Community/highperf/APIhome.html)

and email—

(highperf@artswire.org)

These links are not incidental as two extremes converge: locality—'this place, these people, their stories, here now'—and diffusion—'over the web and everywhere.'

Enter Esther Dyson, 'writer, futurist, philanthropist and venture capitalist',[45] talking about the decline in the market value of 'intellectual property.'

> Let me explain [Dyson says]. In the past, there was a relative shortage of creative work. There was a limited amount of content and people had a limited amount of time, and both were pretty much matched at current price levels. Now [since the Net became popular], there's much less cost associated with the distribution of content. If you put a book or a magazine up [on the Web] all the costs attributable to paper, printing, inventory, holding publications in stores go away. The other thing that is happening is that *everybody* can get up on the Net, sing their own songs, write their own poetry. You no longer

need a publishing house to get a book published. So economics would say that since the supply of content is increasing, the costs of duplication and distribution are diminishing, and people have the same amount of time or less, we are all going to pay less. [. . .]

Q: If intellectual property is to have little monetary value, how will writers, artists, composers make a living?

A: They'll get money for performances, readings, for going on line and interacting with their audience. The free copies of content are going to be what you use to establish your fame. Then you go out and milk it. Also, a lot of creators will get paid by audience gatherers rather than the public. Content will be sponsored somewhat in the way network television programming is today.[46]

Oy-vay, if content is to be determined by the apes who programme network TV conforming to the values of Philip Morris. Quality control to the side, the other face of what Dyson is talking about is that 'presence' replaces content.

A consultant will write a book, hand it out for free [over the net], and then charge higher fees for his services.[47]

The high fee is paid not for 'services,' but for presence, the chance to lay hands on the 'one of a kind real person.' That this 'real person' is performing herself is almost beside the point. Or the point is that we are living on a mobius strip where you really can't tell what's real and what's Memorex.

The imaginary is given presence, virtual realities and identities are put into play (as Butler asserts). Playing around/ playing with, subverting fixed identities, proposing alternative identities and realities. Who is 'me' in the world of MOOs and internet identities; and where does such an 'I' reside? A dizzying liminality in between realities and fictions, not quite really real, not quite really fiction. Pushing this slippage is the notion of the performative. This kind of thing reverberates with my subject because so much believed-in theatre is about inventing presence: local knowledge, the testimony of blood, enacting a better world in a TO workshop, Grotowski's doer fetching both a personal and an ancient truth, *Arbeit Mach Frei*'s encounter with its specific sites and defined audiences, the Colquitt 'dialect' of Swamp Gravy. The Web is the identical opposite of all this, the doppelganger of believed-in theatre.

The believed-in theatre I've discussed shows a strong, conscious relationship to 'history,' 'truth,' 'authenticity,' 'origins,' 'presence,' 'experience,' 'lived-through,' and so on. These terms, and terms like them, have been 'problematized' by post-structuralists. The makers of believed-in theatre either are unaware of this vein of thought, ignore it, or reject it. I am fascinated by how far away from academic theoretical concerns the practitioners of believed-in performances are. The makers of believed-in theatre actually believe; and to believe one must entertain the possibility of truth, wherever it might be found: in your town's history, in your own experience, in a supposedly surviving fragment of an ancient ritual, in the horrific events of the twentieth century, in the flow of your infected blood.

Much has been written about the increasing performativity of everyday life, about how theatre has influenced and infiltrated religion, politics, medicine, the professions, sports, and almost anything else you can name. What I am writing about is motion in the other direction. How the authenticity, real or supposed, of religion, commitment, belief, and the like have helped form an emergent believed-in theatre, a kind of theatre where the people performing and the people receiving ('spectators' or 'audiences' are too passive) are invested through and through in what they are doing. The stories are theirs, the characters are themselves or people they know, the situations pertain directly to them, the places they perform are part of specific communities, the actions they make are often consequential. In believed-in theatre, real life has invaded theatre.

This genre stands close to religion on the one side and judicial testimony on the other. Close to, but different from. Believed-in theatre operates within the theatrical-dramatic paradigm. The people making believed-in theatre tell stories by means of roles; they use dialogues and/or songs; they enact conflict and display emotions; they prepare their work through rehearsal, use varying amounts of technical means; they present work to a public, often enough a paying public, who receive what is done not as religion, not as a town meeting, not as anything but theatre. Even Grotowski, who tries as much as anyone to distance himself from the theatrical-dramatic paradigm, keeps returning to it:

> Art as presentation and Art as vehicle should exist: one visible—public—and the other almost invisible. Why do I say 'almost'? Because if it were entirely hidden, it could not give life to the anonymous influences. For this, it should remain invisible but *not entirely*.[48]

As the venues and occasions of orthodox theatre shrink in relation to film and video, believed-in theatre increases. At site-specific, event-specific, audience-specific performances, people gather as co-creators, participants, actors, spectators, witnesses, citizens, activists . . . doers. The occasions are frequently more social or personal or quasi-religious (ritual-like) than aesthetic. Sincerity and making an honest effort are appreciated. Direct address is standard. At such occasions, 'truth' is more highly valued than 'beauty,' though the two often go hand-in-hand, as John Keats said. Such performances are not make-believe enactments of fictions. They are individual or community or group 'testimony.' Often, the performer is at risk, socially, psychologically, and physically. The 'body' as a frail and multivalent vessel of life and meaning is exposed, played with, compromised, celebrated, penetrated, pierced, covered, pressed—done with in innumerable ways. Yet the bodies are also persons, living subjects who are more than the objects of performance. These persons are, to use Bill T. Jones' phrase from his controversial 1994 piece, 'still here.' Persistent in their presence, present as concrete physical, transphysical, and metaphysical beings, these persons are makers and receivers both, doers together, the creators of believed-in theatres.

In 1974, in 'From Ritual to Theatre and Back' (Chapter 6), I explored the dyadic relationship in performance between 'entertainment' and 'efficacy.' I said that in certain historical periods entertainment was dominant, at other times, efficacy was. I linked efficacious performances with ritual, a major component of which I am now calling 'believed-in theatre.' I theorized that efficacy was overtaking entertainment in the 1960s and 1970s; and I predicted that this trend would accelerate. It has.

Notes

1 Butler, Judith, *Gender Trouble* (London: Routledge, 1990), p. 25.

2 see Golub, Spencer, *Evreinov*: *The Theatre of Paradox and Transformation* (Ann Arbor: UMI Research Press, 1984), Deak, Frantisek, 'Russian Mass Spectacles,' in *TDR* (1975), vol.19, no. 2, pp. 7–22, and Gerould, Dan 'Historical Simulation and Popular Entertainment: The *Potemkin* Mutiny from Reconstructed Newsreel to Black Sea Stunt Men,' in *TDR* (1989), vol. 33, no. 2, pp.137-60.

3 see Schechner, Richard, *Between Theater and Anthropology* (Philadelphia: University of Pennsylvania Press, 1985), Snow, Stephen, *Performing the Pilgrims* (Oxford: University of Mississippi Press, 1993), and Kirshenblatt-Gimblett, Barbara, *Destination Culture* (Berkeley: University of Californa Press, 1996).

4 Kirshenblatt-Gimblett, Barbara, op. cit., 1996.

5 Interestingly, at Plimoth several of the actors playing Wampanoag Native Americans are Native Americans. When I was there in 1995, one of them told me he was a Wampanoag. Stephen Snow, whose *Performing the Pilgrims* (1993) is the best text on the subject, is himself a descendent of Pilgrims. He writes: 'It was both ironic and unexpected that I ended up choosing the restored village at Plimoth as the subject of my study. [. . .] A serious illness in my family brought me back to Plimoth. My mother was stricken with cancer and, after her death in January 1984, I decided to stay on with my father, in Plymouth, and to take a position as an interpreter at Plimoth Plantation. [. . .] I had vaguely known that I was a descendant of the early English settlers of Plimoth but had not paid much attention to the fact. What I did know before I began my study was that Nicholas

Snow, the progenitor of my father's line in America, had actually lived in the original Pilgrim village in 1627'. (xxiv-v). Snow never performed his own ancestor, however.

6 The title combines the grisly ironic 'Work Makes You Free' motto wrought in iron by the Nazis over Auschwitz's main gate, with the sardonic commentary added by the Akko Theatre: '. . . in Deathland Europe.'

7 Rovit writes specifically about *Arbeit*'s showings in Berlin, and how the Akko group adapted the production for a predominantly German rather than Israeli audience.

8 Urian, Dan, '*Arbeit Mach Frei* in Toitland Europa,' in *TheareForum* 3 (Spring, 1993), pp. 61-62.

9 Rovit, Rebecca, 'Emerging from the Ashes,' in *TDR* (1993), vol. 37, no. 2, pp. 167.

10 Urian, *TheatreForum* 3, pp. 60-61.

11 The intervention reminded me of the Living Theatre's 'exemplary actions.' In these, spectators were invited to intervene and show the way violence could be intercepted or blocked. Of course, it was all make-believe: no Living Theatre violence matched what the police, or others, did; and I doubt that practising intervention on a stage promoted such actions in real life.

12 Urian, *Theatreforum 3*, p.61.

14 Quoted in Geer, Richard Owen, 'Out of Control in Colquitt: Swamp Gravy Makes Stone Soup,' in *TDR* (1996), vol. 40, no. 2, p. 109.

15 Ibid., p. 131.

16 Ibid., p. 117.

17 Ibid., pp. 124-125.

18 Ibid., p. 122.

19 *Appalshop Notes* (Whitesburg, Kentucky: Appalshop, 1996), p. 2.

20 Ibid., p. 2.

21 Ibid., p. 5.

22 see Barba, Eugenio, *The Floating Islands* (Holstebro, Denmark: Drama, 1979) and Barba, Eugenio, *Beyond the Floating Islands* (New York: PAJ Publications, 1986).

23 The two works are not both in repertory. *Downstairs Action* originated in Grotowski's Objective Drama project in the mid-1980s. It was superseded by *Action* in the 1990s. Mercedes (Chiquita) Gregory made a film of *Downstairs Action* which Grotowski continues to show,

especially when he is outside of Pontedera lecturing or meeting with groups. No film yet exists of *Action* which, thus far, has been performed only in Pontedera.

24 The history of this development is presented in detail in Schechner and Wolford, eds., *The Grotowski Sourcebook* (London: Routledge, 1997).

25 Not adequately rendered as 'I and thou' because 'thou' is too formal, distant, and awesome. The German 'du' is the intimate, personal form of addressing the other: close friends, lovers, family.

26 Richards, Thomas, *At Work with Grotowski on Physical Actions* (London: Routledge, 1995), pp. 115, 122.

27 Grotowski calls the performer 'doer.' In noh, the main actor is also called the *shite*, literally 'doer.'

28 Richards, *At Work with Grotowski*, p. 125.

29 Osinski, Zbigniew, 'Grotowski Blazes the Trails: From Objective Drama to Ritual Arts,' in *TDR* (1991), vol. 35, no. 1, pp.96.

30 See Grotowski, Jerzy, 'Performer' in Wolford, Lisa, *Workcenter of Jerzy Grotowski*, (Pontedera, Italy: Centro per la Sperimentazione e la Ricerca Teatrale, 1988), pp. 36–41. Privately distributed pamphlet.

31 Wolford, Lisa, 'Action: The Unrepresentable Origin,' in *TDR* (1996), vol. 40, no. 4, pp. 146.

32 Ibid., p. 27.

33 Boal, Augusto, *Theatre of the Oppressed* (New York: TCG, 1985), p. ix.

34 Ibid., p. 139.

35 Boal, Augusto, *Games for Actors and Non-Actors* (London: Routledge, 1992), p. 19.

36 Boal, *Theatre of the Oppressed*, p. 141.

37 Taussig, Michael, and Richard Schechner,, 'Boal in Brazil, France, the USA,' in Schutzman, Mady and Jan Cohen-Cruz, ed., *Playing Boal* (London: Routledge, 1994), p. 27.

38 Robyn Brentano has provided a fine thumb-nail sketch of the development and scope of performance art:

Performance has been a powerful catalyst in the history of twentieth-century art not only because it has subverted the formal conventions and rational premises of modernist art, but also because it has heightened our awareness of the social role of art and, at times, has served as a vehicle for social change. [. . .] The term 'performance art' first appeared around 1970 to describe the ephemeral, time-based, and process-oriented work of conceptual ('body') and feminist artists that was emerging at the time. It was also applied retrospectively to Happenings, Fluxus events, and other intermedia performances from the 1960s. Over the past thirty-five years, many styles and modes of performance have evolved, from private, introspective investigations to ordinary routines of everyday life, cathartic rituals and trials of endurance, site-specific environmental transformations, technically sophisticated multimedia productions, autobiographically based cabaret-style performance, and large-scale, community-based projects designed to serve as a source of social and political empowerment. From Brentano, Robyn, 'Outside the Frame: Performance, Art, and Life' in *Outside the Frame* (Cleveland: Cleveland Center for Contemporary Art, 1994), p. 31-32.

39 McGrath, John, 'Trusting in Rubber: Performing Boundaries During the AIDS Epidemic,' in *TDR* (1995), vol. 39, no. 2, pp. 26.

40 Ibid., p. 27.

41 Ibid., pp. 35-36.

42 Ibid., p. 38.

43 Ibid.

44 Durland, Steven and Linda Frye Burnham, 'Publisher's Notes,' *High Performance* 19, 1996, 1: inside front cover ff.

45 Dreifus, Claudia, 'The Cyber-maxims of Esther Dyson,' *The New York Times Magazine*, 7 July 1996, pp. 16–19.

46 Ibid., pp. 17-18.

47 Dyson in Dreifus, 'The Cyber-maxims of Esther Dyson,', p. 18.

48 In Richards, *At Work with Grotowski,* p. 135.

Rasaesthetics

Where in the body is theatricality located? What is its place? Traditionally in Western theatre, the eyes and to some degree the ears are where theatricality is experienced. By etymology and by practice a theatre is a 'place of/for seeing.' Seeing requires distance; engenders focus or differentiation; encourages analysis or breaking apart into logical strings; privileges meaning, theme, narration. Modern science depends on instruments of observation, of ocularity: telescopes and microscopes. Theories derived from observations made by means of ocular instruments define the time-space continuum. From super-galactic strings on the one hand to molecular and subatomic wave-particles on the other we 'know' the universe by 'seeing' it. See=know; speed=space; distance=time; diachronicity=story.

But in other cultural traditions there are other locations for theatricality. One of these, the mouth, or better said, the snout-to-belly-to-bowel—the route through the body managed by the enteric nervous system—is the topic of this essay. The mouth-to-belly-to-bowel is the 'where' of taste, digestion, and excretion. The performance of the snout-to-belly-to bowel is an ongoing interlinked muscular, cellular, and neurological process of testing-tasting, separating nourishment from waste, distributing nourishment throughout the body, and eliminating waste. The snout-to-belly-to-bowel is the where of mixing, intimacy, sharing of bodily substances, mixing the inside and the outside, emotional experiences, and gut-feelings. A good meal with good company is a pleasure; so is foreplay and lovemaking; so is a good shit.

THE POETICS *AND THE* NATYASHASTRA

Aristotle's *Poetics* and Bharata Muni's *Natyashastra*, a Sanskrit manual of performance and performance theory, occupy parallel positions in European and Indian performance theory (and by extension, throughout the many areas and cultures where European-derived or Indian-derived performing arts are practiced). Both ancient texts continue to be actively interpreted and debated, theoretically and in practice. Both are at or near the 'origins' of their respective performance traditions, both have evoked 'after texts' or 'counter texts' aimed at enhancing, revising, or refuting their basic principals.

But similar as they are in some ways, the two texts differ profoundly. Aristotle was an historical figure (384–322 BC), the author of many key philosophical texts affecting, even determining, Western thought in various fields as far-ranging as the physical sciences, politics, social thought, aesthetics, and theology. The Macedonian-Greek philosopher's writings have been actively debated for nearly two-and-a-half millennia. He specialized in dividing knowledge into knowable portions; he formulated the syllogism. Bharata Muni is a mythic-historical figure, the name of the author or compiler of a very detailed compendium concerning the religious-mythic origins and practices of *natya*, a Sanskrit word not easily translatable, but reducible to dance-theatre-music. The precise date of the *NS* remains in question—scholars have placed it anywhere from the sixth century BC to the second century CE. Exactly how much of the *NS* was the work of one person and how much the lore of many will probably never be known. Bharata Muni, whoever he was, if he was at all, wrote only the *NS*.

Furthermore, the *NS* is a 'sastra,' a sacred text, authorized by the gods, full of narration, myth, and detailed instructions for performers. The *Poetics* is secular, focused on the structure of drama, and dependant on the logical thinking that its author helped invent. The *Poetics* is so laconic, running in English translation about 30 pages, that some believe it to be lecture notes compiled by Aristotle's students after his death rather than the philosopher's own finished work. The *NS* takes the form of an extended disquisition (345 pages in the Rangacharya translation) by Bharat in answer to sages who asked him to explain natya. Bharat begins with the story of how natya came about, what its proper subjects are, and for whom it was made.[1] Then he goes on to detail everything from theatre architecture to how to perform the various emotions to the structure of dramas, and more.

Some centuries after it was completed, the *NS* was 'lost'—fragmented, submerged, misplaced, and unread. The *NS* comes to modern Indians not directly and not as a single text. The *NS* comes down in performance practice and as a series of interpretations. The most important interpreter is the tenth-century Kashmiri Shaivite (worshipper of Shiva), Abhinavagupta. Through Abhinavagupta scholars discern earlier interpretators of the *NS* such as Bhatta Lollata, Srisankuka, Bhatta Nayaka, and Bhatta Tauta. As for the *NS* 'itself,' according to Kapila Vatsyayan, 'not many texts have been systematically collated and edited and published. Hundreds [. . .] lie as manuscripts in public or private collections, in India and abroad, and an equal or larger number are in fragments'.[2]

But this fragmentation ought not to be read as 'neglect.' The *NS* tradition is active, oral, and corporeal. It is present in performers, their teachers, and their performances. We must distinguish the absence of the *NS* as a text (a book brought to light in modern times mostly by Western orientalists)[3] from its presence in actual performances where it has been absorbed into, and forms the core of, a multiplicity of genres such as kathak, kathakali, odissi, and bharatanatyam which, taken together, comprise Indian classic theatre-dance. The *NS* is much more powerful as an embodied set of ideas and practices than as a written text. Unlike the *Poetics*, the *NS* is more danced than read.

Thus the *NS* and the *Poetics* are different in style, intent, and historical circumstance. The *Poetics*, written nearly a century after Greek tragedy's heyday, constitutes only a small portion of Aristotle's enormous output. The *Poetics* lacks descriptions of actual performances; it is mostly about drama, not theatre, focusing on one play, *Oedipus*, which Aristotle offers as a model for the right way to write plays. Framed as 'rational' and 'historical,' the *Poetics* is not regarded as sacred, although it has been, and remains, remarkably influential. On the other hand, the *NS* is a hybrid of myth and down-to-earth performance knowledge, far-ranging and detailed. Its author and protagonist, the semi-divine Bharata Muni, is almost certainly a pseudonym for a collective oral tradition.

But the greatest difference between the *Poetics* and the *NS* is that the Indian book deals in detail with performance: emotional expression as conveyed by specific gestures and movements, role and character types, theatre architecture, music. The *NS* considers drama (chapters 20–21), but that analysis is not the core of the sastra. Many Indian artists subscribe to the ideal of a theatre that integrates drama, dance, and music. Traditional genres accomplish this integration in ways that do not privilege plot (as Aristotle advised) over dance, gesture, and music. And then there is rasa.

RASA, FIRST TAKE

Of rasa, the *NS* says:

> There is no natya without rasa. Rasa is the cumulative result of *vibhava* [stimulus], *anubhava* [involuntary reaction], and *vyabhichari bhava* [voluntary reaction.] For example, just as when various condiments and sauces and herbs and other materials are mixed, a taste is experienced, or when the mixing of materials like molasses with other materials produces six kinds of taste, so also along with the different *bhavas* [emotions] the *sthayi bhava* [permanent emotions experienced 'inside'] becomes a rasa.
>
> But what is this thing called rasa? Here is the reply. Because it is enjoyably tasted, it is called rasa. How does the enjoyment

> come? Persons who eat prepared food mixed with different condiments and sauces, if they are sensitive, enjoy the different tastes and then feel pleasure; likewise, sensitive spectators, after enjoying the various emotions expressed by the actors through words, gestures, and feelings feel pleasure. This feeling by the spectators is here explained as the rasas of natya.[4]

There is a lot going on here, and I do not intend at this time to go into a detailed explication of rasa theory. I want here to outline an overall theory of flavour as it pertains to performance, what I call 'rasaesthetics.'

Rasa is flavour, taste, the sensation one gets when food is perceived, brought within reach, touched, taken into the mouth, chewed, mixed, savoured, and swallowed. The eyes and ears perceive the food on its way—the presentation of the dishes, the sizzling. At the same time, or very shortly after, the nose gets involved. The mouth waters in anticipation. Smell and taste dissolve into each other. The hands convey the food to the mouth—either directly as in the traditional Indian way of eating with the fingers or somewhat indirectly by means of utensils (a latecomer everywhere). The whole snout is engaged. In the snout all the senses are well-represented. The lower part of the face contains the mouth, in the centre is the nose, above are the eyes. The ears are side-centre, but focused forward.

Rasa also means 'juice,' the stuff that conveys the flavour, the medium of tasting. The juices of eating originate both in the food and from the body. Saliva not only moistens food, it distributes flavours. Rasa is sensuous, proximate, experiential. Rasa is aromatic. Rasa fills space, joining the outside to the inside. Food is actively taken into the body, becomes part of the body, works from the inside. What was outside is transformed into what is inside. An aesthetic founded on rasa is fundamentally different than one founded on the 'theatron,' the rationally ordered, analytically distanced panoptic.

ETYMOLOGIES AND DISTANCED KNOWING

Before more on rasaesthetics, something on Western notions of theatre. The word 'theatre' is cognate with 'theorem,' 'theory,' 'theorist,' and such, all from the Greek *theatron*, itself from *thea*, 'a sight," and from *theasthai*, 'to view'; related to *thauma*, 'a thing compelling the gaze, a wonder; and *theorein*, 'to look at'.[5] *Theorein* is related to *theorema*, 'spectacle' and/or 'speculation'.[6] These words are thought to be related to the Indo-European root *dheu* or *dhau*, 'to look at'.[7] The Indo-European root of 'Thespis'—the legendary founder of Greek theatre—is *seku*, a 'remark' or 'saying,' but with the implication of a divine vision; and from *seku* derive such English words as 'see,' 'sight,' and 'say'.[8] Greek theatre, then, and all European types of theatre derived from it, are places of/for seeing and saying. What marks this kind of theatre (and after it, film, TV, and possibly the Internet) is its specularity, its strategies of 'gazing.'

These etymologies reveal the tight bond linking Greek theatre, European epistemology, and seeing. This binding of 'knowing' to 'seeing' is the root metaphor/master narrative of Western thought. If the humans in Plato's cave were ignorant, it was because all they saw of 'truth' were shadows cast on the wall. True reality was so much brighter even than the sun that no human viewer could look at it directly. What Plato said could be known through dialectics, scientists since the Renaissance have tried to do by devising finer and finer instruments of observation. A single net holds Plato's allegory, Galileo's observations, the Hubble Space Telescope, electron microscopes, and the super-colliding super-conductor particle accelerator.

Where does seeing take place? Only at a distance from what is being seen. There is both a logical and a practical difference necessary, keeping what is observed separate from the observing instrument (and/or observer). 'Objectivity' can be understood as the desire to keep things at enough distance from the eyes to allow whatever it is to 'take shape' perceptually: to see things 'in perspective,' to 'focus on' them. The 'indeterminacy principle' linking the instrument of observation to what is observed does not dissolve the distance between observer and observed so much as it asserts that what is observed is indissolubly linked to the means of observing. What 'moves' the particle is the light that is needed to observe it.

At a more everyday level, as an object is brought close to the face, one loses focus and finally the object blurs, loses its visual shape. And, of course, one mustn't put things into one's eyes. Poking out the eyes is a terrible thing both legendarily (Jocasta, Oedipus, Gloucester, et al) and actually. But a child learns early to see something, focus on it, reach for it, grasp it, and bring it to the mouth. The mouth replaces the eyes as the end point of exploring the 'outer' world and relating it to the 'inner' world. The 'transitional object'[9] is how the infant first experiences the sameness/difference between the world outside herself and the world inside herself: from the breast, to the fingers, to the grasped-tasted-chewed whatever, to the security blanket, to the favourite object. Even before birth, as *in utero* photographs show, the pre-born suck their fingers and toes. Can we doubt that the pre-born enjoy this activity? Nor is the mouth a singular conduit connected solely to the brain (as the eye is via the optic nerve). The mouth opens to the nasal cavity and the whole digestive system; the mouth—including lips and tongue—intimately engages the senses of touch, taste, and smell. The ocular system is extraordinarily focused, while the snout system is wide open, combining rather than separating.

The Greek theatre that Aristotle based his theories on was fundamentally a seeing place. Architecturally—as is evident from what is left of the Theatre of Dionysus on the hillside of the Akropolis, the almost wholly intact theatre at Epidaurus, and from other sites and restorations—the Greek theatre was immense. Most scholars place the number in the audience at the ancient festivals at between 14,000 and 17,000. And although Aristotle favoured the drama over the theatre, the actual experience of being in a classical Greek theatre strongly includes the spectacle—dancing, singing, and reciting. The Greek theatre was also, and perhaps mostly, a focus of competition. The Athenians were an intensely competitive people. The *agon* was for them the motor, source, and energy of creation, a model of becoming.[10]

Whatever Aristotle may have wanted, the living heart of Greek tragedy was not plot as such, but a particular kind of storytelling, the *agon*. To sort winners from losers, the judges (and those judging the judges, the spectators) had to see clearly and base their opinions on 'objectivity.' Of course, there may have been all kinds of politicking and pressures. Maybe even bribes and cheating. But, as in today's spectator sports (with or without instant replays), clarity in presentation and reception was absolutely essential. The goal of the shows was to determine winners and losers—both in the dramas and in the competitions among actors and poets.

RASIC PERFORMANCE IS DIFFERENT

Rasic performance has as its goal not separating winners from losers, but extending pleasure—as in an endless banquet or an always-deferred 'almost' sexual orgasm. It accomplishes this in a way comparable to cooking: the combination/transformation of distinct elements into a something that offers new and/or intense and/or favourite flavours or tastes. Rasic performance values immediacy over distance, savouring over judgment. Its paradigmatic activity is a sharing between performers and partakers (a more accurate term than 'audiences' or 'spectators,' words that privilege ear or eye). The rasic performance event is more a banquet than a day in court. The *NS* puts it this way:

> Those who are connoisseurs of tastes enjoy the taste of food prepared from (or containing) different stuff; likewise, intelligent, healthy persons enjoy various *sthayi bhavas* related to the acting of emotions.[11]

The Sanskrit word that is translated as 'connoisseur' is *bhakta*, which can also mean a person ecstatically devoted to a god, particularly Krishna who is celebrated by means of singing, dancing, and feasting. The *sthayi bhavas* are the 'permanent' or 'abiding' or indwelling emotions that are accessed and evoked by good acting, called *abhinaya*. Rasa is experiencing the *sthayi bhavas*. To put it another way, the sweetness 'in' a ripe plum is its *sthayi bhava*, the experience of 'tasting the sweet' is rasa. The means of getting the taste across—preparing it, presenting it—is *abhinaya*. Every emotion is a *sthayi bhava*. Acting is the art of presenting the *sthayi bhavas* so that *both* the performer and the partaker can 'taste' the emotion, the rasa.

In chapters six and seven, the *NS* gives the eight rasas and their corresponding *sthayi bhavas*:

Rasa	**Sthayi Bhava**	**English**
sringara	rati	love, desire
hasya	hasa	humour, laughter
karuna	shoka	pity, grief
raudra	krodha	anger, rage
vira	utsaha	vigour, energy
bhayanaka	bhaya	fear, shame
bibhasta	jugupsra	disgust, revulsion
adbhuta	vismaya	surprise, wonder

Abhinavagupta added a ninth rasa, shanta, 'peace' or 'bliss.' From Abhinavagupta's time onward, many Indians speak of the 'nine rasas.' But shanta does not correspond to any particular *sthayi bhava*. Rather, like white light, shanta is the perfect balance/mix of them all; or shanta may be regarded as the transcendent rasa which, when accomplished, absorbs and eliminates all the others. A perfect performance, should one occur, would not transmit or express shanta (as it could transmit or express any of the other rasas), but allow shanta to be experienced simultaneously and absolutely by performers and partakers.

It is not my aim in this essay to investigate the many connections between the *sthayi bhavas* and the rasas. It is enough to note that 'emotions' in the Indian aesthetic performance system, far from being personal—based on individual experience, or locked up and only accessible by means of an 'emotional memory' exercise or a 'private moment' (Stanislavsky and his disciples)—are to some degree objective, residing in the public or social sphere.

In the rasic system, there are 'artistically performed emotions' which comprise a distinct kind of behaviour (different, perhaps, for each performance genre). These performed emotions are separate from the 'feelings'—the interior, subjective experience of any given performer during a particular performance. There is no necessary and ineluctable chain linking these 'performed emotions' with the 'emotions of everyday life.' In the rasic system, the emotions *in the arts*, *not in ordinary life* are knowable, manageable, and transmittable in roughly the same way that the flavours and presentation of a meal are manageable by following recipes and the conventions of presenting the meal.

When I spoke to kathakali actors, for example, some told me they felt the emotions they performed, others did not feel the emotions. There is no yes or no answer to Diderot's question, 'Do actors feel the emotions they communicate?' Feeling the emotions is not necessary though it is not a bad thing either. Whether it happens or not to any particular performer does not necessarily make the performance better or worse. What is relevant is making certain that each 'partaker' receives the emotions; and that these emotions are specific and controlled. The emotions, the *sthayi bhava*, are objective; the feelings (what an individual performer or partaker experiences) are subjective. What is shared are the rasas of a single emotion or combination of emotions.

It is not easy to clearly differentiate 'emotions' from 'feelings.' Basically, emotions are communicated by means of *abhinaya*; feelings are experienced. So: the rasas themselves (as flavours of moods) are feelings, but what is communicated or transmitted by means of rasas are emotions. One 'has' emotions even if one is not feeling them; one 'experiences' feelings even if sometimes disconnected to emotions ('I don't know why I am feeling the way I feel'). The links between emotions and feelings are usually manifest, but not always. When an actor's *abhinaya* is strong, the emotions are communicated, audience members feel feelings—whether or not the actor is feeling something. In expressing the emotions by means of *abhinaya* one may or may not create feelings in oneself, but a good actor always creates feelings in the partakers (audience). In order for rasas to be shared, performers must enact the *abhinaya* of a particular emotion or concatenation of emotions according to the traditions of a specific genre of performance. The feelings aroused may be personal, intimate, and indescribable; but the emotions enacted are consciously constructed and objectively managed.

According to Stanislavsky-based Euro-American acting, one does not 'play an emotion.' One plays the 'given circumstances,' the 'objectives,' the 'through line of action,' the 'magic if.' If this is done right, 'real' feelings will be experienced and 'natural' emotions will be displayed. But according to my interpretation of the *NS* rasic system, one can work *directly* on the emotions, mixing them according to 'recipes' known to the great acting gurus (which means, simply, 'teachers')—or even by devising new recipes. From a Stanislavskian vantage, such direct work on the emotions will result in false or mechanical acting. But anyone who has seen performers thoroughly trained in the *NS* rasic system knows these performers are every bit as effective as performers trained in the Stanislavsky system.

If performing rasically is to offer emotions to partakers in the same way that a chef offers a meal to diners, then the effectiveness of the performance depends very much on an active response from the partakers. The *NS* is very emphatic in its insistence that natya appeal to people of all stations in life, affecting different people differently.[12] The more knowledgeable the partakers, the better the experience. To respond to the fullest, partakers need to be connoisseurs of whatever performance genre they are taking in—as wine tasters need to know vintages, bottling procedures, and ways of sampling in order to fully appreciate a wine. There is a sliding scale of how much one needs to know. In the rasic system, each person enjoys according to her abilities; the higher the level of knowledge, the greater the enjoyment (or disappointment, if the performance is not up to standards). Japanese noh actors study the audience immediately before entering the stage and then adjust their performances to the particular partakers on hand. All performers know this. The best performers save their best performances for the most discerning partakers and those who know the most expect the best. In India, at least, the active response of the partakers is expected. At dance or music concerts people quietly beat out the *tal*, or rhythm, sing under their breath, and sometimes move their hands in harmony with the *mudras*, or hand-gesture system. At the Ramlila of Ramnagar, many persons carry texts of Tulsidas's *Ramcharitmanas*, following along, even singing, as the Ramayanis chant. The same is true of sports or pop music connoisseurs. The 'home team advantage' is a direct measurement of how the active participation of the crowd can impact the level of performance.

Oral Pleasures, Rasically

Fundamentally, the attainment of pleasure and satisfaction in a rasic performance is oral—through the snout, by combining various flavours and tastes; and the satisfaction is visceral, in the belly. How can this be since the Indian theatre, like the Western theatre, is presented visually and sonically? First, the Indian theatre, both in earlier times and today, is not based on the *agon*, on formally determining winners and losers, either within the dramas (in classic Indian plays often everyone wins) or in terms of competitions among dramatists and actors. In that ancient theatre of India, there were no judges formally ensconced on front marble benches as in the Theatre of Dionysus. Thus there was no attempt to quantify the performing experience, to bring it under the theatron's aegis of visuality. Second, many performances were part of the feasts of the rich or royal, and continue to be offered at weddings or other happy celebrations. Religion itself has a feasting quality interweaving performing, worshipping, and eating. Separating work from play, and the sacred from the profane, has always been more a Western than Indian phenomenon. Third, until the arrival of Islam and then the English, there was no anti-theatrical prejudice or Puritanism in India. Far from it, the arts infused with intense sexual pleasure were often part of the religious experience.

India today is less open to the rasic mix of art, sensuousity, and feasting than before the advent of the Mughals and the British. But imagining performances from the period of Sanskrit drama (fourth–eleventh centuries CE) as indicated by sculptings and paintings at such sites as Khajuraho, the shore temple of Mamallapuram, or the 'theatre caves' of Ajanta can get us closer to the kind of experience I am talking about.

The Ajanta style approaches as near as it is likely for an artist to get to a felicitous rendering of tactile sensations normally experienced subconsciously. These are felt rather than seen when the eye is subordinate to a total receptivity of all the senses. [. . .] The seated queen with the floating hand is drawn so that we obtain information which cannot be had by looking at her from a single, fixed viewpoint. [. . .T]he logic of this style demands that movements and gestures can only be described in terms of the area or space in which they occur; we cannot identify a figure except by comparing its position with others around it. [. . .] It could be said that the Ajanta artist is concerned with the order of sensuousness, as distinct from the order of reason.[13]

Richard Lannoy argues that Sanskrit drama—some form of which is described and theorized in the *NS*—is like the Ajanta paintings:

> The structure and ornamentation of the caves were deliberately designed to induce total participation during ritual circumambulation. The acoustics of one Ajanta *vihara,* or assembly hall (Cave VI), are such that any sound long continues to echo round the walls. This whole structure seems to have been tuned like a drum.[14]

This tuning was not fortuitous. The Ajanta caves are human-made, excavated and carved out of solid rock. Lannoy continues:

> In both cases [the caves, the theatre] total participation of the viewer was ensured by a skillful combination of sensory experience. The 'wrap-around' effect [of] the caves was conveyed on the stage by adapting the technically brilliant virtuosity of Vedic incantation and phonetic science to the needs of the world's most richly textured style of poetic drama.[15]

What the *NS* supplies are the concrete details of that style, which at its core is not literary but theatrical, not plot-dominated or driven. Indian classical theatre and dance does not emphasize clear beginnings, middles, and ends but favours a more 'open narration,' a menu of many delectables—offshoots, sidetracks, pleasurable digressions—not all of which can be savoured at a sitting. The performances the *NS* refers to took place over periods of days or weeks. They were festivals, part of multifaceted celebrations, that also featured feasting and audience participation integral to the whole performance complex. Some of this continues today, as experienced in such popular religious festive forms as Ramlila, Raslila, and bhajan–singing/dancing, with their circumambulations, hymn-singing, trance-dancing, food-sharing, and wrap-around or environmental theatre staging.

It's not all one way or the other. There is a lot of movement—actual and conceptual—from one kind of action to another. There are phases of these festive performances where partakers stand back and watch or listen and other phases where they participate. This blending of theatre, dance, music, eating, and religious devotion is to many participants a full, satisfying, and pleasurable experience that cannot be reduced to any single category—religious, aesthetic, personal, or gustatory. This kind of an event yields experiences that dissolve differences, if only for a little while. This kind of experience is hard to measure from the inside or observe from the outside. It is this experience of an 'all-is-inside' theatricality that most sharply distinguishes rasaesthetics from orthodox Western aesthetics derived from the Greek theatre and its reinterpretations in the Renaissance and variations in the drama-based proscenium or frontal-stage work of today. Rasaesthetics is experienced 'in the gut,' a formulation involving the enteric nervous system.

THE ENTERIC NERVOUS SYSTEM

Take a step into neurobiology. According to recent studies, there is a brain in the belly, literally. The basic research in this area has been conducted by Michael D. Gershon[16] whose work was summarized in the *New York Times* by Sandra Blakeslee:

> The gut's brain, known as the enteric nervous system [ENS], is located in sheaths of tissue lining the esophagus, stomach, small intestine, and colon. Considered a single entity, it is a network of neurons, neurotransmitters, and proteins that zap messages between neurons, support cells like those found in the brain proper and a complex circuitry that enables it to act independently, learn, remember, and, as the saying goes, produce gut feelings.[17]

The ENS derives from the 'neural crest,' a bunch of related cells that forms in mammals and birds early in embryo genesis: 'One section turns into the central nervous system. Another piece migrates to become the enteric nervous system. Only later are the two nervous systems connected via a cable called the vagus nerve'.[18] According to Gershon:

> The ENS resembles the brain and differs both physiologically and structurally from any other region of the PNS [peripheral nervous system]. [. . .B]oth the avian and mammalian bowel are colonized by émigrés from the sacral as well as the vigil level of the neural crest. [. . .] The PNS contains more neurons than the spinal cord and, in contrast to other regions of the PNS, the ENS is capable of mediating reflex activity in the absence of central neural input. In fact, most of the neurons of the ENS are not directly innervated by a preganglionic input from the brain or spinal cord. The functional independence of the ENS is mirrored in its chemistry and structure.[19]

And again, as summarized by Blakeslee:

> Until relatively recently, people thought that the gut's muscles and sensory nerves were wired directly to the brain and that the brain controlled the gut through two pathways that increased or decreased rates of activity [. . .]. The gut was simply a tube with simple reflexes. Trouble is, no one bothered to count the nerve fibers in the gut. When they did [. . .], they were surprised to find that the gut contains 100 million neurons—more than the spinal cord has. Yet the vagus nerve only sends a couple of thousand nerve fibers to the gut.[20]

What this means is that the gut—esophagus, stomach, intestines, and bowels—has its own nervous system. This system does not replace or preempt the brain. Rather it operates alongside the brain, or—evolutionarily speaking—'before' or 'underneath' the brain. Gershon:

> The enteric nervous system is [. . .] a remnant of our evolutionary past that has been retained. [It] has been present in each of our predecessors through the millions of years of evolutionary history that separate us from the first animal with a backbone. [. . .T]he enteric nervous system is a vibrant, modern data-processing center that enables us to accomplish some very important and unpleasant tasks with no mental effort. When the gut rises to the level of conscious perception, in the form of, for example, heartburn, cramps, diarrhea, or consti-

> pation, no one is enthused. Few things are more distressing than an inefficient gut with feelings.[21]

But what about emotional feelings? In December 2000, I emailed Gershon about 'rasaesthetics' and the ENS. He replied:

> Thank you for your letter. You touch a bit of raw nerve. You are certainly correct in that we in the West who consider ourselves 'hard' scientists have not taken Eastern thought very seriously. The problem with a great deal of Eastern thought is that it is not based on documentable observation. You cannot quantify ideas about strong feelings or deep power. We therefore, either ignore Eastern ideas about the navel, or take them as metaphors, which are not very different from our own metaphors about 'gut feelings.' On the other hand, I have recently become aware of quantifiable research that establishes, without question, that vagus nerve stimulation can be used to treat epilepsy and depression. Vagus nerve stimulation also improves learning and memory. Vagus nerve stimulation is something physicians do and is not natural, but 90% of the vagus carries ascending information from the gut to the brain. It is thus possible that vagus nerve stimulation mimics natural stimulation of the vagus nerve by the 'second brain.' This relationship is particularly important in relation to the human condition of autism. Autism affects the gut as well as the brain. It is thus conceivable that autism could be the result in whole or in part of a disturbed communication between the two brains.
>
> In short, I now take the possibility that the gut affects emotions very seriously. This seems much more likely to me now than it did when I wrote my book. A dialogue between us might be of mutual interest.

The dialogue has not yet progressed beyond the email quoted, but it is destined.

Let us suppose, in light of ENS research, that when someone says, 'I have a gut feeling,' she actually is experiencing a feeling, a neural response, but not one that is head-brain centred. Let us suppose that her feeling is located in, or emanating from, the 'second brain,' the brain in the belly. When expressed, this feeling is an emotion. Can such feelings be trained? That is, what are the systems converting 'gut feelings' into expressible emotions? Gershon is interested primarily in the therapeutic value of vagus nerve stimulation, of causing or evoking feelings in autistics who suffer from lack of affect or lack of range of affect. The rasaboxes exercise is a kind of ENS training suitable for 'normal' or 'artistic' uses.

The presence and location of the ENS confirms a basic principal of Asian medicine, meditation, and martial arts: that the region in the gut between the navel and the pubic bone is the centre/source of readiness, balance, and reception, the place where action and meditation originate and are centred. A related place is the base of the spine, the resting spot of 'kundalini,' an energy system that can be aroused and transmitted up the spinal column. Gaining an awareness of and control over the gut and lower spine is crucial to anyone learning various Asian performances, martial arts, or meditations.

Phillip Zarrilli has for many years researched both in a scholarly and in a practical way the relationship between what in the Keralan martial art *kalarippayattu* is called the *nabhi mula* (root of the navel) and performance art training, psychophysical centring, and ayurvedic medicine. According to Zarrilli:

> When impulses originate from the *nabhi mula* [. . .they] are 'grounded,' 'centred,' 'integrated,' 'filled out,' 'dynamic.' The *nabhi mula* of kalarippayattu is identical to the *svadhisthanam* of classical yoga. Its location is two finger widths above the anus and two finger widths below the root of the navel. It is at this center that both breath and impetus for movement into and out of forms originate.[22]

Zarrilli emphasizes that the *nabhi mula* is important 'psychophysically,' as the source of feeling-and-movement, a kind of 'gripping' (*piduttam*) or firmness of body, spirit, and feelings that affect the whole human being. The Chinese notion of *ch'i* and the Japanese 'activating force' *ki* are closely related to the *nabhi mula* and the sense of *piduttam*. In noh theatre, the *tanden*, located 'in the belly two inches below the navel'[23] is the energy centre. The point is that this 'centre' is a radiating spot:

> The actor is engaged in his total being in a psychophysical process where his internal energy, aroused in his vital center below the navel, then directed into and through the embodied forms of external gesture (body and voice) is of course fundamentally the same [in noh] as the interior process of the kathakali actor. This despite the fact that the exterior manifestation of the interior process is different.[24]

I could cite many more examples. But it all comes down to what Zarrilli so nicely summarizes:

> In all such precise psychophysical moments, the 'character' is being created—not in the personality of the actor but as an embodied and projected/energized/living form between actor and audience. These Asian forms assume no 'suspension of disbelief,' rather the actor and spectator co-create the figure embodied in the actor as 'other.' The 'power of presence' manifest in this stage other, while embodied in this particular actor in this particular moment, is not limited to that ego. That dynamic figure exists between audience and actor, transcending both, pointing beyond itself.[25]

The rasic system of response does not preclude the eye and ear during actual performance, but during training especially, it works *directly and strongly* on the ENS which, under different names, has been very important and well-theorized in various Asian systems of performance, medicine, and the martial arts—all of which are tightly related in Asian cultures. Thus, when I say the rasic aesthetic experience is fundamentally different than the eye-dominant system prevalent in the West, I am not talking metaphorically.

THE 'RASABOXES' EXERCISE

But if not metaphorically, how? Let me answer that first in terms of training, then in terms of public performances. Over the past five years I and several of my colleagues at East Coast Artists,[26] especially

Michele Minnick and Paula Murray Cole, have been developing the rasaboxes exercise [see Appendix A and B]. This exercise is an application of some of the ideas in this essay.[27] It is based on the assumption that emotions are socially constructed while feelings are individually experienced.

The rasaboxes exercise takes many hours to complete; in fact it is open-ended. It can't be done in one session. It continues from one day to the next. The exercise proceeds as an orderly progression of steps:

1. Draw or tape a grid of nine rectangular boxes on the floor. All rectangles are the same; and each ought to be about 6 ft x 3 ft.

2. In variously-coloured chalk, inside each rectangle write the name of one rasa. Use chance methods to determine which rasa goes where. Write the names in Roman alphabetized Sanskrit. Leave the centre or ninth box empty or clear.

3. Very roughly 'define' each rasa. For example, 'Raudra' means anger, rage, roaring; 'bibhasta' means disgust, spitting up/out, vomiting.

4. Have participants draw and/or describe the rasas. That is, ask each person to interpret the Sanskrit word, to associate feelings and ideas to it. Emphasize that these 'definitions' and associations are not for all time, but just 'for now.' Emphasize also that drawings, abstract configurations, or words can be used. In moving from one box to another, people must either 'walk the line' at the edge of the boxes or step outside the rasabox area entirely and walk around to the new box. There is no order of progression from box to box. A person may return to a box as often as she likes, being careful not to overwrite someone else's contribution. Take as much time as necessary until everyone has drawn her fill. When a person is finished, she steps to the outside of the rasaboxes area. This phase of the exercise is over when everyone is outside the rasaboxes area. Sometimes this takes several hours.

5. When everyone is standing at the edge of the rasabox area,

time is allowed for people to 'take in' what has been drawn/written. Participants walk around the edge of the rasaboxes. They read to themselves and out loud what is written. They describe what is drawn. But they can't ask questions; nor can anything be explained.

6. Pause. Silence.

7. Self-selecting, one person at a time enters a box. The person takes/makes a pose of that rasa: for example, the pose of *sringara* or *karuna* . . . or whatever. The person can do as few as a single rasa or as many as all eight named rasas. (Remember the ninth or centre box is 'clear.') A person can move from box to box either along the edge or on the lines—in which case the movement is 'neutral.' But if a person steps into a box, he must take/make a rasic pose. This phase continues until everyone has had at least one chance to enter and pose within the rasaboxes.

8. Same as 7, but now the pose is supplemented by a sound.

In steps 7 and 8, there is no 'thinking.' Just take/make a pose and/or a sound. Whatever is 'there' in association to the rasa. Move rather quickly from one rasabox to the next. Don't worry how 'pretty,' 'true,' or 'original' the pose/sound is. Just do it. But once one is outside the boxes, reflect on how you composed your rasa and what it felt like to be in a composed rasa. In other words, begin the exploration of the distinction between feelings (experience) and emotion (public expression of feelings). Don't worry which came first. It is a chicken-and-egg question with no correct answer.

In fact, the first poses/sounds often have the quality of social clichés—of the 'already known' that fit the rasas as casually understood. Big laughs for hasya, clenched fists for raudra, weeping for karuna, and so on. The distance between stereotype and archetype is not great. Sooner or later, the social stereotype/archetype will be augmented by gestures and sounds that are more intimate, personal, quirky, unexpected. Practice leads one towards these. The road from outer to inner = the road from inner to outer.

9. Move more rapidly from one box to the next. Quick changes, no time for thinking it out in advance.

Here we are beginning to grapple with Antonin Artaud's call for actors who are 'athletes of the emotions.' Actual athletic competitions come to mind. A basketball player sits on the sidelines, quiet, a towel draped over his shoulder. But when called on to enter the game, he explodes with energy, performs at a high level of skill, and is entirely focused on his task. A whistle blows, and the athlete relaxes. The time out is over, he jumps back into the game. One of the goals of the rasabox exercise is to prepare actors to move with the same mastery from one emotion to another, in a random or almost random sequence, with no preparation between emotional displays, and with full commitment to each emotion. What happens at the feelings level is left indeterminate—as with the performers in India: some doers of the rasabox exercise will 'feel' it, others will not. [See Appendix A and B for what Cole and Minnick write concerning their experiences with the rasabox exercise].

10. Two persons enter, each one in his or her own box. At first, they simply make the rasas without paying attention to each other. But then they begin to 'dialogue' with the rasas—and shift rapidly from one box to another. So, sringara confronts vira and then vira moves to adbhuta; after a moment sringara rushes along the line to bibhasta and adbhuta jumps to bhayanaka.

At step 10, many new combinations appear. People begin to find things that are far from the social clichés. Those on the outside are often amused, sometimes frightened, or moved. 'Something' is happening, though it can't be reduced to words. A few people are hesitant about going into the boxes at all. The exercise is both expressive and a scalpel that cuts very deeply into people. Paradoxically, in performing different emotional masks, the participants discover aspects of their beings that had remained hidden—sometimes even from themselves.

11. Participants bring in texts from outside—that is monologues from known plays or stuff written just for the exercise. Scenes from dramas are enacted by two or even three people.

> The text remains fixed, but the rasas shift—with no preplanning. So, for example, Romeo is all sringara but Juliet is karuna; then suddenly Juliet springs to bibhasta and Romeo to adbhuta. And so on—the possible combinations are nearly endless. Occasionally, Romeo and Juliet are in the same box.

At this stage, actors test out the many different possibilities of any given text. Or rather, the texts are revealed as not being fundamental, but permeable, open, wildly interpretable.

> 12. Scenes are enacted with one underlying rasa, on top of which are bits played in different rasas.

Here one begins to see how a whole production could be mapped as a progression of rasas. The progression could be scored or improvised each performance.

There are even more possibilities. The rasabox exercise is designed to be unfinishable. It is not intended to be a 'true example' of a *NS*-based performance. Indeed, what comes from the rasabox exercise is not at all like what one sees at any traditional Indian performance. The exercise actually points to the creative possibilities suggested by the underlying theory of the *NS*. It 'comes from' rather than 'is an example of' that theory.

THE EMPTY BOX

What about the empty box at the center? Historically, there was no 'shanta rasa' until Abhinavagupta added it some centuries after the *NS* was compiled. In the exercise, as in the historical development of rasa theory, the 'ninth rasabox' is special. What happens there? In the exercise, a person can enter that box—the shanta space—only when the person is 'clear.' What that means is not for the one directing the exercise to say. Each person will have her own criteria for total, whole clarity. In the years that I've directed the rasabox exercise, 'shanta' has been occupied very rarely, one or two times. There can be no challenge to such a position. So what if it is 'not really so' that the person is 'clear'? How can another person tell? And maybe it is so, maybe the participant has surpassed all *samsara*, all the clutter of feelings, the confusion of mixed emotions, the noise of change. I will not judge.

RASAESTHETICS IN PERFORMANCE

Now let me turn from training to performance. Indian theatre, dance, and music are not banquets. In odissi, bharatanatyam, kathakali, kathak, and so on performers dance, gesture, impersonate, and sometimes speak and sing. Occasionally, there is burning incense thickening the air with odour. But for the most part, the data of the performance is transmitted from performer to partaker in the same way as in the West (and elsewhere): through the eyes and ears. How is this rasic?

Watching traditional Indian genres, one sees the performer looking at her own hands as they form different *hastas* or mudras—precise gestures with very specific meanings. This self-regarding is not narcissism in the Western sense. *Abhinaya* literally means to lead the performance to the spectators—and the first spectator is the performer herself. If the self-who-is-observing is moved by the self-who-is-performing the performance will be a success. This splitting is not exactly a Brechtian *verfremdungseffekt*, but neither is it altogether different. Brecht wanted to open a space between performer and performance in order to insert a social commentary. The rasic performer opens a liminal space to allow further play—improvisation, variation, and self-enjoyment.

The performer becomes a partaker herself. When she is moved by her own performance, she is affected not as the character, but as a partaker. Like the other partakers, she can appreciate the dramatic situation, the crisis, the feelings of the character she is performing. She will both express the emotions of that character and be moved to her own feelings about those emotions. Where does she experience these feelings? In the ENS, in the gut—inside the body that is dancing, that is hearing music, that is enacting a dramatic situation. The other partakers—the audience—are doubly affected: by the performance and by the performer's reaction to her own performance. An empathetic feedback takes place. The experience can be remarkable.

In orthodox Western theatre, the spectators respond sympathetically to the 'as if' of characters living out a narrative. In rasic theatre, the partakers empathize with the experience of the performers playing. This empathy with the performer rather than on the plot is what permits Indian theatre to 'wander,' to explore detours and hidden pathways, unexpected turns in the performance. Here rasa and raga (the classical Indian musical form) are analogous. The partakers' interest is not tied to the story, but to the enacting of the story; the partakers do not want to 'see what happens next' but to 'experience how the performer performs whatever is happening.' There is no narrational imperative insisting on development, climax, recognition, and resolution. Instead, as in kundalini sexual meditation, there is as much deferral as one can bear, a delicious delay of resolution.

I am here expounding a theory of reception—even to the extent that the performer's self-regarding is a reception of her own performance. This needs further elaboration. One treatise on *abhinaya* instructs the dancer to sing with her throat, express the meaning of that song with her hand gestures, show how she feels with her eyes, and keep time with her feet. And every performer knows the traditional adage: Where the hands go, the eyes follow; where the eyes go, the mind follows; where the mind goes, the emotions follow, and when the emotions are expressed, there will be rasa. Such a logically linked performance of emotions points to the 'self.' Not the self as personal ego, but the *atman* or profound absolute self, the Self that is identical to the universal absolute, the *Brahman*.

Eating in a traditional manner in India means conveying the food directly to the mouth with the right hand. There is no intermediary instrument such as fork or spoon. Sometimes a flat bread is used to mop up or hold the food; sometimes rice is used to sop up a curry. But in all cases, the food on the index and third finger is swept into the mouth by an inward motion of the thumb. Along with the food, the eater tastes his own fingers. The performer regarding her mudras is engaging in a kind of 'theatre feeding.' As with self-feeding, the emotions of a performance are first conveyed to the performer and the partakers by means of the hands.

Orthodox Western performing arts remain invested in keeping performers separated from receivers. Stages are elevated; curtains mark a boundary; spectators are fixed in their seats. Mainstream artists, scholars, and critics do not look on synchronicity and synaesthesia with favour. Eating, digestion, and excretion are not thought of as proper sites of aesthetic pleasure. These sites—aside from rock concerts, raves, and sports matches—are more in the domain of performance art. In early performance art there were Carolee Schneemann, Allan Kaprow, Shiraga Kazuo, Hermann Nitsch, Chris Burden, Stellarc, Paul McCarthy, and others. Later came Mike Kelley, Karen Finley, Annie Sprinkle, Ron Athey, Franko B. all of whom insisted on making 'the body' explicit.[28] Their work began to elide differences between the interior and the exterior; to emphasize permeability and porosity; to explore the sexual, the diseased, the excretory, the wet, and the smelly. Performances used blood, semen, spit, shit, urine—as well as food, paint, plastics, and other stuff drawn from the 'literal' rather than the 'make believe.' This work is not very Asian on the surface, but at an underlying theoretical level, it is extremely rasic.

These kinds of performances need to be studied in terms of rasaesthetics. That means paying attention to the increasing appetite for arts that engage visceral arousal and experience; performances that insist on sharing experiences with partakers and participants; works that try to evoke both terror and celebration. Such performances are often very personal even as they are no longer private.

What I'm asking for goes beyond performance art. Rasaesthetics opens questions regarding how the whole sensorium is, or can be, used in making performances. Smell, taste, and touch are demanding their place at the table.[29] Thus I am making a much larger claim—and sending out a more general invitation. I am inviting an investigation into theatricality as orality, digestion, and excretion rather than, or in addition to, theatricality as something only or mostly for the eyes and ears. I am saying that performance practice has already moved strongly into this place and now is the time for theory to follow.

Notes

1 At the very start of the text, Bharata claims for the *NS* the status of a *veda*—the most sacred of ancient Indian texts. This is not all that unusual. Such claims to being the 'fifth veda' were used to validate and strengthen a text. Tradition finally of course assigned the rank of 'sastra' to the *NS*, a position well down the hierarchical ladder of

sacred writings. As for the framing origin myth itself, which is told in chapter one—the story of Brahma's composition of the 'fifth veda,' its transmission to Bharata and his sons, and their performance of the 'first natya' on the occasion of the Mahendra's flag-festival (the victory celebration of Indra's triumph over *asuras* and *danavas* [demons])—much can be made of it. The demons are enraged by the performance of their defeat, they rush the stage and magically freeze 'the speeches, movements, and even the memory of the performers' (Bharata Muni, *The Natyasastra*, Adya Rangacharya tr. and ed., New Delhi: Munshiram Manoharlal, 1996, p. 3). Indra intervenes, thrashing the demons with a flagpole that is then installed as a protective totem. Brahma instructs the gods' architect Visvakarman to construct an impregnable theatre, well-guarded by the most powerful gods. This having been done, the gods say it is better to negotiate with the demons than to forcibly exclude them. Brahma agrees, approaches the demons, and inquires why they want to destroy natya. They reply, 'You are as much the creator of us as of the gods, so you should not have done it' (omitted them from *natya*) (Ibid., p. 4). 'If that is all there is to it,' Brahma says, 'then there is no reason for you to feel angry or aggrieved. I have created the *Natyaveda* to show good and bad actions and feelings of both gods and yourselves. It is the representation of the entire three worlds and not only of the gods or of yourselves' (ibid., p. 4). Thus natya is of divine origin, all-encompassing, and consisting of actions both good and bad. For an extended and highly sophisticated interpretation of the *NS* framing myth, see Byrski, Christopher, *Concept of Ancient Indian Theatre* (New Delhi: Munshiram Manoharlal, 1973).

2 Vatsyayan, Kapila, *Bharata*: *The Natyasastra* (New Delhi: Sahitya Akademi, 1996), p. 115.

3 According to Kapila Vatsyayan (ibid., pp. 32–36) and Adya Rangacharya, whose recent English translation of the *NS* is the most readable, in 1865 the American Fitz Edward Hall unearthed and published several chapters. In 1874, the German Wilhelm Heymann (or Haymann, as Vatsyayan spells it) wrote an influential essay that stimulated further translations of several chapters by the French scholar, Paul Reynaud (or Regnaud as Vatsyayan spells it). But it was only in 1926 that the Baroda critical edition was commenced. The whole text—in Sanskrit—was not in print until 1954.

In spite of all these results, the final text is contradictory, repetitive

> and incongruent; there are lacunae too, but, what is worse, there are words and passages that are almost impossible to understand. [. . .] It is not only modern scholars who suffer this inability to understand; even almost a thousand years ago [. . .] Abhinavagupta [. . .] displayed this tendency. (Vatsyayan, *Bharata: The Natyasastra,* p. xviii)

Vatsyayan (180ff) provides a 'Database of the *Natyasastra*' locating and listing all 112 known extant texts and fragments. All the texts are Sanskrit but transcribed in a variety of scripts: Newari, Devanagari, Grantha, Telugu, Malayalam, Tamil, Kanarese. Thus we know that from an early time the *NS* was widely distributed across the subcontinent.

4 Bharata Muni, *The Natyasastra*, pp.54–55.

5 Partridge, Eric, *Origins: A Short Etymological Dictionary of Modern English* (London: Routledge and Kegan Paul, 1966), p. 710.

6 Shipley, Joseph T., *Origins of English Words: A Discursive Dictionary of Indo-European Roots* (Baltimore: Johns Hopkins University Press, 1984), p. 69.

7 Partridge, *Origins*, p. 710.

8 Shipley, *Origins of English Words*, p. 353.

9 Winnicott, D. W., *Playing and Reality* (London: Tavistock Publications, 1971).

10 'In Presocratic thought the prerational notion of agon is used to describe the natural world as a ceaseless play of forces or Becoming'—Spariosu, Mihai, *Dionysus Reborn: Play and the Aesthetic Dimension in Modern Philosophical and Scientific Discourse* (Ithaca: Cornell University Press, 1989) p.13.

11 Bharata Muni, *The Natyasastra*, p. 55.

12 According to the first chapter of the *NS* Brahma created the *natyaveda*:

> to show good and bad actions and feelings of both gods and yourselves [humans]. It is the representation of the entire three worlds [divine, human, demonic] and not only of the gods or of yourselves. Now dharma [correct living], now artha [warring], now kama [loving], humor or fights, greed or killing. Natya teaches the right way to those who go against dharma, erotic enjoyment to those who seek pleasure, restraint to those who are unruly, moderation to those who are self-disciplined, courage to cowards, energy to the brave, knowledge to the uneducated, wisdom to the learned, enjoyment to the rich, solace to those in grief, money to business-people, a calm mind

to the disturbed. Natya is the representation of the ways of the worlds using various emotions and diverse circumstances. It gives you peace, entertainment, and happiness, as well as beneficial advice based on the actions of high, low, and middle people. (Bharata Muni, *The Natyasastra*, chapter 1; English adapted from Ghosh and Rangacharya translations)

13 Lannoy, *The Speaking Tree*, p. 48–49.

14 Ibid., p. 43

15 Ibid., p. 54.

16 Gershon, Michael D., *The Second Brain* (New York: Harper Perennial, 1998).

17 Blakeslee, Sandra, 'Complex and Hidden Brain in the Gut Makes Cramps, Butterflies, and Valium' in *The New York Times*, 23 January 1996, C1.

18 Blakeslee, *The New York Times*, C3.

19 Gershon, Michael D., Alcmene Chalazonitis, Taube P. Rothman, 'The Neural Crest to Bowel: Development of the Enteric Nervous System' in *Journal of Neurobiology* 1993, vol. 24, no. 2, pp. 199–214.

20 Blakeslee, *The New York Times*, C3.

21 Gershon, Michael D., *The Second Brain*, p. xiv.

22 Zarilli, Philip, 'What Does it mean to "Become the Character": Power, Presence, and Transcendence in Asian In-Body Disciplines of Practice' in *By Means of Performance*, Ed. Richard Schechner and Willa Appel (Cambridge: Cambridge University Press, 1990), p. 136.

23 Nearman, Mark J., 'Kakyo Zeami's Fundamental Principles of Acting'in *Monumenta Nipponica* 1982, vol. 37, no. 3, pp. 346.

24 Zarilli, *By Means of Performance*, p. 143

25 Ibid., p. 144

26 East Coast Artists is a company I formed in New York in the early 1990s. Productions I've directed with ECA are *Faust/gastronome* (1992), *Three Sisters* (1997), and *Hamlet* (1999). The rasabox exercise was developed both during ECA rehearsal workshops and at workshops I ran at NYU in the 1990s. In the late '90s, I worked very closely with Michele Minnick and Paula Murray Cole in relation to rasaboxes. Minnick and Cole have led several rasabox workshops in New York and elsewhere. The exercise is dynamic. It continues to change.

27 The exercise is not based on the theory, exactly; nor does the theory result from the exercise, exactly. Rather, there is a convergence and an interplay between what I am thinking and what I am doing. This interplay is open—that is why both the exercise and the theory are 'in development' and not 'finished.'

28 See Schneider, Rebecca, *The Explicit Body in Performance* (London: Routledge, 1997) and Jones, Amelia, *Body Art: Performing the Subject* (Minneapolis, University of Minnesota Press, 1998).

29 The work of Constance Classen and David Howes and the group of scholars associated with them is well worth noting. They are developing an anthropology and an aesthetics of the senses. See *The Variety of Sensory Experience* (1991) edited by Howes, and Classen's *The Color of Angels* (1998). In April 2000, Classen, Howes, Jim Drobnick, and Jennifer Fisher convened 'Uncommon Senses: An International Conference On the Senses in Art and Culture' at Concordia University in Montreal with 180 presenters.

Appendix A

Rasabox Actor Training / Michele Minnick

WHETHER WE ACCEPT THE IDEA of 'rasa' as a literally gustatory experience, or simply understand food-rasa as a metaphor for the process of theatre-rasa, the practical question still remains as to how one can achieve this shared experience between actor and spectator in the time-space of performance. What of *abhinaya* (the actual behaviors of a performance), the very concrete art of the actor? What are the 'ingredients' at her disposal? How does she know when to add one thing, how much to add, how fast to stir it, how long to let it cook? And how does this idea of rasa as the space *between* serve the Western performer? These questions can be partially answered by the rasaboxes.

Fascinated with the idea of rasa, and challenged by Antonin Artaud's demand that the actor be an 'athlete of the emotions,' my teacher, colleague, and co-artistic director of East Coast Artists, Richard Schechner, designed the rasaboxes exercise, in which the performer's emotional/ physical/vocal expressivity and agility could be trained. In our work performing, directing, and teaching workshops with East Coast Artists, Paula Murray Cole and I have continued to develop this work, using it as a tool not only for training, but for performance composition.

How do the rasaboxes work? The key to their design is the spatialization of emotions. What makes our use of rasa 'Western' is that rather than codifying the expression of emotion in particular gestures and facial expressions, which are always performed in the same way as in classical Indian dance, we use space to delineate each rasa, and allow the individual performer to find her own expression of the emotion/s contained within it.

For a description of the rasaboxes as such, see Schechner's 'Rasaesthetics' essay. The first steps towards movement improvisation involve getting into one box at a time and creating a 'statue' or fixed pose for each rasa. We then establish the rule that you cannot be in a rasabox without expressing it dynamically. Participants then move from one box to the next, embodying each rasa by means of the pose they have chosen, or go into the 'neutral' space outside the grid, or walk the lines dividing the boxes to move between them. The idea is to move from one box to another with no 'daylight'—no period of transition—between them. This develops an emotional/physical agility the actor can use to transform instantly from expressing rage to love to sadness to disgust, etc. Once participants are comfortable with being statues, we introduce breath and then sound and finally movement and sound together. What starts as a fairly controlled exercise develops into a very free improvisation, involving a wide range of interactions or 'scenes' between different people in different boxes.

Since I was introduced to the rasaboxes in 1996, I have been fascinated by their power to free performers (myself included) to experience ranges of physical and emotional expression that might have otherwise seemed unavailable to them. It is possible through this training to develop an incredible range of expressiveness, from very subtle film-style acting to performing of operatic or grotesque proportions of histrionics, without sacrificing the element of greatest concern to Western performers: 'sincerity' or 'truth.' I have found, in fact, that because of its focus on physical embodiment/expression, rasaboxes training can serve to deepen a performer's ability to find authentic emotional connections.

The rasaboxes externalize what is often considered an 'internal' process, proving that 'real' emotion does not have to be kept inside, but is actually a physical as well as a psychological process. In this way, rasa training serves as a bridge for the actor between his psychophysiology and his expressiveness. Because it acts as a link between the individual, physical body of an actor and his emotions, and the emotional/physical relationship to the environment and other performers, rasa technique can serve as a multi-directional training ground, where old habits and patterns can be brought to light and new ones can emerge. Unlike many other forms of actor training—in which the actor is encouraged to lose himself, to act on impulse, to give way to inspiration—the rasaboxes encourage the actor to approach his craft as a conscious, body-oriented process, in which he holds the keys and the tools for his own development. In drama therapy terms, he is the 'observing ego,' experiencing the process and observing the process at the same time. In Somatic Fitness terms, he develops 'a body that knows itself.'[1]

When they have first experienced the rasaboxes, people often comment on the 'therapeutic' aspect of the exercises. Indeed, they are therapeutic; in my experience, many forms of actor training are therapeutic insofar as they promote health and balance, developing the body's energy-giving functions as well as its expressiveness. The rasaboxes have, in fact, been adapted by some practitioners of drama therapy, to provide their clients with a safe space in which to explore emotions. But in the context of performer training, ultimately the point of the exercises is to go beyond, rather than to indulge in the personal side of emotion. When I am engaged in the work, I do feel the sense of being connected to a deep well—a kind of universal emotional source, which allows emotion to move me, and move through me and beyond me to an audience who can mutually share the experience. It is no longer 'my' emotion. A paradox emerges: by going deeply into the intimate details of a particular body, we can go beyond that particular body, past the mundane personal/psychological realm to a transpersonal realm, a mythic realm.

Ultimately, a performer experienced in the training can internalize the structure, and is able to transform from one rasic state to another without the physical map. It is possible with such a performer to change the emotional quality of a moment, a speech, or a scene at any point without necessarily changing her place in space. 'Emotion', like space, time, and other physical elements of staging, becomes simply another tool to be used in the process of exploring and developing performance work. The rasaboxes can free performers from questions about 'motivation,' allowing them to think of and use emotion in a more playful adventurous way. Finally, emotion—which so often is blocked, or internalized in Western acting—moves into the body, where it can energize the space *between* one performer and another, and between performer and spectator.

The rasaboxes are not meant to supplant other forms of actor training. A rasa-trained actor is not necessarily going to do away with objectives, throughlines, creative improvisations, and other widely used Western approaches. If these methods are used to answer the 'what' questions of acting, the rasaboxes can be used in combination with them to answer the 'how' questions. Qualitative changes can be made by applying the idea of rasa to a character, a scene, even an entire play. At times it is useful to think of rasa as a kind of tonality, or rhythm of performance, which can be shifted as the pitch/key or tempo/rhythm can be shifted for a piece of music.

One of the things I have discovered in working with the rasaboxes is that contrary to the training we have inherited from Stanislavsky, emotion—when fully played out through the body—is very active. Also, I learned from this process that on stage, as in life, emotion is not necessarily psycho-'logical' in the simplistic sense that we often associate with realistic acting. One discovers in working on a scene or a monologue in the rasaboxes, that often the least 'logical' of emotions is the one that makes the scene most interesting one in which to play a scene. Sometimes, one discovers new layers of emotion; one played with laughter on the surface may have rage lurking beneath. The rasas can also serve as a kind of emotional baseline for character. A Blanche Dubois played with karuna (grief and compassion) as her baseline would be very different than a Blanche played with raudra (rage) or bhayanaka (fear) as the baseline. She would have a different breath, a different voice, a different body, and these details of her characterization would affect the tone of the entire character interpretation.

Now we are beginning to explore new material in the rasaboxes. Composer/choreographer and East Coast Artists associate Liz Claire is working with music for a piece we are making about Russian poet Marina Tsvetaeva. The rich sounds and rhythms of her violin in bhayanaka, or karuna expand my work as a performer in those emotional spaces—pushing my body and voice into new territory, and multiplying the textural layers of the piece. Here, rasa becomes a terrain for dialogue between actor and musician, blurring the boundaries between our roles and the techniques available to us.

In my work as a movement analyst, I have also begun to explore the application of Laban ideas about movement to performers' work in the rasaboxes. This detailed physical work can refine the body's work of emotional expression, challenging the performer to find light, quick rage, for example, or bounded, strong fear. With its categories of Body, Space, Shape, Effort, and Relationship, Laban Movement Analysis provides the tools to allow the performer to go beyond her 'patterns' in training, developing a greater range of expressiveness toward constructing very specific character details or physical scoring in performance. The possibilities are endless. As Bharata says in the *Natyashastra*: 'It is impossible [. . .] to know all about natya since there is no limit to bhava-s (emotions) and no end to the arts involved [in natya]. It is not possible to have a thorough knowledge of even one of them, leave alone so many of them.'[2] It is with this spirit that I enter, and ask others to enter and re-enter the rasaboxes, always knowing there are new worlds to be discovered there.

Note

1. This idea was introduced to me by Martha Eddy, a Body-Mind Centring practitioner and teacher. *Somatic* refers to *soma*, or cell, which according to this way of thinking, contains its own wisdom. This approach to the body's wisdom, or knowledge is a wonderful way to approach the rasaboxes, where the different parts of our bodies are in constant dialogue with one another as we search for ways to physically contain and express emotion.

2 Bharata Muni, *The Natyasastra*. Adya Rangacharya tr. and ed. (New Delhi: Munshiram Manoharlal Publishers, 1996), p. 53.

Appendix B

Experience Rasaboxes / Paula Murray Cole

I'd like to describe what it feels like to experience the rasas as we explore them in the rasaboxes exercise and apply them to our rehearsals and performances. First however, let me help you to understand what a rasa experience feels like by relating a recent experience.

Not long ago, I spent a week and a half studying the therapeutic uses of essential oils. As part of an introductory exercise, our class was asked to experience and respond to the smell and effects of various oils, to notice what parts of our bodies were most affected by each oil; what memories, images, or associations were evoked; and to guess each oil's therapeutic uses.

During the exercise, I observed the expressions on the faces and bodies of my classmates as they related to each oil. I noticed that their responses were immediate and extremely physical. Robert took a whiff of German chamomile, a heavy dark blue oil, and was instantly, violently repulsed. His body jolted and jumped backward, his face contorted with disgust. 'Auggghhhkk,' he exhaled as he spat. He quickly replaced the cap on the bottle and put it far from his body. Steve uncapped the rosemary and his body and face widened, his spine lengthened, his breathing became large and even. 'Wow,' he said, and he reported that he felt stimulated, powerful, energized. We took turns smelling the substances. After about five minutes, the oils' essences were not only contained inside each bottle, but had diffused throughout the room, transfusing into our bodies and affecting our psycho-physiology.

So it is with rasa. Rasa means 'essence,' and that essence has the power to move us, to transform and shape our responses. It comes from outside our bodies, is smelled, tasted, ingested. Its particular properties change us, transform our chemistry and shape our psycho-physical expressive behavior.

In 1999, I played Ofelia in East Coast Artist's *Hamlet* directed by Richard Schechner at the Performing Garage. I often used the rasa karuna (grief/anguish/compassion). Here's a description from my rehearsal notes about what it felt like to experience karuna:

> *I breathe in karuna, taste it, smell it.* [. . .] *My body folds on the first long exhale as my knees sink to the ground, my belly tightens and rounds my spine/my throat tightens/my breath heaves/my head bows* [. . .]. *One hand reaches up to cover my eyes while the other supports the rest of my weight as it drops further into the floor. I breathe in the karuna that is all around me. I sink into the feeling, my eyes well up with tears. I want to surrender my breath to the openness and expanding relief that sounding this pain would bring.* [. . .] *I tighten and fight against that feeling of vulnerability and exposure. The sound squeezes out anyway, a high keening noise. I breathe again and my mind rifles through the baggage of remembered and created associations I have with this feeling: A muscle memory? An emotional imprint? I can see the image of myself here on the floor. Then I see myself set out on the ice floe.* [. . .] *Then mourning the death of my father.*

Now I am playing a bit of Ofelia's 'mad scene.':

> *The tears stream, I seek relief by crouching closer to the floor, squeezing my guts trying to support an insupportable sorrow.* [. . .] *The experience is as if it were happening to me, karuna is moving me according to its demands. I am not taking myself on an intellectual journey through my own personal psychology, to remember a time when I felt a similar feeling (though those memories may surface while I am working). I am simply and completely connecting with the rasa, working in relationship to the rasa, from the outside until it is the inside and back again.*